Geoarchaeology

Geoarchaeology

The Earth-Science Approach to
Archaeological Interpretation

George (Rip) Rapp, Jr., and Christopher L. Hill

Yale University Press
New Haven and London

Set in Janson type by Tseng Information Systems, Durham, North Carolina. Printed in the United States of America by BookCrafters, Inc., Chelsea, Michigan.

Library of Congress Cataloging-in-Publication Data
Rapp, George Robert, 1930–
Geoarchaeology : the earth-science approach to archaeological interpretation / George (Rip) Rapp, Jr. and Christopher L. Hill.
p.   cm.
Includes bibliographical references and index.
ISBN 0-300-07075-6 (cloth). —
ISBN 0-300-07076-4 (paper)
1. Archaeology—Methodology.   2. Archaeological geology.   I. Hill, Christopher L., 1959– .   II. Title.
CC77.5.R37   1998
930.1'28—dc21   97-16880

10   9   8   7   6   5   4   3   2   1

To Malcolm H. Wiener, a
philanthropist and archaeologist
with a keen vision of the role of
natural science in archaeology

Every archaeological problem starts
as a problem in geoarchaeology.
—Colin Renfrew

Contents

Preface xi

1 Theoretical and Historical Overview 1

The Domain of Geoarchaeology 1

A History of the Interaction Between Earth Sciences and Archaeology 4

Foundations: The Eighteenth and Nineteenth Centuries 5

Collaboration: The First Half of the Twentieth Century 8

Integration: The Second Half of the Twentieth Century 12

2 Sediments and Soils and the Creation of the Archaeological Record 18

Sediments 18

Weathering 19

Transportation 19

Postdepositional Changes 20

Archaeological Sediments 20

Classification of Sedimentation Products 21

Clastic Deposits 21

Chemical Deposition 27

Organic Matter 29

Soils and Buried Soils 29

The Soil Profile 31

Soil Types 32

Paleosols and Buried Soils 34

Inferring Environments from Physical and Chemical Parameters 36

Color 36

Cementation and Induration 38

Texture 38

Structure 43

Composition 44

Boundaries 48

3 Contexts of Archaeological Record Formation 50

Stages of Site Formation 52

Initial Landscapes and Original Occupation 53

Sedimentary Settings 53

Desert Depositional Systems 54

Lakes and Associated Basin Settings 57

Alluvial Depositional Systems: Flowing Water 59

Cave and Rock-Shelter Depositional Systems 66

The Glacial System 71

Coastal and Marine Depositional Settings 74

Postdepositional Processes 81

Mass Wasting 82

Cryoturbation 82

Clay Expansion and Contraction 83

Bioturbation 83

Contents

4 Paleoenvironmental Reconstructions: Humans, Climates, and Ancient Landscapes 86

Lake Records and Geoecology 87

Inferring Environmental Change 88

Ecology and Landscape Change 89

Plant Remains as Clues to Environmental and Climatic Change 90

   Pollen 90

   Floral Macrofossils 92

   Phytoliths 93

   Diatoms 95

Animal Remains as Clues to Environmental Conditions 96

   Invertebrates 96

   Vertebrates 100

Other Ecological Accumulations 103

   Pack-Rat Middens 103

   Peat 103

Isotopes and Chemical Ratios as Environmental Indicators 104

Environmental Change and Archaeological Interpretation 105

   Human Habitats and Geoecology 105

   Tectonics, Climates, Landscapes, and the Human Past 107

   Human Interaction with Environment and Its Effects on Climate 108

Microclimates 111

5 Raw Materials and Resources 112

Minerals 112

   Chert and Chalcedony 112

   Semiprecious Stones 114

   Other Archaeologically Important Minerals 116

Metals and Ores 118

Rocks 122

Shells 124

Clays 125

Building Materials 126

   Building Stone 127

   Burnt Brick 128

   Mortar 128

Other Materials 128

Rock and Mineral Recovery 129

Water 131

6 Provenance Studies 134

Geologic Deposits 135

Materials Used in Geologic Sourcing 137

   Obsidian 137

   Granite and Related Igneous and Metamorphic Rocks 139

   Chert 139

   Marble 140

   Clay 140

   Temper 141

   Amber 142

   Soft Stone, Other Rock, and Semiprecious Minerals 142

   Native Copper 142

   Complex Copper Minerals 144

   Tin 144

   Lead, Silver, and Gold 146

Methods Used in Geologic Sourcing 147

   Trace-Element Analyses 147

   Petrographic Analysis 149

   Statistics and Data Analysis 151

7 Estimating Age in the Archaeological Record 153

Stratigraphy 153

   Rhythmites (Varves) 154

Paleosols in Loess and Alluvium 155

Tephrochronology 158

Dating Techniques Based on Animal and Plant Remains 159

Paleontology 159

Dendrochronology 160

Dating Techniques Based on Chemical Accumulation 160

Chemical Analysis 160

Patination and Desert Varnish 161

Temperature-Affected Dating 161

Amino Acid Racemization and Epimerization 161

Hydration (Obsidian) 162

Radiometric Dating 163

Potassium-Argon and Argon-Argon Dating 163

Uranium-Series Dating 164

Radiocarbon Dating 165

Datable Materials and Geoarchaeological Applications 168

Radiation Dating 169

Fission-Track Dating 169

Paleomagnetic and Archaeomagnetic Dating 169

Electron Spin Resonance and Thermoluminescence Dating 171

Dating Exposed Surfaces 174

8 Geologic Mapping, Remote Sensing, and Surveying 175

Geologic Maps and Mapping 175

Reading the Landscape from Topographic Maps 179

Settlement Patterns 180

Remote Sensing 181

Geophysical Prospecting 182

Seismic Profiling 189

Aerial Photography 190

Satellite and Airborne Remote Sensing 191

Core Drilling 192

Geochemical Prospecting and Analysis 194

Geographic Information Systems 196

The Complexities of Scale 197

9 Construction, Destruction, Site Preservation, and Conservation 198

Ancient Geotechnology 198

Construction 199

Dams 199

Canals 199

Roads 201

Excavation 201

Natural Burial of Sites 202

Destruction 203

Rock Properties 204

Weathering 204

Water 207

Erosion 208

Land Subsidence 209

Seismic Disturbance 210

Floods and Flood Legends 213

Volcanoes 214

Site Preservation 215

Site Preservation Problems 216

Reservoirs 216

Hilltops or Slopes 218

Seismicity 218

Site Stabilization 218

Earth Burial 219

Historic Cultural Resource Preservation 219

Conservation 220

Materials Preservation 220

Corrosion 221

The Future 222

Contents

Appendix: Geologic Time Divisions 223

Notes 227

Glossary 237

Bibliography 241

Index 255

Preface

This book was written primarily for archaeologists in the formative stages of their careers and secondarily for geologists who, in increasing numbers, are assisting in the solution of archaeological problems. Finally, we hope it might also be of value to senior archaeologists, as well as to historians, anthropologists, ethnologists, and Quaternary scientists whose scholarship requires some understanding of the physical context of the remains of past material culture, as represented in the artifactual record.

It is generally believed that no academic discipline has been spared the experience, at some stage of its development, of sometimes bitter and wide-ranging disputes over method and theory. Archaeology has witnessed such disputes since the 1970s. Because the methodology inherent in most geoarchaeology is geologic, it is possible that this subdiscipline can avoid these disputes. Geology settled its fundamental differences about method and theory a long time ago. (This is not to say that there are not current differences of emphasis and priority.)

Rapp co-edited a book published in 1985 by Yale University Press entitled *Archaeological Geology*. This volume is called *Geoarchaeology*. We take these names to have somewhat different meanings. A narrow definition of *archaeological geology* would be geology performed with at least the partial objective of being useful to archaeology. A good example would be the determination (using core drilling, sedimentology, and geomorphology) of the varying positions of shorelines during the Late Quaternary near important archaeological sites. This is mainstream geology, whether or not there are archaeological sites in the vicinity. In contrast, *geoarchaeology*, narrowly defined, is the use of geologic concepts, methods, and knowledge base in the direct solution of archaeological problems. Geoarchaeologists do archaeology. Obviously, there is some overlap in actual practice between the two.

To distinguish the remains of human activity from those of natural (geologic) agencies is perhaps the first task of the geoarchaeologist. We start from the premise that most of the interpretation of archaeological materials, sediments, and site settings requires a broad understanding of several related methods and concepts. This is the first book to take an integrated and comprehensive approach to these areas. The discussion of each geologic concept or knowledge base is framed within an archaeological context. The principal aim is to provide concepts and data derived from the earth sciences that are essential to solving archaeological problems and aiding interpretations of the archaeological record. We hope that this book demonstrates the necessity of taking an earth-science approach to the examination of diverse archaeological settings, ranging from single occupations to complex, multicomponent habitations. Our examples illustrate how earth science is used to resolve archaeological problems associated with artifact identification and description, the integrity of artifact sets, chronological context, paleolandscape habitat, and human-environment interactions.

When dealing with an interdisciplinary area, it is tempting to explain every phenomenon drawn into the discussion. We have tried to limit our exposition to the geologic aspects of the topic.

For example, radiocarbon dating is of great importance in archaeology. However, only certain aspects of carbon-14 (^{14}C) dating are explicitly geologic, and texts abound that cover this field at every level of detail and depth. Therefore we focus on its geologic components.

Nomenclature and basic data (such as chronological periods) from many fields must be imported into an interdisciplinary text. We have therefore added a glossary and appendixes so as not to unduly interrupt readers' concentration by forcing them to consult specialized dictionaries and encyclopedias. Words in the glossary are set in **boldface** type at first mention.

We intend this to be an introductory textbook for advanced-level undergraduates and graduate students in archaeology and geoarchaeology. It is not a scholarly treatise written for colleagues nor a book-length review containing exhaustive references. Some of the material—for example, the discussion of basic rock types in Chapter 5— is rudimentary; more advanced readers may skip this chapter. The authors faced the choice of offering a text with hundreds of references interrupting the discussion or one containing only the specific references from which significant data, unique ideas, or quotations were drawn. Like most textbook authors we chose the latter; in addition, we replaced the standard author-date reference style (Jones and Bryant 1992) with endnotes and a bibliography to make the reference material readily available but unintrusive.

Scientists have begun to drop the -al from many scientific adjectives, like *topographic, stratigraphic, geomorphic,* and *climatalogic,* and geologists now tend to prefer *geologic* to *geological.* We have followed this practice. Archaeologists who reviewed the manuscript, however, overwhelmingly requested that we retain the traditional *archaeological.* So we did.

Our perspective is unabashedly geologic. Hence, other equally important aspects of the broad interdisciplinary field of archaeology are often not mentioned, even when they contribute to the archaeological examples we have used. This is not to minimize their importance but rather to focus on the geologic aspects. There is no shortage of good books and articles covering these other components of archaeology.

Rapp has done field geoarchaeology in Greece, Turkey, Cyprus, Israel, Egypt, Tunisia, Ukraine, and China, as well as in North America, and has visited geoarchaeological sites in Italy, Germany, Great Britain, Russia, India, Thailand, Iran, and elsewhere. Hill has done geoarchaeological fieldwork in Egypt, Turkey and Israel, as well as in North America. We are more comfortable with examples that fall within our range of experience, but this special knowledge has biased the examples given in the text. For this we ask the reader's indulgence.

Early drafts of many chapters were used in a class in geoarchaeology at Boston University in the fall of 1993; later drafts of all the chapters were used as the text for a class in geoarchaeology at the University of Minnesota, Duluth, in the winter of 1995; and still later drafts were used in a geoarchaeology class at the University of Minnesota, Twin Cities, in the spring of 1996. We acknowledge the valuable comments and suggestions of students in these classes. The Duluth class pressed for the inclusion of cost data for chemical analyses and geophysical techniques. We have resisted this because of the many variables involved and because costs constantly change.

We are indebted to many colleagues. Doris Stoessel was instrumental in keeping everything under control and editing the final stages of the manuscript. Russell Rothe created most of the computer illustrations. Elaine Nissen drew some of the figures, while Zichun Jing, Emine Kucuk, and Jennifer Shafer assisted with other illustrations. Jean Thomson Black and Edward Tripp of Yale University Press persevered during the long gestation of this book. Mr. Tripp was the spark behind this volume. Our two anonymous reviewers were tough and insightful, and our Yale University Press editor, Susan Laity, made this a much more readable book.

Hill would like to express his gratitude to Rapp for providing the opportunity to help contribute to his vision of an introductory text in geoarchaeology, and for more than twenty years of support and friendship. In addition, many other individuals have contributed directly or indirectly to this work. Charles Matsch initiated Hill into the wonders of geology and introduced him to Rapp. He also reviewed versions of many of the chapters of this book. David Meltzer provided a critique of an early version of Chapter 1. During graduate studies at Southern Methodist University, Hill was guided and supported by Fred Wendorf. Claude Albritton and the Institute for the Study of Earth and Man provided a framework for geo-archaeological studies at SMU. Romuald Schild guided Hill in the application of a geoarchaeological approach to field studies in African prehistory. The Museum of the Rockies at Montana State University provided a wonderful setting in which to complete the text. Hill would also like to acknowledge with thanks the help given him by students in the anthropology department at Tulane University and in the department of earth sciences at Montana State University in developing some of the ideas presented in this book.

CHAPTER I

Theoretical and Historical Overview

Geoarchaeology is of major importance in understanding the archaeological record. Indeed, the earth sciences play a pivotal role in interpreting this record in terms of both methodology and theory. This chapter begins with an assessment of what is meant by the term *geoarchaeology* and then presents a short examination of some of the historical and theoretical interactions between the earth sciences and archaeology. The antecedents for using a geoscience approach in evaluating the archaeological record lie in the history of the disciplines, beginning with the concern in the eighteenth and nineteenth centuries for chronology and the development of basic principles, moving into the twentieth century with the collaboration between natural scientists and archaeologists, and coming up to the present with the convergence of the two disciplines in a number of areas. Throughout the history of their interaction, concepts and techniques derived from the earth sciences have been used to analyze the processes involved in the formation of the sedimentary archaeological record, to try and establish the paleoenvironmental settings associated with archaeological sites, to develop chronological frameworks, and to ascertain the physical parameters of artifacts and geofacts. Here we offer a brief overview of this history and explore how the geoarchaeological approach attempts to evaluate and understand the archaeological record and the dynamic forces that produced it.

The Domain of Geoarchaeology

The term *geoarchaeology* (or, less commonly, *geo-archaeology*) has been used with increasing frequency since the 1970s to designate a variety of types of research that use geoscience techniques in the evaluation of the archaeological record. The categorizing of research as an aspect or a subsidiary of geoarchaeology depends in part on whether the term is used to designate a more narrow, focused set of concepts and methods or a broader, more inclusive set. There are many different viewpoints concerning what can appropriately be called geoarchaeology. Lars-Konig Konigsson, for example, contrasts geoarchaeology with archaeogeology. In his view, archaeogeology is a complementary science that is useful in describing deposits related to archaeological material. It is seen as having an advisory role in archaeological interpretation. Konigsson describes geoarchaeology, in contrast, as a study in which the geologist tries to determine the "cultural" development of an area; geologists are not in direct collaboration with archaeologists and rely exclusively on geologic materials and methods.[1] Reid Ferring's definition of geoarchaeology emphasizes the changes in archaeological perspective since the advent of Lewis Binford's New Archaeology. As practiced, Ferring sees geoarchaeology as a "grossly empirical approach to archaeological problems" or the "new empiricism."[2] In perhaps its broadest sense —and the way the term is used in this book— geoarchaeology refers to the application of any earth-science concept, technique, or knowledge base to the study of artifacts and the processes

1

involved in the creation of the archaeological record. Geoarchaeology thus becomes "the geoscience tradition within archaeology . . . [that] deals with earth history within the time frame of human history" or that "implies archaeological research using the methods and concepts of the earth sciences."[3] However, the term has also been limited specifically to the study and interpretation of sediments and physical landscapes.

Also disputed is the question of geoarchaeology versus archaeological geology. Our view is that geoarchaeology is part of archaeology—the part that uses geologic methods, concepts, and knowledge base. The *geo-* modifies the noun *archaeology*. An example of geoarchaeology would be the study of archaeological sediments in an excavation: the framework and questions posed are strictly archaeological. On the other hand, we define archaeological geology as geologic research that has direct relevance to one or more archaeological contexts. Coastal change studies that determine shoreline migration, the filling in of estuaries, or the expansion of deltas in archaeologically important areas fit this definition. Geologists routinely investigate the changes in land-sea boundaries that have transpired over hundreds of millions of years. This research is not archaeological per se. However, when paleogeomorphic maps of dramatic landscape changes in such significant archaeological terrain as Ancient Troy, Ancient Carthage, or the east coast of North America are undertaken because of the sites' archaeological importance, such studies can be termed archaeological geology. Many kinds of geologic investigations in archaeological contexts lie between these two extremes. The geoarchaeology label has been applied by researchers from a wide range of earth-science disciplines (in addition to archaeology itself), including stratigraphy, sedimentology, geomorphology, pedology, petrology, petrography, geochemistry, geophysics, paleontology, marine geology, geochronology, and climatology. Almost every subdiscipline in geology has concepts, methods, and a knowledge base that can contribute to the solution of archaeological problems.

Geoarchaeology in its widest scope or most encompassing form is the application of these earth-science disciplines and subfields to the study of the archaeological record. The key criterion is that *archaeological* interpretations are produced using *earth-science*-based ideas or methods. Because *geo-* modifies *archaeology*, geoarchaeology must be defined as a type of archaeology, one in which the fundamental goal of archaeology is understood to be the study of the artifactual record and where any physical object, feature, or landscape either made or altered by humans (including extinct hominids) is considered an artifact. We are aware that this is a rather strict, bare-bones definition of archaeology, designed to accommodate research focused on inferring past anthropological behavior as well as research that seeks to evaluate nonbehavioral features of the archaeological record. A major goal of archaeology is to evaluate and understand past human behavior, but a broader goal is to understand the processes which produced the final artifactual context available for observation and study.

Where geoarchaeology belongs in relation to other disciplines and subdisciplines has been the subject of a surprising amount of discussion. When viewed from the broad definition, geoarchaeology would include many aspects of archaeometry, environmental archaeology, archaeological science, Quaternary geology and geography (including geomorphology, physical geography, geoecology, and biogeography), **taphonomy,**[*] and bridging (middle-range) theory. From one perspective, geoarchaeology is part of the framework for an ecological or contextual approach to archaeology (not to be confused with the very different "contextual archaeology" as an aspect of postprocessual archaeology).[4] There have even been those who would classify archaeology as a subdivision of the natural sciences or natural history or as branch of Late Quaternary geology, where geology is understood, following Amadeus W. Graubau, as "the science of the entire earth."[5] (For a chronological chart of the geologic time divisions, see Appendix.) The viewpoint expressed by Frederick H. West supports such an archaeogeologic perspective: "Archaeology . . . is an earth science."[6]

[*]Words set in boldface can be found in the glossary.

What might be argued, then, is that geo-archaeology represents a particular focus of archaeology which may be considered, along with hydrology, lithology, and ecology, as a subdivision of earth science in the broadest sense. Indeed, it has been suggested that archaeological sites are really geologic sites containing remains that are of interest to archaeologists.[7] Aspects of geoarchaeology, in turn, can be considered from the viewpoints of "dynamics," "structure," and "chronology" (in the sense of the historical natural sciences). Dynamics deals with the effects of physical and chemical forces and is process-oriented; structure deals with composition and arrangement of materials; and the historical natural sciences are concerned with time, origins, and development. Archaeology has been considered a natural science of the archaeological record,[8] and it can be viewed as a division of the earth sciences, especially in terms of some methodological practices.[9] However, the archaeological record can be evaluated and interpreted even more thoroughly by considering dynamics, structure, and history (both chronology and development through time). In contrast to most other physical and natural sciences, geology (in the restricted sense), paleontology, and archaeology share these concerns.

The behavioral aspects of archaeology are the focus of anthropological archaeology—a traditional field of interest in the United States and England. From a geoarchaeological perspective the goals of anthropological archaeology—inferring past human behavior from the artifactual record—can be attained only by examining the contextual association of the artifacts and attempting to evaluate the behavioral and nonbehavioral factors that have produced the record. Under these circumstances, even the application of such terms as *culture* for what is in reality a collection of items that may or may not reveal patterns created by human behavior may not be always appropriate.

The terms *geoarchaeology* and *archaeological geology* have also been used since the 1970s to designate the natural-science aspect of prehistoric studies, with the recognition that evaluations of prehistoric behavior rely on contributions from the earth sciences.[10] Throughout this period Karl Butzer advocated an ecological or broadly contextual approach to archaeology that emphasized the application of what he called geoarchaeology: "It has been said that archaeology is anthropology or it is nothing. . . . I beg to differ with this view. Archaeology . . . has been equally dependent on geology, biology, and geography . . . during its development . . . [and] is heavily dependent on . . . the natural sciences."[11]

This is similar to the point of view expressed by Mortimer Wheeler, when he wrote: "Archaeology is increasingly dependent on a multitude of sciences and is itself increasingly adopting the methodology of a natural science. It draws today upon physics, chemistry, geology, biology, economics, political science, sociology, climatology, botany."[12]

A more restricted use of *geoarchaeology* would make it analogous to *zooarchaeology*. In this sense, geoarchaeology is primarily focused on soils and sediments (instead of life forms). This is the standpoint of both Bruce Gladfelter and Michael Waters. Gladfelter characterizes geoarchaeology as primarily geomorphology and sedimentary petrography, while Waters considers the most fundamental aspects of geoarchaeology to be the field aspect of stratigraphy, site formation processes, and landscape reconstruction.[13] Fekri Hassan sees the study of site formation processes as a way of interpreting the "cultural" significance of archaeological remains by elucidating the role cultural and natural factors played in shaping the archaeological record. He argues that the study of formation processes has proven that archaeologists cannot assume that artifact collections correspond to a settlement, ethnic group, or cultural activity. The study of formation processes should convince archaeologists to be careful about making cultural interpretations on the basis of the archaeological record.[14] Broader connections between the earth sciences and archaeology—dating techniques, provenance of artifacts, site location, and the like—have been assigned by some practitioners (Waters, for example) to the realm of archaeometry. In the broader geoarchaeological approach that we advocate, such aspects of archaeometry as dating, provenance, and site location become part of geoarchaeology when they represent the application of earth-science methods to archaeological problems.

The fluidness of the definition of geoarchaeology is a manifestation of the classification process within science. One can consider geoarchaeology as a component of prehistoric archaeology that, in turn, may be considered a part of geoecology or paleogeography, which is an aspect of Quaternary geology, and so on. These research fields and subdisciplines can be considered "facies" within a broader framework of natural history and natural science focused on the evaluation of the complete Late Cenozoic record. The primary connecting point may be that these research areas attempt to observe systematically the dynamic processes that occur on the earth and to apply these observations to the inference of past conditions. In this sense archaeology is an aspect of the historical sciences in much the same way paleontology is. Archaeology is distinct from anthropology, on the other hand, in the sense that past processes cannot be directly observed but must be inferred from the available record. Both ethnological anthropology and physical geology allow direct observation of dynamic processes, which in turn can be applied to an interpretation of the structural matrix of the archaeogeologic record. From this matrix the chronological and contextual sequence of events that form prehistory can be inferred.

A History of the Interaction Between Earth Sciences and Archaeology

The historical connections between archaeology, especially prehistoric archaeology, and the geosciences extend back at least through the nineteenth and eighteenth centuries.[15] We can identify several phases in this interaction, which fit into three overlapping periods.

The first of these periods was characterized by an integrative approach to prehistory; it can be viewed as a period where the primary concern was with issues involved in the determination of human antiquity. The nineteenth century traditionally has been characterized as a time when

interest focused on evidence concerning early human occupation of Europe and America during the Ice Age. From about the 1840s through the 1920s, geology and archaeology were united in the study of evidence for human antiquity. In addition to the interest in relative chronologies, archaeosedimentary sequences (strata containing artifacts) were studied to determine what processes were involved in their formation and how to evaluate associations between artifacts and remains of extinct fauna.

During the second phase, from the end of the nineteenth century to about 1950, interest in paleoenvironmental and paleoclimatologic conditions expanded the sphere of interaction between prehistoric archaeology and the geosciences. Collaboration between geologists and archaeologists continued to be an important facet of Paleo-Indian studies in North America after the late 1920s, and a major characteristic of Old World Paleolithic research. Sedimentary sequences or stratified deposits continued to be studied for their site formation and chronological implications, but until about the 1950s, the collaboration appears to have emphasized the use of geoscience methods to evaluate the paleoclimatic and geochronological contexts of archaeological sites. This second period was characterized by a shift away from the integrative approach (in which the various scientists would together publish a single report) and toward collaboration between specialists (in which each scientist would publish a separate report). We can differentiate three variants of archaeogeologic efforts during this period: regional geomorphologic studies aimed at developing paleoclimatic and geochronological frameworks; laboratory studies of ecological and artifactual materials; and site-specific studies of deposits containing artifact sequences.

Around the beginning of the second half of the twentieth century, a third phase of interaction began. Although scientists continued to pursue mutual interests in chronology and climatologic change, they also began to combine new emphases and interests in prehistoric archaeology and the geosciences. These new interests had a common theoretical basis that emphasized the "context" of archaeological sites. Archaeologists and prehistorians also believed that the natural sciences could help answer new questions derived from these theoretical developments. This period of convergence owes its existence to a concern for the processes that have transformed the original context of the artifacts into the archaeological record.[16]

Foundations: The Eighteenth and Nineteenth Centuries

In their review of the development of archaeological geology, John Gifford and G. R. Rapp, Jr., delineated a period in which interdisciplinary research was implicit, rather than overt.[17] This period, already initiated by the 1840s, was characterized by an interest in human antiquity and, consequently, stratigraphic chronology. In both the Old World and North America the natural-science perspective was reflected in the efforts of individuals, mostly geologists by training, who in their studies of the prehistoric record took for granted that artifacts found in geologic deposits had been used by humans. In his history of archaeology, Glyn Daniel notes: "Many great nineteenth-century archaeologists were in the first instance geologists and natural scientists," and nineteenth-century archaeology "was essentially geological in outlook."[18] Edward Harris apparently concurs with this; he claims that during this time archaeological work "was dominated by theories of geological stratigraphy."[19] The early recognition of the importance of understanding the context of artifacts is reflected in the report that John Frere wrote in 1797 concerning the discovery of stone hand axes within a stratified sedimentary sequence in England. Frere describes the location of the artifacts and the sequence of sediments, and he discusses the implications of these observations: "The manner in which . . . [the hand axes] lie would lead to the persuasion that it was a place of their manufacture and not of their accidental deposit. . . . It may be suggested that the different strata were formed by inundations happening at distant periods."[20] In Frere's report the horizontal bedding and the density of artifacts in the deposits are delineated. His observations clearly establish that from the beginnings of Paleolithic research, an awareness of the value

of evaluating artifacts within their stratigraphic context was understood.

The history of the demonstration of the contemporaneity of humans and extinct animals (and consequently the acceptance of the presence of humans during the Ice Age in Europe) provides many early examples of the employment of techniques derived from the earth sciences in the study of artifacts. The events leading to this demonstration and acceptance have been chronicled since the mid-1800s. Research initiated by Jacques Boucher de Crèvecoeur de Perthes in 1837 at Somme Valley in France and continued by Marcel Jérôme Rigollot illustrates the critical interaction between geologists and prehistoric archaeologists. Both included profiles that indicated the stratigraphic context of Stone Age artifacts; and their observations demonstrated the contemporaneity of stone tools and extinct animals, although these observations did not convince everyone. It was after the excavations of Brixham Cave in England in 1858, directed by William Pengelly and supervised by a group that included the geologist Charles Lyell (figure 1.1), that geologic opinion began to support the archaeological acceptance of the presence of humans during the Ice Age.[21] Human artifacts were found in direct stratigraphic association with fossils of extinct animals or geologic deposits of Ice Age antiquity. British geologists Joseph Prestwich and John Evans traveled first to Abbeville and later to St. Acheul during 1859 to view the sites studied by Boucher de Crèvecoeur de Perthes. At St. Acheul they were able to observe stone artifacts embedded in sediments containing the remains of extinct animals. They were convinced by this evidence that humans had lived at the same time as extinct animals. Lyell also visited France in July 1859 and confirmed their observations, which were quickly published. They believed that the stone artifacts could validly be associated with the remains of extinct animals; this association lead them to conclude that humans were present during the Ice Age.

Just how thoroughly this approach—which from a present-day perspective would be considered geoarchaeological—was ingrained in the ideas of the middle part of the nineteenth cen-

Figure 1.1 Sir Charles Lyell
If geoarchaeology has a "father," it is Charles Lyell, best known for his multivolume, multi-edition *Principles of Geology* and for his unswerving dedication to the concept of uniformitarianism. His *Geological Evidences of the Antiquity of Man* is both the first book on geoarchaeology and a defining text: it sets out the archaeological problem and then applies geologic knowledge and principles. An Englishman who, along with Charles Darwin and Georges Cuvier, effected the great nineteenth-century revolution in our understanding of human and natural history, Lyell carefully documented, in a uniformitarian geologic context, all known remains of prehistoric humans and their artifacts. (Drawing by Elaine Nissen, from a photograph in the University of Minnesota Archives)

tury is exemplified by the works of Lyell and John Lubbock. Both provided detailed reviews of the evidence for the human antiquity in Europe based on evaluations of the contextual integrity of the artifacts. Lyell's *Geological Evidences of the Antiquity of Man* (1863) clearly established the role of geology in archaeological inquiry. In his 1865 monograph *Pre-Historic Times*, Lubbock divided the Stone Age into the Paleolithic and Neolithic, dividing the artifactual record into an Old Stone Age and a New Stone Age. The Paleolithic was subsequently separated into three more sub-

divisions, Lower, Middle, and Upper, by Edward Lartet and Gabriel de Mortillet, both of whom were greatly influenced by the concepts and practices of geology. A similar review by James Geikie a few years later deals specifically with the climate and geologic age of Paleolithic deposits.[22] The historical importance of geologic thought in prehistoric archaeology has been commented upon by Daniel, who writes: "Antiquarianism was . . . securely bedded . . . [in the] advance of natural science. . . . There could be no real archaeology before geology." Daniel describes archaeology as the child of geology and writes about "the geological beginnings of archaeology." In his view, geology initially "defined the limits and set the problems of prehistoric archaeology." For some early prehistorians, "the Paleolithic . . . was a matter of geology"; "prehistoric archaeologists . . . [thought] of themselves as natural scientists." The geologic approach was exemplified by de Mortillet's attitude that prehistory was "entirely an extension of geology." Daniel reinforces this argument with the suggestion that "the de Mortillet system with its geological background . . . became the orthodox system of prehistory."[23]

During the second half of the nineteenth century other areas of archaeology became concerned with chronology and stratigraphy, as is evident in the work of classical archaeology. In 1860 Giuseppe Fiorelli began to conduct excavations at Pompeii that laid emphasis on stratigraphic control. Alexander Conze showed similar concern for stratigraphy in the 1873 excavations of Samothrace, as did Ernst Curtius in the 1875 excavations of Olympia. At Hissarlik (Troy), starting in 1871, Heinrich Schliemann became the first to excavate a multilayered **tell**. After 1882 the technique of stratigraphic excavation at Troy was firmly established by the efforts of Wilhelm Dörpfeld. During the late 1800s Augustus Henry Pitt-Rivers stressed the critical importance of stratigraphic observation in excavations conducted in England. Another of the main founders of "modern" archaeological methods of excavation was William Matthew Flinders Petrie, with his excavations in Egypt and Palestine.

It has been argued that, perhaps because of the Europeans' early adaptation and refinement of stratigraphic excavation techniques, geologic principles seem to have been more widely applied in Europe than in the United States. As early as the 1840s, however, Ephraim G. Squier and Edwin H. Davis provide a valuable example of how American archaeologists were implicitly using geologic principles during the mid-nineteenth century.[24] The two used stratigraphic methods to determine whether anthropogenic or other natural processes had created mounds found in the Mississippi Valley. Their research proves that attention to the geologic context of artifacts (the method favored by Boucher de Crèvecoeur de Perthes and Rigollot) was being applied to the understanding of the prehistoric record in America at essentially the same time it was in the Old World. According to Bruce Trigger, "all the chronological methods used in Europe were known in America and had been successfully applied by archaeologists."[25] From the 1870s onward, shell-mound studies were reported by Jeffries Wyman, Steven Walker, and Clarence B. Moore from the southeastern United States and by William H. Dall in Alaska. During the 1880s, after the work by Squier and Davis, Cyrus Thomas used stratigraphic principles to study mounds, as did William Henry Holmes and Frederick W. Putnam in their research into the possibility of an American Paleolithic.[26]

North America's first great mining boom during the 1840s provided early evidence of other forms of prehistoric use of natural resources. In the Keweenaw Peninsula of northern Michigan it became apparent that the miners were not the first to exploit the rich veins and surface nuggets of native copper. The "ancient diggings," as they were called in the Lake Superior region, were copper mines from a time well before European contact. In the debris of the ancient pits were stone hammers with marks of hard usage. A large proportion were broken but some had been new or unused when abandoned. These discoveries were reported by professionals in the early 1850s and brought geologists into the picture as they sought to explain the context of these remains.[27]

A prominent example of the application of geologic methodology during this early period is Lyell's observations concerning human remains and their association with deposits containing extinct fauna in Mississippi. Lyell conducted field studies of the area in 1846 and concluded that the association was probably a product of redeposition or mixing. This emphasis on describing the processes that contributed to the final state of the artifactual record was a crucial facet of the "American Paleolithic" issue in the late nineteenth century. The American Paleolithic controversy focused on the effect that natural processes might have on the integrity of the archaeological record, and the validity of arguments regarding the antiquity of artifacts or human remains relied mainly on the stratigraphic context of these finds.[28] The search for human antiquity and the question of an American Paleolithic involved as much geologic as archaeological knowledge.

To understand what happened to the "early man" controversy during the last two decades of the nineteenth century, we must turn to the geologists of the U.S. Geological Survey (USGS) and the archaeologists of the Bureau of American Ethnology (BAE). Both agencies were created through the efforts of the geologist, geographer, and ethnographer John Wesley Powell in 1879. The BAE, in Powell's conception, was to provide a permanent anthropological survey for the United States. The critical role of geologists in the founding and early development of the Bureau of American Ethnology should not be underestimated. After founding director Powell left in 1902, the geologist W. H. Holmes became director, a position he held until 1910. Holmes led the BAE into the important new fields of physical anthropology and cultural-resource preservation.

The key to the early-man controversy lay in the definition of a relative sequence of glacial-age deposits for North America—one of the goals of USGS geologists in the 1880s. European glaciologists had recognized the existence of glacial and interglacial stratigraphy, and Americans also began to discern regional sequences as large areas of the midwest and the Rocky Mountains were mapped by state surveys and by the USGS.

Throughout the last decade of the nineteenth century, the reliability of the geologic context for potential paleolithic artifacts was considered to be of critical importance. Holmes wrote: "Advocates of a paleolithic . . . in America have been forced to give up the idea that there is any other reliable test of the age [of an artifact] . . . than that furnished by geology. . . . The antiquity . . . [is a] question germane to the field of geologic research."[29] This appears to have been a consensus idea, despite differences in the actual evaluations of the geologic contexts of "paleoliths." Powell had earlier written: "The first appearance of mankind in . . . the continent . . . must rest on geologic facts."[30] Regarding Quaternary sediments, Charles C. Abbott stated: "He is no archaeologist whose training falls short of the ability to study intelligently the history of these superficial deposits."[31] Haynes echoed Abbott on the importance of a full understanding of the context of artifacts: "Whether any . . . object can be identified as a . . . paleolithic implement . . . is a question for geologists to answer."[32] So did Rollin D. Salisbury: "Were the 'paleolithic implements' so introduced? This is a geological, not an archaeological question."[33]

By 1892, George Frederick Wright had advocated an American Paleolithic based in part on a review of the geologic context of the purported artifacts.[34] Critics of Wright's ideas equally consistently based their arguments on geologic criteria. The application of geologic methods to buttress the argument that humans existed in America during the Ice Age is exemplified by Holmes's 1893 *Journal of Geology* and *American Geologist* articles concerning contextual problems associated with potential Paleolithic sites in Ohio and Minnesota. The archaeologist David Meltzer considers these papers important because they represent "a shift" from arguments based on artifact morphology to "a dependence on geology."[35]

Many other leading figures of North American geology in the late nineteenth century found the geologic aspects of the early-man controversy compelling and made significant contributions to the resolution of questions about the glacial context of human and artifactual remains. Prominent among them is the first state geologist of Minnesota, Newton Horace Winchell (figure 1.2). While working out the glacial geology of Minnesota, Winchell became interested in the ancient remains of the indigenous Indian tribes. Winchell's interest culminated in a large volume, *The*

Figure 1.2 Newton Horace Winchell
In 1872 Newton Horace Winchell became the first State Geologist and director of the Geological and Natural History Survey of Minnesota. One of Winchell's outstanding contributions was his estimate of the length of time since the last ice sheet retreated from Minnesota, based in part on his evaluation of the rate of recession of St. Anthony Falls, which he gave as 8,000 years. After he completed the final survey reports, he devoted much of his time to the archaeology of the state. From 1906 until his death in 1914, he worked at the Minnesota Historical Society, where he was in charge of the Department of Archaeology. (Drawing by Elaine Nissen, from a photograph in the University of Minnesota archives)

Aborigines of Minnesota, published in 1911. In addition, he summarized many of the questions about the geologic context of early humans in North America in his presidential address to the Geological Society of America on 20 December 1902.

Collaboration: The First Half of the Twentieth Century

As researchers began to conduct more planned, systematic excavations of archaeological sites and became more specialized in their training, the focus on interaction lead to a period of straight-forward collaboration. These years show a re-finement of the field methodologies employed during the 1800s, such as those used by Rigollot at St. Acheul, in France. Geoscience specialists increasingly worked with archaeologists in collaborative efforts not only to evaluate the contextual and chronological situation of artifacts and other fossil remains but also to obtain information concerning paleoenvironmental and paleoclimatic changes. Collaborative efforts were also undertaken in the study of artifactual raw materials and remote sensing.

The collaboration or multidisciplinary co-operation that characterizes this period can be divided into three types. Most prominent, geoscientists (commonly but not exclusively Pleistocene geologists and vertebrate paleontologists) coordinated their efforts with archaeologists working in the same geographic area. These earth scientists were primarily interested in regional studies that could be used as the basis for paleoclimatic interpretations and building a chronological framework that could also be applied to dating archaeological sites. The emphasis on the use of geomorphic, stratigraphic, and paleontologic criteria was a critical aspect of the chronological studies—indeed, this second period ends with the introduction of "absolute" dating methods.

The second kind of cooperation was between specialists involved in the laboratory analysis of geologic samples and artifacts and those who provided the specimens. In the third, the collaboration was between individuals who might be termed "geoarchaeologists" in the sense that they were archaeologists who evaluated the site-specific archaeosedimentary context of artifact localities.

In Old World studies this period of cooperation began roughly at the start of the twentieth century. The years 1900–1950 have been identified as a period of growth in interdisciplinary work on the Pleistocene. The investigations of the Grimaldi Caves and the Grotte de l'Obsérvatoire at Monaco represent pioneering efforts in which natural scientists took direct part in archaeological excavations. These studies were led by the paleontologist Ami Boué. This type of effort can be seen as expansion and refinement of the

work conducted in England at Kent's Cavern and Brixham Cave by geologists Hugh Falconer and William Pengelly in the late 1850s and the development of archaeological excavation techniques in the work in Turkey of Dorpfeld, in Egypt of Petrie, and in England of Pitt-Rivers during the last part of the nineteenth century.

In addition to the advancement of excavation methodologies in early twentieth-century archaeology, there was an increasing emphasis on the examination of all materials recovered from the excavation. Reliance on specific expertise from other natural sciences in the fields of petrography, metallurgy, botany, zoology, pedology, and geochronology to study archaeological materials increased. The joint research of the geologist Raphael Pumpelly and the archaeologist Hubert Schmidt at the site of Anau in southern Turkmenia in 1904 can be considered an example of an early effort at adding what we consider a geoarchaeological perspective to archaeological interpretation. Excavations were conducted on a Neolithic/Chalcolithic through Iron Age sequence using a refined procedure that included screening and vertical and horizontal control of finds. Specialists in ceramics, vertebrate paleontology and human skeletal remains, botany, the analysis of metal artifacts, geomorphology, and climatology participated in the excavation. Pumpelly applied what he called the rules of geologic reasoning to archaeology.[36]

Chronology and environmental and climate change, along with their relation to human adaptation as reflected in artifactual remains, were archaeology's principal concerns. The pollen-analysis methods developed by Lennart von Post revealed climate intervals associated with postglacial environmental change. Tree rings were employed to estimate chronologies by the dendrochronologist Andrew E. Douglass after 1901 —although DeWitt Clinton had used tree rings to date earthworks in New York State as early as 1811.[37] In the Old World, the technique of varve analysis was applied by Gerard J. de Geer in 1905 in Sweden and later by Matti Sauramo in Finland. In North America, the Quaternary geologist Ernst Antevs was the first to use varve analysis (see Chapter 7).

During the 1920s to the 1940s geoscientists

collaborated in a variety of Old World prehistoric investigations. The first phase of geoarchaeological research was archaeological site sedimentologic studies, as described by geoarchaeologists Julie Stein and William Farrand. These are represented in such site sedimentology studies as those conducted by archaeologist Dorothy A. E. Garrod and paleontologist Dorothy M. A. Bate between 1929 and 1934 during their excavations in the southern Levant. Stein and Farrand categorize these as "archaeological geology."[38] Evidence of multidisciplinary interaction in the Old World is reflected by Zeuner's use of prehistoric archaeology for its geochronological and climatic implications, in an approach reminiscent of the earlier works of Lyell, Lubbock, Geicke, and Wright.[39] Zeuner's efforts represent specific attempts to work in an area that falls between the natural sciences and human prehistory. Glyn Daniel and Colin Renfrew describe Zeuner's *Dating the Past* as "one of the first books exclusively dedicated to archaeological science. . . . The approach was largely geological, as it had been since the early days of the last century."[40]

In Europe, the perspective for the study of prehistory appears to have enlarged during the first half of the twentieth century. De Morgan expressed the view that prehistory was not a discipline narrowly focused on the study of artifacts; rather, "Geology, zoology, botany, climatology, anthropology and ethnography are the bases of prehistory."[41]

Remote-sensing techniques were applied during the early part of twentieth century in the form of aerial photography.[42] In 1906 aerial photographs of Stonehenge revealed buried features not visible from the surface. In the Middle East, aerial photographs were used to record the outline of an irrigation system. During the 1920s a major effort to use aerial photography to discern archaeological features was conducted in England, while in North America, Charles Lindbergh took aerial photographs of the American southwest. Atkinson's use of electrical conductivity in 1948 pioneered the use of resistivity meter surveys for the location of such buried site features as structures, pits, and ditches.[43]

The application of natural sciences in the analysis and study of materials recovered from ar-

chaeological excavations—including soils, pollen, metal, stone, and plants—also increased. Examples of such applications include Thomas's petrographic analysis of stones from Stonehenge, Watson's examination of the fossil faunal remains (bones) from the site of Skara Brae, and the work by Danish scientists on prehistoric grains.

Elaboration of the principles involved in stratigraphic studies continued. Wheeler's use of section drawings during the 1920s, which has been considered a turning point in archaeological methodology, is a primary example.[44] This approach was more fully explored in Wheeler's *Archaeology from the Earth*, published in 1954. Important continuities between the European natural-science perspectives that were developed in the nineteenth century and American archaeology in the beginning of the twentieth century can be seen by the expanded use of stratigraphic excavations in America. Influenced by the European geologic approach to prehistory, Manuel Gamino and Nels C. Nelson employed stratigraphic principles at American sites.[45] Alfred V. Kidder, influenced by Nelson's fieldwork, applied the techniques of stratigraphic excavation at the famous site of Pecos, New Mexico.[46]

During the early part of the twentieth century, the issues concerned with verification of potential Ice Age artifacts and human remains continued to dominate archaeological/geologic studies. Purported Pleistocene human remains or artifacts, for example, had to be verified by unquestionable stratigraphic evidence. Interactions between American archaeologists and geologists during this period are exemplified by the publication in 1917 in the *Journal of Geology* of a collection of articles dealing with human remains found in association with remains of extinct fauna at Vero, Florida. As with other potential Pleistocene sites containing evidence of the presence of humans, the basic discussions revolved around the sedimentologic context of the materials and the validity of their association. Rollin T. Chamberlin and George G. MacCurdy both concluded that there was evidence that the faunal remains lay in secondary deposits, but Chamberlin also believed that there was evidence to support the association between the extinct fauna and the human remains. The physical anthropologist Aleš Hrdlička, on the other hand, believed that the Vero discovery could not be supported because of the depositional context of the remains.

The discoveries at Folsom, New Mexico, in 1927 showed that human occupation in North America dated to the Late Pleistocene. The primary criterion for acceptance of the Folsom evidence was that the context of the discovery indicated a primary association between undisputed artifacts and extinct fauna, with no evidence that the associations were caused by secondary depositional processes. The resurgence of a geologic interest among American archaeologists can be traced to the Folsom discovery.[47]

One can recognize the strongest natural-science orientation in American Paleo-Indian studies; within this realm a geoscience perspective has been pervasive in North American archaeology. This growth in interest is exemplified by the efforts of Edgar B. Howard, Elias H. Sellards, Antevs, and Bryan. Howard provided a comprehensive study and review of early human occupation in the American Southwest using geologic and archaeological evidence that included excavations at Burnet Cave and Carlsbad, New Mexico, and a study of Late Pleistocene ephemeral lake sediments between the towns of Clovis and Portales.[48] His synthesis employed a variety of data derived from natural sciences to infer the Late Pleistocene environment on the Llano Estacado. In addition, he gave a critique of Paleo-Indian artifact typology and a review of the chronological and climatic theories associated with the end of the Pleistocene.

The geologic and archaeological aspects of the Clovis-type site were studied by Antevs when he was a member of Howard's expedition in 1934. Antevs was influential in employing geologic techniques to develop paleoclimatic models that could be related to archaeological studies.[49]

Following the research at Vero, Sellards continued to conduct studies documenting the presence of humans in America during the Pleistocene (figure 1.3). Vance Holliday described this as the first regional, interdisciplinary group of studies of Paleo-Indian archaeology and their associated environments.[50]

From about 1925 to 1950 Kirk Bryan dominated research at the interface between geology and ar-

Figure 1.3 Elias H. Sellards
Elias H. Sellards is perhaps best known for his advocacy, when he was State Geologist of Florida, of the association of human remains with those of extinct vertebrates in Pleistocene deposits at Vero and Melbourne, Florida. Although Sellards was probably wrong, the well-publicized dispute provoked careful studies of the vertebrate assemblage, studies that applied more sophisticated excavation techniques than was common in American archaeology. (Drawing by Elaine Nissen, from a photograph in the Texas Bureau of Economic Geology archives)

chaeology in North America. C. Vance Haynes, designating the period the "Antevs-Bryan years," demonstrates that like Bryan, Antevs had a great deal of influence in the geochronological study of Paleo-Indian sites.[51] Bryan and Antevs initiated what Stein and Farrand call the second phase of archaeological sedimentology, in which geoscientists were largely concerned with geochronology and the paleoenvironment of a site.

In the 1920s Bryan investigated evidence for environmental change at Chaco Canyon, New Mexico. Later he became active in assessing the geologic setting of Paleo-Indian sites. Quaternary stratigraphic studies conducted in western Texas made extensive use of Paleo-Indian occurrences. Although a major facet of Bryan's work was his focus on the application of paleoclimatic chronologies to date Paleo-Indian sites, these efforts were also used to delineate the paleoenvironmental settings of Pleistocene archaeological sites. The interpretations of the settings were largely based on evaluations of the processes of sedimentary deposition affected by climatic processes. The reports by Bryan and Antevs on the human remains found within possible glacial-age deposits in western Minnesota show their concern for the processes of deposition in evaluating the archaeological record.

Bryan's influence can be seen in the application of geologic techniques to archaeological studies by his students in both New and Old World sites. The geologist Sheldon Judson carried out a geologic study of the San Jon site and its Plainview artifacts in northeastern New Mexico under Bryan's supervision. The Midland study, led by prehistorian Fred Wendorf with the cooperation of geologist Claude Albritton and archaeologist Alex Krieger, has been called a model of the working collaboration between scientists. John Miller and Wendorf extended Bryan's alluvial chronology to the Tesuque Valley in New Mexico. Bryan had also initiated the investigations of the rock shelter at La Colombière in southeastern France, which were later completed by Hallam L. Movius and Judson. In 1947 Bryan's student Herbert E. Wright, Jr., studied the geology of the Paleolithic occurrences at Ksar Akil, Lebanon. It is reasonable to state that by the beginning of the second half of the twentieth century Bryan and his students had effected a convergence of Pleistocene studies and archaeological studies through an explicitly paleogeomorphic approach to archaeology.[52]

The nature of the interaction between archaeology and geology in America during the first half of the twentieth century is encapsulated in the volume *Early Man* published for the 125th anniversary of the Philadelphia Academy of Natural Sciences.[53] It contains essays by Hrdlička on the skeletal evidence for a human presence in America during the Pleistocene and an evaluation of the Vero finds by Sellards. There is an essay on the significance of profiles of weathering in stratigraphic archaeology by geomorphologist Morris M. Leighton, another on the use of pollen for dating archaeological deposits by paleobotanist Paul Sears, an essay on climate and "early man" by Antevs, and a discussion of the geology of Folsom deposits by Bryan. The volume demonstrates that many approaches derived from the natural sciences were being applied in early twentieth-century prehistoric studies.

Integration: The Second Half of the Twentieth Century

Throughout the nineteenth century and the first part of the twentieth century, earth-science interactions and methodological concerns with archaeology were largely focused on chronological interests. Without question the contribution of radiocarbon dating initiated by Frank Willard Libby in the late 1940s and extensively used from the 1950s onward was a critical contribution of the natural sciences to archaeological interpretation. Other influential technical innovations during the 1950s and 1960s from the field of geochronology include the application of chemical tests like those that verified the Piltdown fraud and research that used potassium-argon (K-Ar) measurements to establish the chronological context of hominid fossils associated with East African igneous rocks.

Another arena of interaction was in the identification of raw material. H. H. Thomas had initiated these studies at Stonehenge (see Chapters 5 and 6). Other studies of raw-material characterization in the Old World were Frederick R. Matson's analysis of the clays from which pottery was made, the study of Bronze Age metals by Edward Sangmeister, H. Otto, and others, and the explorations of Renfrew, J. R. Cann, and others into obsidian sources and trade. New World raw-material characterization studies include the work of David Williams on the petrography of pottery tempers and his investigations with Robert E. Heizer of the rocks used in Olmec monuments from Mexico.

Along with the methodological interaction between the earth sciences and archaeology, a trend toward theoretical convergence developed during the last half of the twentieth century. Archaeology went through a period of change. In part this reflected a major emphasis on the development of a theoretical basis for archaeological studies. The change also came from the realization by archaeologists of how much paleoanthropology depended on an understanding of the geologic context of an archaeological deposit. A critical component of the new emphasis on context was the geoscience perspective. The transformation from a period of collaboration to a period of theoretical convergence in archaeology and the earth sciences is evident in Stein and Farrand's third phase of archaeological sedimentology, "geoarchaeology."[54]

Several prominent developments suggest the explicit integration of an archaeogeologic perspective into archaeological studies during the second half of the twentieth century. The first is a movement toward, and then direct attempts at, formulating a theoretical framework in archaeology that would allow for a geoarchaeological perspective. The second was the merging of methodological interests and the formulation and application of these interests in field and laboratory studies.

At least two subphases within the development of a theoretical framework can be recognized. The initial subphase is characterized by statements made in the 1940s and 1950s on the potential role of geoscientists in archaeology; the second by more formal statements made in the 1960s through the 1990s. In the first phase fall the writings of Movius, Robert J. Braidwood, Herbert E. Wright, Jr., and Ian W. Cornwall;

combined, these works indicate that the benefits of interactive collaboration between geologists and archaeologists were established by the end of the 1950s. This view is illustrated in Old World paleolithic archaeology by Movius, who stressed the bond between prehistoric archaeology and the natural sciences. One goal of archaeology to investigate human adaptation to natural environments, Movius emphasized, could be achieved through natural-science studies concerned with the sequence and correlation of Pleistocene events. He argued for the importance of environmental reconstruction, noting: "Prehistoric archaeology cannot be divorced from its background with the natural sciences without denying it the very key to the solution of its fundamental problem: the reconstruction and interpretation, insofar as possible, of human activities of the past."[55]

In a volume edited by Walter W. Taylor, Braidwood envisioned a new field of "Pleistocene ecology," or "Quaternary geography," consisting of interrelated disciplines that would include archaeology and studies of the environment. In the same volume Wright emphasized that the most useful contributions geologists could make to archaeological problems lay in the interpretation of the physical and climatic environment. He noted the importance of this approach to the study and evaluation of the whole archaeological site and suggested that Pleistocene geologists would be most interested in the climatic environment and chronology associated with archaeological sites. And Judson also recognized the value of collaboration between Pleistocene geologists and archaeologists.[56]

An influential study that demonstrated the potential sediments and soils offered in archaeological analysis and interpretation was Cornwall's *Soils for the Archaeologist*. Butzer describes Cornwall's work as the first systematic attempt at geoarchaeology.[57] Cornwall argued for contextual studies in archaeology that used the geosciences. Edward Pyddoke wrote in his *Stratification for the Archaeologist*: "It should be the task of the archaeologist to interpret and understand not only man's activities and artifacts but also the nature of the natural strata on, in, and under which they are discovered."[58] The books by Cornwall, Pyd-doke, Wheeler, and Zeuner show that a pervasive geoarchaeological perspective was established in the study of Old World prehistory by the 1960s.

The conceptual framework produced by the writings of Movius, Braidwood, and Cornwall provided a foundation from which Butzer's views could be elaborated. Butzer gave the designation "Pleistocene geography" to his view of the natural-science approach. He characterized Pleistocene geography as "environmental reconstruction as applied to an understanding of the ecological setting to prehistory."[59] In addition to stratigraphy and chronology, Butzer placed an emphasis on environmental reconstruction. The role of geology in Pleistocene paleoecology and archaeology was discussed by C. Vance Haynes, Jr. (figure 1.4), when he emphasized the importance of the geologic stratigraphy, interdisciplinary cooperation, and the geologist's role in paleoecologic interpretations.[60]

Beginning in the 1960s, prehistorians, archaeologists, and anthropologists focused on the theoretical and methodological problems of attempting to use the archaeological record to infer prehistoric human behavior. Anthropologist Lewis Binford emphasized the fact that archaeological sites vary in their depositional context and history.[61] Archaeologists recognized the importance of evaluating all potential processes that could affect the final character of the archaeological record to infer past hominid behavior. Prehistorian Glynn Isaac focused on investigating sedimentologic processes to interpret Acheulian occurrences at Olorgasailie in Kenya.[62] Robert Acher looked at disturbances of the archaeological record and the discontinuities between past behavioral systems, the artifacts produced and deposited because of these activities, and subsequent events that affected these materials.[63]

In Greece during the 1960s, William A. McDonald included earth scientists in his wide-ranging survey of Messenia, bringing in first Bryan's student Wright, a geologist and paleoecologist, then Rapp to complement the physical geographers. The resulting publication was subtitled "Reconstructing a Bronze Age Environment."[64] Along the Nile valley, Wendorf

Figure 1.4 C. Vance Haynes, Jr.
One of the few long-time full-time geoarchaeologists in the United States, C. Vance Haynes, Jr., holds dual appointments in geology and anthropology/archaeology at the University of Arizona. He has contributed to the solution of a broad range of important geoarchaeological problems in the southwestern United States and Egypt. (Drawing by Elaine Nissen, from a photograph by Christopher Hill)

(another student of Bryan's) organized a multidisciplinary team of scientists (including geologists Jean de Heinzelin and Albritton and paleontologists Francine Martin, Achilles Gautier, and P. H. Greenwood) to study the Paleolithic of Nubia.[65] Similar efforts at integrating researchers from other natural sciences into archaeology are exemplified by Richard MacNeish's work in Mesoamerica and Braidwood and Robert McCormick Adams' in the Middle East. The theoretical development of concepts associated with processual archaeology may be strongly linked with the increased tendency to view archaeology as a natural-historic science. It became clear that the archaeological record could not be used directly to observe human behavior but instead that the record could be used to infer the past processes that had created it. The early stages of processual archaeology were influenced by the ecological orientation of Leslie A. White and Julian H. Steward and the reappraisal of American archaeology by Taylor. The increased interest in ecological and spatial patterns and their relation to process was noted by Joseph Caldwell in 1959, but Binford's arguments focused attention on the development of archaeological theory toward a processual view.[66]

The later theoretical arguments of both Binford and Michael B. Schiffer advocated a focus on the natural transformational processes involved in creating the archaeological record and the usefulness of a natural-science approach in assessing them.[67] With the goal of providing insights into the accurate interpretation of archaeological record, Binford argued that "archaeology must face up to the nature of the data it employs . . . [and] adopt the methods of the natural sciences." He added: "It is much more likely that archaeological remains will be found within geological deposits. . . . [The] materials within (i.e., artifacts) derive from events during the deposits formation, none of which is necessarily representative of a behaviorally interrelated set of conditions."[68]

On the assumption that the archaeological record was a product of diverse sets of natural and anthropogenic processes, Schiffer differentiated between the archaeological context and the systemic context, proposed a model based on transformation theory, and focused on identifying the processes involved in creating the archaeological record. Whether advocated as bridging (middle-range) theory or as part of environmental archaeology, the focus on processes has become recognized as an important facet in the study of prehistory. Following the lead of Binford, L. Mark Raab and Albert C. Goodyear argue that the principles of processes have become virtually synonymous with middle-range theory in archaeology.[69]

The strong connections between prehistoric archaeology and geology were stressed by Hassan. He argued that reconstruction of site development history using sedimentologic analysis was a contribution "pertinent to the contemporary theoretical orientation of archaeological research."[70] For Hassan, understanding the human past included evaluating artifacts in both their physical context and behavioral matrix in order to interpret their final location.

Quaternary geologists, prehistorians, and archaeologists have attempted to develop a conceptual base for geoarchaeology and its relation to archaeology by building upon Butzer's contextual or ecological archaeology.[71] Influenced by the ideas of David L. Clarke, F. G. Fedele also used the interactions between the human ecosystem and the external paleo-land system to develop a geoarchaeological approach.[72] These ecological attempts paralleled approaches to employ system theory in the earth sciences and archaeology.

During the late 1980s and 1990s opinion has consolidated concerning the importance of a natural-science perspective in archaeology.[73] Our review of historical areas of research and theoretical concepts in this chapter reflects this consensus. Archaeological data appear as the product of varying proportions of human behavioral activities and natural geologic processes. The necessity of differentiating these phenomena is now recognized as crucial to deriving knowledge from the prehistoric evidence. Archaeological occurrences can be understood more fully when the paleoenvironmental context and the processes involved in creating the archaeological record are documented and evaluated.

The methodological convergence of the geosciences and archaeology is characterized by the expansion of the application of technical tools in support of archaeological research. In addition to increased interest in applying sedimentologic and stratigraphic principles to locating and delimiting archaeological sites and features, geochemical and geophysical techniques have become popular.

As we conclude this appraisal, it seems appropriate to return to the question of what geoarchaeology is and what use it has for creating a theoretical base for archaeology. Several theoretical perspectives appear useful for encouraging attempts to understand the archaeological record.

In an extreme perspective, archaeology is a branch of earth science that consists of processes, structure, and chronology. In another viewpoint, it is an independent natural science parallel to geology. Archaeology is a distinct discipline in that one of its main goals is the study of human behavior, but this behavior is not directly observable in the archaeological record. In the field of prehistoric archaeology there are no direct observations of human behavior; all activities and processes must be inferred from evidence that is directly observable. As stated by Clarke, archaeology is "the discipline with the theory and practice for the recovery of unobservable hominid behavior patterns from indirect traces in bad samples."[74] In some sense then, archaeology is closely connected with historical geology and paleontology. These fields seek to understand the history of life on earth. Archaeology may also be understood on its own terms, as many have advocated since the late 1960s and early 1970s.

If the function of geoarchaeology is to solve archaeological problems using earth-science techniques, concepts, and knowledge base, then we must understand the problems that archaeology seeks to resolve. The following chapters give an indication of the diverse methods and knowledge derived from the earth sciences that are used to infer past conditions from archaeological data. Among these are the location of sites and features, the distinction of artifacts or archaeological features from naturally occurring forms, the evaluation of assemblage integrity and the environmental setting, the establishment of the ages of artifacts and the duration and intensity of occupations by identifying materials found in the archaeological record, and the sourcing of raw materials and artifacts.

This brief review of the historical and theoretical interaction between the earth sciences and archaeology prompts a consideration of what the phrase "archaeological record" signifies.[75] The archaeological record can be viewed as a nonrandom sample of past human activity biased by behavioral and physical factors. Any study of artifacts or use of archaeological evidence or data needs to acknowledge the weaknesses and

strengths of the archaeological record. But what, then, is the nature of the sample that comprises the archaeological record? The archaeological record preserves a minute fraction of the initial dynamic, systemic behavioral associations of past humans. Certain conditions are more conducive to the preservation of more complete records of the initial systemic context. What kinds of artifacts are preserved and what factors affect how the record is biased by preferential preservation and subsequent diagenetic alterations?

With the exception of sites like Pompeii, there may be few if any isolated "cultural" deposits, but there are many artifactual deposits that may have "cultural" consequences. If we describe deposits containing artifacts or archaeological features that may have patterns associated with a human social or cultural system, we may be applying unwarranted interpretations to the data, since a primary goal for archaeology is to infer what kind of behavioral signal is present within the artifactual record.

The relation of geology to archaeology can be considered from the complementary perspectives of physical geology and historical geology. As with physical geology, archaeological problems can be approached with an emphasis on understanding the natural (geologic) processes that have affected the record. Here there is an emphasis on process and structure. As with historical geology, the systematic study of past sequences of events, many archaeological problems are related to the continuum that includes stratigraphy, paleontology, geochronology, and Neogene paleoenvironmental studies. Geoarchaeology may best be considered a meeting ground where the full range of earth sciences is applied to artifactual evidence to infer past processes and events. In the late 1930s F. J. North described the historical recognition of overlap in the fields covered by archaeology and geology. He cited John Aubrey's paper of 1695 that suggested that the occupations and even the characters of people might be determined by the soils that existed where they lived. Aubrey went even farther: he attempted to explain the distribution of witches and religious instability on the basis of geology. North concluded: "What, then is the archaeologist to do? Is an advanced course of geology to be regarded as a necessary part of his equipment? I would suggest that what he needs is sufficient knowledge of geology . . . to enable him to deal with straightforward matters . . . to determine whether masses of stone are likely to owe their shape and position to natural agencies or human activities . . . to appreciate the geologic significance of a site . . . [to acquire a] nodding acquaintance with stratigraphy [and the ability] to recognize the rock types most frequently represented by the relics of early man."[76]

At the end of the twentieth century archaeology appears to be struggling for the kind of scientific footing that physics achieved in the eighteenth, geology in the nineteenth, and medicine in the twentieth. Much of the recent struggle has focused on philosophical disputes that only tangentially affect the everyday practice of archaeology. Perhaps when archaeology embraces archaeological science to the same extent that it has embraced classical and anthropological traditions, it will find its footing.

CHAPTER 2

Sediments and Soils and the Creation of the Archaeological Record

The deposits where artifacts are found provide information on the age, landscape, and environmental setting of human occupations and on the processes that formed the archaeological record. Most archaeological data are recovered from sedimentary deposits or associated soils. In terms of process, artifacts can be considered sedimentary particles that contribute to the final character of the archaeological record. Sediments accumulate either mechanically or chemically. Mechanical accumulation includes the **deposition** of fine sands and mud particles that bury human occupations on floodplains alongside rivers. Artifacts in these sites may also be eroded, transported, and redeposited as sedimentary particles. Lime mud in lake basins and other chemical accumulations can cover and protect former sites of human occupation that were once situated near the shoreline. Other natural processes, including human behavior, may alter sediments after deposition. For example, humans may add chemical elements like phosphorus to sediments and soils at a later period.

We offer here an introduction to some principles, processes, and attributes of the sediments and soils that may contain artifacts or other archaeological features reflecting past human behavior. From a geoarchaeological perspective, artifacts that form archaeological sediments are a special kind of geologic deposit. They are a biostratigraphic deposit. Because the same principles apply to sedimentary settings regardless of whether they contain artifacts or other archaeological features, archaeologists need to understand sedimentologic concepts so that they may better evaluate the environmental context of sites and conditions that affect the final archaeological record. Sediments and soils also provide a systematic framework in which to describe the deposits associated with artifacts. This chapter offers an introduction to the origin, classification, and description of sediments and the soils that can develop on them.

Sediments

An understanding of the steps involved in the formation of sedimentary deposits gives an insight into events that contribute to accumulations of artifacts. The major steps involved in the formation of sedimentary deposits are the weathering of the source rocks, the transportation and deposition of particles, and postdepositional alteration (figure 2.1), which includes changes caused by processes of soil formation. These three basic processes affect archaeological materials as well. Pottery, stone artifacts, and archaeological features can be weathered, sometimes to the extent of being destroyed. Artifacts can also be moved and redeposited.[1] Artifacts that are found in the exact position where they were last used or affected by human behavior are designated as being in *primary context*. In contrast, archaeological materials that have been removed from the primary context by biologic or geologic agencies are designated as being in *secondary context*. Most archaeological materials and features can be influenced by postoccupational and postdepositional processes like soil formation, **bioturbation,** and **diagenesis** (see Chapter 3).

Weathering

Sedimentary deposits are composed of materials derived from the weathering of preexisting rocks or sediments. The initial destruction of rocks can either be physical (also called mechanical disintegration) or chemical (also called decomposition). Rocks and artifacts disintegrate because of frost action, development of joints and cracks, and abrasion by organic, aqueous, cryogenic, or eolian (wind) processes. The mechanical disintegration of rocks within caves and rock shelters contributes to the fill on the floor of the cave, burying the remains of prehistoric occupations. Mechanical disintegration and chemical decomposition can also destroy artifactual records. These same chemical processes can be useful in dating artifacts (see Chapter 7). Weathering processes produce the clay minerals that were widely used by humans to make ceramics, one of the most important categories of artifacts (see Chapter 5). Another product of weathering is the in-place alteration of rocks and sediments to produce soils. Soils form on exposed, stabilized surfaces that also serve as the locations for human activity and the accumulation of artifacts. When buried by younger deposits, ancient soils are key locations for isolating potential living surfaces of prehistoric human occupation.

Transportation

Once materials have been weathered, they are subject to erosion and transportation by running water, wind, or ice. Transported particles and artifacts are eventually deposited in one of many types of sedimentary environments. Whether a particular artifact or particle will be eroded, transported, or deposited is generally dependent on the size of the object and the energy of the transporting agent. Smaller or lighter objects can more easily be transported. The amount of energy within the system will influence which artifacts are removed from their primary, behavioral context. Higher energy levels lead to increased erosion and the transportation of larger or heavier objects.

Objects can be removed from their primary contexts and transported in many ways. Rain, which causes surface wash, or running water in streams or along the shores of lakes or seas may result in water transport. Strong winds can transport and deposit sands and finer materials forming dunes and **loess** deposits. Volcanic eruptions lead to the transport and deposition of ash, such as the Terminal Pleistocene Glacial Peak ash or the Early Middle Holocene Mazama ash in western North America. Ash deposits from volcanic eruptions that were transported by wind in east Africa serve as important **marker horizons** in the dating and correlation of artifact and fossil-bearing Quaternary deposits (see Chapter 7). Glaciers slowly transport particles of all sizes and have been known to bury or move artifact-bearing deposits.

Gravity flows can also initiate translocation and deposition, as well as **slumping,** such as at the Calico Hills site near Yerma, California, in an alluvial fan.[2] This is a controversial locality; some scientists contend that it contains evidence of humans in America as long as two hundred thousand years ago (see Chapter 7). At this site, geologic processes of transportation seem to have created naturally fractured rocks, which resemble stone artifacts in Pleistocene fan deposits consisting of mud and debris flows. Skeptics argue that processes of transportation in mud and debris flows can create naturally fractured rocks that have the appearance of objects flaked by humans but that are not artifacts.

This type of earth movement can also bury entire human occupations, as happened at the Ozette site in the state of Washington.[3] Here, during periods of high rainfall, the ground became saturated with water. This caused a hillside to collapse, and the mudslide buried prehistoric and early historic dwellings. One of these mudslides, which happened around 1750, buried and preserved a village. Earth slides can also dam streams, causing lakes to form, along which human occupations might be preserved.

Biologic processes—like the trampling of land surfaces by humans or other large animals—also transport sediments and artifacts. In one site study, it was found that in sandy deposits artifacts of different sizes were displaced by trampling in different ways.[4] Larger artifacts were moved upward, in contrast to smaller artifacts,

Initial or Primary Context

   Original sedimentary deposit or bedrock

   Original composition, configuration, and patterns in artifacts and archaeological features

Weathering

   Disintegration or decomposition of parent materials, artifacts, and features

Transportation and Secondary Deposition

   Movement and size sorting of sedimentary particles, including artifacts

Alteration

   Changes after last deposition
     More weathering
     Soil-forming processes, including mixing

Final Context: Condition at time of discovery and study

Figure 2.1 The Formation of Sedimentary Deposits
The initial context consists of unaltered bedrock (igneous, sedimentary, or metamorphic) or the original artifactual patterning derived from human behavior. During the weathering stage, bedrock and artifactual materials begin to break down into smaller particles; sometimes they are destroyed. After weathering, artifactual and other clastic particles can be moved and deposited in secondary context. More weathering or alteration of the materials can occur after the final deposition event, before discovery and study.

which were pushed downward in the sediments. Mixing, caused by the root action of small plants and the burrowing of animals, is another way biologic agents can move particles. At an Archaic shell mound situated near the Green River in Kentucky, Julie Stein's research showed that mixing caused by earthworms nearly obliterated the boundaries between archaeological and stratigraphic features.[5] People living in the area from about 5149 B.P. to 4340 B.P. created the mound, which consists of a 2-meter-high pile of discarded

debris. The mixing of this debris by earthworms created a gradational boundary between the sediments underlying the mound and the overlying midden material. It also eradicated the boundaries of pits within the midden and made it difficult to distinguish the plow zone.

Postdepositional Changes

After deposition a variety of changes can occur within a sediment or archaeological layer. Such alterations are superimposed on the original makeup of the sediment and its constituents and reflect postdepositional and postoccupational environments and climatic settings. Occasionally the weathering cycle begins again. In the new cycle, the weathering leads to the development of soils and the production of secondary alterations and accumulations. Although they are disruptive of primary relations, secondary accumulations like carbonate crusts on artifacts can provide minimum ages for the artifacts and can furnish evidence of changing environmental conditions. Alterations like **diagenesis** and **lithification** include the processes of cementation and recrystallization of the deposited materials. The introduction of substances like calcium carbonate, iron oxide, and silica causes cementing. In aqueous solution these substances infiltrate and lithify deposits. This lithification can slow later weathering, contributing to the preservation of archaeological sites. Such hardening can also be a hindrance to the excavation and recovery of artifacts.

Archaeological Sediments

The term *archaeosediment* is used to distinguish deposits which form the part of the sedimentary record that results *directly* from past human activities. Archaeosediments are artifacts or archaeological features that are in primary context. Archaeosediments include the charcoal and burned areas of a hearth or fill deposits that have not suffered postoccupational disturbances.

It is sometimes difficult to ascertain when artifacts are not in primary context. A buried floor, pit fill, or hearth are all archaeosediments. However, an assemblage of secondarily deposited pottery or stone tool fragments may not be considered archaeosediments. If the artifacts can be inferred to have been redeposited directly by human activity, as with middens or fill, then they are considered archaeosediments. Deposits consisting of stones from fallen walls or objects that have been eroded, transported, and redeposited by other geologic agents would in particular cases be thought of as geologic sedimentary particles. These objects may become so far removed from the original prehistoric behavioral context that the important paleoethologic information is lost. Although the artifacts themselves may still contain valuable insights into past human behavior, many contextual associations will have been modified. These modifications usually take the form of biologic or geologic restructuring of the previous behavioral patterning created by human activity.

Sedimentary deposits can be composed of artifactual materials that have been so greatly disturbed by postoccupational processes that the original patterns produced by human activity have been lost. From a geoarchaeological perspective this is one problem of applying behavioral interpretations to a set of artifacts. The ability to infer past human behavior from isolated or mixed artifacts in redeposited contexts is limited. Gladfelter coined the term **articlasts** to describe disturbed artifacts and to compare them to geologic clasts or **clastic** particles in general.[6] Articlasts are objects once used by humans that are found in sedimentologic situations far removed from their original human context.

Classification of Sedimentation Products

Sediments and sedimentary rocks consist of three main groups. The first, clastics, are sediments composed of fragments of other rocks and deposited by physical processes. Objects like stone tools, pottery, and bones can be deposited as clastic sediments. The second group consists of chemical deposits. Chemical and biogenic depositions result in the formation of carbonate, evaporate, and organic deposits. A material like phosphate, that was introduced as a byproduct of animal waste, would be a chemical deposit. The

final group, organics, includes decomposed artifacts used by humans that were made from plants and animals.

Classification provides a means to describe in a structured format the strata and features encountered by the archaeologist. In this format, information can be shared and used by other archaeologists and by other earth scientists. These classifications provide a foundation for inferring the past environmental conditions and processes that have contributed to the prehistoric record.

Clastic Deposits

Clastic (or detrital) deposits are sediments that contain fragments or particles derived from preexisting rocks. Most artifacts (including lithics, metal, and pottery) that are part of a sedimentary deposit are clastic particles. Mineral composition and the range of particle size are the two basic attributes used in geology to classify clastic deposits. The term *texture* is used in part to describe the range of particle sizes found in a sediment or soil. Several scales are used to differentiate particle sizes. Figure 2.2 shows the widely used Ingram-Wentworth scale and compares it to size divisions for soils and artifacts. There are three principal size divisions of clastic materials. Deposits composed of large particles are designated gravels, pebbles, cobbles, and boulders. Smaller particles still visible with the unaided eye are termed sand. Very small particles that are not visible without magnification are grouped together as mud. Mud is further separated into silt and clay, again based on size. Many terms have been devised to describe deposits containing a mixture of sizes or varying proportions of mineralogic components. Textural and compositional classifications of clastic sediments and rock can be visualized by means of triangular diagrams or other similar graphic systems. The standard size classification systems are presented in figure 2.3. Other terminologies are employed depending on whether the sediments are indurated (hardened) or not.

Soil scientists have used the same general approach to the size classification of deposits. Unfortunately, the boundaries used by soil scientists to define the divisions between sand and silt and

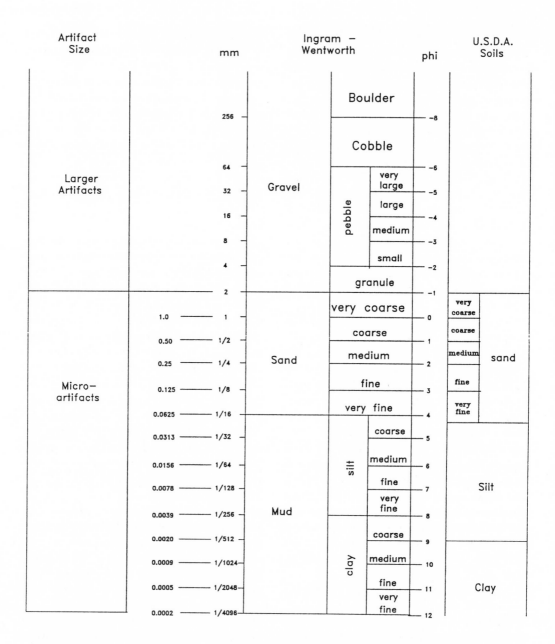

Figure 2.2 Size Categories of Artifacts and Particles
Artifacts fall into two categories, with a boundary at 2 mm. Larger artifacts correspond to the gravel size category of sediments. Micro-artifacts correspond to the sediment and soil fractions of sand or smaller particles.

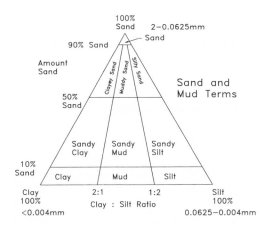

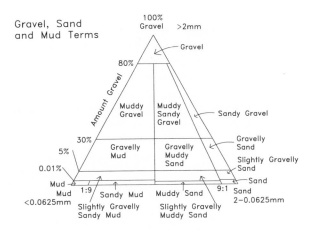

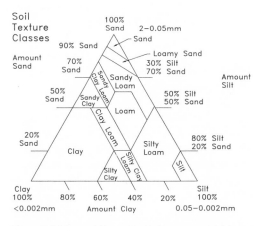

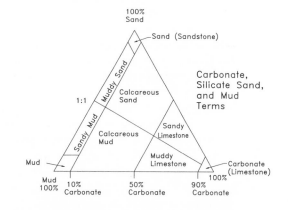

Figure 2.3 Textural Terms for Sediments and Soils
Sedimentologic textural classifications are based on the relative amount of sand and mud (with silt and clay fractions separated). When materials larger than sand are present, terms can be based on the amount of gravel, sand, and mud (with silt and clay fractions combined). The texture classes of soil are based on those between silt and clay are different. The division between sand and silt is designated at 0.0625 mm long in sediments and at 0.05 mm long for soils. The separation between clay and silt is 0.004 mm long for sediments and 0.002 mm long for soils. There is an additional set of terms that refer to the relative proportions of these size categories. If archaeologists come across a stratigraphic description which does not explicitly state the taxonomic system being used, however, helpful clues are available. The term *loam* is different designations and employ the term *loam* for soils containing various mixtures of sand, silt, and clay. An alternate method of categorization is to classify sediments on the basis of the relative amount of sand and mud silicates as well as the relative amount of the sediment composed of carbonate.

commonly used in soil classifications but is absent from sedimentologic divisions used by geologists (although some European classifications use it). In the same way, the term *mud* is used in sedimentologic classifications but is not used as a soil class (see figure 2.3).

Gravel
Particles that are at least the size of gravel (coarser than 2 mm, larger than sand) indicate high energy levels in aqueous transport or transport in a

highly viscous medium. High-energy aqueous conditions are associated with greater possibilities for mixing and mechanical abrasion. Gravel-sized particles can be deposited as screes and debris flows, as rockfall, in streams, along shorelines of basins, and by glaciers. Most objects used by humans, even if broken into fragments, would be in pebble, cobble, or boulder-sized fractions. The gravel size category is important because deposits containing these sizes are a source of **geofacts**. Geoarchaeologists use this term to designate geologic objects that have the appearance of artifacts.[7] Geofacts are nonartifactual objects that have been shaped exclusively by geologic processes. Genuine artifacts found within coarse-grained deposits may have been transported and redeposited from a primary context. Such articlasts may be found as isolated pieces within a coarse-grained **matrix** or as sets of fairly uniform sized artifacts in a size-sorted artifact assemblage. Where geofacts are concerned, a variety of processes can influence the appearance of sedimentary particles to such an extent that distinguishing them from stone that has been altered by humans may be difficult. These naturally fractured rocks have played an important role in archaeology, especially in the determination of the criteria used to evaluate the existence of early Stone Age sites in the Old World and late Ice Age sites in America. The critical question is whether particular sets of objects represent lithics manufactured by humans. In Europe and Africa there are collections of objects made by archaeologists who selectively chose specimens that looked as though humans created them but which were actually formed by mechanical abrasion.

A test case for distinguishing artifacts from geofacts was identified by Peacock.[8] Possible Paleolithic (Clactonian) artifacts were recovered in England from what seem to be beach cobble deposits affected first by wave action and later by freeze-thaw processes. The battering of the cobbles by waves and the splitting of them induced by thermal change created flakes that showed percussive marks, which gave them the appearance of artifacts. These flakes were compared with lithic material from two known archaeological sites. The comparison of attributes of the known arti-fact assemblages with those of the potential artifactual flake sets indicated that some flakes were probably artifacts.

The question of whether objects are geofacts or articlasts has concerned archaeologists since the late 1800s, and some objects may always be in dispute. Several important criteria are employed to distinguish between artifacts and geofacts. These include assessments of whether the object could exist where it was found had it not been transported by humans (that is, Are there geologic processes that could have introduced the object into the deposit?). Another criterion is whether some other kind of geologic or biologic processes could form what appears to be the flaking on stone objects. Some fragments of chert may show haphazard "retouch" created either by the trampling of animals or by thermal events. Such objects could be considered artifacts if they were trampled by domesticated animals or if the heating and freezing were caused by human activities, although humans may not have caused the alterations deliberately. In this sense, a burned layer representing an ancient forest fire could be considered an archaeological feature if it could be determined that it was caused by human activity.

Take, for example, the difficulty in evaluating evidence that humans existed in the New World before about 12,000 B.P. In South America, at the Pedra Furada site in Brazil, natural processes of abrasion may have created objects that have been identified as pre-Clovis artifacts. Objects from what has been designated the Pedra Furada phase have been dated from about 48,000 to 14,300 B.P., but whether they are artifacts or stone fractured by nonhuman processes is debatable.[9] All the objects consist of quartzite cobbles. The source of the quartzite may be a conglomerate that exits about 100 meters above the site. It is possible that the flaked stones were created when cobbles eroded out of the conglomerate and fell to the site, where they were flaked and fractured.

Sand
Sandy deposits contain particles that range in size from 2.0 to 0.0625 mm, or for soils from 2.0 to 0.05 mm long (see figure 2.3). Although textural terms like *sand* refer to a size category and are in-

dependent of mineralogic composition, in most instances, sand is largely composed of quartz. Except for very small objects like beads and seeds, few items used by humans are less than 2 mm, but debris derived from manufacture, use, retouch, and breakage of larger artifacts can be this size. Such artifacts are designated micro-artifacts. The identification of objects as micro-artifacts may be the first indication of a previously unrecognized artifact zone in a deposit. The presence in a deposit of micro-artifacts alone is a strong indication either of a very specific type of human activity—surface sweeping, lithic artifact retouch—or of size sorting by geologic or biologic processes. Micro-artifacts can be used to identify potential surfaces of human occupation, especially when these artifacts come with supporting evidence like larger artifacts, buried soils, or fossil fauna. In such cases, attention should be given to any processes which might form geofacts in the same size range. Mechanical abrasion of sedimentary particles can produce micro-geofacts, which even have bulbs of percussion similar to lithic artifacts.

A variety of human activities can cause the deposition of micro-artifacts. One such is the flaking of rocks to produce lithic artifacts.[10] This activity can create considerable microdebitage—sometimes more than 99 percent in sizes smaller than 1 mm. Even when the larger lithic flakes have been carried away, these accumulations of lithic debris remain within permeable sediments and provide a trace of past human activity.

Micro-artifacts can provide evidence of past human activities that larger artifacts do not show. At the Bronze Age site of Nichoria in Greece, techniques for recovering materials smaller than 2 mm long were applied that uncovered artifacts that influenced archaeological interpretations.[11] Although the archaeologists did not discover actual smelting features, the presence of small fragments indicated evidence for metal working at the site through identification of slag within the sediments. Bone and teeth of microfauna; botanical remains like seeds, flint, and obsidian; and spatters of copper discovered at the site provided a more comprehensive record of human activity.

In addition to providing micro-artifacts, sand-size sediments are important in archaeological interpretations for other reasons. They can be assigned to specific depositional contexts or environments like fluvial (river) settings, shore zones of lakes and oceans, and windblown sands in caves or rock shelters. In fluvial settings, sands are an indication of high-energy floods or channel deposits.

A major problem of interpretation for geoarchaeologists can be the determination of whether artifacts were part of the initial deposit or were introduced later, either by human activities or by mixing processes. If there is evidence of soil development or other indications of a surface of past human activity, artifacts found on or in the top part of a sandy deposit may be in primary context. On the other hand, if the sands contain larger objects that can confidently be considered part of the sediment, axial-orientation comparisons of the artifacts with the particles known to be transported may indicate whether the artifacts were deposited as part of the initial sedimentologic event or afterward.

Another, related problem involves artifacts that form part of a deposit containing soil development. There are at least three possibilities here. First, the artifacts may be associated with the event that deposited the surrounding sedimentary matrix and so be in secondary context. Or the artifacts may have accumulated before the beginning of the soil development. In this instance, they could either be in primary context or pedogenic processes could have moved them. A third possibility is that the artifacts could have been deposited during or after the period of soil development within the sediments. Sometimes crusts or other surface features on the objects, or the spatial patterning and size sorting of artifacts, can help us choose among these possibilities.

The presence of a range of artifact sizes in sands of a uniform size does not necessarily help the archaeologist decide whether the artifacts are in primary or secondary context. The transportational and depositional energies indicated by the sandy matrix provide only a minimum estimate of the size of particles that could be moved. If feasible, archaeologists should conduct studies of

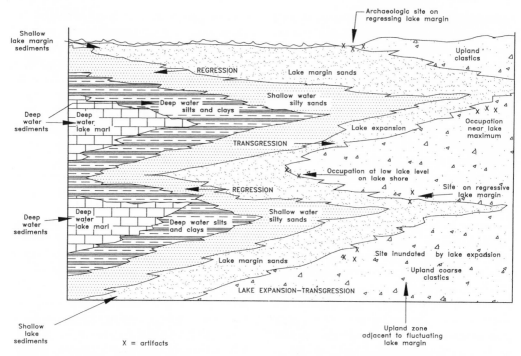

Figure 2.4 Sedimentary Sequences and Facies
Sedimentary sequences can contain evidence of both contemporary (lateral) and temporal (usually vertical) variation of depositional environments. Sediments can be deposited simultaneously in a variety of laterally adjacent settings. Coarser clastics may be associated with shore zones of a lake, while deeper parts of the lake may be associated with the deposition of muds or marls. As the size of the lake fluctuates, the location of characteristic types of deposition changes. Archaeological sites situated on lake shorelines move from place to place as a result of the changing location of the water's edge. During lake expansion, sites will eventually be buried by sediments deposited nearer the center of the basin. During periods of lake reduction, sites may be buried by basin margin deposits like beach sands and dunes.

the technological integrity or refit analyses of the artifact assemblages in addition to the sedimentologic analysis to obtain a more comprehensive site formation evaluation. These types of studies can help evaluate whether spatial patterns are a result of past human activity or geologic restructuring.

The classification of sands and sandstones can be applied by geoarchaeologists not only to the strata associated with artifacts but also to archaeological materials themselves. The blocks that make up the pyramids in Egypt can be so classified. For archaeologists this type of classification provides a standardized approach to the description of sand-dominated rocks and sediments, and it helps in the evaluation of their origin within a stratigraphic sequence. The same type of system could also be used to describe pottery or such construction materials as mud brick.

Mud
Sediments and rocks dominated by clastic particles less than 0.0625 mm long are muds and mudstone (see figure 2.2). They are also called argillaceous deposits. Muds can further be divided into larger particles called silts and smaller particles called clay. These are separated at the 0.004 mm boundary. Further subdivisions of muds can be based on mineralogic content. If detrital muds contain significant amounts of calcium carbonate, they are called marls. If they are indurated they are called marlstones. Marls often originate as biogeochemical deposits in the bot-

toms of lakes and ponds. Lime mud and detrital silts and clays are generally deposited nearer the central part of a lake basin and may also be indicators of climate change. One example of the close connection that can exist between carbonates and silts and clays is provided by a stratigraphic sequence at Bir Sahara in Egypt. The sequence shows a change in depositional circumstances associated with the Middle Paleolithic site known as E-88-2. Sediments deposited during the period when the basin contained its greatest amount of water are high in carbonate and contain the highest amounts of silt and clay. This represents a **retrograding** sequence of deeper water sediments overlying shallow water sediments (figure 2.4). These **transgressive** conditions are reflected on the margin of the basin by a calcareous sandstone. The **prograding** sequence (for example, beach or dune sands deposited above muds in deeper water) is associated with artifacts. At Bir Sahara the lake deposits are overlain by sands containing Middle Paleolithic artifacts. At this site the hominid occupation seems to have occurred after the transgressive event. Wetter climatic intervals can also cause lake expansions that inundate prehistoric occupation sites situated on former shorelines. In these circumstances the sites can be covered with biogenic marls or clastic muds.

Depending on the circumstances, fine-grained sediments can be indicators of either low or high energy levels of transportation. Fine-grained clastic deposits are indicators of very low-energy depositional conditions in aqueous conditions. These are typical of backwater floodplain deposits. The erosion and transport of silt-sized particles by wind would imply higher energy levels. These finer, well-sorted particles typically exhibit little internal stratification and are termed loess. On occasion windblown loess accumulation is interrupted by an interval of landscape stability that provides conditions for weathering and organic and chemical accumulation. Soil zones, called pedogenic horizons, that lie within a top section of silt-dominated loess are an indication of climatic change and are also potential surfaces of ancient human occupation.

Muds have also been used by humans in a number of important ways. Muds are a common constituent of such construction materials as bricks. Muds are also the primary constituent of pottery and figurines. Living surfaces composed of mud, whether humanmade or deposited by geologic means, can influence the spatial arrangement of artifacts. Artifacts moving vertically through a sandy deposit can be impeded by a mud layer, creating a secondary artifact zone. Since mud layers are more impenetrable and less susceptible to mixing by trampling, many separate occupations may be superimposed on a single surface. In addition, artifacts on hardened mud surfaces are more easily moved and rearranged than those on sandy surfaces.

Chemical Deposition

The second major category of sediments consists of minerals that have been deposited by precipitation from solution. The most common of these minerals is calcite (calcium carbonate, or $CaCO_3$). A wide range of chemical deposits exists that can assist us in evaluating paleoenvironmental settings. Many, such as iron oxide, manganese oxide, sulfate, silica, and phosphate, have been important resources for humans. Humans and human activity are also important contributors of chemicals into sedimentary systems.

Calcareous Precipitates

Sedimentary deposits can consist of a mixture of clastic materials and chemically precipitated minerals, such as calcium carbonate or silica. Like silica (quartz, or SiO_2), carbonate can be detrital, but its initial formation was as a chemical precipitate, which is how it is most often studied. Calcite is common in some sandstones as a secondary cementing agent, and it is an indicator of diagenetic conditions. Carbonates are also chemically introduced into a sedimentary deposit as a product of pedogenic processes. Constituents like calcium carbonate that are introduced after the primary detrital depositional event provide clues to the later climatic, hydrologic, biologic, and chemical processes that have affected artifact accumulation (see Chapter 3).

Various terms have been used to designate the many forms of carbonate found as sediments.

These names are applied to sediments and rocks on the basis of their textural and compositional character. *Limestone* designates rocks that contain more than 50 percent nondetrital carbonate (carbonate formed within the basin of deposition). Marls and marlstones contain approximately 40–60 percent calcareous matter, with the remaining constituents being detrital mud particles. *Marl* is a synonym for calcareous silts and clays. Special names are given to carbonate rocks with high fossil contents. A slightly cemented sediment composed chiefly of fossil debris that has been sorted is termed *coquina*. *Chalk* is used for carbonates of marine origin with at least 90 percent calcite.

Although compositional and textural criteria have been used to define some types of carbonates, terms like *tufa* and *travertine* sometimes have particular genetic connotations. Porous and spongy calcium carbonate deposits in a **terrigenous** context are called tufa, whereas travertine is massive and relatively dense. Tufa forms by the precipitation of calcium carbonate from spring water on growing plants. Travertine forms as spring deposits and is also precipitated from solution in caves. Carbonate precipitated in caves is sometimes called flowstone. Travertine in caves seals underlying deposits, thus separating and protecting artifact-bearing deposits; this in turn provides opportunities for dating (see Chapter 7).

Noncalcareous Precipitates

Noncalcareous chemical precipitates and evaporates play a major role in archaeological interpretation. Evaporates are produced by precipitation from evaporating solutions. Evaporates include calcite, gypsum (hydrous calcium sulfate), anhydrite (anhydrous calcium sulfate), and halite (sodium chloride, or NaCl). These sediments are important indicators of environmental conditions associated with human habitation. Under evaporative conditions minerals precipitate out of solution in a particular order. The identification of the mineral precipitation sequence in a stratigraphic profile is used as an indicator of evaporative conditions and changes in water chemistry within a basin. In addition to their use as indicators of past environmental conditions, such evaporate minerals as salt (halite) are important resources that

have been extensively used by humans in the past (see also Chapter 5).

Other minerals or mineral groups used as resources by humans are useful environmental indicators. These include iron oxides, silica, phosphates, and manganese oxides. Depositional environments for manganese oxides are near springs, in natural and artificial wells, in bogs, and in lakes. Iron in sedimentary rocks is primarily derived from the weathering of **mafic** igneous rocks and can be transported as soluble **ferrous** salts or **colloidal ferric** oxides. In freshwater conditions iron is deposited as the mineral limonite, while in saline settings iron oxide may be deposited as the mineral hematite (see Chapter 5). Phosphates have been the subject of much study because they are a biologic (including human) contribution to the sedimentary system. Their spatial variation and concentration have been used as indicators of locations of human activity.

Robert Eidt proposed that the relative proportions of different kinds of phosphate could be related to past human land use.[12] Very soluble phosphates were associated with lands used for crop production—specifically, mixed vegetable cultivation. These lands contained small amounts of two other types of phosphate: tightly bound iron and aluminum phosphate, and apatite and calcium phosphates. In land used as forests there were small amounts of apatite and calcium phosphates but roughly equal proportions of easily soluble iron and aluminum phosphates. In abandoned residential land-use areas the amounts of the three types of phosphates were about the same. From this we can infer that some chemicals may produce spatial patterns indicative of particular human uses of the landscape.

Chemical elements may be added to a human occupational area by specific activities. Dena Dincauze's interpretation of the soil chemistry at the eight-thousand-year-old Neville site in New England provides one example.[13] In deposits associated with the Archaic occupation of the site, chemical analyses indicated the presence of high amounts of mercury. These high concentrations of mercury were interpreted as indicators that the area had been used during the Archaic to process fish.

Organic Matter

Decayed and decomposed plants and animals form another critical component of the sedimentary system. Organic material is vital to soil-forming processes and a valuable indicator of past environmental conditions. Because it contains carbon, organic material is critical for radiocarbon dating (see Chapter 7). Organic matter in sediments can reach levels of nearly 100 percent in some Quaternary peatlike deposits and may be an indication of freshwater-marsh conditions. Sediments containing high amounts of organic matter are termed *carbonaceous*. After it has been deposited, organic matter can be used by plants and animals, undergo biochemical decay, or be destroyed by **oxidation**.

When organic matter shows no signs of extensive alteration or destruction, it can be an indication of an environment with a high rate of sedimentation, where rates of burial were rapid. It is also an indication of **anoxic** conditions, which inhibit organic activity. Extremely well-preserved human remains, wood objects, cloth, and skins have been recovered from bogs where anoxic conditions exist.

In Europe depositional circumstances have led to extraordinary preservation of organic materials associated with human prehistoric occupations. Perhaps the best-known sites are the Swiss lake dwellings, but there are others, such as Starr Carr in northern England.[14] Research at this Mesolithic site showed that it was a lake-margin settlement occupied some ten thousand years ago. At both the Swiss Lake dwellings and Starr Carr, organic material was preserved because of inundation by rising water levels.

Wet boglands have also preserved prehistoric human remains in northwestern Europe and Florida.[15] Perhaps the best known are the remains of a man hanged about two thousand years ago that were found near Tollund, Denmark. The organic preservation was so good that it was possible to determine what he ate for his last meal (porridge made of barley, linseed, herb seeds, and wild seeds). Preservation of these organic materials appears to have been the result of several factors. First, the body lay in water deep enough to protect it from scavenging animals and anoxic

enough to keep it from bacterial decay. Second, the water in the bog contained enough tannic acid to preserve the outer layers of the body. Finally, the water was cool enough to slow decay and rot. In Florida, waterlogged peats at the Windover site have preserved human remains and organic items dating to seven thousand years ago. The site had been used as a burial ground, one where bodies were deliberately placed in the pond. Clothing, wood artifacts, human hair, and brain tissue were preserved as peats filled the pond.

Anoxic settings can also preserve pollen and macrofossils, which provide another set of indicators of paleoenvironmental conditions (see Chapter 4).

Soils and Buried Soils

As Vance Holliday has succinctly written: "A soil . . . is the result of the complex interaction of a variety of physical, chemical, and biological processes acting on a rock or sediment over time."[16] Soils are a product of biologic activity and weathering. Because they indicate the presence of stabilized landscape surfaces, soils mark locations of possible human occupation and artifact accumulation.

The upper part of a sedimentary deposit can contain pedogenic materials, which are weathering profiles developed within preexisting sediments. Soils are the result of horizontal sequences superimposed on sediments. Weathering, alteration, and accumulation create these sequences in the top part of a deposit (figures 2.5 and 2.6). The five soil-forming factors are: 1) parent rock, 2) organisms (including humans), 3) topography, 4) climate, and 5) time. Although parent rock influences soil development, especially by governing the chemical constituents available, the same soil types can form on diverse parent rocks. For example, in Greece, soils called Alfisols have formed on underlying limestones, limestone conglomerates, marine marls, clays, sands, and silts.

The onset of cultivation and agriculture during the Neolithic ushered in a more intensive use of the earth's surface, and available soil types became vital to human affairs. An understanding of soils is

Geologic Units

Biostratigraphic Units

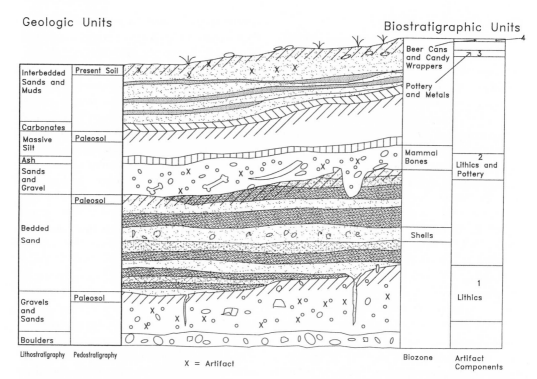

Figure 2.5 Geologic and Biostratigraphic Units
Sedimentary layers can be categorized according to their geologic characteristics or their biologically derived components. Geologic units include strata defined on the basis of their rock or chemical composition and size or lithostratigraphic units and pedostratigraphic units (strata based on secondarily derived char- acteristics associated with soil formation and in situ weathering). Biostratigraphic units include biozones, defined on the basis of organic remains, or sets of artifacts, designated artifact components. The same stratigraphic sequence can be described in more than one way, depending on whether geologic or biologically derived characteristics are available for observation.

equally vital to archaeology. Unfortunately, in archaeology the word *soil* is used for two very different things. Incorrectly, *soil* designates many kinds of surface and near-surface sediments. More precisely, soil is the portion of earth-surface material that supports plant life and is altered by continuous chemical and biotic activity and weathering. The lower limit (depth) of an upper soil zone can often be associated with the lower limit of biologic activity. It may be useful to think of sediments as being, for the most part, biologically dead. In contrast, most soils develop in sediments that are alive, that is, biologically active. Soils represent a zone of biotic interaction. A cubic meter of agricultural soil may contain more than a million living creatures, which will affect

chemical inputs and mixing. Most sediments do not have active biologic constituents; those that do are being affected by soil-forming processes.

Soils often show direct effects of rock weathering. They reflect the composition of the underlying (parent) rock, as it has been modified by climate and biologic activity through time. Soil formation results in the development of a "soil profile" that exhibits a vertical series of horizons (see figure 2.6). A soil horizon is "a layer of soil, approximately parallel to the soil surface with characteristics produced by soil forming processes."[17] There is also a series of roughly horizontal layers that are due to primary clastic and chemical depositional phenomena. It is imperative that the primary depositional phenomena

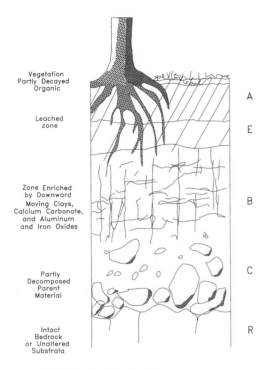

Vegetation
Partly Decayed
Organic

A

Leached
zone

E

Zone Enriched
by Downward
Moving Clays,
Calcium Carbonate,
and Aluminum
and Iron Oxides

B

Partly
Decomposed
Parent
Material

C

Intact
Bedrock
or Unaltered
Substrata

R

Figure 2.6 A Standard Soil Profile
Some of the "horizons" that can be seen in a soil profile. The unaltered parent material (R) decomposes,
forming a C horizon. With the contribution of organic
materials, an A horizon is formed, marking the upper
part of the soil. Beneath the organic-rich A horizon is
a light-colored E horizon. This is common in leaching
environments like conifer forests. In contrast to the
E horizon, zones characterized by the accumulation of
clays or carbonates are designated B horizons.

that form sediments not be confused with postdepositional alterations, including soil-forming
processes. In the field, soils (like sediments) can
be described by such properties as color, texture,
structure, boundary characteristics, and horizontal continuity. Archaeologists must concentrate
on determining which properties represent postdepositional soil-forming phenomena imposed
on the primary deposit.

The Soil Profile

The properties of soils change both vertically
and horizontally. In general they are more easily
observed locally along the vertical dimension by

differences in physical, chemical, and biotic attributes (see figure 2.6). Thus, the soil profile
is the vertical sequence ranging from the original underlying parent material to the overlying
surface-interaction zone. The causes of the vertical differentiation of earth's surface materials into soil horizons are both geologic (parent
rock composition and stratification) and pedogenetic (biotic and climatic). Soil scientists have
given several master horizons standardized symbols designated by capital letters, starting with
bedrock (R) or unaltered parent material (C).
B horizons often are developed in R or C horizons and are overlain by O, A, or E horizons. The
B horizon is a mineral zone that shows few of the
characteristics of R or C, either because of the in
situ **illuvial** accumulation or the development of
secondary structures. E horizons are characterized by the loss or accumulation of components,
while A horizons tend to be darker, primarily
because they contain higher amounts of organic
matter along with mineral matter. O horizons
occur on the surface; because they contain high
amounts of organics, they are very dark in color.

Based on the in situ accumulation of particular components, B horizons can be characterized more specifically, as can other horizons.
A standardized set of symbols is used as suf-
fixes to denote these compositional differences in
soils. These lowercase letters describe the master
horizon. An accumulation of highly decomposed
organic matter is signified by the symbol a. An
illuvial accumulation of iron and/or aluminum is
denoted by s. Clays are denoted by t. The accumulation of exchangeable sodium is signified by n.
B and C horizons with accumulations of calcium
carbonate are designated by k (calcic), those with
gypsum, by y. The presence of salts that are more
soluble than gypsum is indicated by z. Combinations of these subordinate symbols can be used to
describe a horizon. For example, a natric horizon
(significant clays with sodium) is denoted Btn.
Petrocalcic zones (K) are well-cemented calcium
carbonate–dominated horizons.

The record of past environments as recorded in
sediments is biased toward regions of active deposition, called **aggradation**. Soils, on the other
hand, are a record of the "quieter" times of land-

scape stability that come between events like floods, which cause rapid deposition or erosion. These intervals of nonaggradation result in a relatively stable surface for human activities like agriculture. Any major disturbance caused within a soil by such human activities as plowing or digging creates a visible change in the soil horizons. Thus, it is possible to reconstruct past events by studying the morphology of soils on a site and comparing it with the undisturbed morphology of an offsite setting.

New deposition on the surface of a soil can be recognized in the field by several characteristics. An unusually thick *A* horizon (the mineral horizon formed below the organic surface horizon or the surface containing both mineral and organic matter) may indicate the introduction of sediments. Other indicators of renewed deposition are sediments that cannot be related to pedogenic processes, the presence of carbonates in the surface layer that are missing from the horizons immediately below, and distinct color changes.

Plowing mixes the upper horizons of a soil profile and makes it impossible to distinguish them from one another. Nonhuman **turbation** processes can have the same effect. Artifacts within the disturbed zones may have originally been associated with distinct chronological intervals, but they lose their original temporal and behavioral context because of disturbance. There is often a distinct, nongradational boundary between an overlying plowzone and undisturbed underlying soil horizons or sediments. An ancient burial that was covered with soil from the immediate vicinity often shows a distinct change in character at the foot of the artificial mound. This criterion should distinguish natural mounds from burial features. Frequent disturbances of the soils in habitation areas can prevent the pedogenic horizons from forming, as can such bioturbation as earthworm activity.

Soil Types

Soil scientists have developed an extensive nomenclature. A few general soil types within this taxonomic nomenclature are important in geoarchaeology. Identification of the current soils and reconstruction of past soils is essential for grasping the nature and extent of early agriculture and inferring past environmental and climatic conditions. Among the important soil types are Entisols, Vertisols, Inceptisols, Mollisols, Alfisols, Ultisols, Spodosols, Aridosols, and Histosols.

Entisols Present-day soils that are not fully developed or are weakly expressed are called Entisols. These soils may be undeveloped because they are too young or because erosion has removed material as fast as or faster than pedogenic horizons can form. Conversely, newly deposited material may be added faster than soil can develop. Entisols show little evidence of pedogenesis and characteristically have few diagnostic horizons. They usually consist of mineral or organic surface horizons developed on slightly altered parent material or bedrock. For example, major floods of the Yellow River in China deposit so much silt that the new material overwhelms the existing soil profile. Entisols are also common on steep slopes in mountainous regions or in deserts or sandy regions. They currently make up about 20 percent of the earth's land area.

Vertisols Vertisols are usually dark clay soils or soils with a high clay content. Vertisols shrink and swell, often in accordance with seasonal variations in moisture. This shrinking and swelling is caused by a high clay content, typically more than 35 percent. The clay consists mainly of expanding clays like montmorillonite. (See Chapter 5 for an introduction to clay minerals.) Large cracks may develop for part of the year in these thick, clayey soils, producing a hummock-and-swale topography with a subsurface expression of a disrupted structure. Many Vertisols have formed on igneous terrains with intermediate to basaltic composition.[18]

Because of their capacity to absorb water, Vertisols retain surface water. Therefore, their agricultural use has been for pasturage rather than forest growth. Worldwide, most Vertisols presently lie between 45° north and 45° south latitude. Vertisols can play a role in artifact **taphonomy;** the expansion and contraction of clay beds causes vertical movement and the mixing of artifacts.

Inceptisols Embryonic or immature soils similar to Entisols (but with slightly more pedogenic development) are designated Inceptisols. Typically Inceptisols have an *A* horizon with an underlying, weakly developed *B* horizon. This *B* horizon has little remnant structure and tends to be redder in color because of the accumulation or leaching of minerals. Inceptisols may not develop "normal" profiles because of resistant parent materials, extensive deposition of volcanic ash, or some other inhibiting condition. Inceptisols form in low, rolling parts of the landscape and in the foothills of mountain fronts. In sequences of alluvial terraces, Inceptisols form between the Entisols nearest the river and the better-developed soils farther away. Inceptisols are widely distributed throughout the world, and many are in equilibrium with their environment. Agricultural uses of Inceptisols have been diverse: Inceptisol vegetation ranges from forest to tundra.

Mollisols   A dark-colored, humus-rich, deep **epipedon** (surface horizon) is characteristic of Mollisols. They are the well-known grassland soils of present-day short-grass steppes and long-grass prairies. Most deep, dark soils with relatively fertile topsoil are formed under grassland vegetation. The exceptions are the poorly drained Mollisols associated with low-lying hardwood forests. Most Mollisols are found in low, rolling, or flat country. They form under a wide range of temperatures, in areas ranging from the equator to the poles. In addition, they form on a wide variety of parent rocks, although they prefer clay, marl, and basalt. Earthworm activity is often extensive in Mollisols, and the consequent mixing affects archaeological sites by altering artifactual spatial patterns. Early farmers realized that these soils could produce a rich variety of foods after the tough sod had been broken by plowing.

Alfisols   A subsurface horizon with high clay content (*Bt*) but no humus-rich surface horizon (no Mollic epipedon) is characteristic of an Alfisol overlain by a thin *A* horizon. Alfisols are the alkaline forest soils (they may sometimes be slightly acid) that form when sufficient clay accumulates in the subsoil to create an argillic (clay-rich) horizon. Alfisols form only in the absence of conditions that favor the formation of Mollisols or Spodosols. They can be found in many present-day climatic regimes but are most common in humid or subhumid environments on young, stable land surfaces that have been free of major erosion or pedoturbation for thousands of years. Alfisols are normally young enough to retain most of their chemical nutrients. Consequently, they are used for cultivating crops, as well as for pasture and forest land.

Ultisols   Like Alfisols, Ultisols have an argillic horizon, but unlike Alfisols they are low in chemical **bases.** These are among the less-alkaline soils formed under hardwood or pine forests. They develop deep, reddish soil profiles in warm, humid regimes on old terrain. Ultisols have a potential for agricultural production but are subject to rapid depletion of nutrients because of deep weathering. They tend to form on older parts of the landscape like exposed bedrock, high alluvial terraces, or tops of plateaus. The natural vegetation of Ultisols is coniferous or hardwood forest.

Spodosols   Spodosols accumulate subsurface concentrations of aluminum and organics. Often iron oxide and silica cementation is also extensive. These are the "white earths" that used to be called Podzols, in contrast with the "black earths" that were called Chernozems. ("Chernozems" included many soils that now have separate names.) Spodosols are often acidic, ashy-gray, sandy soils. They respond quickly to changes in vegetation. Hence, they form more rapidly than most other soil types.[19] Spodosols may take only a few hundred years to form on quartz-rich sands. Spodosols are naturally infertile and therefore provide only a limited basis for cultivated crops. Coniferous forest is their most common vegetation.

Aridosols   As the name implies, these are the soils of the arid regions that occupy about a third of the earth's current land surface. Aridosols are dry for more than three-quarters of each year. Their organic content is low, primarily because of the restrictive moisture conditions, which inhibit biotic activity. Their soil horizons are usually well oxidized. Caliche—horizons of calcium carbonate—may form within and on them. The surface horizons of Aridosols are light-colored, soft, and often vesicular. The lack of water limits their natural vegetation to plants like cactus, yucca, sagebrush, and muhly grass. Aridosols form mostly in low-lying areas; steep slopes in arid regions tend to be eroded down to bedrock.

Aridosols can be irrigated for cultivation but at the risk of salinization.

Histosols Histosols are the widely distributed organic soils that form wherever the production of organic matter exceeds its conversion or destruction. This comes about when an almost continuous saturation with water inhibits rapid oxidation and slows the decomposition of organic matter. Histosols support bog, swamp, and marsh. They may be drained for cultivation. Peat Histosols have been used throughout history as a source of fuel.

More than 75 percent of stratified and preserved prehistoric archaeological sites in the eastern United States are located in alluvial valleys. In these places, an understanding of the sedimentation and the soil-development sequences is critical to the interpretation of site formation processes. Soil formation on alluvial terraces is usually quite different from that on floodplains. In his discussion of alluvial soil formation and geoarchaeology, Reid Ferring points to the concentration of sites in alluvial valleys, the importance of soils in defining and correlating stratigraphic units, and the use of alluvial soils for paleoenvironmental reconstructions.[20]

In addition, the number of soils in a stratigraphic sequence and their degree of development can be important in assessing the duration and integrity of the archaeological record at an alluvial site. The boundaries of a pedostratigraphic unit can be time transgressive, whereas chronostratigraphic units, by definition, are synchronous. It is also important to note that the stratigraphic Law of Superposition, inviolate in sedimentary sequences, does not apply to soil horizons.

Paleosols and Buried Soils

A paleosol is a soil that formed on a landscape at some time in the past. Buried soils in a stratigraphic sequence are valuable indicators of an interval of nondeposition. Paleosols can either be buried soils or surface soils that have developed for several generations under fluctuating climatic conditions. Paleosols occur frequently in the geologic record and are well represented in archaeological contexts. Archaeologically, they correlate with times of landscape stabilization and surfaces

of human occupation. Buried soils are important as position and time markers of these stable landscape environments where ecological (and sometimes human) forces dominated, rather than erosion or deposition. Rapid burial by windblown loess or overbank floodplain silts can result in the preservation of land surfaces and can also create paleosols.

For some scientists the definition of buried soils is restricted by the depth of burial. Peter Birkeland defines paleosols as soils that are buried deep enough to be unaffected by current pedogenic processes.[21] The U.S. Department of Agriculture classifies a buried soil as one covered by a mantle of new material that is 50 cm or more thick, or between 30 and 50 cm thick if the mantle thickness is at least half that of the diagnostic horizons preserved in the paleosol.[22]

There is no simple set of criteria by which to recognize a paleosol. Rather, one must identify a developed horizon or weathering zone resulting from past soil-forming processes. In addition to clarifying local archaeological stratigraphy, the identification of a paleosol can enable stratigraphic correlation and chronological resolution.[23]

Paleosols can be recognized by the occurrence of fossil root traces, an accumulation of phytoliths (see Chapter 4), calcareous nodules, bioturbated layers with gradational contacts (relic soil horizons), and an increased organic content in a darker fossil *A* horizon. Major- and trace-element analyses offer additional clues to the identification of paleosols. Protracted humid weathering can produce enrichment in TiO_2, Al_2O_3, and Fe_2O_3, with accompanying loss of CaO and MgO. In addition, the covering vegetation would have absorbed much of the K_2O and P_2O_5. The most important factor in the distribution and redistribution of trace elements is what elements were released from the parent material. Available arsenic shows an affinity for organic materials but is depleted in leached horizons. Both vanadium and zinc concentrate in clays.

Pedogenic calcium carbonate in paleosols is usually reduced to about half the quantity found in unburied soils, a decrease that is probably related to soil moisture. Most paleosols are wetter than unburied soils (they often occur beneath the water table). Water facilitates the leaching of carbonates and salts from the system. An increase in soil moisture will cause some clayey soils to swell.

Paleosols tend to have yellower hues and lower chromas (lighter colors) than unburied soils. The differences in color result from a lessening of the oxidation processes, **gleying,** and the changes in the structures of organic compounds. Water-saturated horizons preserve organic carbon.

Burial creates compaction, which causes the structure of paleosols to coarsen. The damage to archaeological materials because of this compressive loading depends on the depth of burial, the compressive strengths of the archaeological materials and of the earth matrix, and the orientation of the artifacts and features with respect to the direction of loading. It should be noted that differential strain rather than stress is the primary reason that artifacts break. Hence, where there are differential compressibilities in the matrix or in matrix-artifact combinations, the potential for damage is greatest.

In areas where sediments have been newly deposited or where fresh rock has been exposed by erosion, a progressive invasion occurs, first by herbaceous plants, then shrubs, and finally trees. This biotic activity, aided by hydrogeochemical weathering, creates a soil profile by the incorporation of decaying organic matter (A horizon) and also by the migration downward and the redistribution of soluble compounds and fine particles.

Features of fossil soils similar to present-day soils include traces of roots, pedogenic horizons, and pedogenic structures. But because of the increased importance of time as a factor, certain attributes of the original soil development, unlike those of current soils, may have been altered or lost. In addition, the vegetational and climatic patterns that form present-day soils cannot be assumed to have existed in the past. Different soil-forming contexts in the past would create paleosols with characteristics different from those of present-day soils. Overlying deposits may compress paleosols, changing original thicknesses and causing cracks or other deformation structures. A soil that may originally have been loose or friable might become indurated because of the addition of a cementing agent. This can result in the formation of nodules or **hardpans**. Recrystallization of mineral components, as well as replacement or **authigenic** mineralization, may occur. Dissolution, dehydration, and oxidation may affect the preservation of paleosols. Organic matter might not survive in buried A horizons, but the former A horizon can be recognized sometimes by higher amounts of turbation compared with underlying horizons. An **eluvial** (E, formerly A1 or albic) horizon in a paleosol profile would underlie an A horizon and possibly be lighter in color, more massive, or more indurated, depending on the removal of clays, organics, or sesquioxides. B horizons are composed of illuvial accumulations (see figure 2.6).

Because the classification of present-day soils is based in part on parameters that do not survive in the geologic record, and because certain climatic conditions must be known for proper classification, earth scientists have developed a classification system specifically for paleosols that focuses on features likely to be preserved and attempts to minimize the use of interpretation.[24] The presence of dark organic matter (but not coal) designates a carbonaceous paleosol. Two types of paleosols exhibit poor horizonation: Protosols, which are relatively immature soils, and 2) Vertisols, which lack horizonation because of the effects of turbation. Where the horizonation is good but the environmental conditions are oxidizing or **reducing,** the paleosol may be termed a Gleysol.

The accumulation of minimal insoluble minerals can produce paleosols called Calcisols and Gypsisols. Calcisols have a prominent calcic (calcium carbonate) horizon; they include calcretes and caliche. Gypsisols are rich in authigenic sulfate. Paleosols high in clay may be termed Argillsols, while those high in organic matter and iron are termed Spodosols. Extensive in situ alteration of minerals may cause the formation of Oxisols.

Some of the subordinate modifiers that can be applied to paleosols include albic (eluvial horizon present), argillic (t, presence of illuvial clay), calcic (k, pedogenic carbonate), ferric (presence of iron oxides), gleyed (g, presence of reduced iron), gypsic (presence of pedogenic anhydrite or *y*, gypsum), silicic (*q*, pedogenic silica), vertic (desiccation cracks, **slickensides**), and vitric (presence of glass shards or pumice).

Despite the alterations that affect soils as they become paleosols, the attributes of present-day soils provide hints about what those attributes found in paleosols indicate about environmental conditions. It should be kept in mind, however, that consideration of these attributes in making inferences about past conditions relies on the assumption that analogous conditions existed in the past. This is demonstrably not true in many instances. Weakly developed paleosols (with Entisol or Inceptisol characteristics) can result from conditions where biota were in early stages of succession, or possibly from early stages of mixed woodland or grasslands. Mollisol characteristics in paleosols may indicate open grassland conditions. Paleosols that have characteristics similar to Alfisols may be an indicator of past forests and woodlands, while characteristics associated with Oxisols and Ultisols may be an indicator of more humid rain-forest conditions. Spodosol characteristics in paleosols may indicate humid temperate or alpine settings with needleleaf forests. Distinctive postdepositional features like patterned ground, frost heave, or ice wedges in paleosols may be an indication of **taiga** settings. The past presence of marsh conditions and waterlogged areas (swamps) could be inferred from the presence of carbonaceous paleosols (peat accumulations, for example).

Inferring Environments from Physical and Chemical Parameters

Description and analysis of sediments from archaeological sites and the areas surrounding them provide a means of identifying depositional processes and environments, as well as postdepositional alterations. Environmental interpretations can be developed from an evaluation of the contexts of the sediments and from the study of their composition. Paleoenvironmental interpretations are based on comparisons of the attributes of sediments with the characteristics of current environments and other sedimentary or strati-

graphic contexts. Here, we provide a review of some environmental conditions associated with specific sedimentary attributes found in deposits.

Color

One of the most obvious attributes of an archaeological deposit is color. The factors that most influence color are the source rocks, the conditions of weathering, the physical and chemical conditions at the site of deposition, and postdepositional changes. Archaeologists have long used the pattern of colors in excavation profiles to differentiate layers and horizontal disruptions. Throughout the history of archaeology, archaeological sediment and related soils have been described by such inexact terms as *grayish brown* or *reddish brown*. With the increasingly scientific orientation of archaeology since the 1950s, the Munsell color notation has become the standard.

The Munsell color-order system is defined in terms of three coordinates: hue, value, and chroma. Hue is the quality of color described by the words *red, green, blue, yellow*, etc. It is the color of pigment that must be mixed with black and white (or shades of gray) to produce the color being matched. Value is the quality of lightness or darkness of the color, measured against a series of gray samples that range from white to black. Zero indicates absolute black; ten, absolute white. Chroma defines the degree of color saturation from a gray of the same value. In other words, it is the amount of pigment that must be mixed with a specific value of gray to produce the particular color. Pure gray colors have zero chroma.

Munsell color charts were adopted by the U.S. Soil Survey program in 1949, and the International Society of Soil Science recommended their use about ten years later. A chart for colors of wet soils (gleys) has been added since. Although the adoption of Munsell charts and related names has significantly improved field descriptions of soils and sediments, the results should not be considered precise. In addition to the standard problems of operator variability and errors endemic to any observations, soil and sediment color are affected by such factors as the quality of the light, the moisture content, and dimensions of the areas of individual colors.

Soil color is best determined in sunlight, with

the light coming over the shoulder. Dry soil or sediment is usually about two units higher in value than the same soil or sediment when moist. There may be a difference of one in dry and moist chromas of a soil or sediment. The hue generally remains the same.

The color of soils and archaeological sediments usually depends upon the content of the organic matter and ferric oxides. The thicker the organic matter and ferric oxide coating the grains, the darker the soil. Another generalization is that red soils are older than yellow soils, and they indicate the presence of drainage.

Iron oxides are good indicators of sediment and soil-forming environments because the iron oxides include several different minerals, which have different colors. As well, the specific mineral formed is a result of the geochemical environment, regardless of whether it is natural or anthropogenic, primary or secondary.

It must be emphasized that redness is not related to the amount of iron oxide present but rather to the hematite content. It should also be understood that typical iron oxide colors may be missed if they are masked by the darker (blackish) colors of humic materials or manganese oxides.

The important sediment and soil iron oxides are goethite, hematite, lepidocrocite, and maghemite. Goethite, alpha $FeO(OH)$, is by far the most common iron oxide in soils. When it occurs as the only iron oxide (which is frequently the case) it can be recognized by its Munsell 10YR to 7.5YR hue, as long as it is finely distributed. *Goethite* is nearly ubiquitous in soils, irrespective of climatic zone. It is frequently the cement in concretions.

Hematite, alpha Fe_2O_3, formed at fairly low temperatures, is usually blood-red, with Munsell hues ranging from 5YR to 5R. Hematite often coexists with goethite. Higher temperature, lower water availability, a near-neutral pH, a high iron content of the parent rock, and a rapid turnover of biomass all favor hematite over goethite in pedogenic situations.

Lepidocrocite, gamma $FeO(OH)$, usually has a hue of 7.5YR—which can also be due to a mixture of goethite with a small quantity of hematite. Although lepidocrocite is metastable with respect to goethite, it still occurs in soils, particularly clayey,

noncalcareous soils that undergo anaerobic conditions sometime during each year. Goethite is favored in calcareous environments that have a high concentration of carbonate ions in solution.

Maghemite, gamma Fe_2O_3, has a hue between 2.5YR and 5YR—midway between goethite and hematite. Maghemite is ferrimagnetic and can be extracted from a soil or archaeological sediment with a hand magnet. Oxidation of magnetite (Fe_3O_4) leads to the formation of maghemite. Other iron oxides are transformed into maghemite by fire that is in the presence of organic matter and has a limited supply of oxygen. This can occur at depth through root burning.

A color chart for estimating the organic-matter content of *Ap* horizons using Munsell color notations and laboratory-determined organic content is available.[25] The chart consists of five color chips, which correspond to five overlapping organic-matter ranges of 10–20, 15–25, 20–30, 25–40, and 35–70 grams per kilogram. Alexander noted that accurate organic-matter estimations were possible more than 95 percent of the time for medium to fine soils, but that more than 50 percent sand content could cause organic matter to be overestimated.

Other studies have indicated that the relation between Munsell value and organic matter for Ap horizons is predictable within soil landscapes, if soil textures do not vary widely, but that different landscapes often have different relations. Studies also showed that the relation is not predictable if soil texture varied widely within the landscape (sands versus silts and loams) and that it is similar among landscapes having the same soil textures and parent materials.[26]

Darker colors often indicate the accumulation of organic matter in a deposit, but they can also mean that manganese oxide or dark-colored rock or mineral fragments are present. Postdepositional alterations, including contributions from human activities, darken sediments. In occupational deposits, dark colors may be attributable to humans depositing organics in refuse or forming charcoal in hearths.

Postdepositional conditions are reflected in color. Grayish, olive-gray, and brown colorations indicate reducing (gleying) conditions and the presence of ferrous iron compounds. An overall mottled appearance in sediments and soils results from the migration in solution of manganese and iron ions, which leads to patchy accumulations of oxides and hydroxides. These are also characteristic of gley soils or conditions. The seepage of colloids, organic matter, or iron compounds may result in colored streaks and tongues in deposits.

Mottling also occurs in soil horizons that are incompletely weathered. Anaerobic decay of biologic materials in marshes and stagnant lakes produces deposits that are usually quite dark, but manganese oxides can also form blackish coatings in swamp conditions. Green colors can result from the presence of green minerals (mostly hydrous silicates), including epidote, chlorite, and serpentine. Without detailed laboratory studies, it is sometimes difficult to ascertain whether the color is a product of the original source rock, later additions, or changing geochemical conditions.

White or light-gray colors are produced by a variety of conditions. Source minerals may lighten the color of sediments. Sands composed mostly of quartz or calcite are generally light-colored, especially when they have not been affected by changing oxidation states of iron oxides associated with hydrologic and geochemical fluctuations. Light colors may indicate leaching by moving water.

Reddish and yellowish colors result from oxidation because of good drainage and aeration, in contrast to more mottled grayish, brownish, and yellowish colors that are indicative of reducing conditions. Reddish deposits may also be an indication of intense heat caused by either human activities or fires of other origins. Reds in particular can imply the presence of alternating wet and dry environmental conditions (such as on floodplains and lake margins). Reddish colors have also been related to weathering zones, like those created during intervals of nondeposition and soil development.

Cementation and Induration

Natural cementation transforms loose sediments into consolidated rock. The degree of cementation influences the ability to excavate strata and recover artifacts and faunal material. While loose sediments can make maintaining profiles and retaining information on the location and orientation of artifacts difficult, well-cemented deposits tend to result in the preferential recovery of larger artifacts and bones and more fragmentation of the materials recovered. In caves in southern Africa where australopithicene fossils were recovered, the deposits were so indurated that excavators used dynamite to blast away the matrix. Not surprisingly, this resulted in the loss of materials and added to the difficulty of determining the provenience of a particular find. In these situations the highly cemented nature of the sediments containing artifacts affects the recovery of artifacts, which can influence interpretations.

Calcite cement is commonly an indication of initial diagenesis and lithification of sedimentary deposits. Cementation and induration of a sediment may imply that at one time the deposit was saturated with water. Lithified materials may be natural substances like stones used by humans for structures, or they may be materials like mud brick that are consolidated because of the activities of humans. Cementation of deposits overlying artifact-bearing deposits provides protection from weathering and erosion, thus helping to preserve surfaces of occupation intact.

Texture

Texture of sediments refers to the size, shape, sorting, and orientation of particles. The principles used to characterize the texture of a deposit are applicable to archaeological components within sedimentary deposits, especially since artifacts are a specific kind of sedimentary particle. The particle-size frequency distribution in a sediment provides an indication of the transport and depositional systems that resulted in the accumulation of the sediments and artifacts (see figures 2.7–2.9). Particle-size distributions provide some information on the general hydrodynamic conditions at the site of deposition. In archaeological contexts they are useful for distinguishing between high-energy and low-energy site formational environments. Thus, they can be used to determine whether there is potential preferential bias in the artifact components.

Size distributions of sediments and artifact

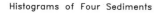

Histograms of Four Sediments

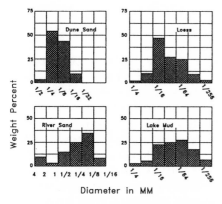

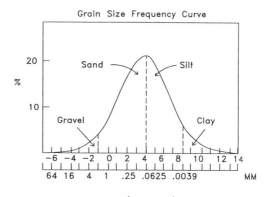

Grain Size Frequency Curve

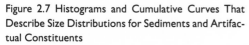

Cumulative Curves of the Sediments

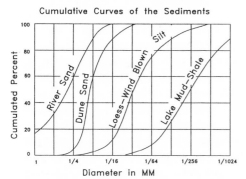

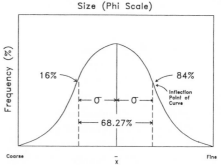

Figure 2.7 Histograms and Cumulative Curves That Describe Size Distributions for Sediments and Artifactual Constituents

Histograms and frequency curves show the relative amount of particular size categories within an artifactual or other deposit. Cumulative curves can also be used to compare the relative proportion of different size fractions in deposits. They have also been used in comparisons of the relative frequencies of types of artifacts among archaeological assemblages.

accumulations depend on five conditions: 1) the type of source rock and the original sizes of the grains or artifacts; 2) the type of transporting medium; 3) abrasion and solution during transportation; 4) sorting of size fractions before deposition; and 5) the depositional environment. Postdepositional mixing and pedogenic processes alter the initial size distribution of sediments. Examples include the downward migration and accumulation of finer particles and the upward movement of larger particles like artifacts. Various methods of data presentation and different statistical measures have been employed to help determine which combination of these conditions is reflected in a sediment's particle-size distribution.

Measurements of artifact size distribution like skewness (symmetry) and mode may be extremely useful in archaeological interpretations. The size distribution of debitage from the Kalambo Falls Acheulian site in Zambia helped indicate that some of the patterning of the artifactual record may have been produced by stream action. At first glance the presence of a relatively large amount of unmodified flakes and fragments, along with certain reduction-stage categories, seemed to indicate that the artifact set could imply stone flaking at the site. But the size distribution of the debitage revealed a strong unimodal peak in the 4–8 cm fraction. Experiments on stone flaking show that there is a strong negative skew toward smaller debitage. The Kalambo Falls debitage, in contrast, had normal skewness. The median, mean, and mode of the debitage size distribution were all in the 4–8 cm range. There were hardly any particles of less than 2 cm in size, although in experiments large amounts of this size range are created by flaking. The size distribution in-

39

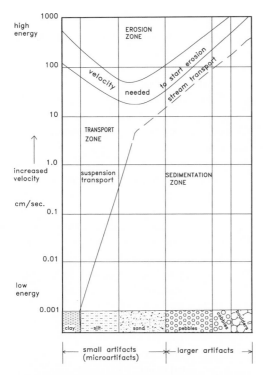

Figure 2.8 Grain Size Versus Energy in Water Transport
At different energy levels, different-sized artifacts
can be eroded, transported, or deposited. Sand-sized
micro-artifacts need lower energies (velocities) to
erode, compared with larger artifacts (artifacts in the
pebble, cobble, or boulder range). The larger the artifact, the higher the velocity needed to keep it from
being deposited. Larger artifacts will be deposited
when energy levels are at velocities of 10 cm per second or less, while sand-sized micro-artifacts can still be
transported at velocities lower than 1 cm per second.

dicated a strong sorting of the larger flake sizes.
One likely interpretation is that the size distribution was the result of stream action.[27]

Typically, particle-size data are presented either
as histograms or as cumulative curves, to show the
relative abundance of size fractions and to allow
statistical measures to be derived (figure 2.7).
Interpretation of these measures of clastic (**exogenic**) sediments are used to infer the energy
of the transporting agent at the point of deposition (figure 2.8). Principal depositional sites of
coarse-fraction clastic sediments include deserts,

beaches, river channels, and lake and sea margins
(see Chapter 3). The fine-fraction (small-sized
particles that comprise a sediment) of a sediment
is used to interpret both depositional and secondary contexts. These include transportation/
deposition agents (if the silts and clays are exogenic), as well as postdepositional processes. The
presence of detrital fine sand to clay particles indicates a low-velocity or zero-velocity transport
agent like passive suspension.

Statistical parameters based on grain-size distributions are used to help infer depositional environments. They have been related to different
forms or modes of sediment movement. These
include surface creep or rolling, and sliding or
traction in continuous contact with bed flow in
rivers. In saltation there is intermittent contact
and resuspension of particles, while in suspension there is no contact (figure 2.9). Rolling and
traction transport particles by air or water. This
usually adds to the coarse fraction of a sediment.
These forms of transport move larger artifacts
and micro-artifacts. Saltation is a common system of transport for finer sands. Suspension is the
common mode of transport for silts and clays. In
glaciers, particles of all sizes can be transported
within or next to the ice; they are deposited as the
ice melts away.

Other statistical methods can be used to describe and interpret archaeologically related sediments. These include mean-particle size, modes
and bimodality, sorting, and skewness, as well as
bivariate comparisons of these attributes. Mean-
particle size for particles is related to current
velocity or to the overall energy of the environment. Coarser mean sizes in aqueous and eolian
contexts are indicative of high energy, while finer
mean sizes are related to lower energy settings.
The most common size fraction with a particle
distribution is its mode. If there is a single mode,
it is an indication that the sediment reflects a
single agent of transportation and deposition. Bimodality of size frequencies generally indicates
mixing of sediment from two sources.

Sorting, the separation of particles by size, is
generally a consequence of variations in transport velocity and turbulence. In well-sorted sediments, particles are of a similar size, while poorly

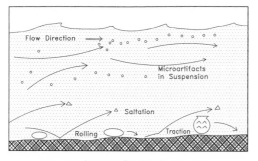

Aqueous Transport

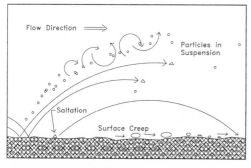

Eolian Transport

Figure 2.9 Velocity and Modes of Transport of Archaeological Particles
Artifacts can be moved within a water column or in an air column by similar methods. In water or by aqueous transport, artifacts roll along without leaving the earth's surface. Similarly, artifacts can be transported by wind by means of surface creep. At progressively higher energies or for smaller artifact particles, saltation or suspension in water or air can be the means of transport.

sorted deposits consist of a wide range of particle sizes. Sorting is an indication of entrainment and transport by water or air currents. Eolian micro-depositional environments have excellent sorting. Dunes typically consist of coarse to fine sand with good sorting. They can exhibit internal sorting, which causes **cross bedding,** in contrast to loess deposits, which can be so well-sorted they appear massive. Because loess deposits are so well sorted, erosional features or soil development are often needed to help the stratigrapher make subdivisions of them. Sandy beaches tend to be well

sorted. However, where energy levels fluctuate and sediments are not continuously reworked, sediments on beaches or dunes can be less well sorted. Spring, lake, and marsh sediments commonly exhibit poor to good sorting, primarily because of fluctuating energy levels. Sediments deposited by glaciers, called till, are poorly sorted. They typically contain very large particles in a finer matrix.

One measure of sorting that can be useful to archaeologists is reflected in the ratio of different artifact categories that are characterized by particular size ranges. In the reduction stages for the making of stone tools, for instance, two of the byproducts are cores and debitage. Cores are larger particles than most debitage or flaking debris. Extremely well-sorted artifact assemblages could either consist of a preponderance of cores or be composed entirely of smaller debris. In both instances, the well-sorted character of the accumulation may indicate geologic patterning of the artifact set. Artifact sets that are less well sorted or are poorly sorted (where both larger and smaller artifacts are present) may represent artifactual patterns that were a direct result of human behavior.

The measure of asymmetry of a grade-size distribution, termed *skewness*, has also been related to selective transport of sediment size fractions. Variations in transport energy seem to affect the extremes of a particle size distribution and influence skewness. Beach sediments can be negatively skewed (contain more coarse particles). Dune and river sands are positively skewed (contain more fine).

Besides interpretations based on statistical parameters of a single particle-size distribution, inferences are made by comparing two or more attributes. Relations like the ratios between coarse and fine clastics are used as a means to differentiate sedimentary **facies**. Relations between kurtosis (peakedness of the distribution curve) and skewness provide an expression of sediment/energy response which may be applied to lacustrine (lake) and other environments. Diagrams that plot two statistical measures of size distribution have been used to distinguish depositional environments. In deposits consisting of

Roundness

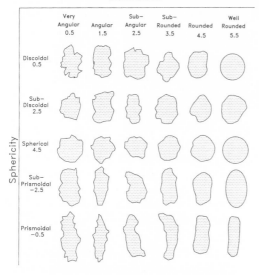

Figure 2.10 Measurements of Particle Morphology
Clastic particles can be described in terms of sphericity and roundness. Particles, including artifacts, become more rounded as they are abraded, unless forces
are strong enough to cause fractures. (Numbers are
median rho values.)

sand-sized particles, for example, eolian dune, lake beach, and river sands have been compared for sorting and skewness. Beach sands are distinguished by negative skewness and good sorting. River sands tend to be positively skewed and less well sorted. Dune sands have positive skewness and are finer grained than beach sands.

In addition to size and sorting characteristics, the morphology of sedimentary particles is an important attribute that is useful in examining artifacts as well. Sedimentary particles are described in terms of sphericity and roundness (figure 2.10). Shape can be an important indicator of conditions of transportation and deposition. Whether the edges of a particle or an artifact are sharp and angular or rounded can be an indication of the amount or intensity of transportation it has undergone. Such surface features as pitting or abrasion marks also indicate the amount and method of transportation.

The property of roundness, or the amount of curvature on the edges and corners of an artifact, changes during transportation in an aqueous sys-

tem. The shape of pottery changes as it is transported by water. In addition to the possibility of being broken, artifacts can be rounded and smoothed by coastal or stream processes. Allen used a quantification of the amount of wear as indicated by roundness as a way of analyzing and interpreting Romano-British pottery assemblages. These artifact sets were found in what is now an intertidal coastal deposit and in subfossil wetland deposits. Allen's study indicated that the Wadell projection technique of measuring roundness was suitable for analyzing transposed and transported pottery sherds.[28]

Another method for studying the properties of abrasion on artifacts caused by stream transport is microscopic measurement of the width of ridges on artifacts. Fresh, unabraided artifacts have narrow, sharp ridges. The ridge width increases or becomes increasingly flattened with abrasion, and this can be measured. The rate of abrasion depends on the shape and hardness of the artifact as well as on the velocity of the current and on the kinds of particles being transported along with the artifact. In the early stages of artifact abrasion during transport, chipping and grinding of the edges is more active. Stress cracks can appear. With further transport the ridge width increases. By using methods of identifying roundedness and abrasion it may be possible to discover the depositional environments associated with artifact accumulation. We could then evaluate whether artifacts are in primary behavioral context. Shackley examined a late Lower Paleolithic assemblage found in a river gravel deposit. Microscopic examination showed that what on a macroscopic level appeared to be unabraided artifacts in fact were artifacts with signs of rounding caused by stream transport. She concluded that the set of artifacts was a selective accumulation produced by deposition and not a distinctly behaviorally induced typologic assemblage.[29]

It appears that for larger artifacts like cores, the properties of sphericity and roundedness play an important role in the amount of potential transport by water. Artifacts that are more spherical, and rounded clasts, such as hammerstones or chopping tools made on fairly spherical cobbles, are more susceptible to transport. They can be more easily moved from primary contexts be-

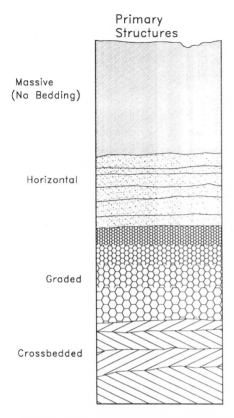

Primary
Structures

Secondary
Structures

Massive
(No Bedding)

Horizontal

Graded

Crossbedded

Frost Wedges

Liquefaction
Feature

Microfaulting

Convoluted
Bedding

Desiccation Cracks

Slickensides

Figure 2.11 Primary and Secondary Structures
Primary structures are created as a direct result of deposition. Secondary structures are created after the sediment has been deposited. Primary structures provide clues to the conditions present at the time the particles stopped being transported. Secondary structures can be used to infer the processes or events that affected the sediment sometime after initial deposition.

cause it takes lower flow velocities to start them going, and it is easier for them to keep moving. More angular objects do not begin to move as easily and are more easily stopped during transport.[30]

Structure
Sedimentary structures are usually small-scale variations in texture or composition. These are created during deposition (exogenic), after deposition within sediments (**endogenic**), by fauna and flora (biogenic), or during pedogenesis or lithification (figure 2.11). Well-known examples of depositional stratification are layering or bedding. Depositional sedimentary structures can be the result of minor variations in conditions of transport and deposition. These variations result in differences in the size of the particles. In certain sedimentologic situations archaeologists will notice very thin beds, generally less than 1 cm thick. These thin beds reflect slight transportational or depositional variations. *Laminae* are the smallest, thinnest layers of original clastic deposition. They can range from >30 to <1 mm. *Lamellae*, in contrast, may be postdepositional structures. They can be features produced by translocation or movement of clay-sized particles within a developing soil profile. Iron oxide deposits can be also be translocated. This movement can produce small-scale banded structures, and it is associated with postdepositional alterations.

Postdepositional structures include mud cracks, faults, and convoluted bedding. Mud cracks and other cracks result from sediments drying up.

43

Frost wedges can also produce cracks in the earth as a result of freezing and drying. Stress within strata can lead to the development of faults. Some postdepositional deformational structures occur when the sediments are in a plastic, water-saturated state. Geologists have inferred that these structures reflect regional tectonic events or deformation associated with overlying deposition of sediments. Liquefaction features have been interpreted as indicators of earthquakes. Sediment intrusions, such as sandstone dikes, are caused by the injection of liquefied sand from below. When very dense strata lie over less dense strata, it causes other load structures. The pressure of heavy overlying deposits squeezes the underlying deposits and causes convolutions to form. Lighter sediments expand upward into heavier layers, which creates such deformation features as convolute laminations. Contorted sediments also can be associated with spring deposits.

Vertical shafts or horizontal tunnels that appear as structures within sediments or soils may result from biotic activities. These kinds of structures are created by plant root systems or burrowing by large and small animals. The presence of these kinds of biogenic structures is an indication of land stabilization and high levels of moisture.

Postdepositional processes also form pedogenetic structures in which soil particles bond together to make various types of aggregate clusters. These soil aggregates are called *peds*, while aggregates formed by disturbances like digging or plowing are termed *clods*. Clods are archaeosediments because they result from human activity. The soil aggregates (peds) have been classified into four types. Roughly horizontal peds arranged in a plane are termed platy. Natric B (*Btn*) horizons have relatively flat vertical surfaces. These vertical surfaces may develop as a result of wetting

and dehydration. Blocklike structures that are usually found in argillic B (*Bt*) horizons have particles aggregated in fairly equidimensional blocks. Spheroidal (granular and crumb) soil structures are associated with *A* horizons and, as a consequence, with organic matter and bioturbation.

Composition

The composition of a deposit refers to the clastic, chemical, and organic constituents of a sediment or soil, as well as to fossil and artifact inclusions. Geologists select physical and chemical properties on the basis of their relation to present-day geologic processes to describe and interpret deposits. The proportion of clastics (sedimentary particles) to authigenic components (minerals formed after clastic deposition) can be used to distinguish different sedimentary depositional environments. Clastic particles derived from an external source area are exogenic. In contrast, endogenic materials are derived from material in solution or near the point of deposition. Figures 2.12, 2.13, and 2.14 illustrate how the proportion of clastics to carbonates can be used to infer changing depositional conditions. These compositional changes are from Pleistocene age basins associated with the Middle Paleolithic occupation of the Sahara.

The types of minerals precipitated from solution can be used to infer environmental settings associated with archaeological accumulations. The principal endogenic phase and dominant carbonate mineral in freshwater and brackish water lacustrine sediments is calcite ($CaCO_3$). The first minerals to form in closed lake basins undergoing evaporative concentration are **alkaline earth** carbonates. "Nonpedogenic" **calcrete** (caliche) can form by **capillary rise** of groundwater and loss by evaporation when the water table lies near

Figure 2.12 Compositional and Size-Fraction Data Used to Infer Past Depositional Conditions
Changes in sediment particle size and composition can be used to infer changes in past environmental conditions. Here the proportion of carbonates to clastics composed of silica and the different sizes of the clastic particles indicate the presence of at least three lake cycles. The peak for each lake cycle, or the time when the lake was at its largest, is indicated by high values of carbonate proportionate to the amount of siliclastics. These same intervals are also associated with higher amounts of smaller particles (silt and clay) in the clastic fraction. Larger, sand-sized particles were deposited when the lake was smaller.

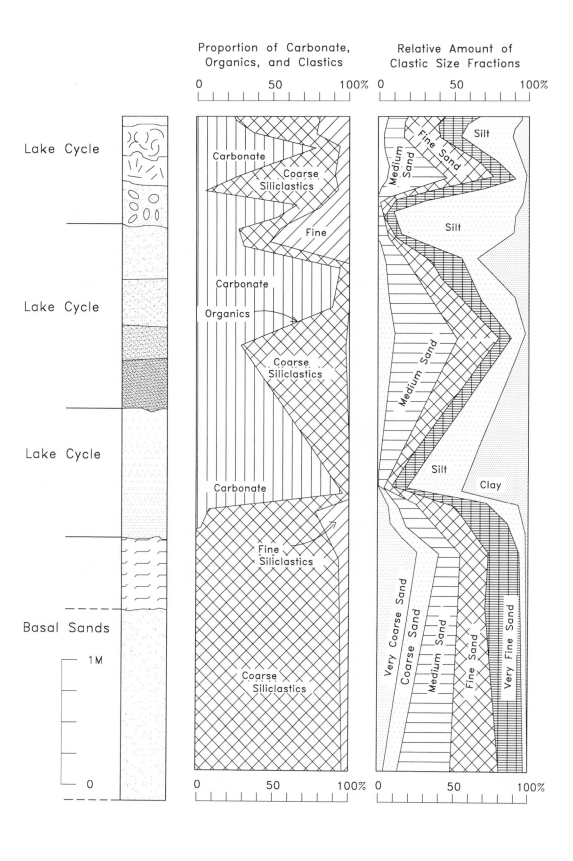

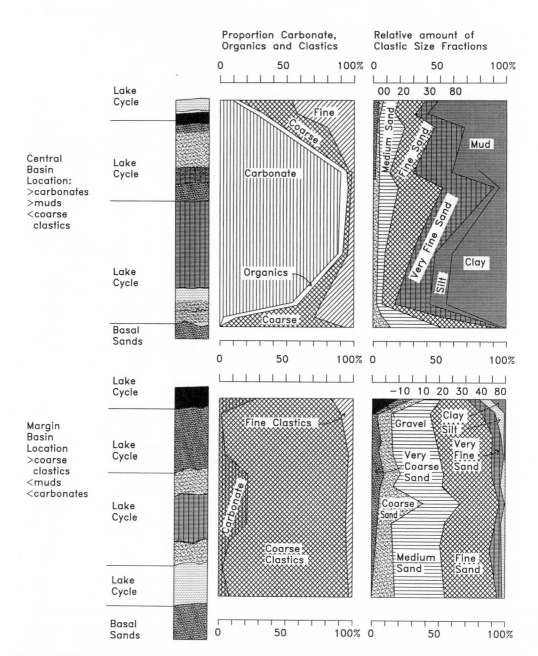

Figure 2.13 The Central Basin and Margin Sediments in Lakes

Variation in the composition and size of sedimentary particles can be the result of different energy levels at different places during a particular time interval. The lower sedimentary sequence was near the edge of a lake basin. It is dominated by coarser particles. Higher amounts of carbonates and smaller particles were de-posited when the lake expanded in size. The upper sedimentary sequence was closer to the center of the basin. Here the quieter, lower energy levels resulted in the deposition of high amounts of carbonate. Notice that there are three peaks of mud (silt and clay) deposi-tion indicating three expansions or maxima associated with three lake cycles.

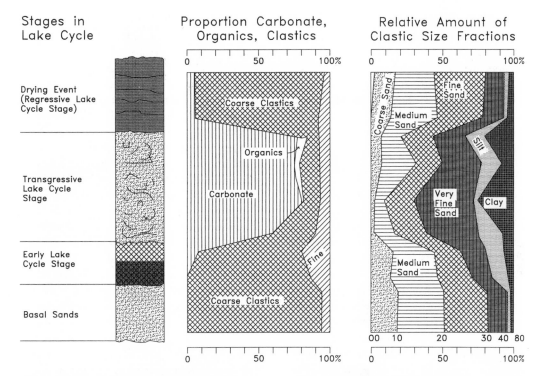

Stages in Lake Cycle	Proportion Carbonate, Organics, Clastics	Relative Amount of Clastic Size Fractions

Figure 2.14 Inference of Lake Cycles from Changes in Relative Amounts of Constituent Materials

The beginning, maximum, and ending of a depositional cycle can be inferred from the composition and size distribution of sediments in a stratigraphic sequence. Here the variations can be linked to the initial, early, maximum, and regressive stages of a single lake cycle. The basal sediments not associated with the later lake event consist entirely of clastic particles, mostly medium or fine sands. During the early stage of the lake, small amounts of carbonate and increasing amounts of fine clastics were deposited in a small body of water. High amounts of carbonate indicate a major expansion of the lake, while two peaks of clay deposition indicate two pulses of increasing lake size during this interval. Coarse particles and a decline in carbonate content mark the end of the lake cycle and the decrease in the size of the lake.

the surface. Pedogenic calcrete can be formed by downward migration (illuvation). In early stages, caliche can form powdery or indurated isolated nodules of carbonate. With time, these can become extensive horizons of carbonate. Various stages in this progression have been used as indicators of age and climate.

Organic matter in carbonaceous deposits reflects the past presence of plants or other biota. Peats, composed chiefly of organic material, form in freshwater environments, although they can also develop in salt marshes or slightly brackish waters. Sapropels, consisting of dark, organically rich sediments, form under more diverse conditions of organic decomposition in lake basins.

Plant and organic matter are also introduced into sedimentary contexts as part of the detrital component. This can complicate the use of basin sedimentary sequences for developing paleoecologic and chronological interpretations. Pollen stratigraphies, as an example, may represent regional watershed environmental conditions instead of the local, site-specific setting (see Chapter 4). In other instances, "dead" carbon may be washed in; when this happens, radiocarbon measurements produce dates that are too old for the archaeological record (see Chapter 7).

Fossils and artifacts are also sedimentary components that can be regarded as either unique particles in a depositional system or inclusions.

Regardless of whether they are in primary or secondary context, they can provide information about depositional contexts. The artifact or fossil taphonomy and sedimentology of these inclusions are critical aspects of archaeological interpretation (see Chapter 3). Both fossils and artifacts can be used as biostratigraphic markers as long as taphonomic agencies of redeposition are taken into account.

Boundaries

Sedimentary deposits, as well as archaeological features like walls and floors, are separated from one another by boundaries that can be of great interpretational value. Many terms are used to describe contacts between deposits, among them *interfaces* and *discontinuities*. Abrupt contacts in sediments can indicate changes in transportational depositional systems. Gradational contacts, in contrast, reflect more time-transgressive environmental changes. Undulating and broken boundaries indicate postdepositional, postburial deformations like the erosion of the upper surface.

Discontinuities between sedimentary deposits can be either *conformable* or *un- or nonconformable*. Where there are bedding plains between sedimentary layers and no apparent break in deposition, the contact is conformable. These types of boundaries occur where there is continuous deposition—or at least there have been no major erosional events. Conformable boundaries can be abrupt or gradational. Artifacts found along such contacts could either be redeposited sedimentary particles or the result of a past human occupation surface that became buried quickly during an interval of essentially continuous deposition.

Nonconformable boundaries are contacts formed by an erosional surface or an interval of nondeposition (like a stabilized or a soil surface). They represent the passage of time between the deposition of the lower layer and the overlying bed. Artifacts found in these settings could have been mixed as a result of being redeposited or, if they seem to be in primary context, could represent many superimposed occupations on a stabilized surface.

Unconformities include different forms of discontinuities. They represent an interval of nonsedimentation. Unconformities can be recognized in a stratigraphic sequence by several attributes. The presence of **lag** deposits may indicate an unconformable surface. The lag deposit may represent a set of artifacts resting on a deflated surface formed by wind erosion. Another indication of an unconformity is the presence of a buried soil or weathered zone. Changes in the dip of the bedding between sedimentary units can also indicate an unconformity. Geologists are usually more explicit than archaeologists in recording and defining unconformities. Although recognizing time gaps is more difficult in archaeological excavation than in most geologic contexts, more attention should be paid to this question. These time gaps may be hints that can help explain time-dependent patterns in the archaeological record. Boundaries represent time.

Where there is a boundary between sedimentary units that cuts across bedding planes, the contact is called a *truncation* or an erosional *disconformity*. Disconformities indicate erosional events that might be the result of deflation, running water, or shore processes. They are prevalent in some archaeological settings. A disconformity could result, for example, from the regression of a lake and subsequent subaerial erosion. Disconformities are good indicators that the artifacts associated with these types of contacts may have been eroded and redeposited and are not in primary context.

The surface topography of boundaries is of particular help in interpretations of postdepositional processes like erosion, burial, deformation, and mixing. Smooth upper boundaries can indicate erosional truncations. The upper boundaries of units can be buried, eroded, or stabilized. Where the upper surface is stable, soil-formation processes like weathering or the accumulation of organic matter can occur. Artifacts found along the interface between an upper boundary of one deposit and the lower boundary of the deposit above could have resulted from one of two situations. The artifacts could have been deposited on the surface of the lower deposit, perhaps because of a human occupation on that surface, or they could have been part of the lower deposit and eroded from it. Artifacts found in the lower part of the upper unit might have been redeposited from the lower layer. Many surface and near-surface processes can add to, alter, or remove components from sediments (see Chapter 3).

Once the observable characteristics of the sediment-soil sequence containing artifacts has been described, "inferential units" can be proposed using Walther's Law of Correlation of Facies. Inferential units reflect our interpreta-tions, and these interpretations transform observations about static physical and chemical properties and spatial relationships of deposits into a dynamic story of the past. This transformation of the prehistoric record from the observation of properties to the interpretation of past dynamics connects the study of the human past (archaeology) with the study of past life (paleontology) and the study of the evolution of the earth (geology).

CHAPTER 3

Contexts of Archaeological Record Formation

It is necessary to study both the human activities and the other natural processes that contribute to the formation of the archaeological record to understand it fully. One of the most powerful conceptual approaches in geoarchaeology is the application of artifact taphonomy. This is an interpretational perspective based on the study of formational processes that affect the final spatial pattern and compositional character of the archaeological record. As indicated in Chapter 2, because archaeological materials are recovered from sedimentary deposits, the geomorphic and sedimentologic processes that are associated with these deposits affect the interpretation of the artifacts within them. The initial landscape and resource settings play a critical role in human behavior. Where humans will live and what forms of human behavior will occur are in many circumstances a result of the landscape context. This context also plays a role in affecting how human behavioral patterns embodied in artifacts become the archaeological record. That is to say, the character and spatial distribution of particular activities reflected in the archaeological record are largely dependent upon the original habitat setting. This landscape setting also influences the visibility and preservation of the record. As with any set of materials distributed across the earth's surface, the evidence of human activities

recorded in artifact patterning is subject to processes that can transform the original behavioral signal. Weathering, transportation, redeposition, and postdepositional alteration change the patterns imposed on the archaeological record by human behavior. In this chapter, we use the principles of sediments and soils introduced in Chapter 2 to describe landscape contexts and processes in depositional systems that directly influence the nature of the archaeological record.

Interpretations of the archaeological record based on a geoarchaeological site formation approach are founded on methodologies focused on artifact taphonomy. Originally applied to physical biotic remains in the study of the fossil record, taphonomy involves the study of objects as they move through a trajectory from being part of a living, dynamic context to being a static accumulation or assemblage of materials (figure 3.1).[1] From a strictly paleontologic perspective, taphonomy involves studying the processes which change biotic communities into fossils. The usefulness of a parallel application of the taphonomic approach to the archaeological record should be clear. The principles of artifact taphonomy provide a framework for evaluating the events and processes that affect objects as they travel from the dynamic contexts associated with human behavior through the transforming events after they

Figure 3.1 The Effects of Human-Environmental Interactions on the Archaeological Record
Evidence of human activity in the archaeological record is a result of biosphere and lithosphere interactions. The biosphere includes human behavioral or systemic contexts and the ecological habitats formed by communities of plants and animals. The physical habitat or landscape context is part of the lithosphere and is the result of both strictly geologic and biologic and atmospheric processes. Artifacts are deposited as a

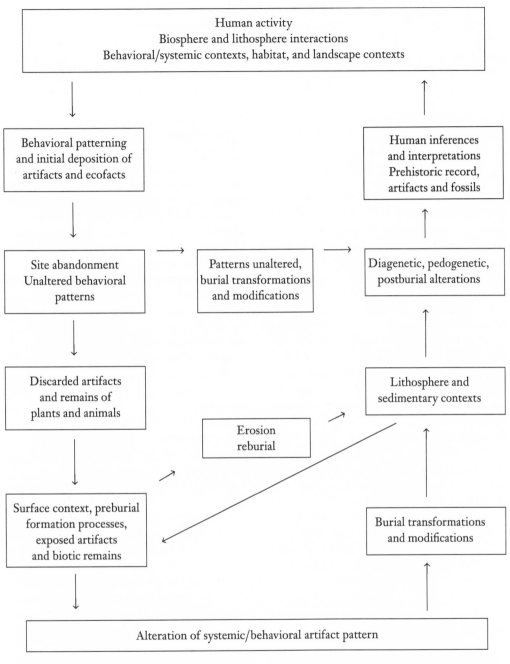

| Human activity
Biosphere and lithosphere interactions
Behavioral/systemic contexts, habitat, and landscape contexts |

Behavioral patterning
and initial deposition of
artifacts and ecofacts

Human inferences
and interpretations
Prehistoric record,
artifacts and fossils

Site abandonment
Unaltered behavioral
patterns

Patterns unaltered,
burial transformations
and modifications

Diagenetic, pedogenetic,
postburial alterations

Discarded artifacts
and remains of
plants and animals

Lithosphere and
sedimentary contexts

Erosion
reburial

Surface context, preburial
formation processes,
exposed artifacts
and biotic remains

Burial transformations
and modifications

Alteration of systemic/behavioral artifact pattern

result of human behavior. After people leave, these patterns resulting from human behavior can remain exposed or become buried. If left unburied, the patterns of behavior can remain unmodified, or they can be transformed by surface and pedogenic processes. Artifacts that are buried become part of the sedimentary context. Through erosion, these artifacts can become part of the surface context or be buried again, forcing increased modification of the original systemic or behavioral patterns recorded in artifactual patterning. Artifacts in sedimentary context can also be influenced by postburial alterations.

become part of the geologic context to the point at which they form the patterns that become the archaeological record.

The development of a theoretical framework using what has been variously called a taphonomic, transformational, or bridging theory approach to interpreting the archaeological record was discussed briefly in Chapter 1. This framework signaled a convergence between earth-science principles and methodology and the explanatory, process-oriented goals of anthropological archaeology. Behavioral interpretations of the artifactual record should rely on considerations of the transforming events that influence the initial patterns of variability produced by human activities before changing them to the variability observed in the archaeological context. An understanding of the sources of variability and patterning represents a critical contribution of earth sciences to archaeological interpretation.

The orientation or bearing of artifactual remains can be used to infer the processes associated with the accumulation of materials at archaeological sites. For example, Todd and Frison used the direction of mammoth long bones to interpret the Colby site in northern Wyoming that contained the remains of seven mammoths associated with Clovis artifacts. The orientation of the long bones were plotted in the form of a rose diagram. The bones showed a nonrandom pattern: they were oriented roughly parallel to the direction of the drainage channel. A possible explanation of the nonrandom orientation of the mammoth long bones was stream action, but although some of the bones seem to have been rearranged by stream action, some of the larger bone accumulations did not appear to have been created by these types of processes.[2]

Stages of Site Formation

A variety of terms are used to describe the stages in the trajectory of an object or feature as it moves from interaction with the dynamics of human behavior to become part of the archaeological record. In the most straightforward scenario, the trajectory can be separated into two stages. Human activity imposes patterns, and then physical (geologic and biologic) processes influence these patterns or impose additional patterns upon the artifacts. Objects may have participated in both these stages more than once before they are studied as part of the archaeological record. In fact, the archaeological investigation itself is a return to participation in the "human activity" stage.

The initial stage of artifact patterning dealing with human activity has traditionally been the focus of anthropologically oriented archaeological interpretations, where the goal has been to infer past human behavior. This stage, where objects are interacting as part of a human behavioral system, is called the systemic context.[3] The systemic context includes all the processes of human behavior or transformational activity that occur before the site is left unoccupied by people. A variety of behaviors can influence the artifact patterns that exist at the end of this stage, including artifact reuse and reclamation, artifact discard and site abandonment (human deposition), and disturbance (trampling, plowing, or excavation). These factors all result from direct human behavior and can greatly influence the character of the archaeological record. Artifact sets that reflect only processes associated with the systemic context, in which no rearrangement or restructuring by geologic and biologic forces took place, are primary archaeological deposits.

In addition to human activity, a variety of geologic and biologic processes introduce patterns into the archaeological accumulations. The stage where natural physical environmental processes alone affect artifacts is called the archaeological context. After the patterning imposed by human behavior has occurred and humans have abandoned the site, geologic and biologic processes can modify the artifactual record. These are transformations imposed either by surface processes or during or after burial. In contrast to primary archaeological deposits, secondary deposits contain artifacts modified by redepositional or diagenetic processes. Understanding the effect of these postoccupational physical-transformation processes is critical to deriving inferences and meaning from the archaeological record.

The composition and configuration of the archaeological record are greatly influenced by formation processes. Basic properties of individual artifacts like size, shape, spatial orientation, and surface features are all affected by formation processes. Postoccupational factors affect the quantity and diversity of artifactual materials preserved in artifact assemblages. Besides influencing whether relics of past human behavior will be preserved, postoccupational processes affect the visibility of the artifacts. Wherever archaeological occurrences are preserved, formation processes have directly influenced the spatial distributions (vertical and horizontal distributions and density) of artifacts. Interpretation of the patterns of variability within the archaeological record requires an understanding of both the behavioral and the physical conditions that influence the final character of the prehistoric record.

Initial Landscapes and Original Occupation

The present distribution and visibility of archaeological sites are based initially on the environmental conditions which existed at the time of human occupation. These conditions made a particular functional activity possible and provided the circumstances which later transformed or preserved the artifactual evidence of human behavior. Many functional activities that take place at a site are related to the landscape context or habitat setting and the resources available at that location. Certain types of activities are restricted to the availability or distribution of resources across a landscape. Specific types of archaeological manifestations are likely to be associated with these landscape patterns. Perhaps the most obvious of these are locations related to the availability of a spatially restricted resource or activity context. For instance, procurement activities associated with stone and mineral sources result in the location of quarry sites near sources of raw materials. Similarly, campsites and butchery sites can be expected in settings connected with animal migration routes or near water-related resources.

An understanding of the landscape context

at the time of human occupation of a particular locality provides important information for determining what types of behavioral activities might have prevailed. In many instances site setting is strongly related to function and use. Whether considered in terms of regional environmental conditions, the physiographic setting immediately surrounding the site, or the local microenvironmental context, the landscape setting directly influences the location of a site and the activities that occur there. The depositional systems discussed below provide contexts for evaluating why humans have used particular settings. They also help us understand what processes might enable primary sites (systemic artifactual patterns) to be left intact, or at least sealed by burial. Some conditions within these depositional settings are more conducive to the preservation of primary sites, while other circumstances are more closely associated with secondary redeposited assemblages.

Sedimentary Settings

Results of present-day depositional environments are used in comparison with those of past environments to infer past conditions. The attributes like color, texture, composition, and lateral and vertical associations described in Chapter 2 help identify specific sedimentary environments and depositional conditions associated with the presence of artifacts and other archaeological features. The major depositional systems that can be related to past human behavior are settings and processes which affect deserts, lakes (and other water-filled basins), flowing water, caves and rock shelters, glaciers, and sea coasts. In addition, artifacts in postdepositional alterations affect these systems. Humans have been involved with these systems as they use both imbedded and mobile resources, and the remnants of these activities are preserved as part of the artifactual record. The sedimentary settings discussed here are considered depositional and postdepositional settings in terms of their implications for archaeological site formation.

The interpretation of archaeological materials

associated with specific depositional settings re-lies mainly on an evaluation of the destructive and preservational processes prevalent in particular sedimentary contexts and how they have affected artifact accumulations. Where weathering and erosion dominate, the spatial arrangement and composition of the artifact accumulations at a site will be modified. Artifacts will be transported from their original contexts and redeposited. They may be abraded, broken, or destroyed. Destruction by weathering or rearrangement by erosion and redeposition removes some or most of the patterns imposed by the systemic context and introduces other patterns of geologic and biologic structuring. Where low-energy erosional and depositional contexts existed, a stronger possibility for retention of structural patterns directly related to the behavioral context also exists. However, even low-energy postburial forces significantly rearrange certain constituents of the archaeological record. As an example, in an overbank flood situation, alluvial sediments may bury larger fragments of pottery and stone while flood waters may remove smaller artifacts and lighter bone.

Desert Depositional Systems

A diverse set of sedimentary deposits exists in arid or semiarid desert systems because at various times different processes operate, depending on the levels and sources of available moisture. What distinguishes desert systems from other systems is the near-absence of water, which directly affects the habitability of desert regions. Available moisture influences where and when human occupation will occur and restricts human use to localized areas that contain water or other important resources.

The timespan of human habitation in desert regions can be related to short-term or long-term changes in available moisture. Human occupation and use of arid and semiarid settings can reflect short-term availability of moisture, such as seasonal precipitation. This seasonal variation in available moisture creates habitats that sustain occupation for certain times of the year. Evidence of past human occupation of currently arid settings can also be related to long-term changes

in available moisture caused by climate changes (see Chapter 4). Climatic fluctuations transform geographic landscape settings and make them conducive to habitation by plants and animals. Past human activity also has resulted in physical changes of the landscape that affected the availability of moisture and created arid or semiarid settings.

The usual lack of water in arid regions alters the focus but not the kinds of sedimentary processes that prevail. The variety of depositional environments and landscape settings integrated into desert systems is reflected in eolian, fluvial, and chemical sedimentary processes. These processes respond to fluctuating moisture availability, causing the erosion, transport, deposition, and burial of sediments and artifacts.

Eolian erosion and deposition are the dominant processes in desert systems. This is especially true during the periods of highest aridity. During intervals of increased moisture, fluvial, lacustrine, and pedogenic processes can occur within the desert setting (figure 3.2). Human occupation of the desert depositional system during extremely arid intervals is usually sporadic, except in areas where surface water or other resources (like a specific stone raw material) are available. Most artifacts in desert settings were initially deposited because of occupation associated with nearby surface water or along routes associated with unique embedded resources.

The Effects of Wind

Wind can bury artifact arrangements associated with the behavioral occupational context of a site under a dune or other deposit and thus preserve it. But usually eolian processes cause major transformations of the archaeological record. This is because of the destruction and abrasion of objects as well as intense erosion. Where stratified sequences of artifact-bearing sediments exist initially, erosion can remove the matrix, a process that permits the collapse of the sequences and the mixing of archaeological components. Smaller artifacts may be destroyed or eroded and redeposited by the wind. Desert pavement surfaces composed of larger particles (lag gravels) initially produced by **deflation** can form a protec-

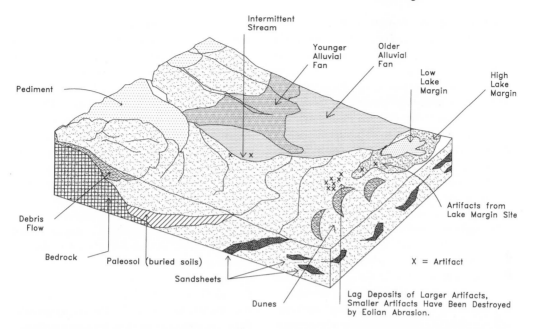

Figure 3.2 Desert System Site Formation
In windblown deposits like dunes, artifacts can lie in secondary deflation lags, and smaller artifacts may be absent because they have been abraded away. Artifact accumulations may be associated around the edges of fluctuating desert-lake margins or in related deposits.

Where there is some physiographic relief, occupation surfaces may be buried under alluvial deposits or debris flows, forming paleosols. Younger alluvial fan deposits may incorporate older artifacts as a result of erosion and redeposition.

tive cover and guard underlying artifact-bearing sediments from more erosion. Dune or sandsheet stabilization after burial may preserve behavioral contexts of occupation surfaces.

Dunes are the most commonly recognized deposit associated with arid settings. A variety of dune shapes can occur, depending on the size of the sediments, the strength and direction of the wind, and the surface on which the material is deposited. Sandsheets and sand seas also occur in arid settings. In addition to these depositional features, erosional features caused by deflation can remove finer materials and leave lag deposits, including artifacts. While finer particles are deflated away, deflation-lag concentrations of coarser particles can form on the surface.

The Effects of Moisture
During intervals of higher available moisture, streams and lakes can form part of the desert depositional system. Arid and semiarid settings

are associated with alluvial fans in places where there is a major difference in the relative elevation on the landscape. These fans consist of cones of sediments that begin in uplands and reach lower elevations. Sometimes they coalesce with other fans to form a **bajada** or a piedmont alluvial plain (figure 3.2). Stream-related sedimentary processes dominate alluvial fans. In addition to stream channel deposits, which result in cut-and-fill accumulations, **sheet flood** and **debris flow** deposits also form alluvial fans. Mass-wasting, the downslope movement of materials induced by gravity, is especially critical for fan development on slopes in arid and semiarid settings. The intermittent depositional events associated with fan development result in the burial of surfaces associated with human occupation.

Localized precipitation in arid and semiarid regions may cause the formation of intermittent streams that produce **wadis** or **arroyos**. These processes can both erode artifact accumulations and redeposit them or bury and preserve them. Artifact assemblages may be transported and sorted during torrential rains or buried by flash-flood deposition.

For human inhabitants, desert lakes can seem either intermittent or permanent on the human timescale. Either way, they are focal points for human occupants and biologic inhabitants of arid settings. Where there is a high degree of fluctuation in the level of the lake, occupation surfaces can be inundated and preserved or washed away by wave action. Intermittent lakes form **playa** deposits because of local precipitation, while more permanent lakes may develop where there is regional groundwater recharge. Short-term desert lakes form from surface water runoff or inflowing streams, either because of catastrophic storms or seepage of groundwater. Because current velocity is generally low in these closed basins, deposition occurs mainly from suspension. Human occupations around the margins of these restricted water bodies may be eroded by intermittent stream flow and sheet wash or buried by retransported sediment. When sand dunes are inundated because of groundwater seepage, interdunal ponds can be created. These are locations for the deposition of organics and fine-grained sediments.

Desert System Site Formation

Although eolian processes are likely to dominate desert systems, processes induced by climatic variation also have a significant influence in desert systems. Archaeological sites in arid settings are commonly preserved around locations associated with the past presence of water. Deposits associated with these settings often contain records of the human occupation of areas that now experience desert conditions. Dune stabilization may accompany increased levels of moisture and, in semiarid conditions, may be associated with increased vegetation cover. Under conditions where there is no vegetation, any local rainfall will have major erosional and redepositional repercussions. Without vegetation cover, ephemeral stream and sheet wash can either erode and redeposit artifacts or bury them. Where seasonal or perennial bodies of water exist in desert systems, fluctuating water levels may erode sites situated along high-energy margins or bury them in quieter, low-energy depositional regimes.

A Middle Paleolithic locality in southern Egypt provides an example of desert system, stream-related artifactual erosion, transport, and redeposition. The artifact assemblage, dated to 100,000–200,000 years ago, was on the edge of a shallow ephemeral stream channel in a setting ideal for stream action to have removed and redeposited artifacts. To determine whether horizontal downstream movement may have occurred, the frequencies and locations of large and small artifacts were plotted. Most of the larger artifacts, consisting of cores and retouched and unretouched flakes, as well as the smaller artifacts, consisting of flaking debris (debitage), were found in a dense upslope concentration. This suggested a horizontal integrity of the artifacts. However, a distribution plot of the ratios of smaller and larger artifacts suggested that more of the smaller artifacts had been eroded and redeposited downslope. In this instance, the smaller artifacts seem to have been transported preferentially downstream during a flood within the channel. Although infrequent and sporadic in desert settings, rainfall can be a major factor in the modification of artifact accumulations. Lack of vegetation enables high energy runoff to occur, and this in turn affects the erosion, sorting, and repatterning of artifact sets.

The nearby Acheulian site at Bir Sahara provides another site formational context associated with desert conditions. Here, eolian processes have deflated sediments which once contained Lower Paleolithic artifacts. The wind removed the sandy matrix and left the larger artifacts in lag position mantling the remnant of a fossil groundwater pond. Few smaller items were found on the deflated surface containing the Acheulian bifaces. The smaller artifacts seem to have been destroyed by the deflation. Excavations were conducted into the deposits not affected by deflation that remained at the site. In these undeflated sediments there was a much higher percentage of smaller artifacts than of larger Acheulian artifacts (hand axes) compared to the surface collection. In terms of archaeological interpretation, the presence of higher proportions of smaller artifacts in the undeflated deposits suggests that hand axes were being used and resharpened at the site. It also implies that the site artifacts may still be in primary context. The Acheulian occupation seems to have been overlain by carbonates deposited in a groundwater-fed pond as it expanded in size. The carbonate protected the underlying sediments from erosion, whereas on the margins of the basin, where there was no protective carbonate, wind could easily erode the sandy deposits.

Lakes and Associated Basin Settings

Lakes are bodies of standing water within basins. Both ancient lake shoreline and basin deposits are areas with high potential for containing archaeological sites. Other archaeologically significant lakelike environments are spring-fed ponds, swamps, marshes, and bogs. These are generally distinguished by water depth and the vegetation associated with it. Lakes are often deep enough to prohibit the growth of vegetation (except for subaqueous plants). Such a fine distinction may be difficult to establish in the geologic record, where the absence of evidence of vegetation can reflect climatic or preservational conditions rather than the depth of the water body. Standing water and the presence of trees characterizes swamp settings, while marshes contain grass but no trees; yet both are difficult to ascertain in the prehistoric record without the application of fossil indicators. Peat deposits characterize bogs, which may be quite visible in the stratigraphic record. All these settings contain resources humans have used in the past and are associated with archaeological sites. Distinguishing among these types of aqueous environments using only sedimentologic or pedogenic data can be difficult in the absence of fossils or other paleoecologic indicators.

Basin Deposits

Lake and other water basin deposits can be classified into two major groups, clastic (essentially exogenic) and chemical (endogenic and authigenic). Organic deposits can be important constituents of each. An idealized picture of sediment distribution in lakes corresponds to potential levels of hydraulic energy, in a scale that ranges from coarse particles around the perimeter in the beach zone, grading into sandy marly muds, and finally grading into muds or deposits high in carbonates (figure 3.3). Organic (carbonaceous) sediments would be expected to occur along the edges of the basins in shallow water marshes, swamps, and bog settings or within ponds. Coarser particles tend to appear in the higher-energy regions around the margin of the basin while fine-grained sediments accumulate nearer the center of the basin.

In addition to the changes in particle size of clastic materials, in saline lakes general vertical and lateral patterns may be associated with the deposition of chemical precipitates. Evaporation sequences begin with the deposition of carbonates (calcite, aragonite, dolomite), followed by gypsum, and finally by anhydrite-halite. Modern perennial saline lakes like the Great Salt Lake, the Dead Sea, Lake Magadi, and Lake Chad are generally restricted to climates that are currently dry. Some of these fluctuate greatly in size, based on seasonal and more long-term climate changes.

Calcite is the dominant chemically deposited mineral in freshwater lakes. Evaporation need not cause carbonate precipitates in lakes. Saturation of the water by calcite can be caused by photosynthesis or temperature changes. Lake sediments can also be created by organisms, mostly invertebrates like pelecypods and gastropods (usually depositing the carbonate mineral aragonite), **diatoms** (siliceous), oncolites (algal), or ostracods.

The lower wave energy in lakes and the fluctuation of water level can produce sediments that are more mixed in size. Waves can develop beaches. Waves that rework coarser sediments and move finer sediments offshore affect the shorelines of larger lakes. Freshwater lake and marsh facies are coarser and more heterogeneous near shores, and finer and more homogenous toward the center. Erosion, transport, and deposition of coarse material are mostly confined to the shallow zone of lakes near the shore, which is also the area where human occupation and artifact deposition are likely to occur.

Plant life can be abundant in shallow basins or at the edges of lakes and may be a resource used by humans. Harvesting these plants by prehistoric people may provide an explanation for the presence of discarded artifacts in settings that

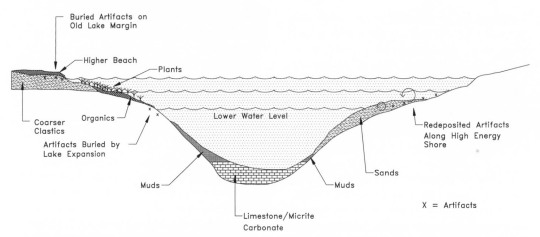

Figure 3.3 Site Formation in Lake Basin Settings
In terms of sediment deposition, higher energies along the edges of the basin result in the deposition of coarser clastics like sands along the beaches. Organics can be deposited in shallow water areas where energy levels are low enough to allow plant growth. Muds and carbonate (limestone and micrite) are deposited nearer the center of the basin. When water levels are low in the basin, human occupation can occur in locations that, with rising waters, can be buried by deeper water sediments. Rising waters can also result in the erosion and redeposition of artifacts that were once part of lower shoreline margins. In the reverse instance, artifacts associated with lake margins formed during high-water levels in the basin will not be affected by shoreline erosion during intervals of reduced lake size. Artifacts on these higher, abandoned lake margins may be affected by other erosional events, but they may also be dated if their existence can be reliably associated with the presence of humans and the creation of the margin feature.

would have contained knee-deep water. Bioturbation is rarer in the deeper parts of lakes: clastic deposition in the center of lake basins usually comes from suspension. Deep-water areas would not tend to contain artifacts unless they had once been the location of basin margins that were later inundated. Artifacts found in deep-water settings may have been deposited on aerially exposed surfaces during a recession of the lake to a lower water level, only to be buried with the next expansion of the lake. Low-lying swamp or marshlike environments are associated with the presence of fossil plant-root structures. These environments contain resources that humans used.

Besides holding the possibility of having primary and secondary artifact accumulations interstratified within deposits caused by the expansion and contraction of water bodies within a basin, the margins of basins can contain sediments and landforms which may be associated with human occupation. Features that indicate the presence of a former shoreline, such as beaches and deltas, are likely to contain archaeological sites. Because the position of lake-margin features can reflect the changing water levels within a basin, they can help date associated archaeological assemblages and explain archaeological site distribution and visibility.

Sedimentologic conditions found in lake and associated environments of deposition (ponds, swamps, springs) are also found in other depositional settings. Depending on the level of groundwater and the amount of seasonal precipitation, playa and more permanent perennial lakes can exist in semiarid and arid desert conditions. Lakes also form in alluvial and glacial settings.

Site Formation in Basin Settings
Lake-related contexts have a variety of microdepositional settings that both protect and destroy archaeological sites. Low-energy settings associated with the flooding of the margins of

water bodies bury and protect sites. Artifacts in higher-energy regimes—along shorelines, river mouths, and spring conduits—are susceptible to erosion and redeposition. Artifacts in spring contexts are particularly susceptible to redepositional processes, which can cause the mixing of artifacts from different periods, although these mixed-component assemblages may be preferentially preserved because of later diagenic processes. Abrasion of artifacts and size sorting is also common in spring contexts. The later deposition of tufa and other carbonates may serve as a protective seal over primary sites. The geologic conditions of spring formation will be discussed in Chapter 9.

Lacustrine shoreline features have a high potential for archaeological occupation, but high energy levels may modify systemic contexts associated with these features. Fluctuating lake margins can either bury sites or erode them. Away from the high energy of spring conduits and shorelines, quieter depositional settings can preserve behaviorally related contexts. The infilling of lakes, which creates bogs and swamps, may preserve archaeological localities. Where lake levels are lowered, successive occupations along the margin should become younger toward the center of the basin. The opposite distributional pattern and the potential for burial are associated with transgressive lake events.

Alluvial Depositional Systems: Flowing Water

Flowing water is a major force in landscape development and the creation of the habitat context of human prehistoric occupations. Sediments deposited by a stream or running water are termed *alluvium*. Fluvial deposits are a specific type of alluvium that has been transported and deposited in a river system. It is no overstatement to say that every major river system in the world contains important archaeological sites. Not only do these settings frequently attract human habitation, but they also undergo sedimentologic processes that facilitate their initial burial and preservation, as well as their later erosion and exposure.

Depositional Contexts

The major depositional contexts of the fluvial system include alluvial fans, stream deposits, and deltas. Fans can be formed in both arid and humid environments. In arid settings fans commonly occur along **scarps**. Fans formed in more humid settings may form **pediments** and generally contain better-sorted deposits. There is a general trend in particle size distributions of fining toward the **distal** segment of the fan. Because the dominant processes in fan development in humid settings are fluvially related, distinguishing between alluvial fans in humid climates and braided stream deposits can be difficult, because multiple channels and bar aggradation characterize both.

Deposits associated with fluvial conditions vary from gravels transported during periods of high energy to muds deposited while suspended in low-energy areas. Dried river beds, whose importance in arid settings was discussed earlier, make up a subcategory of alluvial settings. There are four main types of rivers: straight, braided, anastomosing, and meandering. Straight rivers are probably the least common. Braided streams form a network of branching and reuniting channels separated by islands and bars. Based on sedimentary texture and structure, a wide range of microdepositional conditions can be identified with braided stream deposition. Gravels with cross bedding are characteristic of bars, channel lag, and channel fill deposits. Artifacts coarser than sand found in these deposits are potential articlasts, having been eroded from their systemic context and transported and redeposited with other nonartifactual clasts. Fine sands and finer fractions (silt and clay) are indicative of very low-energy regimes like flood deposits and standing pools. Artifacts in these settings may have been buried soon after human occupation and may be in primary context. Sedimentologic events in braided streams include flooding and channel aggradation with deposition under decreased velocity, development of bars through lateral accretion, and cut-and-fill episodes.

Within an idealized fluvial system, meandering streams are situated between braided streams

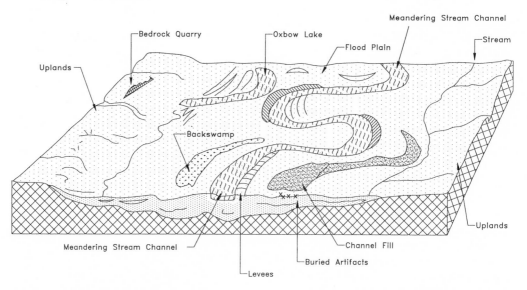

Figure 3.4 Meandering Stream Environments
Levees are created along the banks of river channels as a result of periodic flooding and depositional events. The river channel moves back and forth within the floodplain region, which is sandwiched between uplands. During large floods the river flows out of the channel and over the floodplain, resulting in both erosion and burial of artifacts. Old, abandoned sections of the channel form oxbow lakes and backswamp areas that may be associated with functionally specific human prehistoric activity.

and deltas. A variety of micro-facies can exist within a meandering stream depositional environment (figure 3.4). Within the channel, coarser lag deposits form in the deeper part of the channel while on the inside (convex side) of the meander loop, **point bars** can accumulate. Ridge and swale features that resemble lake strandlines can be present on larger point bars. Sediment can be deposited outside the channel in the form of overbank deposits after extreme discharge events. **Oxbow lakes** form where a meander is abandoned, usually after the river has created a new channel. In these cut-off channels, later deposition contributed directly from the fluvial system will be only low-energy overbank sedimentation. The banks of oxbow lakes are areas with a high potential for containing preserved human prehistoric occupations. The stratigraphic sequence within the lakes may contain such paleoecologic data as fossil pollen, phytoliths, and diatoms (see Chapter 4). Meandering stream conditions are commonly recognized by the textures and structures within a sedimentary sequence. They tend to be texturally upward-fining sequences: larger particles are in the lower section of the sequence and smaller particles are more prevalent in the upper part.

Fluvial terraces are benches or shelflike landscape features along a river valley. They are formed by aggradation and degradation (figures 3.5–3.6). These settings have been the focus of archaeologists since the discoveries of prehistoric artifacts in France and England during the 1800s. Terrace systems can help us understand artifactual assemblages and geomorphic-climatic inferences. However, many traditional techniques of terrace correlation may conflict with detailed lithostratigraphic and chronological research. As can be seen in figures 3.5 and 3.6, a number of different depositional and erosional events can create terrace sequences of similar appearance. One of the longstanding landforms resulting from fluvial environments that is used by archaeologists is the alluvial terrace sequence. Alluvial terrace sequences are steplike platforms which mantle the sides of river valleys. In many instances parallel,

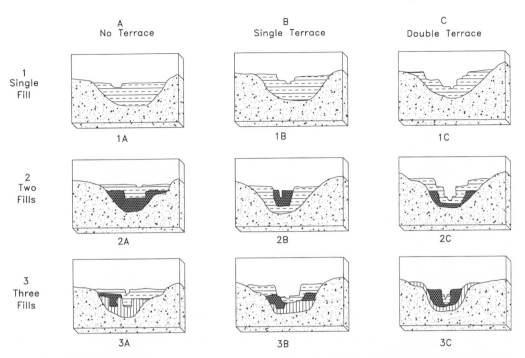

Figure 3.5 Terrace Types and Fill

Fluvial terrace sequences provide critical information for the interpretation of the archaeological record. Where the highest surfaces are the oldest and the lowest terraces the youngest, they can be used as chronological tools. They can also be used to explain the spatial distribution patterns of artifacts. Older artifacts will not appear on younger terrace surfaces unless they have been redeposited. Younger deposits may also bury older archaeological material. Stratigraphic excavations of stream valleys make it possible to understand the events that created the terrace sequence.

same-elevation platform surfaces occur on each side of the valley which appear to be the same age. When these terrace surfaces are traced upstream they generally get higher, while as they are traced downstream they have lower altitudes. In the classic interpretation, the sets of tilted surfaces represent periods of stream deposition and erosion (incision). The times of stream deposition are "fill" intervals. During these times the valley is filled with sediments by so-called aggradational events. The aggradational fill creates a surface which can form a terrace surface.

One way that terraces can form is by erosion of the stream valley fill. Erosion or incision into the fill during a "cutting" episode results in a new, lower surface. Archaeologists have applied the concepts of stream cut-and-fill episodes to help determine the age of artifacts. Although it is not

always the case, usually the highest terrace surfaces are the oldest; the lower and closer to the present-day stream channel they are, the younger they are. Thus, artifact forms and features found exclusively on particular terrace surfaces have value as chronological markers. In addition, the presence or absence of certain artifact types may be explained as the result of the dynamics of terrace formation rather than of past human behavior. For instance, Acheulian artifacts dating to 500,000 years ago might be found on one of the older terrace surfaces but not on a terrace surface created around 30,000 years ago. The absence of Acheulian artifacts on the 30,000-year-old landform surface would not in this instance be the result of a behavioral pattern. Instead, it would be due to the landform's not being in existence at the time of the Acheulian occupation. In this way,

X = Artifact

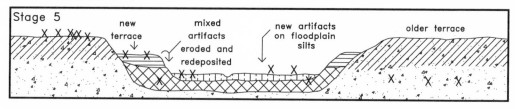

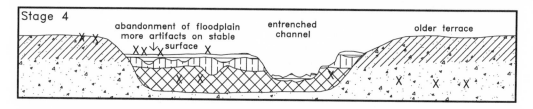

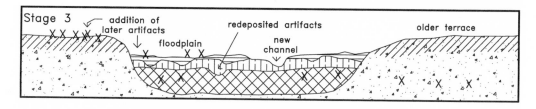

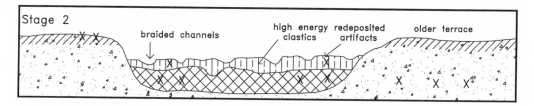

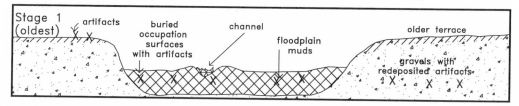

Figure 3.6 Alluvial Terrace Development Stages and Artifact Deposition, Mixing

There are five stages in the hypothetical development of an alluvial terrace system. These stages have important ramifications on archaeological integrity and visibility. At the outset, stage 1, people drop artifacts on both the upland surface and in areas of the floodplain between the upland and the stream channel. Artifacts in the gravels which form the older terrace system are redeposited. Recurrent deposition of floodplain muds bury human occupation surfaces. During stage 2, fluctuating higher energy levels cause the intermittent deposition of coarser sediments and increased erosion and redeposition of artifacts. During stage 3, additional artifacts are incorporated into younger stream deposits as well as on the upland surface. There, artifacts are mixed in a way similar to stage 1 occupation. The stream channel cuts into all the previous artifact-bearing deposits in stage 4, resulting in the erosion and removal of artifacts and their redeposition downstream as a mixed-age accumulation. In stage 5 people deposit artifacts on the new floodplain surface created by the later migration of the channel composed of eroded and redeposited artifacts.

so the model goes, younger lower terraces should have artifact forms that are absent on the higher older terraces. In the same way, in the Americas, we would not expect to see Paleo-Indian artifacts on terrace surfaces formed after about 8,000 years ago.

Stream valleys can have no terraces or many terraces. There are a variety of ways for more than one terrace to occur. In perhaps the simplest scenario, a single fill or depositional episode can be followed by several cutting episodes. Each erosional cut that goes deeper into the fill creates a lower, younger terrace. This progression is illustrated in the top row of figure 3.5, where several incision intervals into a single alluvial fill create first a single terrace (1B) and later a second terrace set (1C).

Where there has been more than one episode of aggradation or fill within a fluvial setting, the story becomes somewhat more complicated, especially with regard to archaeological interpretation. There are two complications. First, certain older cut-and-fill episodes may be completely buried by younger fills. When this happens the surface manifestation of the archaeological record is biased toward younger occupations. Older artifactual records will appear to be absent simply because they cannot be observed unless excavations are undertaken. The second complication has to do with the relations between cut-and-fill episodes and the number of terraces that can be observed without stratigraphic studies. Because older terraces can be completely buried by younger fill, a valley system can appear to have no terraces at all. On the other hand, sometimes there can be a direct relation between the age of the deposit, the terrace surface, and intervals of valley incision.

Some of the ways two depositional events can create different numbers of terraces are shown in figure 3.5. If the earlier cut-and-fill episode is completely buried by a younger fill event no terraces may appear to exist, as in 2A. The same scenario with three alluvial fills is shown in 3A. In both instances the absence of older archaeological materials on the valley surface is explained by their burial by later deposition. In some instances the surfaces of the terraces are the result of two intervals of cut and fill, as shown in 2B. Here older artifacts will be found on the upper higher surface, and younger artifacts will be found associated with the lower terrace. (For three cut-and-fill episodes, see 3C). Sometimes terraces can exist as the result of successive cut-and-fill episodes. Where there are two fills, as shown in 2C, an erosional event after the deposition of an older fill may be completely buried by a single younger fill, which itself has been subjected to several succeeding intervals of incision without intervening fill episodes. For a case where three alluvial fills have been subjected to a variety of erosional events, but only one terrace can be observed without stratigraphic excavations, see 3B.

Anastomosing rivers commonly exist in deltaic or coastal settings. They resemble braided streams because they also consist of channel networks that separate and reconnect around portions of land; but unlike braided streams, anastomosing rivers have deep, narrow channels; long-lived, vegetated islands; and floodplains with backswamps. They also tend to transport a suspended load of fine clastics. The presence of fine-grained sediments and vegetation retards the lateral stream migration, an action that typically leads to vertical aggradation.

Deltas form where sediments are deposited from rivers into still water. Deltas are an alluvial subsetting that is commonly connected with basin-related depositional systems, especially lake and coastal systems. As clastics carried within the stream are moved into a basin, larger particles are deposited first, while smaller particles are carried closer to the center of the basin. Deltas commonly contain a gradation of depositional contexts, consisting of the delta plain, the delta front, and the prodelta. Settings on the delta plain include channels and levees, point bars, **crevasse splays,** and marshes. Waves and longshore currents dominate in the delta-front zone. Prodelta deposits consist of silt and clay deposited away from the shore. In North America, one of the most well-studied reconstructions of a delta setting is at the mouth of the Mississippi River. Over the past 5,500 years there have been seven discernible lobes of the Mississippi Delta.[4]

The fan of the Nile Delta is an important alluvial feature that has influenced human activity for thousands of years.[5] Three **lithofacies** sequences exist from the past 35,000 years of sedimentation. The facies reflect changing transport processes associated with the delta. Strata from the lower sequence range in age from older than 35,000 years to about 12,000 years. They consist of alluvial sands that interfinger with overbank and playa muds. The muds were deposited in areas alongside the fluvial channels during high flood events. The top of this lower set of deposits contains an unconformity: the overlying unit consists of coarse sands and marine shells. It seems to be the product of erosion and redeposition of the older Pleistocene alluvium by waves in a high-energy, near-shore setting. These deposits represent a marine **transgression** dating from about 11,500 to 8000 B.P. The overlying Holocene deposits include deltaic alluvial plain, delta-front, and prodelta sediments.

These deposits help us understand the paleogeographic landscape context associated with the human occupation of this area. From 35,000 to 18,000 B.P., the area seems to have been an alluvial plain with braided channels. As sea level began to rise (about 15,000 to 8,000 years ago), the high-energy shoreline moved inland, reworking the sandy alluvium that had been deposited previously. Archaeological sites that had been part of the braided channel setting would have been subject to erosion and redeposition. The modern Nile Delta began to form about 7,500 years ago. Evidence of human occupation is associated with the Predynastic, dating from about 7,000 to 5,000 years ago. At about 2000 B.P., humans were actively changing the development of the Nile Delta. Human intervention maintained channel branches, while more intense irrigation and wetland drainage modified the delta. The construction of dams in the twentieth century has eliminated the annual cycle of Nile flooding, which deposited sediment into the delta. Thus, delta deposits can be indicators of former lake or sea levels, because they form at the intersection of the stream with the level of the lake or sea. Many archaeological sites are associated with deltas and with related abandoned shoreline features.

Site Formation in Alluvial Settings

Both erosional and depositional processes occur in stream settings, occurrences that could cause either dramatic modification of archaeological configurations or the preservation of patterns derived from human activity. In the past, humans often seemed to have lived on active floodplains and banks next to channels. Although the landscape settings and resources associated with alluvial settings may be considered conducive to the initial presence of artifact accumulations, depositional conditions associated with these settings may result in geologic structuring of the artifact patterns. There is a good chance that artifacts found in channel stream–related deposits have been redeposited, so that many patterns derived from human behavior have been modified or destroyed. This frequently occurs in depositional settings where either vertical or lateral aggradation is common, as on floodplains or meander belts. We would expect occupation surfaces which could have been occupied by humans to have existed on point bars and stream banks but not in active channel areas, except in ephemeral (seasonal, for example) streams. Artifacts are likely to move downstream in channels and in floodplains near channels when they are removed from their setting as part of bank erosion.

Occupations on floodplains next to stream channels can be buried by overbank floodplain deposits. During periods when erosion and deposition do not occur, there are stable surfaces on which occupations can develop. Excellent coherent stratigraphy can be created in contexts where stable surfaces were buried by overbank flood deposits.

The Indian Creek site in the northern Rocky Mountains consists of twenty-eight stratified prehistoric occupations (zones containing artifacts) within a valley floodplain terrace setting. Excavations directed by Leslie Davis exposed 8.5 meters of alluvium and colluvium dating back to about 13,000 B.P.[6] The basal layer consists of a coarse gravel bed of Late Pleistocene age. These gravels are overlain by a unit consisting primarily of fluvial sediments with some colluvium, debris flows, and a volcanic ash deposit dating to 11,125 B.P. The unit consists of a thinly bedded sequence of massive and laminated sands, sandy-silty clays, and gravels that seem to indicate mostly braided stream conditions. The presence of hematic, limonitic, and manganese oxide staining and mottling implies that the unit was intermittently saturated with water. The unit also contains interbedded carbonaceous layers of up to 2 cm thick, some of which contain Paleo-Indian artifacts; but no clearly pedogenic horizons were observed. After about 8340 B.P., artifact-bearing layers interbedded with alluvial fan and braided stream deposits, as well as organic horizons, were deposited. Middle and Late Holocene strata contain artifactual accumulations dated from 7200 to 3000 B.P. They also contain the Mount Mazama volcanic ash dated to around 6900 B.P.

The geologic context of Stone Age sites illustrates another alluvial situation in the Nile Valley. In Wadi Kubbaniya, along an old tributary to the Nile River in Upper Egypt, a small, multicomponent Upper Paleolithic site provides another example of the interaction of fluvial deposition and the preservation of the archaeological record.[7] At this site, designated E–84–1, stone artifacts, bone fragments, and charcoal were recovered in the upper part of a sand dune that dated to around 19,000 B.P. The dune sediments are interbedded with overbank floodplain silts. More floodplain silts overlie the dune deposits nearby and are themselves overlain by lake deposits dating to about 13,000 B.P. Holocene wash deposits cover the lacustrine sediments. A separate set of younger artifacts at the site seems to have been deflated out of these overlying silts or from deposits that are contemporaneous with the lake sediments. The sedimentary dynamics associated with this stratigraphic series represents a classic example of the encroachment of a dune field onto a floodplain and the simultaneous deposition of fluvially derived overbank silts. Eolian deposits containing Upper Paleolithic artifacts appear to have been sporadically covered by flood waters that deposited silts. The dunes later created a dam across the floodplain which created a lake, as well as the deposition of marls and **diatomites**.

Another indication of the complexity of alluvial deposition contexts is presented in the Thames River Valley in England. This extensively studied area contains Pleistocene fluvial deposits and Paleolithic artifacts, dating to about 300,000 years ago.[8] The first hand ax ever recorded was found in gravels beneath Grays Inn in this region in 1690. Studies of the sedimentologic context of Paleolithic artifacts in the Thames Valley have been used to interpret the landscape during the intervals of prehistoric human occupation and to determine the degree of geologic restructuring that has occurred. Most of the artifacts were incorporated into sediments consisting of gravels that were deposited in a braided river setting under cold climatic conditions. Some sediments containing artifacts seem to have formed during more temperate interglacial climatic conditions. These include artifacts found in finer sediments in the so-called Silt Complex, or "brickearth," and sometimes in sand.

Most of the artifacts are in secondary context. They show physical evidence of having been rolled. However, some of the artifacts can be rejoined. Accumulations of unsorted, unabraded artifacts also exist. These seem to imply conditions where transport must have been minimal or of low energy. In terms of artifact taphonomy, it cannot be assumed that the artifacts found in coarser clastics were initially dropped into the sediments from which they have been recovered. Especially under cold climatic conditions, these artifacts could have been incorporated into the sediment by channel migration, overbank floodplain deposition, or eolian or slope-wash deposits. The artifacts could have gone through many cycles of redeposition. It is possible that those found in finer sediments represent actual occupation surfaces. They may represent systemic context patterning that has been buried by younger sediments. However, various processes may have caused geologic restructuring, for example, low-velocity currents may have transported large clasts, including artifacts, on low-angle slopes. Compared to the abrasion that occurs in the collision of gravel-sized clasts in a river channel, the abrasion on these objects was not very extensive.

Human changes to the landscape can alter alluvial systems and cause social change. This has been demonstrated in Mesoamerica, where agriculture has affected the landscape context. Joyce and Mueller have shown how human habitation of the Rio Verde Valley in Oaxaca, Mexico, during the Late Formative (about 400 to 100 B.C.) increased flooding and alluviation, caused a change from meandering to braided stream patterns, and influenced future human populations by increasing the agricultural productivity of the lower valley.[9] In the upper part of the valley, land clearance for farming and settlement caused accelerated runoff and erosion. These human-induced changes to the alluvial system of the upper drainage led to several changes in the downstream part of the system. Flooding and alluviation in the lower valley increased, and a meandering stream pattern changed to a braided channel pattern. Three types of sediments provide an indication of the shifts in alluvial conditions. Lateral accretion resulting from high-energy river-channel settings was inferred from the presence of coarse sands. Vertical accretion related to moderate-to-low energy overbank deposition was reflected by the deposition of mud-sized particles. Infilling of oxbow lakes by low-energy deposition resulted in deposits of organic clay.

The stratigraphic and geomorphic relations between these sediment types made it possible to distinguish two Late Holocene alluvial patterns for the lower valley. The older one consisted of a meandering channel, while the younger channels were part of a braided stream pattern. The meandering channel was abandoned and became an oxbow lake, gradually filling with sediment. Associated archaeological finds date the abandonment of this earlier channel to about 2500–2200 B.P. The younger braided channels are associated with lateral accretion and channel migration.

Changes caused by human activity in the upper part of the drainage made the lower drainage more productive for agriculture. During the meandering stage (before about 2500–2200 B.P.), the floodplain was smaller, and floods that deposited agriculturally useful sediments were less frequent. Only sporadic settlement seems to have occurred before the change in river patterns (during the Early to Middle Formative), although alluviation in the lower valley may have buried or destroyed archaeological sites from this time. The fine clastics deposited on the floodplain as part of the braided stream pattern were well-suited for agriculture. In addition, the oxbow lake that formed in the abandoned meander channels was a year-round water resource that attracted fish and birds. Several sites have been found around these infilling ponds.

Cave and Rock-Shelter Depositional Systems

Caves have been a critical source of archaeological information in both the Old and New Worlds. In the Old World, European cave stratigraphies played an early role in the demonstration of human antiquity, as did similar settings in Asia and Africa. Some candidates for the oldest human occupation site in the Americas are contained in caves or rock shelters; some of these also contain artifacts in an excellent state of preservation. Perhaps the best-known cave site in Great Britain is Kent's Cavern, but there are ten other caves or cave groups that contain evidence that human habitation started in the Paleolithic.[10] Elsewhere in Europe, the best-known caves are in France and Spain—the sites of Lascaux and Altamira, for example. In Australia the best-known sites are in the caves of Devil's Lair and Kenniff Cave. There are many extraordinary cave sites in Africa, including Sterkfontein and Klassies River Mouth in the south and the Haua Fteah in the north. Important archaeological cave sites in southwest Asia include Mount Carmel, Shanidar, and the Dravidian caves. Another cave with a long archaeological record is Zhoukoudian in China. In northern Asia, sites like the Ust-Kanskaiya Cave in Siberia provide evidence for comparison with the earliest sites in the Americas.

Cave settings have been critical to archaeological studies in North America. The extensive study by C. Vance Haynes of the limestone cave of Sandia Cave in New Mexico is a classic, as is the research from Russell Cave in Alabama and in Modoc and Graham Caves in Illinois and Missouri. Caves in arid settings—Danger Cave in Utah, Leonard Shelter and Gypsum Caves in Nevada, and Ventana Cave in Arizona—have preserved many organic remains. The Meadow-

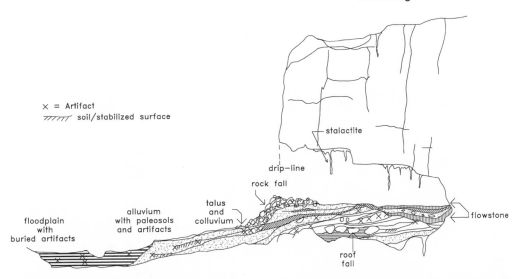

x = Artifact
⁊⁊⁊⁊⁊ soil/stabilized surface

stalactite

drip-line

rock fall

talus
and
colluvium

alluvium
with paleosols
and artifacts

floodplain
with
buried artifacts

flowstone

roof
fall

Figure 3.7 Cross Section of a Typical Limestone Cave
This limestone cave is situated near a small stream system with artifact-bearing alluvial sediments and paleosols. On the alluvial and colluvial scarp leading to the cave entrance is a slope composed of rockfall and talus that has buried a site at the location of an earlier cave entrance. Some of the roof fall near the cave entrance also overlies deposits that continue into the cave. The cave fill consists of several types of sedi-ments. Large rocks are the result of bedrock having fractured and fallen on the surface of the cave. Buried soils and occupation surfaces contain artifacts, while other artifact-bearing deposits are in more disturbed contexts. Several flowstone layers composed of precipitated calcium carbonate seal the different layers and provide one means of dating the stratigraphic sequence.

croft rock shelter in Pennsylvania contains potential evidence of human occupation as early as 16,000 B.P.

Stratigraphic sequences in caves were an early focus of prehistorians and archaeologists. This was especially true in Europe, where stratified cave and rock-shelter deposits provided objects used by humans in association with extinct animal remains, as well as evidence for the change and development of artifact assemblages and fossils through time. Most commonly formed in limestone, caves and rock shelters are significant depositional systems for archaeological studies because they are conducive to burial and potential preservation. They are a critical source of chronostratigraphic and artifactual data (figures 3.7 and 3.8). Although artifact accumulations may be preserved, taphonomic histories of these types of deposits are complicated. As in other depositional settings, many sedimentary processes are involved in creating the materials that fill caves

and rock shelters. Where caves and rock shelters exist, both clastic and chemical deposition occur. In addition to debris deposited by human or animal occupation, clastic materials include washes, fluvial deposition, rockfall, and eolian deposition. The most common chemical precipitates are various forms of calcite deposition, such as flowstone or dripstone.

Limestone Caves
In limestone caves, travertine or dripstone in features like stalactites and stalagmites are produced when calcite precipitates from permeating water (see figure 3.7). These deposits have been used extensively for the construction of artifact-related chronologies and paleoclimate. A major step in cave and rock-shelter development is solution by groundwater. Groundwater creates caves primarily by dissolving the carbonate of the limestone bedrock. After solution, removal, and transport, carbonate may be redeposited as

67

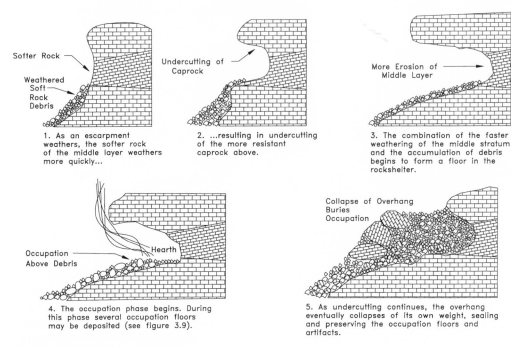

1. As an escarpment weathers, the softer rock of the middle layer weathers more quickly...

Softer Rock
Weathered Soft Rock Debris

2. ...resulting in undercutting of the more resistant caprock above.

Undercutting of Caprock

3. The combination of the faster weathering of the middle stratum and the accumulation of debris begins to form a floor in the rockshelter.

More Erosion of Middle Layer

4. The occupation phase begins. During this phase several occupation floors may be deposited (see figure 3.9).

Occupation Above Debris
Hearth

5. As undercutting continues, the overhang eventually collapses of its own weight, sealing and preserving the occupation floors and artifacts.

Collapse of Overhang Buries Occupation

Figure 3.8 Evolution of a Rock Shelter
Five steps in the hypothetical development of a limestone rock shelter.

travertines and tufas, if evaporation saturates the solution.

In southern Africa a series of caves including Sterkfontein, Taung, Swartkrans, and Kromdraai were formed of dolomite, a calcium-magnesium carbonate. Surface water widened the joints in the bedrock, providing locations for archaeological debris to accumulate. In some instances travertines formed. The remains of australopithecines have been recovered from these caves. The Haua Fteah site in northern Africa is also in limestone. Here, stratigraphy consists of roof fall and sediments washed into the cave.

Some of the most spectacular archaeological features ever discovered were found in the deposits and on the walls of caves in Europe. The rock shelters in the Périgord of France are large cavities in the faces of limestone bedrock situated within river valleys (see figure 3.8). Both chemical solution by water and physical, mechanical weathering have affected these settings. Karstic dissolution by water and frost weathering with re-

sulting rock shatter are major contributors to the formation of limestone caves and rock shelters. **Talus** slopes may form outside these features.

At the site of La Colombière in southern France, sedimentary and artifact-bearing deposits are stratified in limestone bedrock and lie adjacent to the terrace system of the Ain River. Upper Paleolithic (Upper Périgordian) artifacts were recovered in a sandy, angular matrix that was overlain by large rockfall deposits. The rockfall episodes are stratified within clastic sediments and cemented zones.

The Mousterian and Aurignacian artifact-bearing deposits at El Castillo Cave in Cantabrian Spain are also in a karstic setting (figure 3.9). El Castillo was one of several cave settings extensively studied by Karl Butzer, who separated the archaeosedimentary column into nineteen units. Stalagmitic flowstone covers the ceiling of the limestone cave and also the present-day surface within the cave. The sedimentary sequence also contains stalagmitic flowstones interstrati-

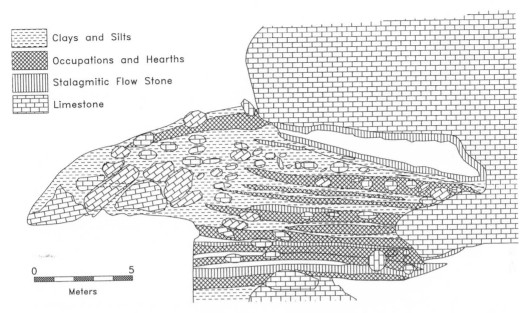

Figure 3.9 Stratification and Natural Interbedding at El Castillo Cave in Cantabrian Spain

The cave is formed in limestone bedrock. Large chunks of the bedrock that once formed the roof of the shelter have fallen and been incorporated into the cave's stratigraphic sequence. Artifact-bearing deposits denote prehistoric human occupation and use of the shelter. Prehistoric human use is also reflected in the presence of layers interpreted as hearths. Interlayered between the artifact- and hearth-bearing deposits are sediments that are predominantly composed of muds (clays and silts), as well as numerous layers of stalagmitic flowstone composed of precipitated calcium carbonate.

fied with occupational levels and silts and clays. Larger limestone rock fragments also form part of the sequence.[11] In Britain, Kent's Cavern is developed from limestone and contains Middle and Upper Paleolithic artifacts that indicate occupation from about 100,000 to 13,000 B.P. At Kendricks Cave in Wales, a solution cave, faunal materials and artifacts occur in a stratigraphic context. Caves in South Wales contain archaeological sites from both the Stone and Bronze ages. The limestone cave of Drachenloch in Switzerland is famous for its bear remains that appear to be arranged in a ritual manner.

There are limestone caves with archaeological remains throughout the world. In Belize, caves with solution features are associated with Mayan occupations. In Peten, Guatemala, and in the Yucatan Peninsula of southern Mexico, caves associated with limestone bedrock, karst hydrologic settings, and solution features also contain archaeological materials. In highland Guatemala, Brady and Veni have discovered the existence of pseudo-karst caves that seem to have been ritual activity centers for the Maya.[12] These caves, carved out of the bedrock, were formed by human activity; they are not the result of water dissolving away bedrock. One of the best-known caves, La Lagunita, was cut into Quaternary sediments high in volcanic ash. It is situated under the central stairway of a major pyramid and underlies the pyramid's central plaza. La Lagunita appears to date to the Protoclassic–Early Classic transition, around A.D. 360–400. Other caves, such as those at the Contact Period site of Utatlan (the capital of the Quiche Maya empire), are cut into the sides of mesas. The pattern of the caves underneath the central ceremonial complex has led scientists to believe that they had sacred and ritual significance. Caves appear to have been sites of ritual significance from the Ice Age, with its cave art and

69

bear cults, to the Late Holocene, and the rites of socially complex groups like the Maya.

Karst solution features in limestone bedrock have been reported at the Hearth and Mordor caves in Australia, where evidence of human occupation includes artifacts and cave paintings. Fraser Cave in southwest Tasmania, a cave associated with karst and solution features, contains archaeological materials. In China, some caves contain a long record of hominid occupation that provides critical records of long-term development of Paleolithic behavior. Other caves, such as Longgu Cave in northern China, contain Upper Pleistocene rock and cave art. In the Chuandong area (Guizhou Province) of southwestern China, caves contain stratified deposits with a variety of fossil fauna and artifacts.

The most important means of sedimentation in limestone caves and rock shelters include freeze-thaw phenomena, solifluction (see below), the breaking off and collapse of large blocks, stream and sheet wash, eolian deposits, carbonate deposition, and biotic inputs. Karstic limestone caves are widespread and consist for the most part of deposits resulting either from weathered material transported into the cave or physical weathering of the cave walls. One of the most extensively studied karstic cave depositional sequences is in the Peking Man Cave in the Zhoukoudian area southwest of Beijing.[13] It is a large, vertical cave formed out of Ordovician limestone and filled with deposits separated into seventeen lithologic units. There seem to have been two main stages of filling. The basal layers are fluvial deposits which filled the cave after karstification processes changed from solution to fluvial deposition. Limestone, breccia, stalactitic, and travertine lenses form the upper part of the sequence. Most of the deposits are Middle Pleistocene in age, and the sequence contains faunal remains (including those of *Homo erectus*), stone artifacts, and ash lenses. The occupational layers are interbedded with sand and clay deposits that were washed into the cave; with roof fall from periodic collapse of bedrock; and with carbonates formed from crystallization in lime-rich waters. Accumulations in the cave probably span at least a 500,000-year period, ending around 250,000–200,000 years ago.

Sandstone Caves and Rock Shelters

One of the most extensive archaeological investigations of sandstone (as distinct from limestone) rock shelters took place at the Meadowcroft Site in southwestern Pennsylvania. The well-defined stratigraphy contains artifact-bearing deposits indicating possible human presence in North America by perhaps 16,000 B.P. Jack Donahue and James Adovasio have outlined the development of these types of settings on the basis of the Meadowcroft rock shelter and other eastern North American sandstone contexts: the sandstone shelters generally occur along the slopes of relatively young valleys, and the development of the rock shelters is related to less resistant bedrock types interbedded with the sandstone, which leaves sandstone overhangs.

Mechanisms of sedimentation within sandstone rock shelters incorporate four major processes, which can be recognized by grain-size distributions and sedimentary structures. These include rockfall, attrition, sheetwash, and flooding. In these sequences, large fragments of bedrock apparently released by the development of joints, freeze-thaw conditions, and possibly biotic activity like root action indicate rockfall (including slab failure and rock avalanche). Attrition and granular disintegration also contribute to the stratigraphic sequence in sandstone rock shelters and may be associated with both physical and chemical weathering. Sheetwash, or slopewash, will contribute poorly sorted size fractions, while floodplain deposits dominated by the finer sizes may come from nearby streams.

Igneous Rock Caves

In addition to the more typical limestone and sandstone caves and rock shelters, there are other forms of caves used by humans that contain artifacts. In western Iceland, caves formed as lava tubes associated with the Hallmundarhraun lava flow contain faunal materials and artifacts. Caves and shelters in Hawaii formed from such volcanic features as lava tubes have indications that they were used by humans: they contain strati-graphic sequences that include artifacts. Caves and tunnels associated with volcanic features have also been the subject of archaeological study near Teotihuacan, Mexico.

Site Formation in Caves

Site formation processes within caves and rock shelters are eclectic because of the types of bed-rock or depositional environments that produce variable depositional, erosional, and occupational events. Differential erosion of bedrock can form caves in areas of high energy, such as those along coastal shorelines and along the margins of stream valleys. Caves at the Sidi Abderrahman quarry along the Atlantic coast of Morocco provide an example of archaeological site formation in a coastal setting. The sedimentary sequence in the cave contains Acheulian artifacts as well as homi-nid skeletal remains. During a time when the sea level was low, Acheulian artifacts were deposited on the beach. As the sea level continued to drop, dunes encroached along the exposed coastal mar-gin and buried the artifacts on the beach. This sediment became consolidated and formed sand-stone. A later rise in sea level eroded the sand-stone and formed a cliff wall that contained caves. Beach deposits inside these caves show that about 300,000 years ago the sea level was 27–30 meters higher than present sea level. After the beach sediments were deposited in the eroded sandstone cave, hominids lived in the caves.[14]

Gorham's Cave, cut into the basal cliffs of the Rock of Gibraltar, is another example of a cave that was directly influenced by coastal formation processes. Artifacts in the cave show that Middle and Upper Paleolithic human populations lived in the cave during the past 100,000 years. A sea-level rise resulting from the melting of large continen-tal glaciers during the last interglacial may have scoured the cave and eroded sediments contain-ing older artifacts. The deposits in the cave dis-play clear connections with the coastal setting.[15]

Mummy Cave, in the Absaroka Mountains of northwest Wyoming, provides another example of a cave created by high-energy erosion. The cave is an alcove cut into a cliff made of volcanic

(tuff-breccia) bedrock on the outside bend of a river. A series of thirty artifact zones covering the past 9,000 years of human prehistory were found in the cave. The cave was formed by lateral cutting of the bedrock through stream erosion along the outside of a meander bend. After the cave was cut, the river shifted its course. More than 12 meters of fill, consisting of redeposited volcanic bedrock from outside the cave, accumulated in its interior over the past 10,000 years.[16]

Many caves containing archaeological materi-als develop as the result of interactions be-tween bedrock and groundwater, especially in limestone-karst landscapes. The groundwater dis-solves the limestone by slow percolation of pre-cipitation through the bedrock or by dissolution along the interface of bedrock with the water table.

Sediments within caves are the result of for-mation processes that produce two categories of deposits: sediments consisting of materials from outside the cave that find their way into the cave and materials that are formed within the cave and deposited there. Areas near the mouths of rock shelters and caves generally have more compli-cated formation histories than those within the interiors of caves. Sedimentary events connected with the region outside the cave are generally represented in the deposits around the mouth of the cave, while deposits within the cave usually exemplify events taking place within the caves.[17]

The Glacial System

Glaciers have also affected the location of human occupation. Pleistocene glaciers covered large areas of land, where they both eroded and de-posited sediments. The growth and melting of continental and mountain glaciers, and the re-lated environmental changes that occurred with these fluctuations, influenced the habitability of certain areas. Indirect glacial-related settings in-clude those formed by both **proglacial** and **peri-glacial** conditions. Each of these related settings shows particular sedimentologic regimes and re-sultant geomorphic context that can be related to prehistoric human occupation (figure 3.10). Here we focus on a short description of glacial settings

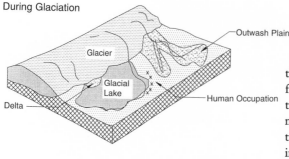

During Glaciation

Outwash Plain

Glacier

Glacial Lake

Human Occupation

Delta

x = Artifact

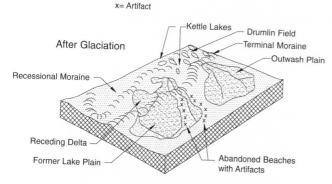

After Glaciation

Kettle Lakes
Drumlin Field
Terminal Moraine
Outwash Plain

Recessional Moraine

Receding Delta

Former Lake Plain

Abandoned Beaches with Artifacts

Figure 3.10 Glacial and Postglacial Landscapes
In the top drawing, glacial ice is shown advancing. Debris eroded and transported by the moving glacier can contain artifacts. Along the edges of the melting ice sheet, sediments can be deposited, to form outwash plains or delta deposits associated with proglacial lakes. The margins of the glacial lakes are potential locations for human occupations. After glaciation, as shown in the bottom drawing, several geomorphic features may be present that can be used to infer the past presence and character of a glacial event. Large mounds of sediments may be left along the edge of the glacier, forming terminal and recessional moraines. Whale-shaped oblong features within the area where the glacier existed, called drumlins, indicate the direction of ice movement. The sediments that fill kettle lakes formed in the glaciated area can help us interpret the timing of deglaciation and the postglacial environment. This helps us understand when the region was available for human occupation and the ecological context of prehistoric adaptation. Archaeological occurrences may also be associated with the abandoned beaches of former proglacial lakes.

associated with prehistoric human activities and the concurrent erosional and depositional processes.

Glaciers are moving accumulations of ice which erode and scour the earth's surface, transporting and depositing sediments and, in some instances, artifacts. The three major types of glaciers are

those formed in mountains, those that spread from valleys and flow along the front of mountains, and ice sheets that cover continents. These moving accumulations of ice result in the formation of erosional and depositional features. Rocks incorporated into glaciers erode the earth's surface, and the eroded and transported debris is deposited as **till**. Unsorted, unstratified till can be deposited directly by glaciers, while glacial meltwater can generate stratified glacial-fluvial deposits.

Till deposited along the edges of glaciers creates **moraines**. Along glacier edges, melting water is associated with **outwash**-related braided streams, delta deposits, and ice-margin (proglacial) lakes. These sedimentologic contexts were the locations of prehistoric human occupation. Glacial tills may be found to overlie, underlie, or incorporate artifact accumulations. Glacial conditions can destroy, modify, or preserve evidence of human occupation. In the southwestern part of the North American Great Lakes region, there is a stratigraphic sequence consisting of till, proglacial lake sediments, and nonglacial deposits. One till is overlain by laminated clays interbedded with silts and sands of an ice-margin lake. A zone containing the remains of the Two Creeks boreal forest (dated from about 12,000 to 10,500 B.P.) has developed on this lake bed (figure 3.11). The forest bed is a detrital zone containing organic matter, with plant debris—including logs and stumps—in the parent deposit. Another lake deposit overlies the Two Creeks bed. The lake appears to have flooded the forest before being overrun by another glacial advance that deposited another till. The till has incorporated material from the forest and is itself covered by more lake sands and eolian dune deposits. It is possible that artifacts lie within the deposits that have incorporated remnants of the Two Creeks forest; human occupation of the North American continent had begun by at least 11,000 B.P. In Europe, where there is stronger evidence of Middle and Late Pleistocene human occupation, there are instances of both the burial and the incorporation of artifact-bearing deposits into glacial sediments.

In Europe glaciers pushed across and deposited till on deposits containing artifacts.[18] In Brit-

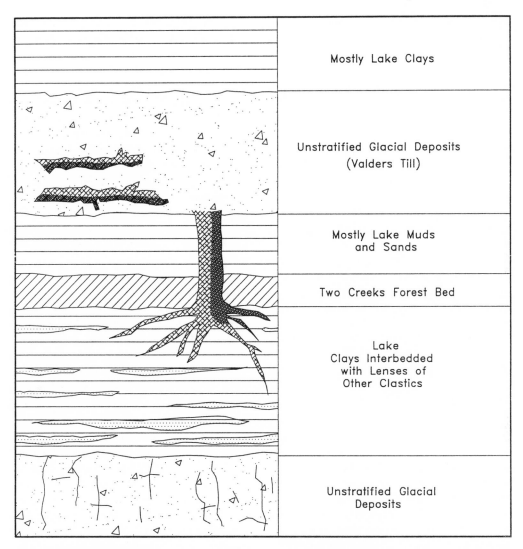

Figure 3.11 Idealized Late Quaternary Sequence Within Two Creeks Bed, Wisconsin

The lowest sedimentary deposit is related to an earlier glacial event. It is covered by a unit largely composed of clays deposited in a lake. The upper part of this lake clay unit contains the roots of plants that grew in the Two Creeks forest. The Two Creeks forest bed over- lies the lake clay unit and is buried by sands and muds deposited in a younger lake. Glacial deposits above these lake sediments contain fragments of plants that are in a redeposited position. Artifacts found in this deposit would probably be associated with a previous time period, such as when the Two Creeks forest was in existence.

ain there are artifact-bearing sediments overlain by tills. At Elveden the lowest deposit overlying chalk bedrock consists of a till ("boulder clay"). The upper surface of this till is an eroded surface overlain by a marl. Over this marl lies a series of clastic units that contain artifacts, including Acheulian hand axes. These clastics represent an old lake or small channel, and the artifacts seem to come from a hominid occupation along the edge of a water body. The top of the clastic series con- taining the artifacts appears to represent a lake setting and consists of calcareous sand. The upper section shows signs of **cryoturbation**. Another till overlies this and contains a superimposed soil in its upper section. Here the artifacts seem not to have been affected by later periglacial conditions or deformed by ice load.

Where glaciers have overridden landscapes that were once occupied by prehistoric humans, and the artifacts have become incorporated into glacial sediments, archaeological interpretation becomes more complicated. As with the Two Creeks stratigraphic sequence, older materials have been incorporated into younger glacial tills. Under these conditions, artifacts assigned to an earlier time are recovered in deposits of a younger glacial advance. The British site of High Lodge provides an example of how to apply geologic interpretations of glacial deposits in the interpretation of Old Stone Age artifact accumulations.[19] For more than a hundred years, the site of High Lodge has been the subject of much discussion because of the presence of Middle Paleolithic (Mousterian) artifacts recovered from fine-grained deposits overlying till. These artifacts were found under deposits containing what were thought to be older Acheulian hand axes. Here, both the Acheulian and the later Middle Paleolithic artifacts had been subjected to secondary disturbance, but of different kinds. Apparently the High Lodge Middle Paleolithic artifacts lay in sediments that the advance of an ice sheet disturbed. This ice advance transported large blocks of sediments, still containing artifacts, intact to the top of a younger deposit. Although the artifacts were fresh, and pieces could be refitted to one another, they were in a disturbed context because they had been transported along with the matrix that enclosed them. The Acheulian hand axe assemblages were also in secondary position. Originally they had been deposited as part of a Lower Paleolithic habitation before the Middle Paleolithic artifacts. After the Middle Paleolithic artifacts had been transported along with their enclosing matrix, the older Acheulian artifacts had been incorporated into **glaciofluvial** and debris flow deposits that later buried the Middle Paleolithic artifact-bearing sediments. The transportation of large chunks of matrix had removed the Middle Paleolithic artifacts but retained their

initial integrity, while the melting of the glaciers had caused the secondary redeposition of the Acheulian materials.

The melting of glaciers can create circumstances other than glacial advance that are key to archaeological interpretations. Ice-margin or glacial meltwater lakes create landscape contexts that are especially suitable for prehistoric human habitation. Geomorphic features along the margins of the basins and the former drainage into these basins are likely areas to find evidence of human occupation. In the western Great Lakes area, lakes and drainage overlying glacial till and outwash deposits provide evidence of Late Pleistocene and Early Holocene human occupation of the region.

In very cold settings postdepositional frost heaving (see below) can result in the formation of rock rings or polygon-shaped features. These form when intervals of extreme cold followed by melting and a freeze-thaw cycle produce contraction cracks at the earth's surface .

Coastal and Marine Depositional Settings

The margins of larger bodies of water—large lakes, seas, and oceans—contain various sedimentary environments that are of archaeological significance. Larger bodies of water have sediments deposited as beaches, backshore dunes, spits and bars, and river-mouth bars and deltas. Changes in the level of the water can either inundate these coastal features or leave them "stranded," forming abandoned shorelines. In either case, these margins are critical settings of past human occupation. Coastal areas that are currently underwater were frequently areas of human habitation during lower water levels. One explanation for the relative absence of sites that date from certain time periods may be that most of them are now under water.

The reconstruction of geologic and ecological environments has provided an increasingly clear picture of the landscapes and habitats that have sustained human development. In these reconstructions, both the geologist and the archaeologist depend on incomplete stratigraphic records and evidence that is frequently insufficient for an absolute chronology. Few areas of the earth's land surface have witnessed long and continuous periods of deposition; on the contrary, erosion is the terrestrial norm.

In coastal areas three geologic processes combine to drive geomorphic change. Changes in sea level have an immediate impact on the coastal zone. Vertical (up or down) tectonic movements offset or augment **eustatic** rise or fall. In addition, erosion or deposition may drive the transgressional or regressional migration of the shoreline.

Ancient writers, including Herodotus, Plato, Strabo, Pausanius, and Livy, noted shoreline changes, but they had no context in which to analyze them. Today we use a number of geologic concepts and methodologies to investigate geomorphic change along active coasts. The initial phase of a paleogeomorphic reconstruction relies on detailed field geomorphology to ascertain the broad scheme of landscape evolution. This may be aided by knowledge of the vertical position of archaeological structures for which we have dates or of horizons or firsthand reports from ancient texts. However, two decades of work on Mediterranean coasts by Rapp and his colleagues have shown that intensive core drilling with detailed analysis of the sedimentary record is necessary to provide an adequate picture of the sequence of coastal environments and the associated chronologies.

Coastal areas host a high percentage of the world's population. Where land and water meet there are often large amounts and varieties of nutrients that in turn supply diverse assemblages of fauna and flora—all in a complex of geologic environments like bays, estuaries, beaches, deltas, dunes, and marshes, with adjacent floodplains. Add to this the high energy available from wind-driven waves, and it is easy to see why constant change is the rule. Figure 3.12 shows the geomorphic evolution of the site of Tel Michal on the coast of Israel.

In investigating Holocene coastal change one must view the landscape in terms of the morphology of sedimentary bodies and erosional features, as well as the vertical and lateral sequences of environments created by the processes operating in the coastal environment. These processes include local **tectonism,** changes in sea level, climatic change, and ocean currents and wave regimes. In addition, one must consider the nature and frequency of catastrophic events; sources, types, and quantities of sediments available; and the nature and intensity of human activity. All environmental processes leave a record of past physiographic change in the local sediments. Microfaunal and microfloral remains in the sediments record such environmental parameters as salinity, water depth, and even pollution. Investigation of them affirms one of the fundamental beliefs of geology—**uniformitarianism.**

Geologists rely on a well-developed concept of sedimentary facies. By *facies*, geologists mean the characteristics of a rock unit that reflect the conditions of its origin and differentiate it from adjacent units. When coastal sedimentary deposits are considered in terms of their lateral and vertical relations, they provide a full chronological-geologic record of the events that resulted in coastal change. For example, the details of the history of a transgression or regression of the sea will be reflected in the vertical sedimentary facies deposited.

The lateral and vertical changes that can be present in archaeological sequences and strictly geologic stratigraphies are described by Walther's Law of Correlation of Facies, introduced by Johannes Walther in 1894. Where different sedimentary facies reflect different environments, shifts in depositional environments through time will eventually cause the deposition of one type of environment over another (figure 3.13). Therefore, relations between laterally contiguous facies (representing environments) can be connected to vertically stacked sediments. In other words, for conformable sedimentary sequences, the facies that occurred laterally side by side will appear stacked within a stratigraphic column. Thus, the deposits formed next to one another on a contemporary landscape, starting inland within a shoreline, followed by nearshore and then deep-water settings, and with shifts in environments caused by an expanding water body, would create a vertical sequence where shore-margin sands are covered by deep-water muds. This is important for paleogeographic interpretations because vertical changes preserved in a sedimentologic

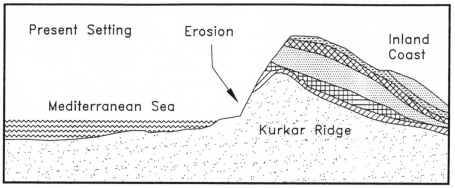

Present Setting — Erosion — Inland Coast — Mediterranean Sea — Kurkar Ridge

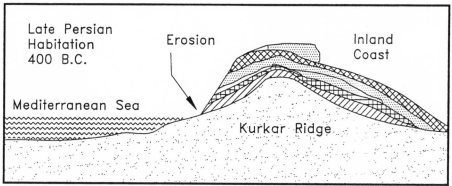

Late Persian Habitation 400 B.C. — Erosion — Inland Coast — Mediterranean Sea — Kurkar Ridge

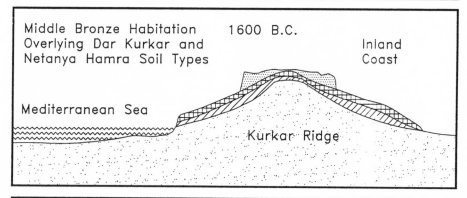

Middle Bronze Habitation Overlying Dar Kurkar and Netanya Hamra Soil Types — 1600 B.C. — Inland Coast — Mediterranean Sea — Kurkar Ridge

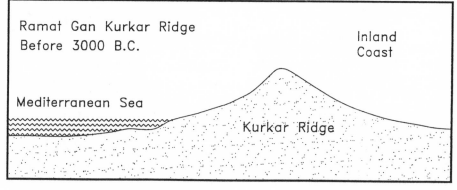

Ramat Gan Kurkar Ridge Before 3000 B.C. — Inland Coast — Mediterranean Sea — Kurkar Ridge

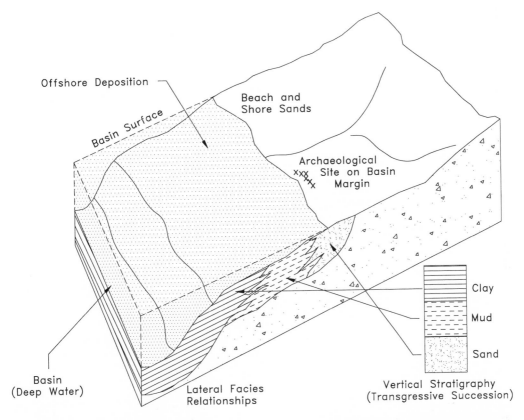

Offshore Deposition

Basin Surface

Beach and
Shore Sands

Archaeological
xxx Site on Basin
x Margin

Clay

Mud

Sand

Basin
(Deep Water)

Lateral Facies
Relationships

Vertical Stratigraphy
(Transgressive Succession)

Figure 3.13 Three-Dimensional Representation of Walther's Law of Correlation of Facies
The internal relations between sedimentary facies and
environments are reflected in vertical stratigraphic sequences. Here the lateral relations show facies associated with beach-margin, offshore, and deep-basin
deposition. The vertical stratigraphy shows these facies
after a flooding or transgression.

record provide clues to the types of environments
that existed adjacent to these deposits, regardless
of whether the lateral deposits are available for
study. Walther's Law can be illustrated in stacked
sedimentary sequences when the element of time
is introduced.

Coastal-change studies draw heavily on Walther's Law, which provides a means of interpreting environmental changes. According to

Walther's Law, only those sedimentary facies
that occur in laterally adjacent environments of
deposition can occur in conformable vertical sequence. Walther's Law gives geologists a powerful tool; it enables them to use three-dimensional
stratigraphic sequences in the reconstruction of
ancient (sedimentary) landscapes through time
and space.

Figure 3.12 Idealized Reconstruction of the Evolution
of the Coastal Site of Tel Michal, Israel
Initially the location consisted of a coastal ridge formed
of kurkar. By 1600 B.C., Middle Bronze Age structures
had been built on top of the kurkar ridge. Between
1600 and 400 B.C., coastal processes caused erosion
of the seaside section of the archaeological deposit.

Human habitation continued through the late Persian
period, increasing the size of the tell at the same time
that coastal erosional processes were destroying it.
Present coastal processes have removed a substantial
portion of the seaward-facing part of the archaeological deposit.

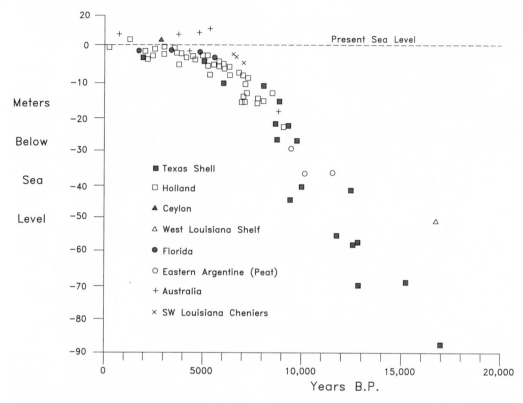

Figure 3.14 Global Sea-Level Change
A global sea-level curve depicting eustatic rise, using radiocarbon-dated samples collected from inferred stable areas. (After Stanley, "A Global Sea-Level Curve for the Late Quaternary")

Coastal Processes and Site Formation

Coastal shoreline processes can erode and redeposit or bury sites of past human activity. **Progradational sequences** can chronologically order sites located next to shoreline features (the oldest will be away from the present margin; the youngest, on the present margin), while transgressive episodes can result in erosional surfaces and the redeposition of artifacts. Coastal settings provide a wide variety of depositional contexts that can influence human habitation and artifact accumulation. Archaeological accumulations have been found in cave stratigraphic sequences associated with sea margins, as well as in shell midden deposits.

In the study of late Quaternary coastal change around archaeological sites adjacent to the world's oceans and seas, nothing is more important than the variation in sea level. Coastal geologists have labored unsuccessfully to construct generic eustatic rise curves. Sea level began rising rapidly at the end of the Pleistocene, when the massive continental glaciers melted. Today only the Greenland and Arctic continental ice masses remain.

During the last glacial low stand, sea level was more than 100 meters below the present mean sea level. Along many continental slope breaks in different parts of the world, there are numerous wave-cut notches at 120 to 125 meters below sea level. Sea level rose rapidly from those levels until somewhere between 8000 and 6500 B.P. (figure 3.14), at which time the rate of rise decreased substantially.[20] Sea-level rise and fall is a major cause of transgressions and regressions. Above, we presented information on how the enlargement and reduction of water bodies can be inferred from changes in the characteristics of sedimentary deposits. Transgressions and regressions can also be correlated with changes in both floral and faunal communities. Transgressions seem to take place much more slowly than regressions; therefore, the latter should have more dramatic consequences on plant and animal communities. In regressions, organisms suffer extinction, changes in diversity patterns, and forced migration. In shallow water areas, the principal paleoenvironmental events are due to transgressions (for example, the development of brackish water). Short-term changes in local faunal communities are usually the consequence of environmental perturbations, because any evolutionary changes in these groups would be too slow to detect. Because of their slow pace, we cannot observe marine transgressions directly, but we can easily see some of the consequences, such as a rising water table.

The Inupiat site of Pingasagruk in northern Alaska is a prehistoric and historic habitation situated on a coastal sandbar that contains artifact distribution patterns which appear to have resulted in part from storms and consequent erosion and transport.[21] Storm waves erode artifacts from dunes, leaving behind larger objects like fragments of coal and cobbles on the beaches of seas. Artifacts eroded from deposits tend to accumulate in secondary concentrations because eddies and turbulence prevent them from washing away. They can concentrate on the beaches of bays. When breakers submerge areas, more artifacts are likely to be carried away. Artifacts like bone, antler, and ivory become water-borne, tumbled and rolled around before they are redeposited. Artifacts transported from the original location can be temporally mixed as well as spatially displaced.

Coastal Landscape Context
In addition to altering artifact composition and spatial patterns, coastal geologic processes can have a major influence on other aspects of archaeological interpretation. For example, the 1,500–3,000-year gap between the Early Formative Valdivia and the earlier preceramic Vegas occupations of coastal Ecuador may not reflect depopulation of the region, as was once believed, but instead may be associated with changes in the position of coastal shorelines. The abandoned

coastline thought to be associated with the Valdivia period contains a variety of features, including uplifted ancient shorelines, cross-bedded beach deposits, and shells. Pottery associated with beach sands and shells indicate an occupation around 5500 B.P., overlain by a Late Valdivia site dated to around 3500 B.P. This indicates that the shoreline environment was previously inland from the current coastline.

Other abandoned coastal features near the site of Real Alto indicate that during occupation it was situated along the shoreline. This geoarchaeological information instigated a reevaluation of Real Alto in Andean prehistory. The site had previously been interpreted as an inland location in which agriculture was the dominant feature of the prehistoric economy. The presence of clams at the site was attributed to their use in constructing a pavement. Now it seems possible that the people associated with the Valdivia assemblages had a diverse subsistence economy that included fishing, hunting, and agriculture. Real Alto seems to have been established to take advantage of coastal resources, and the abundance of clam shells surrounding Early Valdivia dwellings may be the result of onsite refuse disposal by people living near coastal mangrove swamps. The site of Real Alto was probably abandoned because of coastal uplift, which made it an inland location. The land between the site and the present-day coast contains later Valdivia sites, and it is possible to relate the distribution of sites to paleo-landforms. Gaps in the archaeological record appear to be caused by restructuring of the shoreline. Some terrestrial areas were not present during Valdivia times and consequently cannot contain sites of this period.

Another example of what we can learn from coastal landscape change can be seen in the Late Holocene topography of Greece and its relation to available routes of human movement. Conflicts among historians over the Battle of Thermopylae in 480 B.C. between the Greeks (mainly Spartans) and the advancing Persians center around the inconsistencies between ancient sources and the modern topography. There is a discrepancy between the width of the "pass" along the coast at Thermopylae. Rapp and his colleagues used a core drilling program to reconstruct the relevant

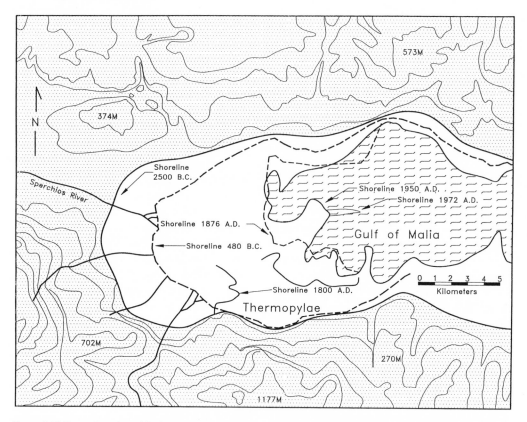

Figure 3.15 Geoarchaeological Reconstruction and the Battle of Thermopylae

View of the ancient and modern shoreline margins in the vicinity of Thermopylae, Greece. The Thermopylae Pass, or coastal route, was much narrower during ancient times because the level of the Gulf of Malia was higher: there was less land between the sea and the upland regions. A dramatic change of more than 2 kilo- meters in the Sperchios River drainage is recorded for the interval between 2500 B.C. and 480 B.C. Around Thermopylae, a large change occurred in the width of the pass between 480 B.C. and the twentieth century. The pass increased in size by several kilometers. The smaller size of the Thermopylae coastal route was a crucial factor in the Greeks' ability to hold the pass.

paleogeography. With the recovery and analy- sis of materials from seven core drilling holes it was possible to delineate considerable variation over time in the coastal geomorphology at Ther- mopylae.

Figure 3.15 illustrates the coastal change of the Gulf of Malia-Sperchios River floodplain at Thermopylae. In 480 B.C. the narrowest coastal pass at the place where the small army of Spar- tans would have had the best chance against the Persian hordes would have been about 100 meters wide, possibly the width of one wagon track. From the point of view of understanding a changing

landscape context, it is critical to recognize that the land surface of that time is currently buried under up to 20 meters of terrigenous clastic sedi- ment and hot-spring travertine deposits. These changes underscore the difficulties encountered by investigators who use only observations of the current landscape to reconstruct earlier land- scapes in areas of high deposition. Without core drilling to determine the location, elevation, and nature of the earlier landscape features, physio- graphic reconstructions will remain interesting guesses.

The sedimentary sequences and paleogeographic reconstructions at Thermopylae also provide information for interpretations of sites of later local battles: Greeks versus Gauls in 279 B.C., Romans versus Antiochus the Syrian in 191 B.C., and others.[22] With additional coring, even more details of the ancient coastal topographies will emerge. However, the basic subsurface geologic data indicate and date the major delta system to the west as well as the sequence of changing environments along the coast.

The ages and sequence of proglacial lake levels in the Lake Superior Basin and their relation to Paleo-Indian sites present a good example of coastal change affecting habitation possibilities and context. Geologists, archaeologists, and geoarchaeologists have investigated these relationships.[23] Paleo-Indian sites on raised beach terraces and strandlines are well documented. Prehistoric groups favored these shoreline sites because of their biologic resources and supply of fresh water. Along the north shore of Lake Superior there was also an abundant supply of lithic resources.

Archaeological interpretations of the sites depend on geologic determinations of the sequence of landscapes and on lake-level chronologies. Habitation possibilities in the area depended not only on water levels in the Lake Superior Basin but on the extent of Glacial Lake Agassiz. Lake Agassiz was the largest of the North American proglacial lakes, inundating nearly a million square kilometers. Fluctuations of the lake greatly affected the size and suitability of the land area between the two lakes. Lake Agassiz beaches and strandlines offered fluctuating travel routes and landscape settings for early human inhabitants.

Postdepositional Processes

After artifacts are incorporated into a sedimentary deposit (whether buried as a primary assemblage or secondarily redeposited), physical and chemical processes alter the spatial and compositional character of the artifactual components. The major physical (geologic and biologic) processes which can affect the spatial distribution of artifacts include mass wasting, cryoturbation, expansion and contraction of clays, deformation,

and bioturbation. Postdepositional chemical conditions can destroy or protect artifacts.

Postdepositional alterations of sediments can be the result of several processes. Subaerial weathering processes include biochemical alteration, **humification,** and **illuviation** and **eluviation** (leaching and accretion). Other processes include **turbation** and the influences of fluctuating groundwater, which are reflected in **oxidation** and reduction mottling, and **authigenic** carbonate deposition.

Soils reflect postdepositional alterations of sediment. As discussed in Chapter 2, pedogenic zones reflect alterations caused by biotic and atmospheric conditions and show vertical differences in characteristics. They are distinct from the original sediment and represent periods of landscape stability, which episodic deposition or erosion can interrupt.

One of the postdepositional processes that alters sediments is the secondary accumulation of carbonate. Pedogenic carbonate enrichment can occur when soil-moisture evaporation is greater than or roughly equal to water infiltration. Chemical processes within a sediment form concretions and nodules by accretion. Calcite can occur as isolated nodules or as coalescing layers and can range from a few centimeters to several meters in dimension. The first stage of calcium carbonate–rich horizons of pedogenic origin occurs when carbonate is deposited on the undersides of gravel particles. Accumulation of calcium carbonate may also result from capillary rise from a **perched** high-water table.

Several types of horizons can be associated with high moisture content or nearness to a water table. Poor water drainage, and consequent low oxygen content, leads to reducing conditions that result in iron and manganese compounds, which form gray and bluish colors of **gleyed** horizons. A fluctuating water table level can produce varying oxidizing and reducing conditions that result in mottling. Soluble salts, iron compounds, and manganese compounds may accumulate at the top of either the water table or the capillary fringe.

Shell middens present a host of both opportunities and problems for the geoarchaeologist. These middens are found in nearly every coastal area of the world. Such deposits are particularly subject to diagenetic change from sea-level variation and saturation by groundwater. Chemical changes affect the porosity, permeability, and alkalinity. Compaction, translocation, and bioturbation disturbance combine with the chemical changes to render stratigraphic and archaeological analysis difficult.[24]

Mass Wasting

Influenced by gravity, sediments can move downslope and mix constituent materials in the deposit. A variety of mass-wasting processes may alter the archaeological record. They can be separated into slow gravity-movement processes like creep, solifluction, and subsidence and rapid gravity-movement processes like mudflows, landslides, and rockfall.

Solifluction is the downslope movement of water-saturated soil and sediments. Under periglacial conditions, solifluction has caused major deformation of archaeological stratigraphic sequences. Solifluction of the sediments overlying an occupation layer caused folding and discontinuities in the artifact layer at the Denbigh site in Alaska, while at the Engigstack site (also in Alaska) this type of movement caused reversals in the stratigraphic sequence.

Soil creep can also have a major influence on the spatial distribution of artifacts by causing a downslope movement of deposits in which heavier and denser artifacts tend to be transported farther.[25] Artifacts can also be buried by soil creep if they were originally situated at the base of a slope. More rapid massive downslope movements can transport large quantities of sediment very quickly, moving artifacts, producing geofacts, and burying archaeological sites.

Cryoturbation

Disturbance of sediments, soils, and artifact-distribution patterns caused by cycles of freezing and thawing is called cryoturbation. Cryoturbated sediments may have several features. Deformation of the earth's surface during a freeze can cause the upward bending of strata. The creation of patterned ground features, consisting of sorted polygon shapes, during frost heaving can

result in the outward movement of objects to the edges, while large objects are thrust to the surface. Cryoturbation is especially critical in periglacial settings but must also be considered as a potential influence in mid-latitude and mountain areas. (For example, the present-day maximum frost penetration in midwest North America between Missouri and Minnesota ranges from about 50 to 250 cm.)[26]

Frost heaving is a cryoturbation process connected to freezing and thawing events that can cause upward movement of earth and artifacts; it also reorients artifacts within deposits either by frost pull or frost push.[27] When groundwater freezes, it expands and can push artifacts. When the ice melts, water surface tension pulls finer sediments together, while artifacts and larger sedimentary particles remain where the expansion of ice pushed them. The presence of size sorting (with larger artifacts closer to the surface) and vertical orientation of the long axes of artifacts within sedimentary sequences may indicate frost heave.

Freezing-induced (cryostatic) pressures can also cause upward and lateral movement of objects. These in turn can cause contortion and deformation of sediments, such as that found at the Dry Creek Site in Alaska, where the stratigraphic sequence shows evidence of cryostatic pressures in the form of involutions and mass-displacement features. Ice and sand wedges are another indication of sediment deformation. Particle size sorting, in which upward sequences become coarser, may result from frost action. This can have critical implications for archaeological components composed of a mixture of artifact sizes. Mechanical abrasion caused by cryoturbation has been proposed as an explanation for geologic "retouch" on flakes in Paleolithic assemblages.[28]

Another set of cryoturbation features, termed *patterned ground*, consists of semi-symmetrical shapes formed along the ground surface by frost-heaved rocks. These features can take the shape of circles and polygons (among others), and it is important to recognize them because they can be mistaken for structures made or used by humans.

Frost action can transform the archaeological record in several ways. It can alter stratigraphic sections, sort both organic and lithic debris, and affect surface distributions of materials. Sediment contortion may obscure stratigraphic boundaries. It may transport larger artifacts upward, and it may transform the patterns of surface artifacts.

Clay Expansion and Contraction

The swelling and shrinking of clays (usually in Vertisols) cause a form of mixing called argilliturbation. During dry intervals, sediments composed of high amounts of expansible clays will shrink and crack. Artifacts lying on the surface of these sediments can fall into the cracks. During moister intervals the clays may expand and push up sediments. Scientists hypothesize that alternate wetting and drying cycles caused the formation of stone pavements and the size sorting of artifacts through the preferential upward movement of larger objects.

Bioturbation

Bioturbation can be divided into two major groups: modifications caused by animals (faunalturbation) and disturbances caused by plants (floralturbation). Postoccupational trampling and other alterations by humans and other animals are forms of faunalturbation that change the initial state of the archaeological record. However, it is likely that most postburial faunalturbation in archaeological sites comes from burrowing by small mammals (mainly rodents), insects, and earthworms (figure 3.16). Different types of animals have different effects on archaeological deposits, depending on their burrowing patterns. Vertical movement of smaller objects may be caused by subsurface foragers like gophers and certain earthworms. Mixing and churning by burrowing animals can cause the disappearance of boundaries between originally distinct layers. Surface foragers like prairie dogs, foxes, ants, termites, and rodents may also cause disturbance by building tunnels and nests.

The effects of pocket-gopher burrowing on the archaeological record illustrate the influence of bioturbation. There are at least four ways that gophers affect artifact accumulations: movement, destruction, impact on sedimentary structures, and organic enrichment. When excavating bur-

rows, gophers push sediment into mounds. This results in vertical and horizontal transportation of sediments and artifacts. Fragile artifacts composed of bone, shell, or plant remains may be broken during burrowing, and materials pushed to the surface may be exposed to weathering. Structures and boundaries within and between strata are disturbed or obliterated by burrowing activity. Pocket gophers collect organic matter from the surface and transport it underground, as well as providing additional organic enrichment by the deposition of feces. In the long-term, gopher burrowing influences the patterns of artifact size sorting, strata disruption, and destruction of fragile remains. Occasionally these have produced distinct artifact assemblages that have been interpreted without consideration of the potential effects of bioturbation. Characteristics used to define particular artifact or "cultural" entities may instead be the result of bioturbation, as at the Milling Stone horizon in California.

Mixing of archaeologically related soils and sediments by plants can be caused by root growth and decay and by tree fall. Root action can disturb archaeological sites by pushing artifacts or leaving cracks within the sedimentary matrix. If a tree is uprooted, artifacts may be brought to the surface. Discrete artifact components can be mixed, and size sorting of artifacts can result when materials adhering to the root system are redeposited. As with patterned ground there is the possibility that topographic features formed by tree throw may be interpreted as the work of humans. Plants also contribute to the stabilization of sediments and the development of soils. Artifacts within soil horizons may have been deposited as part of the original sedimentary matrix or during a later interval associated with surface stability, vegetation growth, and soil development.

Sedimentary contexts provide the initial landscape setting that affects both human habitation and use of a location and what happens to the objects after people use them. In addition to influencing the functional activities that occur at a site, different sedimentary contexts influence the visibility of the site and original site integrity. Many agencies can alter the original primary con-

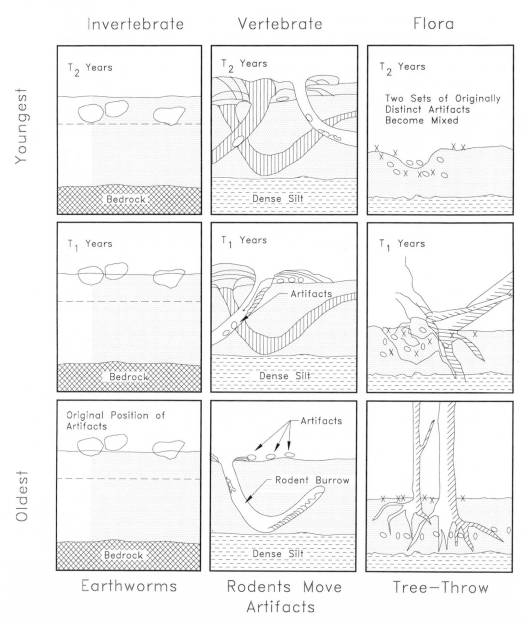

Figure 3.16 Effects of Bioturbation
This illustration shows what happens to the original patterning of the soil in three situations, after a lapse of time T_1 and after a further period of time T_2.

text by erosion, transportation, and redeposition. As well, secondary processes can also affect the site once the materials are within a depositional matrix.

There are several avenues to pursue in trying to determine the kinds of behavioral information available at an archaeological site. Two basic types of information can be used to help interpret the patterning found in the archaeological record. First, one can consider attributes directly associated with artifacts and archaeological features. Second, one can examine the sedimentologic and landscape context of the archaeological materials. The latter is specifically geoarchaeological, and the information can affect how one regards the first type of information. Landscape and sedimentologic data that indicate less disturbance relate to low-energy levels and few opportunities for erosion and redeposition. Greater opportu-

nities for postoccupational site changes occur in higher energy settings. The different sedimentary systems that we have related to archaeological site formation show that the final condition of the archaeological record is a result of a continuum between the primary, systemic context and postoccupational transformational processes.

CHAPTER 4

Paleoenvironmental Reconstructions: Humans, Climates, and Ancient Landscapes

Broad-scale relationships between landscape evolution, climatic fluctuations, and human activities are a critical aspect of archaeological interpretation. Interactions between the physical, geologic environment and biologic organisms, including humans, can be studied from either biogeographic or geoecologic perspectives. A fundamental aspect of geoarchaeology is the interpretation of the prehistoric record in terms of past patterns of interactions and interrelationships between humans, other organisms, and their physical habitats. This area of geoarchaeology is a subset of paleogeoecology, the study of interactions between prehistoric life and environmental landscapes.

Site-specific, regional, and global changes in the physical and biologic environment are reflected in the landscape context and are often directly influenced by climatic factors. Climate change itself is a complicated area of study. Climate change is thought to be the result of global, regional, and local geologic changes that influence atmospheric and hydrologic circulation patterns. Inferred connections between changing depositional environments, geomorphic contexts, and climatic processes are valuable tools for evaluating both spatial and temporal patterns of human behavior. Usually the visibility of an artifactual accumulation will depend on the patterns of landscape development with which it is associated. The sediment-soil system components of the landform environment contain a variety of biologic and chemical components that can be used as paleoecologic indicators (see Chapter 2). These constituents provide a means to infer past environmental conditions and to study their re-

lation to climate change. Human behavior has had an increasing influence on the environmental landscape, as reflected in the sediment-soil record of erosion, deposition, and landscape stability as well as in the paleoecologic indicators found in Quaternary deposits.

The geologic and biologic records of paleoclimates are stored in a variety of materials embedded in terriginous and ocean sediments and in ice sheets. Each of these proxy records provides only a limited local picture, but taken together they present a good general representation of regional and, in some cases, global patterns of Quaternary climates. In North America, for instance, paleoecologic data derived from pollen in lake sediments that have accumulated for the past 12,000 years allows us to reconstruct the habitats of early human occupation. In parts of the Old World there are paleoecologic records of the Plio-Pleistocene that provide clues to the environments associated with early hominids (australopithecines and early and archaic *Homo*), the Late Pleistocene associated modern humans, and Holocene human populations. Accurate time control (see Chapter 7) is essential for paleoclimate reconstruction. For the late Quaternary, especially the past 30,000 years, accelerator mass spectrometry (AMS) dating has helped provide this control. Other methods, such as potassium-argon (K-Ar) and uranium (U) series, have been useful for dating older paleoclimate records and relating them to the artifactual record (see Chapter 7).

Lake Records and Geoecology

Lake data offer paleoecologic information that can be particularly helpful in understanding human behavior and climate change. Because of the special depositional and preservational contexts associated with lakes, lake data provide much of our paleoclimatic and related environmental information. Marine sediments provide information on global climate change, while information on local and regional climate change comes from lake deposits. Organic-rich sediments tend to accumulate on the edges of lakes (or in swamps and bogs), while pollen and other paleoecologic indicators can be found in the sediments deposited in the deep-water portions of lakes. Although the sediments trap trace chemical and particle components from atmospheric deposition, much of this material is derived from the lake catchment area or the landscape surface areas that drain into the lake. In Holocene lake deposits, the trace chemicals incorporated into the basin provide a record of anthropogenic pollution that reflects the changing patterns of human landscape use, including such behavior as farming and the introduction and use of new technologies.

Records of lake-level changes are derived from many kinds of geomorphic, sedimentologic, and biostratigraphic data. These changes can be the result of climatic fluctuations, local geologic events (such as those related to tectonics), or biotic intervention. Animals can have a direct influence on lake levels. For instance, beavers create hydrologic changes by building dams. Humans also have directly affected lake levels: either they raise water levels by impounding waters or lower them by diverting water that would normally flow into a basin. One present-day example of humans affecting lake levels is Mono Lake in California, where inflowing tributaries have been diverted for use in agriculture and urban centers.

In the past, lake levels in the basin fluctuated as a result of climatic change. Major changes in the climate of western North America are recorded not only by geomorphic indicators of lake-level changes but also by the presence of tree stumps. These tree stumps, examples of a macrobotanical remain (see below), are what is left of trees killed by waters that rose because of a change in climate. In many cases shoreline change and variation in water depth can be reconstructed by either biologic or physical and chemical signals. One important aspect of the various forms of paleoecologic data available from lakes is that the different forms of information provide independent checks on the paleoclimatic interpretations. Lake-level interpretations based on remnant shorelines (geomorphic data) or on chemical signals (isotopes or salinity) provide independent sources of climatic information to test climatic inferences from pollen diagrams (a form of biotic data). Together, these geomorphic, chemical, and biotic signals offer a powerful means to help develop a geoecologic perspective of the past.

The most successful studies of lake-level fluctuations and their climatic implications have involved closed lakes (lakes without any outlet) in regions that are currently semiarid or tropical. Many classic studies concern closed basins that held water in the past, like Lakes Bonneville and Lahanton in the Great Basin of western North America. Studies based on lakes with outlets are more complex, and these open basins typically show less dramatic climatic response.

Hiatuses, mineralogic changes, microfossil or macrofossil distributions, organic material distributions, and changes in gross sedimentary stratigraphy all provide paleoecologic evidence from which lake-level changes can be reconstructed. Because sediment composition reflects both hydrologic and biolimnologic processes, the sedimentary evidence must be bolstered by other kinds of information. For example, wind-driven currents are usually the defining factor in establishing the boundary of sedimentation within a lake, because sedimentation is related to the high or low energy of the current. Therefore, paleo-wind directions and velocities, and thermal stratification within the water body will affect the vertical movement of sediments. This is especially true for lakes in temperate to cold climates.

Water-level changes in lakes like the Dead Sea are good indicators of past climate. Sometimes determining what aspect of climate produced the observable record is difficult, since lake levels can change because of variations in either precipitation or evaporation. A single paleoclimatic factor—increased precipitation, say—could cause a lake level to rise. Cooling temperatures, which lead to lower evaporation rates, may also increase lake levels by decreasing net water output. In these cases, biotic or chemical paleoecologic signals would have to be used to interpret the actual cause for the fluctuating lake levels that were indicated by the geomorphic and sedimentologic observations (transgressive and regressive stratigraphies or abandoned shorelines, for example). In our time, human activities control the lake levels of many such lakes. Over the past millennium, the Dead Sea has fluctuated through a range of 50 meters. From about 100 B.C. to A.D. 40 it showed a dramatic rise and fall of 70 meters.

Geologic events can also result in changes in lake levels. In these circumstances lake-level changes may not be directly attributable to climatic or biotic conditions. Changes caused by direct geologic events are typically the result of processes that influence basin drainage patterns. Some of these can be associated with tectonic events and related earth movements. For example, faulting can raise outlets to lakes, or earthquake-induced landslides can block drainages. The tectonically active area of the East African Rift system is an example of a place where faulting, along with climate, has played an important role in producing a record of lake-level fluctuations associated with archaeological remains. In addition, mass movements and earth flows caused by earthquakes are known to block stream drainages and form lakes.

Inferring Environmental Change

A variety of physical and biologic information can be used to reconstruct environmental and climate change. Our understanding of the postglacial ecology of North America rests on a combination of geologic (geomorphic, sedimentologic), chemical (including isotopic), and paleontologic (biotic) evidence. From these types of data we know that, although the last remnants of the Laurentide Ice Sheet in North America did not disappear until about 7000 B.P., the Early and Middle

Holocene (10,000–4500 B.P.) was perhaps warmer than the period since 4500 B.P. (the warmer time is sometimes called the climatic optimum). Some Early Holocene warmth may have been seasonal rather than year-round. Changes in precipitation also marked the first half of the Holocene. An estimated 20 percent decrease in rain led to an eastern extension of the Prairie Peninsula in the Great Plains of North America. Western North America was drier during the climatic optimum. The human response to the changes resulting from this geoecologic, climatic-biotic interaction is reflected in the patterning of the archaeological record. This patterning is partly a result of the geologic processes of erosion, deposition, and soil formation. However, much of the artifactual patterning shows human response to changing ecological habitats. Human adaptation to changing plant and animal arrangements instigated by climate change may explain the variation within the Paleo-Indian–Archaic–Woodland archaeological succession.

In protohistoric and historic times many significant climate changes have affected human habitation and agriculture. In Europe a cool period beginning about 4500 B.P. and ending about 2500 B.P. caused an expansion of mountain glaciation. This cooling interval can be seen in the geomorphic evidence of glacial moraine deposits and in such biotic indicators as pollen. Although a misnomer in strict archaeological terms, this period has been called the Iron Age cold epoch. The climate became warmer during the beginning of the Roman Empire, and the so-called Dark Ages in Europe (500–1000) coincided with a return to colder climates. After the year 1000, a warmer regime allowed the settlement of Iceland and Greenland. Alpine passes between Germany and Italy became free of ice.

Physical and biologic data support the impact of climatic change on human populations during the latest part of the Holocene. One example is the Little Ice Age, in which mountain glaciers advanced. The Little Ice Age began about 1450 and did not conclude until around 1890. The suggestion has been made that if not for the possibility of a human-induced greenhouse effect, the Little Ice Age might have been the start of another interval of global glaciation. This period had two main cold stages, which roughly coincided with the seventeenth and nineteenth centuries. Although it is sometimes thought of as a European phenomenon, the Little Ice Age was global. Other parts of the world experienced changes in precipitation and temperature that had an impact on biotic communities.

The first known European migration and occupation of North America shows how the Little Ice Age directly affected human behavior. During the warmer interval before the Little Ice Age, seafaring northern Europeans could travel and settle along the coasts of Greenland and Newfoundland. But with the onset of the Little Ice Age, sea ice expanded in the North Atlantic around Iceland, and the Norse colony established in Greenland was abandoned. The archaeological record suggests that northern European populations were also present in North America. The application of the geoarchaeological or paleogeoecologic perspective helps to explain this artifactual record. In the Middle Ages, Europeans could live in the New World habitat only so long as the traditions and technology they carried with them adapted favorably to the new conditions. To survive the climatically induced environmental changes caused by the Little Ice Age, these people needed to change their behavior, either by adapting to the new conditions or by seeking more compatible environments.

Climate thus has an important effect on geologic and biotic patterns. Geologic events like volcanic eruptions can cause short-term climate cooling. In addition to the effects volcanic activity has on local and regional environmental habitats, volcanic eruptions can result in global climate change. Acidic and sulfur-rich dust and ash from volcanic explosions have been found embedded in the layers of ice in Greenland, Antarctica, and mountain glaciers. Changes in the amounts of windblown volcanic material have been correlated with changes in climate. By measuring the sulfur content of Greenland ice cores, glacial advances in the past 1,400 years have been correlated to the frequency of volcanic eruptions. The work of Fritts and Bryson indicates that volcanic eruptions are involved in major climatic

transitions and intervals like the Younger Dryas event (around 10,500 B.P.), in which the climate deteriorated, slowing the retreat of continental and alpine glaciers.

Ecology and Landscape Change

Landscape evolution involves changes in both the physical and biologic features of the earth's surface. One must examine the factors associated with the sediment-soil system and the biologic evidence available in the deposits to analyze the evolution of the prehistoric landscape and place it within a geoecologic context. The mechanisms that influence spatial and temporal variation in habitat contexts are critical to archaeological interpretation. In addition to techniques based on sedimentologic and pedogenic evidence, a variety of paleoecologic methods based on biologically derived contents or chemical signals found in deposits can be employed (see Chapters 2 and 3). The inference of past environmental conditions from the remains of plants and animals found in sediments or soils relies on the same kinds of taphonomic and site formation principles used to interpret the archaeological record. The initial, dynamic, living populations of plants and animals can be altered by a variety of pre- and postdepositional processes.[1]

Paleontology is the study of fossils preserved in sediments. Any remains or traces of plants or animals preserved in the sedimentary record are fossils. In this broad sense artifacts, as traces of past human behavior, are fossils. When geology was developing in the early 1800s, geologists used the evolution and extinction of fossil groups to develop the geologic timescale—in much the same way that archaeologists have since used ceramic or lithic typology to develop chronological sequences and correlations. At any one period of time, many separate communities of fauna and flora live in different environments or habitats. Current theory postulates that populations of organisms, rather than communities of organisms, had different responses to environmental change during the Quaternary. This ecological aspect of the study of fossil fauna and flora provides geoarchaeology with a wealth of information on ancient environments.

Changing patterns in ecological materials found within archaeological contexts can reflect environmental fluctuations or evolving human adaptations. These changing patterns can be the result of human behavior on a physical landscape. The opposite can also happen. Changing human behavioral strategies can result from alterations of the environment. The Quaternary prehistoric and geoarchaeological record illustrate interactions that can be better understood by using a geoecologic approach.

A variety of paleoenvironmental and paleoclimatic indicators are found in sediments and archaeologically related deposits. These can be divided into biotic and abiotic indicators. Chapters 2 and 3 introduced many ways to interpret abiotic geomorphic and sedimentologic indicators. Apart from biofunctions of soils, biotic indicators are of two types: plant and animal remains. Common types of fossil plant remains that can be recovered as part of geoarchaeological studies include pollen, floral macrofossils, phytoliths, and diatoms. Fungi and mosses have also been used to infer past environmental conditions. The faunal fossil groups that are used to assist archaeological interpretations are divided into vertebrates (including mammals, reptiles, amphibians, fish, and birds) and invertebrates (like ostracods, mollusks, and insects). Unique accumulation circumstances can provide a combination of paleoecologic elements, such as coprolites and pack-rat middens.[2] In addition, trace-element compositions and isotopic ratios of plant and animal fossils are used as environmental indicators. When integrated with abiotic evidence derived from geologic data, these biotic sources of paleoenvironmental information can illuminate the geoecologic patterns contained within the prehistoric record.

The study of the past relationships between organisms and their environment relies on our knowledge of today's ecosystems. When we interpret the biologic evidence for past ecosystems, we depend on a variety of assumptions, including knowledge of the present-day environmental constraints on comparable biota; how (and whether) these constraints can be applied to past biotic distributions; and whether the fossil assemblages being studied are a true reflection of past living systems.

Plant Remains as Clues to Environmental and Climatic Change

Pollen

Pollen and spores from plants can be preserved in both soils and sediments. The study of these fossils is called palynology.[3] Except for macrofossils, pollen has probably contributed more to archaeological interpretation than any other plant remains. Many issues in the interpretation of fossil pollen assemblages provide insight into the complexities of interpreting other aspects of the prehistoric record, including artifacts and archaeological features. These issues include the application of taphonomic concepts, the connections between the observation of a pollen assemblage and higher levels of interpretation, and the possibility of "disharmonious" or nonanalog ecological patterns.

Securely dated stratigraphic pollen diagrams form a basis for paleoclimatic reconstructions and environmental reconstructions of archaeological sites. Pollen diagrams show the relative changes in kinds of pollen found in the sediment. However, links between pollen deposition and vegetation are not straightforward. The pollen record is a complex linkage of pollination ecology (especially wind transportation) and site formation processes. Pollen obtained from sedimentary sequences of lakes has been used to infer past vegetational landscape settings and paleoclimatic contexts. Other sedimentary contexts generally do not contain pollen unless unique physical and chemical circumstances exist that provide a situation for preservation. In addition, certain postdepositional conditions are more suitable for pollen preservation than others. Oxidizing conditions, calcareous settings, and deposits associated with well-drained alkaline deposits generally are not good for pollen preservation. Transportation and abrasion can also affect the final character of the pollen assemblage. Pollen can best be preserved in acidic, waterlogged areas. As well, the method of transport and the dispersal mechanisms influence the composition of a fossil pollen assemblage.

Pollen analyses in environmental reconstruction rely on a set of basic principles. Plants produce pollen, and a relation can be established between the relative amounts of the pollen initially released and the vegetational landscape. Different plants produce different amounts of pollen, so the absolute abundance of each pollen type has to be considered in relation to plant production. Plants that pollinate by means of wind dispersal produce a lot of pollen. Some pine species produce billions of pollen grains seasonally. Closed flowering and insect-pollinated plants produce much less, perhaps 100,000 pollen grains in a season.

Water can also move pollen. Thus, a specific pollen assemblage may not represent the vegetative setting of a single place but rather a combination of vegetation types within a stream drainage or region of wind transport. Another source of patterning is the size and shape of pollen grains. Particular pollen types may be sorted and settle in different parts of a basin. In this sense, like artifacts, the final pollen assemblage is related to factors associated with clastic deposition—pollen grains are small bioclasts (artifacts are bioclasts, too).

Some portion of the pollen production will eventually be deposited and preserved. After initial deposition (following dispersal and accumulation), oxidation and biologic activity can destroy pollen. Preservation is enhanced if the pollen grains settle in anoxic conditions or in settings where sediment accumulation is rapid, resulting in quick burial. In addition to lake and bog deposits, pollen is preserved in soils, tufas, glacial ice, and cave sediments.

Pollen grains can be diagnostic to the species level based on a combination of characteristics, including size, surface textures, and types of aperture. It is possible to observe changes through time in the frequencies of pollen types if samples can be obtained from a stratified sequence. These temporal changes can be related to past climatic conditions or to the effect of human alteration of the landscape. Where paleoenvironmental chronologies have been developed for pollen stratigraphies, the changing pattern of pollen types

through time has been used as a general chronological indicator. In order to use pollen assemblages as an indicator of time, it is necessary to document enough pollen sequences from a region so that the pollen sequence from the new core can be compared with a securely dated pollen chronology. Sometimes it is possible to examine temporally equivalent pollen assemblages from different locations in order to document spatial variation in vegetation and climate.

Estimates of past vegetational landscapes can be made by comparing past pollen assemblages with similar present-day settings. Estimating past climatic conditions by means of fossil pollen assemblages requires an understanding of the relationship between plant communities and climatic parameters. In order to make these comparisons, one must understand the vegetational and climatic linkages with the presence of particular soil conditions, the amount of precipitation, temperature patterns, and the like. As with any application of present-day observations to the prehistoric record, care must be taken: in some instances no direct analogs can be applied to past ecological circumstances.

We can trace the impact of human activities on the vegetational landscape during the Holocene by applying pollen sequences in Europe and the Near East. Sometimes particular plant types are good indicators of a particular climatic variable, like precipitation or temperature. The onset of the Holocene, around 10,000 years ago, coincided with the beginning of the Neolithic in the Near East. Early Holocene environmental changes caused conditions favorable to the development of agriculture. Ten thousand years ago the Near East had a very different climatic regime from that of the present, which we know in part through interpretations of fossil pollen records. Pollen has been used to infer changes in both precipitation and temperature. From about 20,000 to about 15,000 B.P., the climate was cool and arid, with much of the Near East landscape in steppe.[4] Between 15,000 and about 5000 B.P. temperatures rose, reaching their maximum at the end of that period. At the beginning of the Holocene the climate of the Near East was cooler and more humid than today. In Mesopotamia, pollen data indicate that the temperature increased, but rainfall remained relatively low. In the eastern Mediterranean and Near East the oak pollen frequency curve, considered a proxy for the amount of precipitation, shows that increased rainfall caused an expansion of the forests in Anatolia, the Levant, and the Zagros Mountains. This climatic change may have been the trigger that led to the domestication of plants in this region. Changes associated with Pleistocene to Holocene transition altered the types of plants and animals available for human use. Incipient domestication may have been an adaptive response by prehistoric humans to increase the reliability of food sources as procurement strategies connected with the Pleistocene were no longer useful in the Holocene.

In North America, pollen has been used to reconstruct changing vegetative and climatic patterns throughout the Holocene. The late Pleistocene and the onset of the Holocene in North America are associated with Paleo-Indian populations. Pollen data indicate that in central North America a spruce-dominated forest changed to prairie in the west and to pine in the east between 12,000 and 9000 B.P. This change in vegetative landscape may be reflected in the change in faunal communities and in human adaptations. A series of pollen stratigraphies documents the time-transgressive nature of first the eastward advance and then the westward retreat of prairie during the middle Holocene. An archaeological site that shows the eastward movement of the prairie and forest boundary is the Itasca bison kill site in northwestern Minnesota, where the presence of an open pine forest around 8000 B.P. and its replacement by prairie about 7500 B.P. has been documented.[5] Along with other paleoecologic indicators, pollen studies have figured prominently in a synthesis of North American human prehistory with environmental change.[6] Changes in the levels of biodiversity are reflected in the archaeological succession from Paleo-Indian to Archaic.

The palynology associated with archaeological sites can be used to evaluate the season of occupation, the subsistence, and related aspects of past human behavior. At Shanidar Cave in Iraq, palynologic studies revealed that the remains of a Neanderthal buried in the cave were associated with flowers.[7] In addition to airborne pollen,

pollen from hyacinth, hollyhock, and groundsel were clustered with a pinelike shrub. The flowers also provide an indicator of the time of year of the burial: probably between late May and early July. Later interpretations of this depositional context have posed the possibility that roof fall in the cave may have crushed the Neanderthal, and that mechanisms other than human ritual activity can explain the presence of the pollen.[8]

There are many other examples of pollen being used to infer environmental conditions associated with archaeological sites.[9] At the Acheulian site of Terra Amata, excavators found pollen in coprolites associated with archaeological remains of what appear to have been seasonal hunting camps. The pollen indicated that these sites may have been occupied during the spring.

Disturbance by human alteration of the landscape can also be observed in pollen data. The presence of high amounts of maize (*Zea mays*) pollen found in a pollen stratigraphic sequence in Ontario, Canada, provided evidence for agricultural subsistence patterns associated with Iroquois occupation of the region.[10] Maize and purslane pollen are found in the Crawford Lake pollen diagram starting about five hundred years ago and continuing until about three hundred years ago.

The studies by Hebda and Mathewes demonstrate the direct effect pollen studies can have on the interpretation of artifacts.[11] The two scientists looked at the age range of artifacts thought to have been used for massive woodworking at archaeological sites in the coastal areas of Washington and British Columbia. They found pollen sequences which indicated that between 9000 and 2500 B.P., cedar migrated along the coast northward from central Washington to British Columbia. The pollen indicated a correlation between the presence of artifacts thought to be used for massive woodworking and cedar trees. Hebda and Mathewes concluded that the development of activities associated with massive woodworking were constrained by the availability of cedar.

Floral Macrofossils

Macroscopic plant remains found in sediments include seeds, nuts, fragments of charcoal, and larger objects like tree trunks. Some depositional environments enable these materials to become part of the sediment-soil record. Because of the larger size of plant macrofossils, taphonomic trajectories associated with them are not usually as complicated as those associated with pollen dispersal. However, as with artifacts, depositional and postdepositional circumstances play a part. As an example, seeds of domesticated plants were recovered from charcoal lenses associated with Late Paleolithic artifacts at Wadi Kubbaniya, a tributary to the Nile River in southern Egypt.[12] The charcoal dated to about 17,000 B.P., but the domesticated seeds were dated to the Holocene; they had intruded into the earlier deposits. Careful collection of other plant remains from the series of sites at Wadi Kubbaniya led to the recovery of wood (tamarisk) charcoal and a variety of tubers that were dated by radiocarbon as being contemporary with the Late Paleolithic occupations.

Larger plant remains like tree trunks are used as indicators of both general prevailing environmental conditions (based on the type of tree and its habitat tolerances) and finer-scale fluctuations (based on the variation in ring-width thicknesses).[13] These kinds of materials can be incorporated either as structural features (e.g., the wood beams found in Pueblo sites in the American Southwest) or as sedimentary deposits (such as the Two Creeks forest discussed in Chapter 2). Tree remains also have been used as indicators of climate and as chronological tools.[14] In the most straightforward cases trees from archaeological sites can provide evidence of climate, because the width of tree rings can be directly related either to rainfall or temperature, or to a combination of both. Variations in isotopic ratios of tree rings also provide signals of climatic parameters. Conifers have been used in chronologies going back to the early Holocene in the American southwest (more than 8,000 years). Studies of oak-tree rings in western Europe have pushed back the tree-ring chronologies to around 7000–6000 B.P.

Phytoliths

Plants produce microscopic bodies composed of silica or calcium oxalate, which can be used as paleoenvironmental indicators in accordance with their morphologic assemblages. The microscopic opal or calcium oxalate deposits that form in and between plant cells are called phytoliths (literally, "plant rocks"). Phytoliths can encode significant archaeological and paleoenvironmental information. Unfortunately, phytolith studies have as yet received only limited attention from scientists, so considerable research remains to be done in phytolith systematics.

Plant families that produce abundant opal silica bodies are grass (which includes the cereals), sedge, elm, bean, squash, and sunflower. Cereal-grain phytoliths can be classified into many types, according to cellular origin and shape. Phytoliths tend to be deposited through decay-in-place mechanisms and are more stable than pollen in some depositional environments. This makes phytoliths an excellent complement to pollen.[15] In addition to being useful in the study of early agriculture and as broad paleovegetational indicators, opal phytoliths can differentiate between C_3 and C_4 photosynthetic pathways in grasses.

Phytoliths are classified according to shape (figure 4.1). *Pooid* phytoliths have circular, rectangular, elliptical, crescent, or oblong shapes and occur primarily in C_3 grasses growing in high latitudes or high elevations. A high percentage of Pooid phytoliths tends to indicate cool temperatures. *Chloridoid* phytoliths are saddle-shaped and occur primarily in C_4 grasses. *Panicoid* phytoliths have dumbbells and crosses and also occur primarily in C_4 grasses. Panicoid phytoliths, however, tend to occur in areas with higher moisture than do Chloridoid phytoliths. Therefore, grass phytoliths from soils, paleosols, and archaeological sediments can be used to reconstruct the environment of a site or region. Increased evapotranspiration of hot arid environments promotes increased phytolith formation. Irrigation farming or farming in areas with poor drainage, where additional soluble silica is available from excess soil water, may enhance this process.

Phytoliths have been found in a variety of settings. The phytolith record from Natural Trap Cave of northern Wyoming provides an example from Ice Age deposits.[16] The depositional sequence at the cave contains an environmental and climatic record that includes the last interglacial and the Pleistocene-Holocene transition. Phytoliths produced from grasses were found

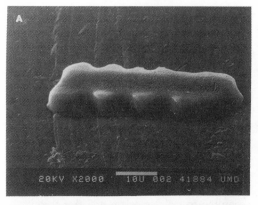
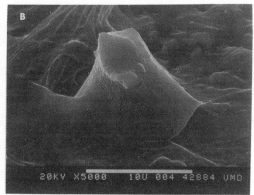
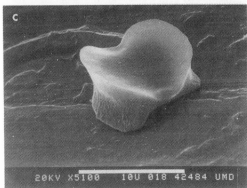
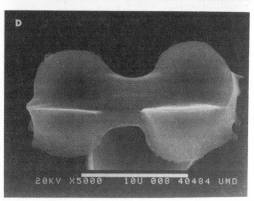

Figure 4.1 Grass Phytolith Types
A) Sinuates (long trapezoid) are characteristic of grasses of the Pooid tribe; B) Rondels (short trapezoid) are widespread in all tribes, particularly in florescences; C) Saddles are characteristic of the Chloridoid tribe but also occur in bamboo and some arundinoids; D) Dumbbells are most often found in Panicoids; bamboo, some arundinoids, and some Pooids also produce dumbbells. Crosses are a particular type of dumbbell.

in deposits thought to range from later than 110,000 B.P. to around 12,000 B.P. Pooid phytoliths dominate the oldest deposits, which contain no Chloridoid phytoliths, a distribution that may mean that the region was cooler and wetter than now. Greater numbers of Panicoid and Chloridoid phytoliths occur in the upper part of the sequence, but the grass phytolith composition of circa 12,000 B.P. does not have a composition similar to the Holocene. Fauna found in the same sequence suggest the possible presence of a montane conifer parkland, with C_3 grasses changing to C_4 in the Natural Trap area about 11,000 years ago.

Phytolith analysis can help solve a specific paleoethnobotanical problem, such as the identification of maize at an archaeological site. Kernels and cobs are common macrofossils at many sites; however, domestication and diffusion of maize are thought to predate the macrofossil evidence in many areas. Maize produces both larger quantities and larger sizes of cross-shaped phytoliths than other grasses. (*Cross* is defined as a body with at least three sides clearly indented in the planar view, and a length of no more than 2 microscope units, or 9.16 micrometers, greater than the width.) In addition to noting the percentage of phytoliths that are cross-shaped and the size of the phytoliths, a dumbbell-cross ratio confirmed that most wild grasses produced fewer and smaller crosses than maize. Phytolith three-dimensional structure is based on the face opposite the cross-shaped face. Other approaches to identifying corn by phytoliths that were used by Irwin Rovner and John Russ have focused on computer-based recognition systems to sort the three-dimensional assemblages.

Phytolith analysis was used to help reconstruct the vegetative history and landscape of the nineteenth-century Harpers Ferry site in West Virginia.[17] The samples collected from prehistoric levels at the site contained nongrass phytoliths that probably derived from deciduous trees and other phytoliths representative of grasses. In the lowest historic levels, dating from about 1800 to 1820, there were fewer phytoliths but higher proportions of grass phytoliths (short-cell Panicoid, Festucoid, and plain-rod types). The number of scrub and tree phytoliths decreased, while that of grass phytoliths increased significantly. In samples dating from about 1820 to 1832 there was an increase in Festucoid types associated with grass. Phytoliths from flood layers were also associated with grass growth. The presence of Panicoid and Festucoid classes reflected these moist conditions.

Phytoliths can provide data about the types of foods eaten by past human populations. At the medieval site of La Olmeda, Spain, which dates from the seventh to the thirteenth century, scientists looked at the surfaces of human teeth. It was possible to identify the presence of a phytolith attributable to the common millet. This was a short-cell or dumbbell-cell phytolith. The phytolith was found through scanning electron microscopy; to verify that the structure was a phytolith, its composition was tested using an X-ray microanalysis system. All the phytoliths that could be classified belonged to the *Poaceae (Graminae)*.[18]

Diatoms

Algae, found in aquatic settings, form cell walls composed of silica. These biogenic silica organisms are called diatoms and can be preserved in sedimentary sequences. Distinct morphologies provide a means for identifying different species of diatoms. Different algae types have distinct habitat tolerances. Their known ecological niches provide useful information about the hydrologic conditions of bodies of water.

Many taphonomic principles that influence a pollen assemblage also affect diatoms. Streams and wind can readily transport diatoms in drainage basins. Freshwater diatoms exposed on dry lakebeds have been eroded and blown by the wind into marine sediments, providing a record of continental environmental conditions in nearby ocean sediments. Diatoms have been recovered from both lake and marine sediments and are especially useful in documenting environmental changes that reflect fluctuations in water levels and transgression-regression sequences.

Diatoms can help document sea-level changes because some species are very sensitive to changes in salinity and consequently are an indicator of transgressive and regressive sequences. Particular species are associated with freshwater, brackish, or marine conditions. Because of this, studies of diatoms can help in evaluations of paleoenvironmental settings connected to coastal archaeological sites.

Diatoms were used as paleoecologic indicators in archaeological interpretations at the Lubbock Lake, a Paleo-Indian site in west Texas.[19] A study was undertaken to determine the sequence of water conditions in the area. Some sediment samples could be correlated with the Folsom artifact-bearing stratum. The results of the diatom study indicated the existence of bog conditions associated with stagnant to slow-flowing water that had considerable variation in salinity levels. One of the more common species of diatom indicated that flowing springs had once existed. The diatoms showed conditions that fluctuated from slightly brackish to much fresher water; these conditions were consistent with climatic changes in precipitation regimes and fluctuating spring flow and water levels.

Another example of the geoarchaeological use of diatoms comes from the study of Montezuma Well in northern Arizona. Montezuma Well consists of a collapsed spring-mound composed of travertine; it has a diatom record of more than 11,000 years.[20] A radiocarbon-dated core from Montezuma Well was studied to evaluate past environmental conditions at the spring and their effect on prehistoric human occupation. Variations in diatom taxa and other information from the core seem to show that before 9000 and after 5000 B.P. there was a moister climate in the region. Between these two dates conditions seem to have been drier. The presence of *Chaconnes placentula* var. *Lineata* throughout the sequence indicated the continuous presence of submerged aquatic plants. The variation in amounts of *Anomoeoneis sphaerophora* suggested periods of high aridity during the intervals of 8700 to 8400, 7800 to 6900, and 2000 to 1000 B.P. The major changes in the diatom assemblages after about 5000 B.P. seem to indicate a change in physicochemical conditions. After about 4000 B.P., the water levels were apparently higher.

There is a possible correlation between the diatom species in the sequence and prehistoric human occupation of the area. The higher values of *Aulacoseira granulata* and *A. islandica* coincide to some degree with the occupation of the Sinagua people. The Sinagua occupied pueblo, cliff dwellings, and pit-houses near the well between about A.D. 750 and 1400 (about 1250–600 B.P.). These diatoms were more abundant between 1500 and 1000 B.P. and are indicators of organic enrichment in the Montezuma Well. Diatoms have also been used to trace landscape change associated with human settlement.[21]

In addition to their function as environmental indicators, diatoms have helped trace the source of clays used to make pottery and, consequently, are useful in the study of exchange systems (see Chapter 6). Diatoms can accumulate in lakes and swamps, which results in the formation of biogenic siliceous deposits called diatomites. An indicator of lacustrine and paludal environments, diatomites have been used as a raw material by humans.

Animal Remains as Clues to Environmental Conditions

Invertebrates

Ostracods

Ostracods are very small (about 0.2–0.7 mm in size) bivalve crustaceans. They are bottom-dwelling organisms, most of which crawl, al-

though some can swim. The presence of ostracods in sediments indicates the existence of aquatic habitats in the past, which can be either saline or freshwater. Chemical signatures contained in ostracods have helped in the evaluation of paleoecologic and paleoclimatic settings. Ostracods have also been used to infer hydrologic changes caused by human activity. Ostracod shells can be preserved in most aqueous depositional environments, including oceans, lakes, ponds, and streams. Because not enough time has passed for **phylogenetic** changes to take place during the Quaternary, freshwater ostracod species cannot be used as chronostratigraphic markers (the same is true for insects). The exception to this would be the occurrence of unique frequency variations in ostracods that can be dated by independent means. Stratigraphic zones based on different ostracod assemblages have been used to document changing environmental conditions in lacustrine settings.

As with most paleoecologic methods, the use of freshwater ostracods to infer past environmental settings relies on a comparison of the morphology of fossil ostracods with physical, chemical, and climatic information about present-day ostracods. Often the present-day habitats associated with ostracods are restrictive, so it is possible to make specific inferences about past conditions from species found in sediments. For example, some species are found predominantly in lakes, others in ponds, and others in moving water. Other parameters that can be derived from present-day habitat associations include salinity and the amount of dissolved oxygen in the water body.

The presence of calcareous ostracod shells provides an indication of past geohydrologic conditions. To preserve calcareous shells, hydrologic conditions need to be buffered based on **pH** levels. Below a pH level of about 8.3 the carbonate in the shell will dissolve; ostracods will therefore not be preserved in many bog and marsh deposits, although they may have been present initially. Ostracods are more likely to be preserved in marl deposits. Ostracods generally do not live in high-energy environments associated with the deposi-

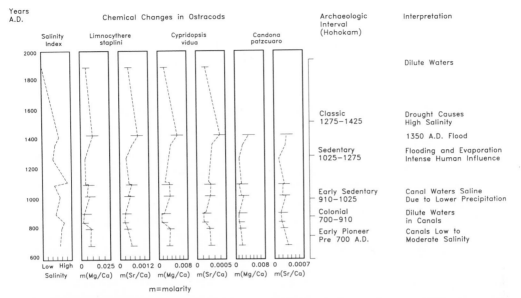

Figure 4.2 Hohokam Canals and Irrigation Reconstruction from Ostracod Chemistry

Geoarchaeological evidence from the chemistry of ostracods is used to infer events associated with the canals and irrigation of the Hohokam. Two chemical ratios in ostracods compare the amount of Mg to Ca or the amount of Sr to Ca. Changes in the proportion of the elements were recorded in three types of ostracods. The salinity index shows several fluctuations from low to high salinity from after 600 to after 1800. When imposed on the archaeological chronology, these changes can be used to interpret prehistoric irrigation from the Early Pioneer through the Classic Period.

tion of coarser clastics. They may be found in fine sands and coarse silt, but they are most common in clays, fine silts, or organically rich areas.

The chemical composition of ostracod shells can throw light on certain environmental parameters. The ratio of magnesium and strontium to calcium is related to salinity. Chemical parameters control the strontium-calcium ratio while water chemistry and temperature both control the magnesium-calcium ratio. Changes in the strontium-calcium ratio within the ostracod shell are related only to fluctuations of carbonate or sulfate in the water body. Where strontium-calcium and magnesium-calcium ratios are both stable, it is an indication that water composition and temperature did not change. This may reflect settings of deeper water.

Palacios-Fest used the levels of magnesium-calcium and strontium-calcium to study changes in a Hohokam age canal, in Arizona; variations in the water chemistry were related to the effects of human- and climate-induced environmental change (figure 4.2).[22] The ostracod samples were collected from canals at the site of Las Acequias in Arizona. Between about A.D. 1025 and 1425, increases in salinity, as recorded by ostracods, may have been a product of human-induced environmental alteration. Ostracods also recorded major climatic pulses, including two floods (one at about 855–910, another at 1350) and a drought (from about 1365 to 1425).

Based on the ostracod species present at Las Acequias and the environmental conditions associated with them, four assemblages were determined, which indicated waters ranging from chemically dilute to calcium-enriched, dominated by sodium, magnesium, and sulfate ions (either low or moderate salinities). Assemblage 1 was associated with slow-flowing waters, 2 with seepage conditions, 3 with slow-flowing and stagnant waters, and 4 with seepage and flowing waters in a human-disturbed environment. From the Hohokam Early Pioneer Period (before 700) to the Colonial Period (700–910), canal waters became more dilute, while during the Early Sedentary Period (910–1025) they became more saline. After 1350, the trace-element chemistry of the ostracods indicates a dramatic increase in water salinity during the Classic Period (1275–1425), followed by more dilute waters in historic times.

The Las Acequias Hohokam irrigation system provides an example of the usefulness of ostracods to an understanding of prehistoric human-land relations. Higher stream flows and more dilute waters and flooding that are probably associated with climate are indicated for the Colonial Period. An increase in salinity during the end of Hohokam occupation (Classic Period) indicated by the ostracods would support the contention that higher temperatures and drier conditions associated with the Anasazi Warm Period were responsible for the abandonment of the area by the Hohokam. Increasing salinization, suggested by the trace-element chemistry in ostracods, may also reflect transformations of the landscape because of Hohokam irrigation and agricultural practices.

Cladocera, another form of small bivalve *Crustacea*, can also help us understand environmental conditions associated with human occupations. Megard used Cladocera samples collected from Terminal Pleistocene deposits in Lake Zeribar in Iran to indicate environmental conditions during an interval when human subsistence patterns changed from hunting to agriculture.[23]

Mollusks

Mollusks are one of the more common types of invertebrate remains associated with Quaternary deposits and archaeological sites. The study of mollusks is called malacology. Gastropoda (snails) and bivalves (including clams) are two prominent types of molluskan invertebrates. Gastropods usually consist of a single conical or spiral shell, while bivalves have a hinged shell. Most mollusks are composed of **aragonite** although some consist of calcite. Different mollusk species

live on land and in water. They can be found in a variety of depositional settings, including loess; caves and rock shelters; stream, lake, and spring sediments; and marine coasts (figure 4.3). Terrestrial mollusks have been recovered from archaeological features like ditches, wells, and occupation debris. Mollusks also form a primary constituent of coastal middens.

Several factors need to be considered in determinations of environmental conditions from assemblages of fossil mollusks. These include taphonomic processes of deposition and preservation (including the potential for mixing), the relative abundance of various molluskan types, sampling, and identification.

Malacology has been used to study the climatic transitions associated with prehistoric human occupations. In northern France the mollusks from several sites covering the late glacial and Early Holocene have been related to the Upper Paleolithic (Late Magdalenian) and Mesolithic archaeological sequence. There were five distinct zones. The bottom of the sequence contained redeposited silt, probably consisting of redistributed loess. It included species that exist in cold conditions and in open, short grassland environments. An overlying organic silt contained a higher number and a greater diversity of mollusks, some of which indicated the presence of relatively warm and humid interstadial conditions and more complete vegetative cover. Humid conditions are indicated by changes in mollusk types in the overlying sediments. The fourth zone, which represents the Early Holocene, reflects a major change. Forest species increased at the expense of open-ground conditions. In the last zone there is a change back to open-land mollusks and a dramatic decrease in forest species. At one site (Holywell Coombe) that had the same characteristics as the fifth zone, the change may reflect human activities associated with forest clearance during the Neolithic and Early Bronze Age.

Mollusks have also been used to infer landscape change. Variations in land molluskan fauna helped in reconstructions of prehistoric land-use change at the Pink Hill archaeological site west of London.[24] The lower deposits at the site con-

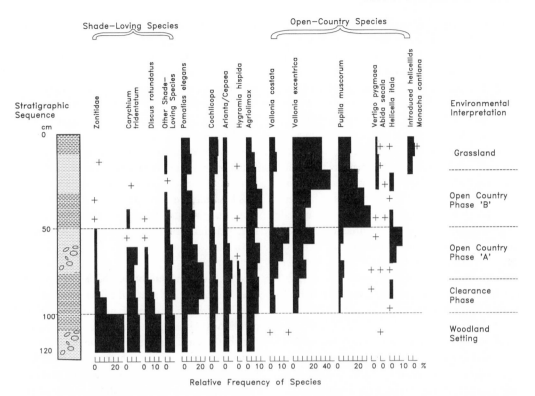

Figure 4.3 Microfaunal Diagrams as Indicators of Environmental Change

Different kinds of terrestrial gastropods are indicative of specific types of environmental settings. In this example, we see the changes in the landscape through time. Greater numbers of shade-loving species indicate the presence of a woodland environment, while greater numbers of open-country species indicate a grassland habitat.

tained shade-sensitive mollusks associated first with woodland habitats and then with initial clearance of the woodlands during the pre-Iron Age. An open-country phase A was correlated with Iron Age agricultural activity, and a phase B with Romano-British agriculture.

Studies of mollusks along the southern New England coast have demonstrated that Late Holocene use of shellfish resources was affected by environmental and climate change.[25] Although human preference has been suggested as an explanation for prehistoric shellfish use patterns, climatic factors may have played a critical role. During the Middle Woodland period, dating from about 1800 to 1600 B.P., the regional climate cooling produced cooler water temperatures, which resulted in changes in molluskan fauna from warmer to cooler assemblages. This led to a corresponding alteration of human resource use.

Insects

Paleoenvironmental and climatic data can also be derived from insect fossils. Insects are a remarkably pervasive group of creatures. They make up more than half the faunal and floral species known today. Insect fossil fauna can be recovered in such depositional contexts as ponds, bogs, lakes (often near the margins), fluvial deposits, and pack-rat middens. There are two underlying principles in the use of insect fossil fauna: first, throughout the Quaternary many insect species seem to have remained unchanged; and second, the habitat associations of insects do not seem to have changed either. Therefore, insects are good indicators of environmental conditions. Because they are so abundant, many insects (flies, bees, beetles, and ants) have been recovered from Quaternary deposits.

Beetles (Coleoptera) have been used extensively in the reconstruction of environmental conditions. Like other Quaternary insects, they combine genetic stability with sensitivity to climate and so live in restricted environmental settings. There are about 350,000 species of beetles. This has been a boon to paleoenvironmental studies, because they are often precisely adapted to narrow environmental niches, but collectively they inhabit nearly all terrestrial and freshwater habitats. In southern Britain, fossil insects from the type site of the last interglacial in Suffolk provided valuable information regarding environmental conditions during the Paleolithic occupation of this region.[26] The twenty-one species of beetles found there indicate that during the Paleolithic occupation the climate was warmer than it is now. Some insects from Britain are extinct while others are now distributed in southern Europe, indicating that the climatic zones shifted southward.

The insect fauna of Middle-Late Holocene England has been studied in relation to archaeological features associated with forest clearance.[27] Underlain by lake deposits of the last glaciation, Thorne Moor is a relict of an extensive bog containing fossil timber that is riddled with insect galleries. A radiocarbon age of about 3090 B.P. dates this to Bronze Age clearance of the mixed oak forest of the region. Insect fauna were recovered from organic silts and preserved trees. The study found a number of insects known to be associated with oak. That some insects found in the moor do not exist in the area today indicates change in climate or change in vegetative cover caused by forest clearance.

The insect fossil record also throws light on the timing and intensity of environmental change associated with the Terminal Pleistocene and Lower Holocene human occupation of western North America.[28] Fossil insects collected at the Lamb Spring Paleo-Indian archaeological site

in Colorado seem to indicate that there were cooler-than-present mean summer temperatures at around 14,000 B.P. Other locations in Colorado and Montana indicate that there was a gradual warming between 13,000 and 10,000 B.P. Rapid warming seems to have occurred after 11,000 B.P. By 9700 B.P. insect fauna from Utah indicate that temperatures were warmer than today. Similar warming intervals are also documented by insect fauna for the late glacial Holocene transition in Europe and eastern North America. The insect fossil assemblages indicate a rapid change in climate that probably affected all biotic communities, including prehistoric human populations.

Vertebrates

Deposits within landforms and archaeological sites also contain a variety of animal remains that may serve as indicators of past environmental conditions. Although the potential value of using vertebrate remains in making general paleoenvironmental inferences is high, attention must first focus on the taphonomic conditions of accumulation. Environmental evaluations of faunal remains are primarily based on comparisons with the geographic ranges and present-day habitats for living species. Morphological attributes and contextual information help to provide indications of past environments of extinct animals.

Mammal Fossil Remains

When using fossil vertebrate remains to infer past environments and climates, there are several points to consider. Generally, many larger mammals have broad habitat tolerances. This is partly because they are warm-blooded (endothermic) but also because they can be highly adaptive. Smaller animals are usually more valuable for environmental reconstruction, because they are more ecologically restricted. In attempting to determine the past habitat tolerances of extinct species, it is helpful to make ecological inferences that rely on a variety of mammal types, not just a single species.

Some habitat associations can be partially determined from anatomical characteristics, but these may not be restrictive enough. The teeth of mammoth and mastodon show marked differences thought to be related to their eating habits. Mastodon have short-crowned teeth and were probably browsers, while mammoth have high-crowned teeth and were likely to have been grazers. Mastodon are thought to be more closely associated with woodland or forest settings while mammoth are associated with steppe and grassland conditions. But the species perhaps were not limited to these settings. Generalities like this are not always clear indicators of environmental habitats. Present-day elephants have teeth similar to mammoth and are grazing animals, but they can live in either savannas or forests and can also browse on trees. Biotic taxa other than humans seem to have adapted and changed their habitat tolerances through time.

Some attributes that enable mammals to be used as chronological indicators make them less useful for paleoenvironmental studies (see Chapter 7). The major characteristic of Late Tertiary (Pliocene) and Quaternary mammals is the generally high morphologic diversity observable in the prehistoric record. This diversity is usually considered the result of adaptation to climatic or environmental fluctuations. Throughout this time major morphologic changes occur in many mammal groups, including primates, elephant types, bison types, deer types, rhinoceroses, beavers, and, in particular, smaller rodents. The morphologic changes mean that mammals can be used as chronological indicators, but these same changes complicate mammals' use in paleoecologic inference.

Morphologic changes are thought to be the result of adaptations to particular physical and biotic habitats. Where the mammalian forms are similar to those of existing animals, it is reasonable to consider observations of present-day habitat preference and behavior when studying the fossil record. For mammoths, living elephant communities are used as a first approximation for understanding the fossil record. The same kind of logic is employed for carnivore behavior. Thus, the behavior of existing felidae, along with independent paleoecologic information derived from the context of the fossils, provides the basis for reconstructing the habitats and habits of extinct felids, like the saber tooth–scimitar cat forms.

Despite the constraints caused by changes in mammalian morphology through time, basic, generalized environmental habitats can be inferred using modern comparisons. Fossil taxa that are physically similar to present-day elk, reindeer, lemmings, musk ox, and polar bear would indicate the probable presence of an arctic or boreal landscape habitat. In the same way, antelope and horse types would be an indication of steppe-taiga landscapes. However, the possibility of major behavioral changes not directly observable by the morphology of the fossil forms should always be a consideration. Thus, the sometimes subtle differences in the morphologic features of fossils grouped into the two hominid genera (*Australopithecus* and *Homo*) reflect diverse adaptations that are probably related to a variety of habitats. It is thus necessary to use a wide array of geoarchaeological tools when developing a geoecologic model of the past. For hominids, the evaluation of the entire environmental context, using strictly geologic and biotic criteria (including artifactual patterns) forms the basis of a paleoecologic reconstruction. A more reasonable estimate of prehistoric environments will be produced when we can rely on the likely habitats of many fossil mammal forms, if we can assume that the fossil assemblage is from a contemporaneous community and not the result of taphonomic mixing.

Generally, smaller mammals are more reliable indicators of local geoecologic conditions than larger mammals. We base this conclusion on the observation of present-day large and small mammals. Larger mammals inhabit more diverse and widespread landscapes. Many have seasonal migration routes or at least extensive areas of potential habitats. Smaller mammals, especially rodents, are typically better indicators of local geoecologic conditions. They are also useful as chronological indicators.

Bird Fossil Remains

Because the ecological constraints of birds are often quite narrow, bird remains can prove useful in ecological reconstructions. Yet despite specific range tolerances, there are problems with using bird remains. These include birds' potential to adapt to changing habitats and their high mobility, which results in their being found throughout a wide geographic range. This is especially true of birds that migrate seasonally. In archaeological contexts the presence of migratory fowl can be an indicator of seasonal occupation. Some bird taxa may be linked to specific landscape contexts. We can thus infer the past presence of a particular landscape on the basis of the bird remains.

Sometimes the distributions of bird fossils provide clues to past changes in geoecologic patterns. Steadman and Miller have argued that changing ecological patterns in North America led to the reduction in the geographic distribution of the California condor.[29] During historic times the California condor was primarily associated with warm-temperate climatic and ecological contexts. Based on several lines of paleoecologic evidence (including pollen and plant macrofossils), it appears that around 11,000 B.P. the bird's range was much less restricted. Evidence from the Hiscock site in western New York shows that the California condor was once able to live in an ecological setting associated with spruce-jack pine woodlands. This boreal, coniferous vegetative landscape may have been associated with colder climatic conditions. Probably condors were able to exist in this environment because of the availability of an important biotic food source, large mammal carrion. The severely restricted distribution of the California condor during the Late Holocene may be linked to the extinction of large mammals during the Pleistocene-Holocene transition that would have reduced the available food for scavenging birds.

Reptile and Amphibian Fossil Remains
The study of reptiles of the past is called paleoherpetology. In comparison with mammals, little morphologic change is observable in the Late Tertiary and Quaternary fossil record of reptiles. Reptilian fauna have been stable; they have undergone little adaptive radiation or speciation. Reptiles can be useful for interpreting paleoenvironments, although reconstructions need to take into consideration reptiles' adaptive abilities.

Fossil remains of morphologically similar reptiles have been found in contexts different from those of their apparent present-day counterparts. Scientists thus conclude that reptiles may be highly adaptable to ecological-habitat alterations induced by climate change. Climatic factors account for most of the changes in the distribution of reptilian forms. Reptile distribution seems to reflect changing patterns of temperature and moisture.

As has been demonstrated for other aspects of the biostratigraphic record, taphonomic processes are important to amphibian and reptile fossil accumulations. In some instances, the presence of other paleoecologic data has led to the conclusion that the reptilian specimens were not originally part of the same community. The presence of fossil assemblages containing animals that now live in different ecological settings led scientists to believe that these were mixed assemblages. The work on amphibian and reptile fossils by researchers like W. H. Holman has led to the conclusion that different ecological patterns existed in the past. Some accumulations, instead of being heterochronic (consisting of bones from different periods), may be indicators of different, nonanalog, geoecologic patterns in the past. Similar interpretations have been made on the basis of other ecological indicators, like pollen stratigraphies and mammal assemblages.

Because reptiles are ectotherms, they have fairly restricted ecological and geographic ranges, especially compared to large mammals. These ecological constraints make reptiles potentially useful in geoecologic reconstructions. Trends in the body size of reptiles have been used as an indicator of either climate or ecological associations. Larger body size has been attributed to higher temperatures (a climate factor), or less stress on populations from predators, while smaller size (dwarfism) has been associated with increased predation. These types of ecological connections demonstrate that morphologic change in fossil forms cannot always be directly attributable to climatic factors. For instance, Pregill interpreted the decrease in the size of lizards living on islands as a result of Holocene human settlement.[30]

Fish Fossil Remains

With due consideration for taphonomic indicators of transport and redeposition, fish remains can be an indicator of the presence of water. Fish can also be used to infer a variety of aquatic conditions. Freshwater fish are associated with two contexts: well-oxygenated bodies of water, such as streams and larger lakes; and poorly oxygenated water, like ponds and swamps, or low-energy fluvial settings.

Because the scales, vertebrae, and ear stones (otoliths) of fish have annual growth rings, it has been possible to use them to study seasonality. For example, Casteel used fish scales to infer a relationship between rates of fish growth and water temperature, with higher rates linked to higher temperatures.[31]

Fish remains can help provide information about prehistoric drainage connections. In southern Egypt, sedimentary deposits containing Middle Paleolithic artifacts also contained the remains of fish. The presence of fish indicated that streams once connected ancient lakes to one another. Van Neer's studies of the fish remains from these deposits were also used to reconstruct the paleoaquatic environment of the Middle Paleolithic sites.[32] The variety of fish found in the deposits was one indication of good hydrologic conditions, but the fish taxa found also suggested that the lakes were large and deep, with sandy bottoms.

Other Ecological Accumulations

Pack-Rat Middens

Pack rats (genus *Neotoma*) are small mammals that received their common name because they pick up a variety of materials and bring them to their dens, where they accumulate as middens. In dry areas, like the Great Basin of western North America, these midden accumulations have been preserved for more than 40,000 years. In 1964 Philip Wells and Clive D. Jorgensen documented the potential uses of pack-rat middens for paleoecologic information.[33] Two characteristics make them useful for studying past environments and climates. Pack-rat middens contain a variety of plant and animal remains, including twigs, leaves, seeds, pollen, and bones. These can be dated, using radiocarbon measurements (see Chapter 7). A major difference between these accumulations and continuous stratigraphies that contain pollen or macrofossils is that pack-rat middens generally represent an isolated interval in time. In addition, pollen stratigraphies can represent regional vegetative patterns, while middens consist mostly of materials within several hundred feet of their location. As a result, one must analyze and date many separate middens in order to interpret regional or chronological variation.

Peat

Peat bogs are a major source of information about Quaternary landscapes for northern latitudes. Although the rate of accumulation varies widely, peat accumulates at about 1 meter every 1,000–2,000 years in a favorable environment. For most peat deposits the sedimentary record is composed of decayed plant remains in a waterlogged environment. Peat deposits extend back as far as 9000 B.P. and contain a continuous record of plant communities, as well as a record of atmospheric deposition, including pollen.

These bogs are some of the most important environments for wetland archaeology. In Europe peat bogs have preserved many tracks, dugout boats, and even fishnets. The best-known discoveries from bogs have been the well-preserved Iron Age bodies like the "Tollund man" of Denmark. Although acid bog waters have dissolved the bones of the "bog people," the skin and the stomach, along with its contents, usually remain.

In North America, Florida's extensive peat deposits have yielded abundant totems, masks, and figurines. A Florida peat bog preserved a skull from 8000 B.P. that had a relatively undamaged brain. The soft tissue remains recovered from bogs provide an important source for DNA studies.

Other waterlogged environments have preserved oak-coffin burials, Viking ship burials, textiles, and the wooden structures from Swiss lake dwellings. In historic archaeology, waterfronts of harbor towns have been preserved. A major problem with waterlogged wood is that it begins to dry, crack, and disintegrate when removed from its burial environment. It therefore requires special preservation measures, such as keeping the wood submerged or using waxes and chemicals.

Isotopes and Chemical Ratios as Environmental Indicators

Because isotopes of a given chemical element have different numbers of neutrons, they have different atomic weights (masses). Isotopes of a particular element will have the same chemical properties, but their different masses cause them to be separated or **fractionated** by certain natural processes.

The element oxygen has been useful in the reconstruction of past environmental conditions. It has three isotopes, each with a different atomic mass (same number of protons but varying numbers of neutrons). The oxygen with eight neutrons has an atomic mass of sixteen and is designated ^{16}O, the isotope with nine neutrons is designated ^{17}O, and the isotope with ten neutrons is designated ^{18}O. When water evaporates, the lighter oxygen isotope (^{16}O) is preferentially incorporated into water vapor, while the heavier isotope (^{18}O) becomes proportionally higher in the remaining water. The fact that ^{18}O is preferentially left in ocean water during evaporation has been used to infer global climatic fluctuations. This has led to a revolution in our understanding of environmental and climatic change during the time of human physical and behavioral development. When these climate changes are dated, they can sometimes be used to ascertain the age of archaeological sites. Isotopic signals contained in marine sediment, calcite veins, and ice-core sequences appear to provide a continuous record of global climatic change for the interval associated with the archaeological record. The isotopic signals have been related to relative sea-level changes and alternating periods of colder global climates (glacials) and warmer global climates (interglacials).

During Ice Ages the ^{16}O isotope of oxygen does not immediately recycle back into the ocean but instead becomes part of the large ice sheets. The heavy oxygen isotope (^{18}O) becomes more common in oceans during these colder intervals. This colder isotope ratio is recorded in the shells of ocean-living organisms. When warmer global climatic intervals prevail, the lighter isotope, which had been trapped in the ice, returns to the ocean. Thus, during interglacials, there is proportionately less ^{18}O in the oceans. The changes in oxygen isotope ratios have been used to connect artifact-bearing deposits with climate chronologies. On the southern coast of the Mediterranean the Paleolithic archaeological sequence at Haua Fteah was correlated and dated with isotopic values. At Klassies River Mouth, Shackleton used oxygen isotope evidence to date shell-midden deposits associated with Middle Stone Age (MSA) artifacts.[34] The variation in oxygen isotopes from the shell-midden deposits was correlated with the deep-sea isotope record. The matches indicated that the MSA I midden contained shell that could be isotopically matched with substage 5e (see appendix A.4) of the continuous marine record. This was a period when the oxygen isotope composition of the ocean was as light as at present. Isotopes of the shells from the younger, MSA II horizon seem comparable to either substages 5c or 5a. Based on these matches, and the estimated age of substages 5e, 5b, and 5c, it is possible to apply the oxygen isotopic composition of the shells to the dating of the MSA I and MSA II horizons using uranium-series techniques (see Chapter 7). MSA I artifacts matched with 5e probably date from about 130,000–120,000 B.P. while MSA II artifacts matched with either the 5a or 5c date from around 105,000–75,000 B.P.[35]

Variation in isotopic ^{18}O measurements has been used to help explain the collapse of the Tiwanaku state in the Andes of South America between A.D. 1000 and 1100.[36] Based in part on the oxygen isotope record from the Quelleccaya ice cap, temperatures can be inferred to have increased beginning around 1000 and continued to at least 1400 (figure 4.4). This temperature rise in South America seems to have been part of a global warming interval that lasted until the Little Ice Age. Higher values of ^{18}O are associated with decrease in ice accumulation. The tempera-

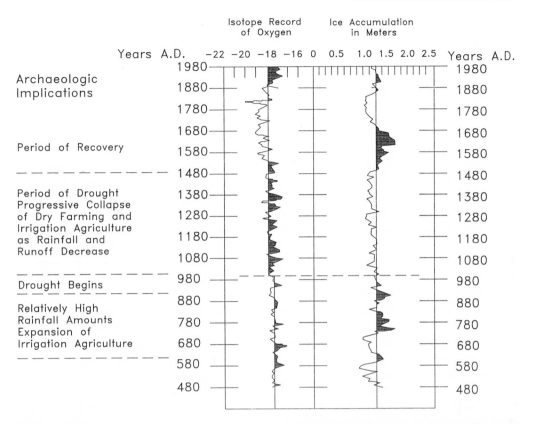

Figure 4.4 Relation of Ice Core Record to Agricultural Patterns
Fluctuations in the oxygen isotope record and accumulation of glacier ice used to interpret the human prehistory of the Andes. High amounts of rainfall before A.D. 880 can be related to an expansion of irriga-

tion agriculture in the region. An interval of increased drought is represented by low amounts of ice accumulation; isotope values above −18 occurred between about 980 and 1480. The human response to this climatic change appears to be reflected by a collapse in dry farming and irrigation agriculture.

ture rise in the Queleccaya region may have been associated with a simultaneous drop in precipitation. These climatic changes appear to have profoundly affected the human populations of South America. The decrease in precipitation may have hurt the agricultural base of the Tiwanaku and ultimately led to the collapse of their political system.

Isotope ratios derived from the remains of plants and animals have also been used to interpret prehistoric human subsistence and settlement systems. Stable carbon and nitrogen isotopic values have been used to indicate the presence of maize and the relative proportion of marine and terrestrial food consumed by prehistoric human

populations. Changes in the environmental landscape inferred from the character of and constituents within sediment/soil sequences can be used to develop models of climate change. These models can then be employed to evaluate the habitat context associated with human occupation.

Environmental Change and Archaeological Interpretation

Human Habitats and Geoecology
Evidence for alternating glacial and interglacial periods and even finer-scaled (short-term) environmental-climatic intervals can be found in

the stratigraphic record using the paleoecologic methods described earlier in this chapter. Since the Late Pliocene changes in global climate are reflected in the fluctuations between glacial and interglacial conditions. Major changes in the behavior of humans may be associated with the end of the last glacial interval and the beginning of the present interglacial, the Holocene. The impact of the earth's environmental and climatic patterns on human physical and behavioral development, and the effect of prehistoric human behavior on changing environmental landscapes, can be pursued by means of a geoarchaeological approach as part of a broader geoecologic perspective.

Human-earth interaction is reciprocal. Environmental conditions have influenced humans, and humanity has had an increasing impact on landscape habitats. The concept of "environmental determinism" was first promoted to explain the origin of agriculture as being climatically influenced in Gordon Childe's *Most Ancient Near East*. At about the same time, Ellsworth Huntington and C. E. P. Brookes argued that major changes in human society were a result of fluctuations in climate. Environmental determinism was out of favor with anthropological archaeologists between 1960 and 1980, but it seems to be regaining some credence—for example, there is strong evidence for a close temporal correlation between climatic change and the origins of agriculture. Gordon Willey and Philip Phillips' 1955 observation about North America that the shift at the beginning of the Early Archaic was not so much cultural as it was environmental, would not now be considered controversial. Paleoecologic research has supported the general idea postulated by Childe in the 1920s that the agricultural revolution in the Near East was a response by people to climatic events.[37]

Changes in climate have affected the physical and biotic contexts associated with human occupation throughout the Quaternary. For example, large lakes that once existed in currently dry areas disappeared because of major regional and global paleoclimatic events. In the hyperarid eastern Sahara of today, sedimentary deposits indicating past **pluvial** conditions during the Middle and Early Upper Pleistocene are associated with Acheulian and Middle Paleolithic artifact assemblages. Many remnants are composed of indurated lake marls that show the earlier presence of large, perennial bodies of water. Fish bones within some of the lakebeds indicate the presence of streams connecting the lakes. No younger Upper Paleolithic artifacts have as yet been found. The absence of artifacts might be explained by a hyperarid interval during the late Upper Pleistocene that made the region uninhabitable. Playa deposits associated with the Terminal Pleistocene and Early Holocene contain Neolithic artifacts marking the return of habitats suitable for human occupation.

Large lakes also appear to have formed in northern Chile around 14,000–9000 B.P. The earliest human occupations of this region are associated with Terminal Pleistocene and Early Holocene beaches of lakes. High lake stands in the Andes appear to be related to glacial retreat and widespread aridity that developed from around 8500 to 5000 B.P. Human occupation appears to have occurred before and after this arid interval (from 11,000 to 8000 B.P. and then again from 5500 to 4000 B.P.).

Loess deposits can provide indications of climate change that may have affected prehistoric human populations (see also Chapter 7, figure 7.3). In Argentina at Cerro La China, the stratigraphic sequence contains three episodes of loess deposition and several soil horizons associated with archaeological materials. Paleo-Indian materials dated to around 10,600 B.P. were recovered from the lowest loess. A soil-forming interval occurred after the deposition of this loess, which lasted to about 5000 B.P., and which was followed by a period of erosion. A second cycle of loess deposition, soil formation, and later erosion occurred in the Later Holocene and was followed by a short eolian episode. There are also important Quaternary loess-soil sequences in China, Europe, and central North America that provide clues to geoecologic conditions associated with human occupation of these regions.

Stratified Holocene sedimentary and archaeological contexts within the Upper Delaware Valley of Pennsylvania also appear to reflect regional climatic change. This sequence consists of Archaic and Woodland components. Sediments containing evidence of several major changes in depositional processes also reflect paleoenvironmental changes. The Early Archaic artifacts are found in deposits dated to around 9000 B.P. A decrease in landscape stability and increase in deposition from flood events occurred during the mid-Holocene and is associated with Middle Archaic artifacts (around 6000–5000 B.P.). Late Archaic and Middle and Late Woodland components are also present in the sequence.

During the middle of the tenth millennium B.P., the site of Starr Carr on the sun-exposed north shore of an ancient lake (Glacial Lake Pickering) in Yorkshire, England, provided a resource-rich location for a seasonal camp of the prehistoric human inhabitants.[38] Almost all of the raw materials (flint, clay, birch bark, glacial boulders) used at the site were no more than an hour's walk away. Abundant red deer apparently provided most of the animal protein for the humans. Geoarchaeological sediment coring has helped us determine the sequence of environments and provided a detailed picture of the geoecologic landscape setting associated with Starr Carr. Where the sediment core showed woody coarse detritus, it was interpreted as representing a former **fen carr**. Reed peat was interpreted as the deposit of a reed swamp. Fine detrital mud was taken to represent a marginal open-water environment, while calcareous mud deposits were interpreted as indicating open water.

The site was located at the mouth of a shallow gully on the southern slope of a low hill of glacial till that extended into Glacial Lake Pickering near the entrance to the lake's narrow outflow channel. The occupation area was situated where the open water most closely approached the shore. It seems that during Early Mesolithic times there was great variation in the vegetation of the lake margin. At about 9800 B.P., open water lapped the shore, leaving only a narrow fringe of reeds and sedges. By 9650 B.P., just before human occupation, a reed swamp extended well into the lake. During the period of occupation (beginning about 9600 B.P.), the reed swamp was replaced by fen, and the area of the site was covered mostly by ferns. The inhabitants put down a wood matte to consolidate ground formerly covered by damp fen. By 9300 B.P. the occupation was over and a fen on which willows were growing covered the site again.

Other ecofacts were employed to infer past environments and the kinds of resources that had been used at Starr Carr. Pollen analyses indicated that at the time of occupation, pine and birch probably covered the surrounding area. Other pollen types indicated the presence of open areas that may have been forest clearings. Antlers from deer and elk were used to establish the seasons in which the site was inhabited. Interdisciplinary paleoenvironmental investigations of this nature allow a clear picture of the ancient landscape setting to emerge.

Tectonics, Climates, Landscapes, and the Human Past

One of the major integrating concepts in the earth sciences is that of tectonics. Many of the geologic and biologic features associated with the archaeological record can be more fully understood within the context of plate-tectonic theory. The basic idea of plate tectonics is that parts of the earth's crust are being created, moved, and destroyed by the internal processes of the earth. At some places, like East Africa, for example, parts of the earth are separating, spreading, or "rifting." At other places, like the Himalayas, the collision of pieces of the earth's crust resulted in the creation of mountain ranges. In yet other areas—along the Pacific coast of South America, for example—oceanic crust has been moved under (or subducted) continental crust, which has led to volcanic activity and mountain building.

Throughout the world the tectonic-related effects of mountain building, faulting, earthquakes, and volcanism have influenced the prehistoric record. Earth movements, or faulting, associated with crustal rifting resulted in the creation of lakes used by prehistoric humans, as well as in the exposure and discovery of sediments containing hominid remains and artifacts. Volcanism associated with rifting or subduction led to the interbedding of fossil and artifact-bearing sediments with datable lava flows and ash deposits. The creation of mountain ranges is thought to have dramatically altered the global climate system, causing both geomorphic and biologic reactions.

There is a consensus among scientists that many large-scale climatic changes inferred from the prehistoric record are a result of tectonic events. The climatic cooling observed in the marine record for the Cenozoic interval (the time since sixty-five million years ago) generally and the fluctuations of climate observed during the Quaternary (the past three million years) in particular can be explained at least in part as the result of crustal movements caused by tectonic processes. Several major climatic cooling events may be the result of the rifting of continental crust or collisions of fragments or plates of the earth's crust (or lithosphere). One of these tectonic connections resulted in the creation of the Isthmus of Panama. This and other tectonic events has been implicated in changes in climatic patterns which resulted in the interglacial and glacial episodes of the past three million years. The climatic fluctuations between glacial and nonglacial episodes affected the physical and biotic habitats associated with human evolution and the formation of the archaeological record.

Climate, through direct expression as temperature and precipitation, or in vegetation, is an important factor in the nature and intensity of geomorphic processes. Major climate changes are particularly significant in the long-term stability of land surfaces and soil formation. Since Holocene climates have deviated significantly from present-day climates, the geomorphic responses will be preserved in sedimentary sequences and in landforms in many places.

On the floodplains of the major river systems, flooding plays a key role in the erosion and transportation of sediments and ultimately in the stability of landforms. Floodplain systems develop a quasi-equilibrium morphology that a change in climate may destabilize.

Data on river runoff and from U.S. watersheds indicate two critical vegetation boundaries of geomorphic significance. In grasslands in the temperate zone, where the mean annual temperature is about 10°C, vegetation becomes sparse when annual precipitation drops below about 500 mm.[39] The second boundary occurs where the mean annual precipitation is about 800–900 mm and mean annual temperature is about

10°C. Under these conditions grassland grades into forest. In undisturbed forests, if the mean annual precipitation is more than 900 mm, there is little overland runoff. Grasslands in good condition are nearly as effective as soil cover in reducing overland flow but may lose this effectiveness in reducing runoff and erosion during droughts.

Past changes in precipitation are less well understood than past changes in temperature. There is a general tendency for middle latitudes to experience increased precipitation during cool climate episodes, the most recent of which was the Little Ice Age.

Regional responses in sediment yields should mirror Holocene climate changes. Such responses vary with the contextual climatic regime. A change to warmer and drier conditions would decrease annual sediment yield in the arid U.S. southwest, while increasing annual sediment yields in the midcontinent grassland. The Holocene flood record can be reconstructed from dated paleochannels.

The intensity of lateral channel migration varies with flood magnitudes. This has a major effect on locations of long-term habitation. Relatively modest changes of mean annual temperature and precipitation have been associated with relatively large adjustments in major flooding in the Mississippi flood record. The erosion, transportation, and deposition of fluvial sediments is an episodic process because of dependency on surface runoff and high-stage flows. These characteristics of floods play a key role in the stability and evolution of alluvial landforms and the ability of humans to live in this important environment.

Human Interaction with Environment and Its Effects on Climate

In the earth-surface environment, the lithosphere is the most stable component. Despite long-term patterns of instability associated with plate movements or short-term instability like volcanic eruptions, earthquakes, faulting, and related events, the lithosphere is far less dynamic than the atmosphere and hydrosphere. Powered by the immense energy from the sun, they are not easily modified by human intervention. But the local climate can be altered. The change from forest to open field alters the local heat balance and produces greater temperature extremes at the soil surface.

The biosphere is the environment most easily modified by human activity. Out of the "wilderness," Neolithic humans created settled communities and agriculture. This was an apparent step forward for the stability of human communities, but it led to new instability for the environment. The widespread onset of human use of fire brought enormous alterations to the floral environment. The forests of the subtropical and middle latitudes are now only a shadow of their primeval selves.

Humans have affected geoecologic systems through the clearing of forest for agricultural purposes. Deforestation in the Mediterranean basin was a long and complex process. Sedimentary sequences in the Mediterranean region appear to reflect two periods of erosion during the Holocene that are associated with human activity. The first erosional and aggradational interval was initiated during the Late Neolithic/Early Bronze Ages and had its strongest signal between around 3800 and 3100 B.P. From about A.D. 200 to 500, a second interval of erosion was initiated because of human abandonment of terraced hillsides. Somewhat contradictory evidence is available concerning the climate during the Bronze Age in central Europe. This was formerly considered a period of cooling after the postglacial thermal maximum. But low groundwater tables during the period strongly indicate a prolonged dry period. (Pollen analyses are probably unreliable over short periods where human interference is strong, because of activities like forest clearance.)

Landscapes in Mesoamerica were also modified because of increased agriculture. Increases in human population and expanded agricultural use of the landscape in Guatemala between about 3,500 and 1,000 years ago have been related to changes in pollen, clays, organic matter, carbonates, and phosphates in lacustrine sedimentary sequences. In western Mexico three intervals of erosion have been correlated with increased human agricultural practices.

A 1995 study provides an excellent review of landscape-human interactions in the Archaic Period in North America.[40] The Archaic (Middle Holocene) was a period of landscape and climate change that accompanied a dramatic evolution in human social organization, technological innovation, and trade networks. This volume should be consulted for its examples of the reciprocal relationship of change across the human and geomorphic-climatic landscapes.

By the later Holocene, along the west coast of North America, prehistoric hunting and plant gathering were facilitated by the deliberate setting of fires. This affected the natural landscape. Burning was used to control the growth of brush and promote the growth of plants and increase deer populations. According to eighteenth- and nineteenth-century accounts, the Chumash people promoted the growth of specific plant foods by burning. In the Great Basin, the Shoshone and other communities burned the natural vegetation to increase the yields of plants, to increase food for game animals, and to drive prey toward ambush. In North America, slightly less than half the area of Canada and the United States was forested when the first European settlers arrived. A third of these forests are now gone.

Within the geoecologic system, vegetation and soil are interdependent. If change occurs in the vegetative cover, the character of the supporting soil will be altered. The human alteration of the landscape is recorded in the soils, paleosols, and archaeological and related geologic sediments. The influence people have on the features of the earth is directly connected to the types of behavior they use to adapt to and function in the environment. Usually, human-earth interaction comparisons are based on the effect particular subsistence strategies had on modifying the original landscape. Hunter-gatherers and foragers are often considered to have had a relatively low impact on the natural environment. This is arguably not so in some instances.

A very early impact on the "natural" landscape by humans may stem from their control and use of fire. Evidence suggests that humans may have used fire about 1.4 million years ago at the site of Cheswoanja in Kenya. Human use of fire resulted in major transformations of the biotic and physical landscape. Another major impact resulted from hunting. Along with climate change, Late Paleolithic human migration into the Americas has been implicated as a factor in the extinction of biotic communities at the end of the Pleistocene. Human hunting also seems to have had a major impact on the vegetation and landscape of New Zealand. Hunting, the domestication of animals, and the initiation of agriculture had significant consequences for Holocene landscapes.

Apart from the instances where direct ethological observations are available, it is difficult to distinguish between natural modifications to the environment and impacts caused by human behavior. It is often difficult to determine whether a fire was natural or deliberately set by humans, but sometimes it is easier to guess than others. The charcoal frequencies found in a sediment sequence in Australia associated with the last interglacial before human occupation are much lower than the frequencies found in Holocene sediments, when humans were present.

Patterns of Holocene erosion and deposition linked to landscape modification caused by human activities have been found in the sedimentologic record of lakes. The biologic, mineralogic, and chemical components associated with lake sediments can be used to infer human activities. Mesolithic and Neolithic landscape use during the mid-Holocene in Britain led to increases in fine-grained clastics and salt concentrations associated with a decrease in forests. Pollen diagrams from northwest Europe have been used to trace patterns of land clearance and cultivation starting in the early Neolithic. In Asia charcoal concentrations from sediments near the central Thailand archaeological site of Khok Phanom Di (around 6000–3000 B.P.) may reflect the deliberate burning of mangrove vegetation during the first occupation and later vegetational disturbances of the Middle Holocene landscape.

Major modifications of the natural environment during the Holocene throughout many parts of the world can be directly related to human behavior. Farming and herding have had an important impact on landscape development because they can disturb the natural hydrologic, pedogenic, and sedimentologic processes that affect the landscape. Human behavior influences the

soil-sediment system in a variety of ways that also affect the processes of erosion and deposition. Devegetation through burning, clearance, and grazing disrupts the natural patterns and increases the effects of precipitation. Soil loosening caused by cultivation or animals also increases surface-water runoff and erosion.

Changes in hydrologic and groundwater conditions and soil-water relations (soil moisture) can have a major impact on the environment. Higher water tables can cause increased leaching. Seasonal dehydration can eventually cause the development of waterlogged areas. Extremely dry conditions, with dramatic drops in the groundwater table (as is currently occurring in the Ogallala aquifer under the American Great Plains), may lead to devegetation and the consequent erosion of previously fertile soils. Irrigation can also lead to the concentration of salt in the soil, making the soil unusable for agriculture.

Human construction activities have had direct effects on the soil-sediment system, primarily by modifying the drainage of water. Terraces, dams, and irrigation ditches used to increase moisture retention also cause the accumulation of sediments. Roads and paths lead to increased erosion, and buildings concentrate runoff, which also increases erosion. The construction of burial mounds, the accumulation of tell debris and middens, and the development of spoil heaps associated with mines also modify landscapes.

One can demonstrate that fluctuating patterns of erosion, deposition, and stability have occurred by means of the soil-sediment record, but evaluating whether human activities or natural processes have caused these patterns is not always as easy. Plowing causes distinct soil horizons to be mixed and leads to increased erosion. Eroded sediments and soils from upland or upslope areas will eventually be deposited in footslope areas, in floodplains, or in deltas: Increased deposition can lead to increases in the thickness of the A horizon or even complete burial of the soil. Intervals of erosion and deposition (aggradation) may be interrupted by periods of stability that can be recognized by the presence of fossil A soil horizons.

In addition to environmental modifications to improve hunting or promote plant growth, some changes in animal populations have been attributed to humans who were hunter-gatherers. Again, it is difficult to differentiate between natural changes and modifications caused by human activity. Perhaps the best-known example of the problem is the controversy over whether climate change or human predation caused the extinction of the large mammals in North America at the end of the Pleistocene.

From a geoecologic perspective it could be suggested that Paleolithic humans (including Paleo-american populations) and the now-extinct large Pleistocene animals were both affected by changing biotic patterns that prevailed during the Pleistocene-Holocene transition. In this sense climatic change can be considered the prime mover in the changes. Different parts of the geo-ecologic system reacted in independent ways, thus causing a variety of interrelated patterns. Climate change resulted in the extinction of Pleistocene plant communities, as individual plant taxa responded to changes in precipitation, temperature, and soil development. Large herbivores were forced either to change their behavior (e.g., migrating with the plants on which they most depended) or to change physically to adapt to the new ecological setting better; or they became extinct. The animals that depended on the larger herbivores (predators, carnivores) or relied on both plants and animals (omnivores) also had to change. In this sense the differences between Paleo-Indian and later artifactual patterns can be viewed as either the extinction of human behaviors predicated upon the ecological patterns of the Pleistocene or the modification (adaptation) of these behaviors to fit the new Holocene ecological habitats.

Microclimates

Microclimates have a far greater influence on life forms than generally realized. Small-scale inter-actions between air, water, solar heat, the earth's surface, rocks and soils, and its vegetation have not received sufficient attention. Although evaluating microclimatic evidence for habitation sites is difficult, some general principles remain, for example: weather is usually much more severe on the windward side of large hills; wind speeds are amplified and accelerated at ridge tops; in the northern temperate zone, solar energy is more abundant on south-sloping hills; and although it is colder higher up in the atmosphere, at ground level cold air and frost settle in low-lying areas.

Microclimates are generated within a relatively thin layer of air near the ground. This is where the atmosphere interacts with soil, rocks, water, vegetation, and human-made objects. Here the atmosphere is influenced by surfaces that either reflect or absorb solar energy during the day and radiate energy back into the air at night. Water retains solar radiation longer than solids, while surface sediments and soils radiate it back into the atmosphere quite quickly. Heat exchanges are most pronounced between land and water bodies. Valleys produce their own wind systems; the greatest variety of microclimates, therefore, are where offshore air meets rugged landforms.

In parts of the earth that receive winter snow, lake-effect snow and the ability of vegetation to trap snow in drifts can account for vast differences in microclimates. In agriculture some crops, such as citrus, are sensitive to low temperatures during certain times of the growing cycle—a freeze can destroy not only the crop but the trees.

Geoarchaeologists are asked to assist in paleo-climatic reconstruction. To do so, they must assess everything from deforestation and microclimatic niches to broad climatic change in developing an environmental context. Chapters 2, 3, and 4 have provided some of the major earth-science methodologies needed to make these assessments.

CHAPTER 5

Raw Materials and Resources

The excavation of an archaeological site usually brings to light only a small portion of the material culture of a society. Because artifacts of rocks and minerals as well as the debris produced during their manufacture are stable in the earth-surface environment, they make up a large part of what is recovered. Most inorganic remains are derived from geologic raw materials. From early Paleolithic tools through building materials and ceramics to sophisticated metal alloys, the source materials are rocks and minerals. By the end of predynastic times the following had been used for stone vessels in Egypt: alabaster, basalt, diorite, granite, gypsum, limestone, marble, schist, serpentine, and steatite. By Neolithic times stone was being used for construction in Cyprus and the Near East. At Tell es-Sultan, near Jericho in Palestine, stone was being used for house walls by about 6000 B.C.

Let us begin with some basic definitions. A *rock* is a specific aggregate of one or more minerals that occurs commonly enough to be given a name (granite, limestone). A *mineral* is a naturally occurring inorganic element or compound having a specific crystal structure and a characteristic chemical composition (quartz, mica). Obsidian is a volcanic glass that has not yet crystallized but in all other respects is a rock. Our section below on rocks describes the three genetic types of rocks recognized by the geologic sciences and provides a basic nomenclature. The word *stone* has many meanings. Within a geoarchaeological context the usage should be restricted to building stone and gemstone.

Archaeologists use the word *lithic* (from the Greek *lithos*, meaning "stone" or "rock") for materials and artifacts made from rocks or minerals.

Geologic nomenclature also makes extensive use of this Greek root: *lithification* (the compaction and cementation of an unconsolidated sediment into a coherent, solid rock), *lithology* (the description of the characteristics of a rock, such as color, mineralogy, and grain size), and *lithosphere* (the solid portion of the earth, as contrasted with atmosphere and hydrosphere).

Lithic resources have been used since our hominid ancestors first threw stones and made stone tools. The ancient Greeks and Romans had specific names for a large number of common rocks and minerals. The Greek natural scientist Theophrastus published his *On Stones* in the fourth century B.C., and the last five books of Pliny's *Natural History* (first century A.D.) are devoted chiefly to the consideration of lithic materials. Pliny discusses approximately 150 separate rock and mineral species and indicates that there are many more that he does not discuss. Many names of common rocks and minerals come down to us from these early times. From Theophrastus, we have derived *alabaster, agate, amethyst, azurite, crystal (quartz), lapis lazuli, malachite,* and *obsidian.*[1] There is a vast array of archaeological lithic materials. Here, we have concentrated on those rocks and minerals that geoarchaeologists are likely to encounter in Old World and New World contexts.

Minerals

Chert and Chalcedony
There are more than 3,000 mineral species. The chemical and structural makeup of the various species gives each a distinct set of physical prop-

erties, such as color, hardness, cohesiveness, and characteristic fracture. Chemical composition is the key characteristic in determining how certain minerals—like the ore minerals, which provide metals—were used in the past.

Long before the development of writing, humans recognized such distinct mineral properties as hardness, cohesiveness, and color. They used hard, cohesive jade for adzes and formed tools and weapons from fine-grained varieties of quartz. Red hematite and black manganese oxide minerals were used in cave paintings. Brightly colored minerals provided ornaments. Technological development led to the mining and smelting of ore minerals to produce copper, lead, silver, and iron.

The hardness of a mineral is defined as its resistance to scratching. Hardness was quantified by the Austrian mineralogist Friedrich Mohs, who proposed the following scale of relative hardness in 1922: 1) Talc, 2) Gypsum, 3) Calcite, 4) Fluorite, 5) Apatite, 6) Orthoclase, 7) Quartz, 8) Topaz, 9) Corundum, 10) Diamond. Each of the minerals lower in the scale can be scratched by those higher in the scale. The scale is not linear; in absolute hardness diamond is three orders of magnitude harder than talc.

Hardness is an important diagnostic property in the field identification of minerals. In addition to the minerals in the scale, the following materials serve as handy references for hardness (on the Mohs scale): fingernail: 2 to 2.5; copper coin: approximately 3; pocket knife: 5 to 5.5; window glass: 5.5; steel file: 6.5.

Rocks, per se, as assemblages of minerals do not have Mohs hardnesses, although some monomineralic rocks like quartzite and marble will exhibit the hardness of their constituent mineral. A rock like granite, composed of orthoclase and quartz, would exhibit a Mohs hardness of between 6 and 7. However, the importance of granite for building stone lies not in its hardness but in its cohesiveness and its mechanical strength. Granite was used for hammer stone as much as for its cohesiveness and lack of tendency to fracture as for its hardness.

Rocks and minerals composed chiefly of quartz make up a large percentage of lithic artifacts. Quartz is the most stable of all minerals under sedimentary conditions and in the earth's surface environment. Few areas of lithic nomenclature are as confusing as that of fine-grained varieties of quartz (SiO_2), and *chert* has been used as a general term for any fine-grained siliceous rock of chemical, biochemical, or biogenic origin. Chert is usually a very hard compact material that fractures conchoidally when struck. (Quartz has a Mohs hardness of 7, and chert can be between 75 and 99 percent quartz.)

In a comprehensive monograph on chert and flint, archaeologist B. E. Luedtke opts for using *chert* as the general term for all rocks composed primarily of microcrystalline quartz.[2] Our approach differs only slightly. For example, we distinguish chalcedony from chert because it has a different structure (fibrous) that is easy to recognize under the petrographic microscope.

Chert occurs as bedded deposits, discontinuous lenses, and nodules that are usually interstratified with chalk, limestone, or dolomite. Chert is microcrystalline quartz composed of interlocking, often roughly equigranular, grains. It can be almost any color and accommodate a wide variety of impurities which affect its workability in lithic manufacture. Grain size also has a significant effect on fracture properties.

The chief varieties of chert of interest in archaeology are flint, jasper, and novaculite. The term *flint* should be used primarily for the gray-to-black nodular chert found in chalk and marly limestone. It is very fine-grained and tough, and it often has directional properties that are of value in flint knapping. Impurities are usually less than 1 percent and consist chiefly of sponge spicules and calcite. The best flints of Europe occur in chalk beds.

Jasper is a common, widespread red chert. It is usually fine-grained and dense, with up to 20 percent iron oxide. Jasper from the eastern desert has been used in Egypt since predynastic times for beads, amulets, and scarabs.

Novaculite is a white, unlaminated microgranular quartz of uniform grain size. It is not common and so is of special archaeological importance when it is found as an artifact.

Chalcedony is also microcrystalline quartz, but texturally it is composed of radiating fibers in bundles. (The texture can be established by microscope examination.) This texture is more porous than that of chert, and in addition, chalcedony has a more greasy luster than chert. Chalcedony has no significant impurities and so tends to be whitish, although many chalcedonies turn red with heating. The name comes from Chalcedon, an ancient maritime city on the Sea of Marmara in Turkey.

Semiprecious Stones

Semiprecious stones are gemstones of lesser value than precious stones like diamond and emerald. They usually have a hardness of 7 or less on the Mohs scale. The most common semiprecious stones used by ancient craftsmen are varieties of quartz. We shall list here only the most important varieties of macroscopic quartz crystals for archaeology.

Amethyst, which is of bluish, reddish, or purplish violet color, can occur in large crystals (15 cm long). It was used in Hellenistic and Roman times for engraved seal stones. The name comes from the ancient Greek word for "not drunken": an amethyst amulet was supposed to protect from intoxication. Amethyst was also one of the twelve gemstones worn by ancient Israelite high priests to represent the twelve tribes of Israel, and amethyst mines in Egypt are known from Old Kingdom times. As early as the First Dynasty (2920–2770 B.C.) in Egypt, amethyst was used for beads (in bracelets and necklaces), amulets, and scarabs. The Romans exploited amethyst from the eastern desert, where it occurs in cavities in a reddish granite.

Rock Crystal is clear quartz in large crystals, used extensively in ancient times for everything from small seals to large vases. Diverse ancient societies (Greek, Roman, Chinese, Japanese) thought of these clear crystals in the same way; each group referred to them as "permanent ice." Predynastic Egyptians mined rock crystal north of Aswan. Ancient Egyptians coveted rock crystal for beads, vases, and filling in the corneas of eyes in statues and coffins.

By the eighth century, the rock crystal deposits of Mutsu Province, Japan, were developed on a commercial scale. Because quartz crystals break with a sharp conchoidal fracture, they were used in North America for projectile points. Some archaeologists have used the term *rock crystal* for the quartz of these points.

Varieties of fine-grained crystalline quartz were also used for seal stones, jewelry, amulets, and related objects. Many of the names date from antiquity. The most important varieties were agate, carnelian, and sard.

Agate is a varicolored quartz; the colors often occur in irregular or concentric bands. Sometimes agate contains mossy or dendritic inclusions that give the impression of landscapes or vegetation. Known from ancient times—its name comes from the Achates River in Sicily—agate has been used for projectile points and mortars, as well as for cups, bowls, and bottles. The Sumerians used agate in ceremonial ax heads. Engraved agates were highly esteemed by the ancient Romans. One Roman two-handled wine cup made of agate had a capacity of more than 550 ml and an exterior carved with Bacchanalian themes. The prophet Muhammed wore a signet of Yemen agate.

Carnelian is a red (sometimes deep blood red) variety of quartz that may be transparent or translucent. Carnelian is found abundantly as pebbles in the eastern desert of Egypt. It was used in Egypt from predynastic times on for beads, amulets, and inlay in jewelry, furniture, and coffins. In the classical world carnelian was used for sealing rings and seal stones. *Sard* is similar to carnelian but more brown and opaque in appearance. It is the *sardion* of Theophrastus, named from Sardis, the capital of ancient Lydia in Anatolia.

Onyx and *sardonyx* are banded forms of silica. In onyx and sardonyx the bands are usually straight and comparatively regular; in onyx, milk-white bands alternate with blackish bands, while in sardonyx, white bands alternate with reddish brown or red, as the name implies (onyx alternating with sard).

A related mineral, *opal* ($SiO_2 . H_2O$), occurs in many colors and has been popular since antiquity. The name is believed to derive from the Sanskrit word meaning "precious stone." The use of opal as a gemstone in antiquity dates back to the fifth century B.C., when it was mined in Slovakia. Its use was prevalent in ancient India, and it was a favorite gem of the Romans, who mined it in Hungary. Opal and onyx were mentioned in the first book of the Bible. In the Americas, gem opal is found in a belt of scattered deposits that stretches from the northwestern United States through Central America to Brazil. Some Mexican opal was taken back to Europe by explorers as early as 1520. It has also found favor as a material for projectile points. Opal cannot long survive exposure to the effects of surface weathering. It tends to lose water and become cracked and opaque. Opal from quarry discard piles becomes chalk white and crazed.

The nonquartz semiprecious stones most commonly found in archaeological sites are lapis lazuli, jade, and turquoise. *Lapis lazuli* is a mixture of complex silicates that exhibits a range of colors from deep blue to azure blue and from greenish blue to violet blue. It has a hardness of 5–6, depending on impurities. It has been used for at least 7,000 years; in predynastic Egypt, it was a favorite material for cylindrical and flat seals, scarabs, beads, pendants, and amulets. Lapis lazuli was also used as a pigment. The most important source was at Baldachin, Afghanistan, a mining area that Marco Polo visited and described in 1271. There it occurs in large blocks and crystals in a white calcite matrix. Although it was popular in antiquity in China, India, Sumer, Israel, Egypt, Greece, and Rome, the modern name dates only from the Middle Ages and derives from the Latin word for stone (*lapis*) and the Persian word for blue (*lazhward*). The Romans and Israelites called it saphiris.

Jade can be one of two minerals: jadeite (a **pyroxene** with a hardness of 6.5–7) or nephrite (an **amphibole** with a hardness of 6–6.5). Jadeite is somewhat more vitreous, nephrite more oily in appearance. Nephrite is generally more cohesive because of its texture of interlocking fibers. The coloring of jadeite comes from minor chromium; it can be a rich emerald green. Jade can also be bluish, purplish, or even reddish. The Chinese have made extensive use of jade since the beginning of the Neolithic; they acquired their nephrite pebbles from Burma (where it occurs in serpentinite in boulders that can weigh up to several tons) and from Chinese Turkestan.[3] Burmese jade occurs in a wide range of colors. The Aztecs and

Mayans also used jade extensively,[4] although it has been found less commonly in archaeological contexts in other parts of North and South America. Throughout history many names have been used for jade, and many materials have been called jade, so considerable uncertainty exists about early references to it. The name in English dates only to 1727 and comes from the Spanish term *piedra de yjada*, meaning "stone of the side"—an allusion to its supposed powers to cure side pains.[5]

Turquoise is a blue or bluish-green mineral with a hardness of 5–6. It is a secondary mineral usually found in small veins in weathered volcanic rocks in arid regions. Some turquoise will change color as a result of dehydration shortly after mining. Turquoise was highly prized by, among others, Pre-Columbian societies of the American southwest, the ancient Egyptians (as early as the Neolithic), and many other groups throughout the ancient Near East. The famous Persian mines were found near Nishapur in the province of Khorasan. The name *turquoise* is French, meaning Turkish, the original stones having come into Europe through Turkey from Persia.

In the southwestern United States—principally New Mexico—turquoise deposits were mined in prehistoric times. In some ancient quarries, stone mauls, pecks, and chisels have been recovered. There is evidence that the common technique of heating and quenching the bedrock was used to free the turquoise. In southern North America (Mesoamerica) turquoise was in common use. Aztec ruins contain many human skulls that were completely covered with turquoise.

The *feldspars* are a group of silicates that are the most common minerals in the earth's crust. They are major constituents of most igneous rocks. Feldspars are generally dull, cloudy, and fairly opaque, so they have not been sought after as ornamental "stones." They have, however, been found in archaeological contexts and as important constituents of igneous rocks. The common feldspars are orthoclase, plagioclase, and microcline. Semiprecious stone varieties of feldspar include sunstone, moonstone, and amazonstone. Indigenous Americans used all three as gems: moonstone by various groups in Mexico, sunstone by the Apaches in Arizona, and amazonstone by the

Aztecs, Mayans, and Indians of Venezuela, Brazil, Trinidad, Wisconsin, and California.

Other Archaeologically Important Minerals

In addition to semiprecious stones of considerable hardness a number of softer minerals were widely used in similar fashion. *Alabaster*, a fine-grained, cohesive variety of the mineral gypsum, usually has a whitish to pinkish color. It is quite soft: its Mohs hardness of 2 is less than that of a fingernail. Alabaster was employed in ancient Egypt from early dynastic times as a subsidiary building material to line passages and rooms. It was also popular for funerary vessels that contained the viscera of mummies. Some Egyptian material called alabaster is actually fine-grained calcite, which has a hardness of 3. Most New Kingdom stone vessels were alabaster (both true alabaster and calcite). The name comes from the Greek word *alabastros;* the Greeks used it to make ointment vases, and the Etruscans for vases, urns, and ornaments.

Malachite is a dark-green copper-carbonate hydrate with a hardness of 3.5–4.5. It was most likely the first mineral ever smelted (see the discussion of ores, below), but it has also been used since the Neolithic for beads and other ornaments. It occurs in the oxidized portions of copper ore deposits, especially in regions where limestone is present. Along with many other green minerals, malachite was much in favor with the ancient Egyptians for ornaments. Malachite was used as an eye-paint as far back as 5000 B.C. in Egypt. The name comes from the Greek *mallow* (resembling the color of the leaf of the mallow), in allusion to its green color.

Although it is not strictly a mineral, *amber* has been used as a precious stone since the Neolithic. Amber is fossilized tree resin from evergreens and lacks crystalline structure. Amber is brittle and breaks with a conchoidal fracture. It is soft enough to be cut easily by any metallic knife. Easy to shape, amber was used for a wide variety of ornaments and amulets. The Greeks and Romans so revered amber that it was reserved for the nobility.

Amber is found in many parts of the world, but the principal supply for Europe and the Near East has been the Baltic region, where it has even been collected from the Baltic Sea because it is buoyant enough to float on salt water. Baltic amber has been found in archaeological contexts as disparate as central Russia, Etruscan Italy, Mycenean Greece, Pharaonic Egypt, and early first millennium Mesopotamia.

The world's oldest amber comes from the Appalachian region of the United States. Other sources in the Americas are Manitoba, Alaska, the Atlantic seaboard, Mexico, Ecuador, and Colombia. A primary source is the Dominican Republic, where it is found in the north, the east, and the center of the country, near the village of Cotui. It was the first American gemstone recognized by Columbus (a necklace of amber was presented to him by the indigenous peoples of the Dominican Republic as a welcoming gift). Amber earplugs and beads were found in Tomb 7 near Monte Alban, Mexico, dating from around 1100. The Aztecs controlled the amber trade from their capital, Tenochtitlan. This trade network went through Chiapas, an outpost of the Aztec Empire. The Codex Mendoza mentions amber as part of the tribute materials paid to Montezuma by certain districts in Mexico. Amber was also in common use by the Eskimo.[6] In southeast Asia the major source of amber was Burma. Burmese amber has been imported into China since the Han Dynasty.

Often mistakenly called "black amber," *jet* is a compact and dense form of fossil coal. Geologists think that jet derives from water-logged pieces of driftwood. High-quality jet has a conchoidal fracture and no foreign matter like pyrite (common in most coal). Because it takes a high polish and is a deep, pure, velvety black, jet has often been used for ornaments. Its Mohs hardness varies between 3 and 4. The jet of Whitby, England, appears to have been used in Britain since pre-Roman times. In North America high-quality jet has been found in southern Colorado and Pictou, Nova Scotia.

The name *mica* derives from the Latin word meaning "to shine." Mica is not one mineral but a group of related sheet silicates, the most important of which is muscovite. Muscovite is colorless and transparent; with one perfect cleavage, it can occur in sheets called *books* that are as large as a meter across. It was therefore used for mirrors in ancient Nubia. Prehistoric societies throughout the Americas used muscovite. It was mined from many deposits in the Appalachian region and Alabama and traded as far west as the Mississippi River. From a single mound of the Mound Builders, more than 250 mica objects were recovered. Its name derives from its use as a substitute for glass in Old Russia (Muscovy).

Many of the large sheets of mica found in Hopewellian ceremonial contexts in eastern North America apparently came from the southern Appalachian region. Mica outcrops in western North Carolina were mined extensively in prehistoric times.[7]

A hydrous calcium sulfate, *gypsum* is a soft mineral that has many uses. It is a common mineral, widely distributed in sedimentary rocks, often as thick beds. The colorless, transparent variety called selenite can be found in large-cleavage sheets that have been used as windows since Roman times. Alabaster is another variety of gypsum. Gypsum has also been used widely as a plaster (its name comes from the Greek word for plaster), and it is the raw material for plaster of Paris. The Minoans used large gypsum blocks as building stone.

Common table *salt*, the mineral *halite* (NaCl) has been the source of salt for human nutritional needs from the beginning of human evolution. It has also served as a preservative, a medium of exchange, and a source of tax revenue. Salt oases lay on the caravan route through the Libyan Desert in the time of Herodotus. The salt mines of ancient India were the center of widespread trade. The salt of its harbor Ostia supplied some of Rome's needs. Those of Caesar's soldiers who were "worth their salt" received part of the pay (their *salarium*) in the form of salt. Throughout the world, salt takes little energy to exploit, and it has always been easily transported. It can be recovered by boiling sea water or merely by allowing the water to evaporate. Large-scale boiling of brine to recover salt dates back to the Iron Age in Europe.

Halite also occurs in major beds in many Triassic sedimentary rocks in central Europe and England. Halite deposits form when arms of the sea are cut off from a supply of water and dry up.

Sea water is about 2.5 percent NaCl. In coastal estuaries evaporation can increase this percentage to about 8 percent. Pliny identified and described the three different raw materials for salt production: rock-salt beds from evaporite deposits, brine, and sea water. In prehistoric Europe the rock-salt mines of the eastern Alps were a major source: the mines at Salzburg, Hallstatt, and Hallein were worked on a scale far exceeding local needs. Miners dug as far as 350 meters into the salt beds of the mountain sides.

In Mesoamerica, Yucatan was the greatest producer of salt. Salt beds extended along the coasts, where the salt was collected at the end of the dry season. Underwater excavations off the coast of Belize have uncovered a site where the Mayans produced salt from sea water more than 1,000 years ago. The salt trade was important in the development of Classic Mayan civilization. Plants have a very low sodium content, so inland agricultural societies need mineral salt. People in the tropics have high salt requirements because they sweat so much. They therefore were forced to import their salt. Salt was also recovered from Guatemalan wells.

Salt deposits can form from the hot brines of hot springs. Since around the year 1000, humans have excavated salt from brines and brine deposits originating in the Rift system in East Africa. Of special note are the deposits at Bunyoro on the eastern shore of Lake Albert.

In the Krakow region of Poland, the earliest salt-making sites date to the Middle Neolithic. Ditches, storage tanks, hearths, pits, and ceramics have all been recovered in association with salt making from brine springs. The brine was channeled through clay-lined ditches to prevent seepage into the sandy soil, into storage tanks, and into ceramic vessels used for heating and evaporation. The Krakow region also has salt mines that have been worked for more than 1,000 years from a layer of salt nearly 400 meters thick lying far beneath the surface. In Romania, many saltwater springs provided salt from the Neolithic through the Middle Ages.

In Japan the environment for salt production is poor. Although surrounded by salt water, the islands of Japan lack coastal flats for evaporation fields; in addition, they have too little sun. As a result, at least for the past 1,400 years, the Japanese have relied on a two-step process for concentration and evaporation. Seaweed soaked in seawater was dried, and the salt that precipitated was rinsed off into more seawater, which produced a more concentrated brine that was evaporated by being heated in clay pots.

It should be noted that the evaporation of sea water will yield not only halite but also the other salts that are dissolved in the sea. The salts produced by evaporation in natural saltpans occur in the following order: calcium carbonate (calcite), calcium sulfate (gypsum), sodium chloride (halite), and potassium magnesium chloride (carnallite), with halite occurring in the greatest quantity. The composition of natural brines varies widely. Many are unsuitable for salt production.

Natron is a naturally occurring mixture of sodium carbonate and sodium bicarbonate. It occurs abundantly at Wadi Natrun (a depression in the Libyan Desert 60 kilometers northwest of Cairo). Each Nile flood vastly increases the supply of water entering the wadi and its string of small lakes. During the dry season evaporation from the lakes causes deposition at the bottom of the lakes and as an incrustation on the ground adjoining them. In Ancient Egypt, as Pliny notes, natron was also prepared artificially, in much the same manner as table salt, except that Nile water rather than sea water was used. The Egyptians used natron in mummification, for purifying the mouth, for making glass and glaze, for bleaching linen, and in cooking and medicine.

Metals and Ores

Of the approximately seventy metallic chemical elements, eight (gold, copper, lead, iron, silver, tin, arsenic, and mercury) were recognized and used in their metallic state before the eighteenth century. Only gold and copper were sufficiently available in their native (metallic) state to be of importance to early societies. In the Old World, metallurgy had its beginnings in the Near East more than 7,000 years ago with copper and gold.

The first uncontested use of metallic copper dates to the late eighth millennium B.C. at an aceramic Neolithic site in southeastern Turkey. Here archaeologists found beads made of native copper. In the New World, Andean metallurgists developed sophisticated technologies that later moved north and flourished from Panama to Mexico. The Andes Mountains contain some of the richest gold, copper, tin, and silver mines in the world. Unlike the Old World focus on copper, metallurgy in Andean societies focused on gold from the middle of the second millennium B.C.

The word *ore* is derived from an Anglo-Saxon word meaning a lump of metal. It is applied to an aggregate of minerals from which one or more metals can be extracted *at a profit*. Therefore, what may be an ore under one set of economic conditions may not be an ore under other economic circumstances, for example, when it is possible to import a metal more cheaply than to extract it from a local deposit. In recent years there has been a tendency to drop the requirement that the desired substance be metallic. The worthless material from an ore deposit is called *gangue*.

Copper and *gold* (Au) were the first metals to be used by humans, primarily because they occur in the native, uncombined state in nature. The ancient Egyptians particularly prized gold for its eternal sheen, and they had a nearby source, the extensive deposits in Nubia. There is also a gold-bearing region between the Nile and the Red Sea. In the ancient world gold was exploited for purely decorative purposes. Deposits in the Taurus Mountains of Anatolia were extensively mined in the Early Bronze Age, and deposits in Greece were worked throughout the Bronze Age. In the New World, the use of gold came much later but reached great volume and artistic heights south of the Rio Grande, in Central America, and in northern South America. Indeed, stories of the abundance of gold objects were the driving force behind the Spanish conquest.

Gold is widely distributed in small amounts. It usually occurs in high silica (SiO_2) igneous rocks and quartz veins. Its exceptionally high density (19.3 g/cm³; more than six times the density of the average rock) causes it to concentrate in what are called placer deposits (see below). Its melting point of 1,063° C means that it can be melted and cast, and its chemical status as a noble metal means that it is free of unsightly corrosion.

Silver (Ag) does occur in the native state, but in ancient times most of it came as a byproduct from the smelting of lead ores. Silver was used in Egypt before 3000 B.C. but was comparatively rare until the Eighteenth Dynasty. In North America, native silver has been found in some Mound Builder (Hopewell) sites. *Electrum* is an alloy of gold and silver. The earliest electrum used was probably natural, although by Greek and Roman times artificial electrum was also used.

Over a considerable span of time, ancient metalsmiths discovered the rewards of applying pyrotechnology to metalliferous rocks. The smelting of *copper* (Cu) ores goes back six millennia in the Old World. Our knowledge of the origins of copper alloy metallurgy is primarily indirect, derived from analyses and interpretations of the composition and structure of artifacts, **slags**, and ores. Because archaeology (particularly Old World archaeology) has focused on the excavation of temples, graves, and habitation sites, relatively few examples of Chalcolithic or Early Bronze Age metallurgical or mining sites are known. Most of these have provided scant evidence of ores or technology. Only since the time of the English chemist and physicist John Dalton (1766–1844), who made significant contributions to our understanding of what a chemical element is, has the concept of chemical elements been used in a scientific or technical sense. The development of alloy metallurgy, therefore, must have come about without the artisans having any clear notion of elements and compounds. Ancient metalsmiths must have been aware of the results of smelting a mix of different "ores," but they must have marveled at the outcome of the results of smelting both metallic-looking and nonmetallic-looking stones.

A variety of scenarios may be proposed to account for the initial discovery that copper can be separated from such nonmetallic looking minerals as malachite and azurite. Bright green malachite or bright blue azurite may have been applied as decoration on the surface of pottery by Chalcolithic artisans. If the pottery were then fired in a **reducing atmosphere,** copper beads would have formed. Malachite and azurite begin to decompose below 400° C. It is likely that the earliest copper smelting was done well below the melting temperature of copper (1,083° C). When ancient metallurgists learned how to smelt the more difficult copper sulfide ores, perhaps about 2000 B.C. in the eastern Mediterranean, they turned to the much more abundant copper iron sulfide, chalcopyrite (see below), for their ore.

North of the Rio Grande prehistoric people did not smelt, melt, cast, or alloy metals, relying instead on the relative abundance of native copper. Copper use began in the Lake Superior region about 5,500 years ago. The native copper occurrences in the Lake Superior region are by far the most extensive in the world. Native copper is found in lode (original) deposits; in river, shoreline, and lag deposits of rounded nuggets; and in nuggets from glacial till. Subject only to surface alteration, native copper is nearly indestructible in the surface geologic environment. Most of the sources of native copper are associated with **mafic** volcanic rocks (e.g., those in the Lake Superior region, in the Copper River in Alaska, on the Coppermine River in the Northwest Territories, and at Cap d'Or, Nova Scotia) and are found in the oxidized zone of copper sulfide deposits (e.g., in southwestern United States and in the Near East, where metallurgy began).

Unlike gold, silver, and copper, *lead* (Pb) does not occur in the native state but must be smelted from its ores, especially lead sulfide (galena), lead carbonate (cerrusite), and lead sulfate (anglesite). Lead becomes molten at 327° C, so it is easily cast. It may have been smelted as early as copper: it is known from the Old World as long ago as the sixth millennium B.P. Lead mining at Rio Tinto, Spain, goes back to about 900 B.C., and at Lavrion, Greece, mining extends at least back to the late prehistoric times. Lead-tin pewter has been used since Roman times.

The Romans used lead for many purposes: storage vats, water pipes, pewter. It was also used as a preservative in wines. This toxic element then found its way into their bodies, causing severe medical disorders and leaving its archaeological trace in their bones.[8] Litharge (PbO), called red lead, has been widely used since ancient times as a red pigment. It too is quite toxic. Natural litharge forms in the oxidized zone of lead ore deposits. By Roman times red lead was also being manufactured from other lead minerals such as cerrusite (lead carbonate).

Cinnabar is a blood-red mineral, mercury sulfide. The Mayans prized it highly as a pigment, probably because its color could symbolize blood and blood sacrifice. Most of the cinnabar probably came from the Mayan highlands. Excavation of a Mayan site in Belize dating to the late ninth or early tenth century uncovered an offering vessel containing more than 100 grams of hematite, 19 grams of cinnabar, and other objects floating in a pool of 132 grams of mercury. Two possible sources for the Belize *mercury* are the Todos los Santos Formation of Guatemala or the Matapan Formation of western Honduras. This suggests that the mercury was acquired locally and not through trade.[9] Native mercury is rare in geologic deposits, and it is not known whether the Mayans mined liquid mercury or smelted it from cinnabar.

Cinnabar was used for the coloring on the famous oracle bones of ancient China. But all the ancient artisans had great difficulty differentiating among the various red pigments. Pliny's account of red mineral pigments is quite garbled.

A deep blue complex copper hydroxycarbonate related to malachite, but less abundant, *azurite* is an easily smelted ore of copper that was used both for its copper content and as a blue pigment, probably as early as the seventh millennium B.C. It forms in the upper oxidized zone of copper sulfide deposits, along with the more common malachite.

As a tin oxide, *cassiterite* is the only ore of tin. (Tin becomes molten at 232° C and was occasionally used in its metallic form in the ancient Old World.) Because of its specific gravity of 7 g/cm³, cassiterite is found in placer deposits, often along with gold. Cassiterite is widely distributed in small amounts, but cassiterite deposits of ore grade are rare. Perhaps the greatest unsolved problem in Old World Bronze Age metallurgy is where the tin came from. The plentiful placer cassiterite from Cornwall was certainly mined for British Isles Bronze Age metallurgy, but we do not know how widely that ore was

traded (see Chapter 7). By Roman times cassiterite from Iberia and Cornwall was available throughout the Mediterranean. The name cassiterite comes from the ancient Greek word for tin.

Galena is lead sulfide. It is recognizable from its perfect cubic cleavage, high density, and silvery metallic color. It is a common metallic sulfide frequently associated with silver minerals. Since Greek and Roman times a large part of the supply of lead has come as a byproduct of ores mined for their silver content. The Romans gave the name galena to this lead-ore mineral.

In North America where in antiquity no smelting occurred to recover metals, the brilliant silvery luster of galena nevertheless attracted the indigenous peoples, and it was used extensively in burial practices and for ornaments. Geologic sources of galena are numerous in the region from the southern Appalachians to the western Great Lakes area, and from Virginia to northeastern Oklahoma.

Galena has been reported from more than two hundred prehistoric sites in eastern North America. The earliest known use was during the Early Archaic. Of the 232 sites reported by Walthall, 60 percent were mortuary sites in which galena was used in a burial association.[10]

Galena rarely occurs in sites earlier than the Late Archaic. During the Late Archaic and Early Woodland periods galena is found in the Great Lakes and Mississippi Valley regions. During the Middle Woodland, a large quantity of galena was moved through regional and long-distance exchange systems. More than sixty Mississippian sites from Illinois to the southern Appalachians contained galena. These artifacts often exhibited ground, rather than natural, facets.

A red iron oxide, *hematite* (hardness 5–6.5) derives its name from the Greek for "blood red." But although the streak (the color of the finely powdered mineral, so called because of the diagnostic test used by geologists of drawing a mineral across a piece of unglazed porcelain and noting the streak) of hematite is red, the color of the mineral itself can be black or, in the case of specular hematite, a silvery metallic color. Hematite is widely distributed in rocks of all ages and is the most abundant and important ore of iron. Engraved cylinder seals of hematite were found in the ruins of Babylon, and it was used extensively by the ancient Egyptians. Red ocher is hematite and has been commonly used as a pigment throughout history. The ancient Egyptians had plentiful supplies of red ocher near Aswan and in the oases of the western Desert.

Most hematite can be ground into a red ocher powder. In North America red ocher, either in the form of lumps or ground into a pigment, accompanied the dead in their burials. In central and eastern North America (the area roughly bounded by Minnesota, Ontario, North Carolina, and Alabama), hematite was used in prehistoric times to make pendants, axes, celts, and edged tools. Celts are the most common and widespread hematite implements in this region. Hematite was recovered from both glacial till and bedrock quarries.

Red ocher has been used for decoration at least since Mousterian times. The pigments for the cave paintings in France contained red ocher. It was used in the Upper Paleolithic in cave painting and since the Neolithic for painted pottery.

Limonite is a field-geology term referring to hydrous iron oxides of uncertain identity. *Goethite* is hydrous iron oxide and a major iron ore. When it is yellow in color, goethite is called yellow ocher. Goethite is one of the commonest and most widespread of minerals and forms the **gossan** or "iron hat" that caps oxidized sulfide deposits. Goethite is common in near-surface sediments and soils as a secondary or concretionary material precipitated from circulating ground water. Our lack of archaeological knowledge concerning iron ore mines of the European Iron Age probably stems from the wide occurrence of small, shallow deposits of limonitic and hematitic iron ores. The exploitation of such ores would have had little lasting effect on the landscape.

At the Nichoria excavation in southwestern Greece, goethite was found in the shape of small rods in Bronze Age contexts. This created quite a stir, because it was conjectured that these might have been pre–Iron Age oxidized iron nails. However, Rapp demonstrated that the rods had a radial cross-sectional structure similar to other known goethite nodules rather than the concen-

tric or structureless cross-section that would have been consistent with a rusted metallic iron nail. Goethite was named in honor of the poet Johann Wolfgang von Goethe.

Magnetite is a magnetic iron oxide; it is iron black with a metallic luster and a black streak. A natural magnet, magnetite is known as lodestone. It is common in small amounts in most igneous rocks. Occasionally there are concentrations large enough to be classed as an ore deposit.

Although most *meteorites* are stony in composition, many are composed of an iron-nickel alloy that is nearly rustproof and easily recognizable as a metal. Meteoric iron is malleable and easily worked. It can be distinguished from smelted iron by its high nickel content, 5–26 percent. Metallic meteorites were picked up and used by humans long before the Iron Age in the Old World and were prized in prehistoric America. Ancient Sumerian texts mentioned meteoric iron, calling it "fire from heaven." Artifacts of meteoric iron are known from the end of the third millennium B.C. in Egypt and the Near East. The Aztecs made knives from iron meteorites.

A copper iron sulfide, *chalcopyrite* is the most widely occurring ore of copper. It is easily recognized by its brass-yellow color. The development of copper sulfide metallurgy—which is more complex than copper oxide metallurgy—allowed the continued expansion of bronze-making in the ancient world. The sulfide ores in copper deposits lie below the oxidized ores, so ancient metallurgists may have been forced into sulfide smelting when the oxide ores were depleted.

The most common and widespread of all sulfide minerals, *pyrite* frequently occurs as crystals and has long been called "fools' gold" for its color, although it is not as golden as chalcopyrite. An iron sulfide, it is easily distinguished from gold by its brittleness and hardness (6–6.5 on the Mohs scale) and from chalcopyrite by its paler color and greater hardness. It is ubiquitous in copper deposits and contributes to the formation of gossan, which marks most sulfide deposits. Pyrite has been found in many archaeological contexts. The Mayans used it to make mirrors, while the Aztecs used it for inlays in mosaics and eyes in statues. The Inuit and others employed it as a firestone be-

121

Table 5.1 Igneous Rocks

	Lighter colored	Darker colored	
	High SiO$_2$ (silica)	*Intermediate SiO$_2$*	*Low SiO$_2$(silica)*
Coarse grained	granite, syenite	diorite	gabbro
Fine grained	rhyolite, felsite	andesite	basalt

cause of its ability to give off sparks when struck. It was also used to make amulets.

Rocks

Just as the silica minerals have always been preferred for tools and weapons, the common durable rocks were the material of monuments, statuary, burial chambers, and buildings.

The major classifications of rocks are *igneous* (from the Latin for fire): rocks formed from molten magma; *sedimentary:* rocks formed from the consolidation of deposited clastic particles or by precipitation from solution; and *metamorphic* (from the Greek for undergoing a change of form): rocks formed by a major alteration of preexisting rocks owing to high temperature and pressure.

Geology has hundreds of names for variations in igneous rocks, but the names in table 5.1, with the addition of obsidian, should suffice for most archaeological work. The difference between granite and syenite lies in the percentage of quartz, with syenite having little or none. Rhyolite is the fine-grained mineralogic equivalent of granite. Felsite is a general term for any light-colored, fine-grained igneous rock, with or without **phenocrysts,** that is composed chiefly of quartz and feldspar. Basalt is sometimes called trap or trap rock. The wide range of igneous rocks used for hammer-stones, axes, and other pounding instruments is too extensive to be discussed here.

There are also hundreds of names for the varieties of the common sedimentary rocks (table 5.2). For example, a sandstone that has feldspar as a major constituent of the clastic particles is

called a greywacke. The pebbles or boulders in conglomerate are often very hard chert or quartz; the ability of prehistoric societies to dress blocks of conglomerate cutting neatly across tough chert boulders (for example, at the Lion Gate at Mycenae in southwestern Greece) is extraordinary. On the other end of the hardness scale, shale was used for beads because it was easy to shape and drill.

And there are many names in the geologic literature to account for mineralogic or textural variation within the major metamorphic rock types (table 5.3). It should be noted that not all quartzites are of metamorphic origin. A quartz sandstone completely cemented with silica can fracture through (rather than around) the grains, thus emulating metamorphic quartzites.

Individual rock types of special interest in geoarchaeology include:

Andesite A widespread fine-grained volcanic rock, named after the Andes Mountains, it is hard and cohesive. **Vesicular** andesite has been used extensively throughout the world for grinding stones for such grains as wheat and corn.

Basalt Fine-grained and often extremely tough and cohesive, basalt has found widespread favor for lithic tools, querns, and, in Egypt, statues. The earliest stone vessels made in Egypt were Neolithic basalt vases. Basalt is widely distributed in Egypt and was used as early as the Old Kingdom as a material for pavements in the necropolis stretching from Giza to Saqqara. Its source apparently was the Fayum, where one can still see the ancient quarry. During Pharaonic times, basalt was used in statues and sarcophagi.

Felsite Felsite is a general term for any fine-grained, light-colored igneous rock composed chiefly of quartz and feldspar. Felsite can be very hard and cohesive. Like chert, it breaks with a

Table 5.2 Major Sedimentary Rocks

Shale	The most common sedimentary rock. Shales are composed of clay and silt and often exhibit a finely laminated structure that resembles bedding.
Sandstone	Rounded or angular particles of sand size cemented together by silica, iron oxide, or calcium carbonate. Sandstones are often quartz and may be well cemented and therefore cohesive or poorly cemented and therefore friable.
Conglomerate	Coarse-grained clastic rocks composed of large rounded pebbles, cobbles, or boulders set in a fine-grained matrix of sand or silt cemented by silica, iron oxide, calcium carbonate, or hardened clay.
Limestone	Calcium carbonate in the form of calcite, formed by either detrital, biologic, or chemical processes. Many are highly fossiliferous and represent ancient shell banks or coral reefs. Chalk and travertine are also limestones.

sharp conchoidal fracture, which makes it valuable as a lithic material.

Rhyolite Almost the same as felsite, rhyolite is the fine-grained mineralogic equivalent of granite. Thus it contains quartz as an essential constituent.

Granite and Diorite Fairly abundant, often mechanically tough and free of cracks, aesthetically pleasing, and capable of taking a high polish, these igneous rocks have been widely used in the construction of large monuments. As early as predynastic times in Egypt they were also used for bowls and vases, and later for statues, obelisks, and stelae. The Pharaonic Egyptians carved single large obelisks from Aswan granite and used diorite for large statues. Diorite has been used in Egypt since Neolithic times for axes, palettes, and mace heads. Not all coarse-grained igneous rocks used in Egyptian statuary that are called diorite by archaeologists are actually diorites— granodiorite, granite, and other rock types have been mistakenly identified as diorite. Granite and diorite vary considerably in composition, texture, color, and durability, however.

Scoria In regions where there has been extensive metallurgical activity, scoria has been mistaken by archaeologists for slag. Scoria is the name applied to very dark, highly vesicular, sometimes glassy rock of basaltic composition. Coal clinker has the same appearance and is sometimes also called scoria. In the eastern Mediterranean region a blackish residue from the melting of kiln walls under reducing conditions has also been mistaken for slag. This latter material, however, has very low density.

Obsidian The name obsidian goes back as far as Pliny, who described obsidian from Ethiopia. It is a volcanic glass, usually black but sometimes of other colors or even variegated. High-silica volcanic rocks are typically fine-grained or glassy. The molten material from which these rocks formed is so viscous that crystal growth is impeded and noncrystallized rocks often form during rapid cooling. Obsidians contain less than 1 percent H_2O by weight because magma at high temperature that is extruded onto the earth's surface, or intruded at very shallow depth, cannot retain much water in solution. However, obsidian can become hydrated (up to nearly 10 percent) by later absorption of groundwater (see Chapter 6 for a discussion of obsidian provenance studies and Chapter 7 for obsidian hydration dating). As a glass, obsidian breaks with a conchoidal fracture. Because it is easily worked into sharp projectile points and other implements, it has had wide use since prehistoric times.

Obsidian was in use as far back as Upper Paleolithic times. It was found in level C of Shanidar Cave in Iraq and dated to approximately 30,000 B.P. Obsidian has been recovered from almost every Neolithic site in the eastern Mediterranean area. It was equally important in New

Table 5.3 Metamorphic Rocks

Transformation of sedimentary rocks through high temperature (→) and high pressure (→)

Limestone → Marble
Sandstone → Quartzite
Shale → Slate → Phyllite → Schist → Gneiss

World contexts. Indigenous miners in central America pursued high-quality obsidian at depth, developing underground mines. The Aztecs made extensive use of obsidian for projectile points, knives, razors, swords, mirrors, and ornaments. There are numerous high-grade obsidian deposits in western North America, such as Obsidian Cliff in Yellowstone National Park and in the volcanic regions of Central America.

Pumice and Ash Pumice is a light-colored, vesicular, glassy, pyroclastic rock that is commonly composed of rhyolite. It is often porous enough to float and has been widely used as an abrasive. Pyroclastic rocks are volcanic rocks that form as particle deposition from explosive eruptions. When particles are smaller than 2 mm in size, they are called ash. Pumice from archaeological excavations can now almost routinely be traced to the volcano of origin and often dated to a particular eruption.

Quartzite Composed chiefly of quartz sandstone with silica cement, this rock fractures conchoidally, which allows it to be worked into sharp tools, just as chert and obsidian are. Quartzite was used in Pharaonic Egypt for statues and sarcophagi. Nubian sandstone, a quartzite, was used by Paleolithic people in the Sahara.

Marble Marble was the preferred statuary and monumental stone of the classical world. In Egypt it was also used for vases. Marble can be found in thick deposits of wide areal extent that are relatively free of cracks and easy to quarry. It takes a high polish. Its chief drawback is its high susceptibility to disintegration under the action of acid rain (modern pollution aside, rain is acid because

CO_2 dissolves in atmospheric water to create a never-ending supply of carbonic acid in rain). Marble is plentiful in western Anatolia, Italy, Greece, and elsewhere in the Mediterranean area, where it was widely used.

Serpentinite A rock composed chiefly of the green minerals of the serpentine group (hardness 2.5–3.5), it occurs widely as the alteration product of mafic igneous rocks. It has been used since antiquity in the Old World for stone bowls, vases, carved figures, and occasionally molds. It was popular throughout North America because it was easily worked.

Siliceous Shale/Slate As with quartzite, this low-grade metamorphic rock fractures conchoidally. Because it is composed chiefly of silica, it has a hardness approaching 7 on the Mohs scale. It was widely used in North America, especially in northern Minnesota, for projectile points and other sharp tools.

Steatite (Soapstone) A fine-grained, compact rock consisting chiefly of the mineral talc (hardness 1) but usually containing many other constituents. It has been favored since antiquity for ornaments and molds because of its softness and cohesion. Nearly all of the North and Central American prehistoric peoples used steatite for pots, bowls, and pipes. The Inuit and others used steatite for lamps. Steatite outcrops are common in many locations throughout the Appalachian Mountains.

Catlinite A red, siliceous, indurated clay that is often called pipestone because of its extensive use in North America since at least the late sixteenth century B.C. for making tobacco pipes. Catlinite is named after George Catlin (1796–1872), well-known painter of Native Americans. Although the best-known quarry is in southwest Minnesota, there are also deposits in Wisconsin, Ohio, and Arizona. The trade in catlinite was countrywide and extended into Canada.

Shells

Along the Atlantic seacoast in North America shells were made into wampum beads that in the Colonial Period were the Native American's form

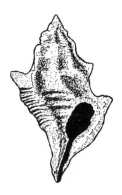

Figure 5.1 Murex Shell

of money. **Crinoid** stems were drilled and worn as beads. Water-tumbled stones of glacial till containing shell fossils were used for such everyday objects as hearth and boiling stones, hammers, anvils, and mullers. Some projectile points from the eastern United States have shell fossils located centrally in the artifact, suggesting its intentional placement as an ornament. Shell fossils and concretions, some stained with hematite, have been found associated with burials and grave goods.[11]

In the eastern Mediterranean region, shells from certain species of the marine gastropod genus *Murex* yielded the royal purple dye of the ancients, especially favored by the Romans. (A substance secreted by murex turns purple when put into heated seawater.) The use of murex purple dye goes back to 1500 B.C. at Ugarit on the Levant coast. Murex shells were found associated with Middle Minoan pottery on the small island of Korephronisi just off Crete, and Cretan use of the purple dye was mentioned by Herodotus. Murex may have been bred in tanks along the ancient south coast of Turkey. Pliny gave fairly good descriptions of the gastropods and their dye. Murex shells are highly ornamented and easily identifiable (figure 5.1).

Clays

The primary raw materials for archaeological ceramics were local clay-rich sediments and soils that were used for the paste and coarse sedi-

mentary particles that were used for the temper. Clay deposits are of two general types: 1) primary deposits formed in situ by the weathering of bedrock like granite or shale, and 2) secondary deposits formed by river (fluvial) or lake (lacustrine) deposition. The secondary deposits are often referred to as transported clays. In soils, clay minerals form as part of the natural chemical weathering of the parent bedrock. Clay minerals are low-temperature hydrous minerals that are stable in the earth-surface environment. They form in soils from the breakdown of minerals that were created in high-temperature anhydrous environments. These primary minerals are not stable at the earth's surface. Plant nutrients become available during this chemical weathering. The supply of potassium (K) in a soil correlates well with the rate of clay formation.

It must be noted that the word *clay* has two meanings: it is both a particle size (smaller than two microns) and the name of a group of silicate minerals that have a sheetlike structure. Because of their small size and sheet structure, clays become plastic when mixed with water. This plasticity allows the mixture to be shaped and to retain the new shape. Whether a clayey raw material will make good pottery—one of the primary uses of clay—depends on which clay mineral predominates, the shape and size distribution of the nonclay minerals, the organic content, the exchangeable ions present, and the size distribution in the whole mass. Good pottery clays also contain fine-grained quartz, which provides the **refractory** backbone during firing.

Crude pottery is relatively simple to make. Many clayey soils and sediments can be fired to form simple, thick-walled vessels that can withstand moderate thermal and physical stress. Fired clay objects are known from the Upper Paleolithic of central Europe. The earliest known ceramics from North America come from Florida and date to about 1700 B.C.

The major clay minerals and their important properties for pottery making are:

Kaolinite, $(OH)_8Al_4Si_4O_{10}$ Kaolinite is the most refractory of the clays and has excellent firing properties. Not only does it have the best high-temperature stability, it can also be heated rapidly, and it has low shrinkage. Because of its restricted chemical composition, kaolinite maintains its white color. It is the clay of fine china. Its particle size and shape—it forms as small hexagonal plates—give it good plasticity. Kaolinite is the only clay that works well alone in pottery manufacture. It is a common and widespread product of the weathering of feldspars in igneous and metamorphic rocks. It can also be found as a secondary clay.

Halloysite, $(OH)_8Al_4Si_4O_{10}$ Although similar to kaolinite in composition, halloysite has thin platelets that curl up, leading to poor workability (for example, it can crack during forming and drying). Halloysite must be heated slowly to prevent fracture during firing. It is a common product of the alteration of feldspars and often occurs with kaolinite.

Montmorillonite/Smectite, $(OH)_2(Al,Mg,Na)_2$-Si_4O_{10} (composition variable) The smectites are the expanding (swelling) clays that can absorb large amounts of water between the sheets in their structure. Their ceramic properties include high plasticity and moderate refractoriness but also high shrinkage. These clays are widespread alteration products of the weathering of volcanic ash and of many high magnesium igneous and metamorphic rocks. They also form as soil clays.

Illite, $(OH)K_4Al_4(Si,Al)_8O_{20}$ (composition variable, usually containing iron and magnesium) Illite has good plasticity, variable shrinkage, and low refractoriness. It is good for **slips.** Illites are the dominant clay minerals in shales and mudstones. They also form commonly in soils from the alteration of micas and other clay minerals and from colloidal silica. Illite is the only clay mineral containing significant potassium.

Other sheet silicates are found mixed with these clay minerals in many deposits, but they all reduce the plasticity. The addition of fine-grained organic material and many varieties of plastic and aplastic tempers can improve plasticity, strength, and firing properties.

To reduce shrinkage and/or improve workability, temper is added to the clayey material before it is formed. Coarse sediments for temper are normally available in nearby streams. Fossil shells also make good temper because calcium carbon-

ate has the same thermal expansion as the average pottery clay. The same is true for marble (also calcium carbonate). Chips of broken pottery, called grog, were also used as temper.

The glaze is a thin layer of material applied to ceramics before firing that becomes a glassy coating at high temperatures. Low-melting materials are necessary for glazes. Sodium and lead are the most common elements used to lower the melting point of the silicates in ceramic glazes. Lead glazes can cause lead toxicity if used for drinking or eating ware. Soluble salts or saline water can be the source of sodium. High-fired glazes usually contain feldspars, calcite, dolomite, or wood ash. Low-fired glazes are usually alkaline (containing sodium or potassium).

Building Materials

The nature of the building materials employed by a society depends primarily on the kind of material available. It was no accident that the great tells of the Middle East resulted from the disintegration of mud-brick buildings. For hundreds of kilometers around, there were neither hard-rock outcrops nor trees available for building. At Çatal Höyük in Anatolia, walls and even built-in furniture were made of clay earth by 6800 B.C. In more northern regions, also lacking sufficient timber and where mud-brick walls would not survive, stone construction was a necessity. Except for timber, almost all building materials reflect the exploitation of minerals and lithic resources. Early in human cultural evolution, we turned to rocks for building, first to improve a cave or rock shelter, later to construct dwellings. In the Near East, rock walls for houses and towns go back more than 7,000 years. In areas where rock masses were scarce, earth plaster and mud bricks were used.

Ancient Egypt, Greece, and Rome were responsible for great advances in the use of quarried and dressed stone for building. By 3000 B.C., the Egyptians had learned to shape their comparatively soft Tertiary limestones into rectangular blocks. Before 2000 B.C., they had learned how shape the more difficult granite and diorite.

By the time of the Third Dynasty in Egypt

(2649–2575 B.C.) there was a marked increase in the use of stone for buildings. Limestone was the primary building material, but large blocks of granite were used in an unfinished pyramid located between Giza and Abusir and in the step pyramid of Djoser at Saqqara. By the Eighteenth Dynasty (1550–1307 B.C.), limestone had largely given way to the more durable sandstone and granite. The great sandstone quarries along the Nile about 60 kilometers north of Aswan bear inscriptions dating from the Eighteenth Dynasty down to Greek and Roman times. The Egyptians removed the surface layers of granite outcrops by burning papyrus on them and then drenching them with cold water, which caused the granite to **spall** and disintegrate. If no natural crack or joint could be exploited in quarrying the granite, a trench was made around the desired block by pounding it with balls of dolerite, a fine-grained basaltic rock. Wooden wedges were inserted in cracks or trenches, driven tight when dry, then wetted.

The Greeks and the Romans developed masonry building in shaped (ashlar) blocks to a fine art. During the Late Bronze Age the Mycenaeans in Greece constructed "Cyclopean" walls by fitting angular blocks neatly together. Sometimes mortar was used in masonry: the Egyptians favored gypsum while the Greeks and Romans used burnt lime (calcium oxide) and clay. Lime plaster was formed by heating limestone (calcium carbonate) at temperatures higher than 900° C to drive off the carbon dioxide. This left calcium oxide. Calcium oxide reacts rapidly with water to form calcium hydroxide. When exposed to the atmosphere, the calcium hydroxide takes up carbon dioxide again, becoming a stable calcium carbonate—hard and cementlike.

The Greeks and the Romans also discovered that certain volcanic ash produced a hydraulic cement when mixed with slaked lime and water. The Greeks used the volcanic **tuffs** from Thera (Santorini), while the Romans discovered around 100 B.C. that the volcanic ash from the village of Pozzuoli on the slopes of Mount Vesuvius was suited for this purpose. Not all volcanic ash has this property; the Roman recipes call the cements made with volcanic ash Pozzolanic cements. These cements can set under water; they were used as early as 144 B.C. to line water channels.

In the early nineteenth century, portland cement was invented in Britain (named after the Isle of Portland in Dorsetshire). The basic materials of portland cement are clay and limestone. Some iron is needed, but this is usually supplied by iron minerals in the clay. The most stringent requirement of the limestone is that it not contain more than about 5 percent magnesium carbonate. Portland cement is hydraulic—water is involved in the basic chemical reactions of manufacture. The first portland cement produced in the United States was in the Lehigh Valley of Pennsylvania in 1875.

Building Stone

A large number of distinct hard rock types (including limestone, sandstone, granite, and gneiss) make good building stone. The necessary characteristics are: 1) structural strength (ability to carry a load without failure), 2) durability (resistance to weathering), 3) ease of quarrying and dressing, and 4) availability (the energy cost of transportation).

By the time very hard rocks like granite, diorite, quartzite, and conglomerate came into use for building stone, the use of abrasives must have become commonplace. The Aztecs worked granite with copper implements with quartz sand as an abrasive. Emery, a grayish-black mixture of magnetite and corundum (which is second only to diamond in hardness), and pumice must have been used as abrasives from early on in those areas where they were available. Emery is abundant in the Near East and some of the Aegean Islands.

On the low end of the structural-strength scale are clays and muds. Yet these were important building materials (with only minor processing) in antiquity. As a geologic term, *mud* is a mixture of silt and clay-sized particles. (The word in common usage describes essentially the same material.) Many natural muds also contain some sand-sized grains. As noted earlier, *clay* has more than one meaning, but the thing to keep in mind is that most clay-sized material is composed of clay minerals.

The optimal sand-silt-clay ratios vary for different types of structures. For rammed earth walls, there should be about 50–75 percent sand in the mixture to prevent excessive shrinking of the plastic components. The size range of the sand and coarse particles is of little importance. In rammed earth walls only a small amount of clay is desirable: more than 30 percent clay results in rapid erosion. The pre-Spanish inhabitants of the American southwest used the **pisé** technique to build layered walls in three-foot (vertical) units of adobe-type mud, rather than making mud bricks.

To make satisfactory adobe bricks, a lithology lying outside the range used for rammed earth walls is needed. Adobe bricks must have a higher percentage of clay and contain straw for binder. Good sun-dried adobe bricks can be made from earth containing 9–28 percent clay. (The Uniform Building Code in the United States requires that the clay content of adobe bricks be greater than 25 percent and less than 45 percent.) Too much clay causes the brick to develop cracks as it dries; too little makes the brick too weak, so that it crumbles easily. Individual clay minerals have different bonding properties, and the lime content as well as the organic content will affect the physical properties. Sand-silt-clay ratios cannot tell the whole story. Compositions suitable for adobe or sun-dried mud brick can be attained by mixing a range of materials, but it is likely that in prehistoric times raw materials for mud brick were primarily clay and organic binders such as straw. In present-day mud-brick making in Egypt and Turkey, bricks are carved out of the soil directly, without going through a molding step. Enough plant material may exist in the soil there to take the place of added binder.

Burnt Brick

For thousands of years stone, clay, or clay plus timber were the dominant construction materials. The use of timber is recorded in archaeology by the abundance of debris in "destruction levels" that result when towns and villages are burnt down. London was destroyed by the Great Fire of 1666 because it was built chiefly of timber and mud. It was rebuilt with brick produced from the abundant high-quality clays available in southeast Britain. The art of baking clay to produce bricks dates from the second millennium B.C. in Mesopotamia, India, and Egypt. It was the Romans, however, who developed the technology of making burnt brick of high quality by carefully choosing and fine-grinding raw materials, then subjecting them to controlled firing. Since the twelfth century brick making has become ubiquitous; clayey sediments and weathering products are widely distributed. Although all clay minerals begin to recrystallize above 1,200° C, the mineralogy of the clay is almost as critical in brick making as in pottery manufacture. The compositions of brick raw materials can vary widely throughout the world. In Georgia in the United States, brick is made from pure kaolinite, some feldspar, fire clay, and bentonite (a rock composed chiefly of montmorillonite). In Great Britain red marls, deltaic muds, and illitic sediments of Jurassic age have all provided raw materials for brick. Throughout the world the most common raw material used for bricks is recent alluvium from the great floodplains of the Yellow, Ganges, Nile, Mekong, and Indus rivers. These alluvial deposits, however, are often high in silt and low in clay, leading to a weak and porous brick—best suited for single-story houses.

Mortar

Ancient mortar, before the advent of cement, usually consisted of clay, gypsum, or lime. Both gypsum and lime mortar required preparation in high-temperature kilns. The ancient Greeks and Romans used lime, whereas Pharaonic Egyptians used gypsum because in a land where wood was scarce, the firing of gypsum plaster was accomplished at lower, fuel-saving temperatures.

Clay mortar was used primarily with mud bricks. Clay, lime, and gypsum all served a dual purpose as mortars and as plaster. The ancient Egyptians mixed clay and gypsum and also clay and fine limestone for wall plaster.

Other Materials

When considering the geologic raw materials that may be found in an archaeological context, it also pays to become acquainted with objects that can

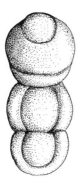

Figure 5.2 Concretions

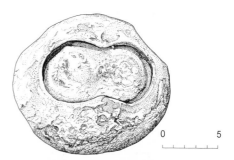

Figure 5.3 Chert Nodules
These nodules form in carbonate rocks that weather away, leaving the nodules lying loose on the surface. This nodule was collected in the Valley of Kings near Luxor, Egypt, by Rapp. The scale is in centimeters.

resemble natural materials in shape or some other aspect but that have a different origin. Chief among these are concretions and dendrites.

Concretions are hard, compact segregations of mineral matter found in sedimentary rocks, particularly shales and sandstones, as well as in soils. They are formed by precipitation from aqueous solution, growing outward from a nucleus, and usually are of a composition somewhat different from the host rock. Concretions represent a concentration of a cementing material, such as iron oxide, calcite, silica, or gypsum. Most concretions are spheroidal, ellipsoidal, or discoidal, although many attain odd or fantastic shapes, sometimes mimicking turtle shells, bones, leaves, or other fossil material. These concretions are often **septarian**. Figure 5.2 shows one concretionary shape. Many concretions have an internal structure similar to that of concentric shells. Chert nodules have similar shapes (figure 5.3).

In soils, concretions cemented by iron oxide are found in better-drained soils but require some moisture to form, whereas calcareous concretions form in dry soils, particularly under alkaline conditions. Concretions range in size from a few millimeters to up to 3 meters. Concretions have been found in many ancient refuse pits and as grave goods on pre-European North American archaeological sites.

Dendrites are near-surface deposits of manganese oxide that have crystallized in a branching pattern along fractures in rocks. They are often

mistaken for fossils. Figure 5.4 shows a common dendrite.

Nearly all the rocks and minerals that hold their color when ground to a powder (most silicates turn white) have been used as pigments. There are too many of these for detailed consideration here. Among the most common are hematite (red ocher), goethite (yellow ocher), malachite, azurite, selenite (gypsum), cinnabar, varieties of coal, calcite, huntite (a rare white calcium-magnesium carbonate), magnesite (a white magnesium chloride), and manganese oxides and graphite.

Maya blue, used since the beginning of the Mayan Late Classic Period, is a mixture of minerals and indigo—a blue dye obtained from various plants. The mineral constituents are palygorskite (formerly called attapulgite), a white clay mineral, and sepiolite (also called meerschaum—from which smoking pipes are made). Both minerals occur as alteration products of serpentine. The dye becomes affixed to the absorbent white minerals after heating. This pigment was unknown in other parts of the ancient world. It continued to be used in central America in mural paintings into the nineteenth century.

Rock and Mineral Recovery

Geologists use the term *outcrop* for rock bodies that jut up at the surface of the earth. It seems a safe assumption that most rock and mineral prod-

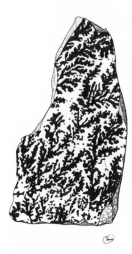

Figure 5.4 Dendrites
These near-surface deposits of manganese oxide that
have crystallized along fractures in the rocks are frequently mistaken for fossils. (Drawing by Elaine Nissen)

ucts used by prehistoric cultures were gathered
from outcrops. When a particularly high-quality
stone or ore deposit was discovered, early humans
developed mining and quarrying techniques to
maximize its exploitation. The miners often made
use of natural vertical joints in the rock in quarrying.

At Rudna Glava in Serbia people of the Vinca
culture mined copper 4,500 years ago from 15-
meter vertical shafts. The mining of copper ores
and minerals in the Egyptian Sinai date to the Old
Kingdom. Underground flint mines that operated
in England more than 5,000 years ago during the
Neolithic had shafts of more than 4 meters deep.

In prospecting for ancient mines the geoarchaeologist should look for evidence of waste
dumps. The surrounding (waste) rock in metal
mining is called country rock or gangue. This
material was routinely discarded at the mining
site so the miners would not have to transport it
to smelting or other metal-processing sites.

A troubling problem in Old World prehistoric
metallurgy has been the dearth of copper slag
dumps from the Bronze Age. Copper smelting
generates large quantities of slag—a waste product. Scientists speculate that later societies re-
smelted or comminuted (pulverized) some of the

earlier slags that retained recoverable copper. Or
perhaps archaeological surveys have been insuffi-
ciently intensive to locate these mounds.

Throughout human prehistory people have
prospected stream gravels for lithic raw materials,
recognizing that the boulders that could survive
the rough-and-tumble ride down water courses
would not shatter easily. In most parts of the
world these boulders were composed largely of
chert and related quartzose rocks and minerals.

Most of the debris from weathering is moved
away from its point of origin by running water.
What size, shape, and density particles can be
transported depends of the velocity of the water.
Larger and denser particles tend to lag behind
and accumulate in low spots in the channel,
where the water velocity is lower. When there is
a sharp change in water velocity—for example,
where a river emerges from a mountainous area
onto a plain—the larger and denser particles are
deposited immediately. These concentrations of
heavier particles are called *placers*. The earliest
gold and cassiterite deposits used by humans were
undoubtedly placers. The California Gold Rush
of 1849 was based on placer deposits formed by
the active erosion of lode deposits and gravels
higher up in the Sierra Nevada Mountains. Placer
mining has led to extensive excavations of alluvial
valleys.

Large blocks of building stone were secured
through quarrying. Quarries are not easily eroded
or removed from the landscape, except when they
are replaced by even larger quarries, so many
landscapes contain ancient quarries. The quarrying of large blocks of rock for building stone was
not possible until the advent of copper and bronze
tools for working the softer rocks like limestone.
Blocks of rock were quarried by isolating a block
on four sides by means of trenches cut in the
rock and then detaching it from below by means
of wooden wedges wetted with water. In Egypt
quarrying probably had its beginnings in the cutting away of limestone to make tombs.

Artifacts recovered from nearly 12,000 years
of occupation of the Cebolleta Mesa region in
New Mexico illustrate the broad range of mineral resources exploited for human needs.[12] Most
of the materials came from the immediate area or

adjacent regions. Use was made of sandstone for masonry blocks and paint mortars; adobe from alluvial soils for building; basalt for tools, mauls, and bowls; clay from clay sediments for pottery; quartzite, chert, chalcedony, obsidian and pitchstone, pipestone, calcite and travertine, limestone, hematite and limonite for pigments; jet and turquoise for ornaments; halite for food; and felsite and metamorphic rock (other than quartzite) for implements. Also recovered were feldspar, quartz crystals, malachite, azurite, galena, and pyrite.

Ball has published an extensive treatise on the mining of gems and ornamental stones by Native Americans before they came into contact with Europeans.[13] He noted that while mineral products were essential to both Indian and European ways of life, the Indians used coal mainly as an ornament and petroleum as a liniment. Ball reports on 84 different geologic materials used for gems and ornamental stones. Similarly, Heizer and Treganza have located and plotted 142 mine or quarry sites where California Indians exploited rock and mineral resources.[14]

The use of petroleum by Native Americans is well documented from archaeological sites. Asphalt was used as a mastic in the Ohio Valley and elsewhere. Many fossil hydrocarbon deposits (oil shale, tar sands, tar springs) were used as fuels in pre-European North America. Fossils, fossiliferous rocks, quartz crystals, galena cleavages, and sheet mica all have been found as grave goods.

The most necessary lithic material in Precolumbian North America was quartzose material, which was used for projectile points. The continent contains innumerable lithics that are good to excellent for this purpose, and large quarries were operated in what are now Ohio and New York for chert, Pennsylvania and New Jersey for jasper and rhyolite, New York for quartzite, and Minnesota for a slightly metamorphosed high-silica siltstone.

Water

For geoarchaeologists, water is perhaps the most important and the least understood compound. It is key not only to keeping organisms alive but to climate, weathering, agriculture, and transportation. Habitation sites have always depended on a supply of potable water.

The appearance of natural water reveals only part of its total composition and potability. Suspended and dissolved matter imparts color to water: turbidity from abundant suspended clay particles imparts a yellowish color, abundant phytoplankton will generate a deep green, iron oxide a rusty red. The dark colors of swamps and bogs are due to suspended humic material and tannic acid. All surface and near-surface waters contain bacteria in concentrations of up to hundreds of thousands per cubic centimeter. Even unpolluted water contains large quantities of dissolved matter and dissolved gases, particularly O_2 and CO_2, that have been picked up from the atmosphere. Most natural rainwater—unaffected by acid pollution—is acid because the carbon dioxide it picks up in the atmosphere forms carbonic acid. This phenomenon has major archaeological consequences including the dissolution of buried bone, the corrosion of monuments (especially marble and limestone) and metal artifacts, the decay of organic matter, and the formation of caves and rock shelters.

Rainfall that does not run off or evaporate seeps into the ground, where it has an important effect on human economy. It provides the medium for chemical and biochemical soil development, chemical and physical transport in soils, and nutrients for plant growth. Water not removed by plants returns to the surface by **capillary rise,** where it evaporates, returns to rivers or the sea by lateral flow, or, emerging as springs, is retained as groundwater. The top of the zone where the groundwater saturates the earth is called the water table. Because of modern-day drainage of low-lying areas for land use and the heavy pumping of groundwater for agricultural and other uses, contemporary water tables are much lower than in prehistoric or early historic times.

The quality of the groundwater is of critical importance for domestic uses. Usually, groundwater that is not near urban areas is free from bacteria because it is naturally filtered as it flows through near-surface strata and soils. Pure water

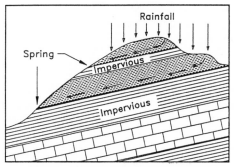

1. Charged aquifer above or between dipping impervious strata results in springs where lower edge of aquifer breaks surface.

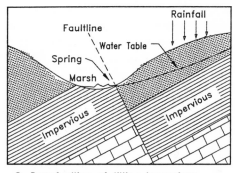

2. Downfaulting of tilting impervious strata results in subsurface impondment of trapped groundwater with overflow breaking surface as spring.

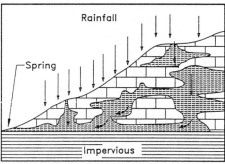

3. Percolating groundwater in karst areas is trapped above impervious strata and forms springs where impervious strata break surface. Common near the floor of river valleys.

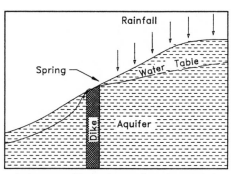

4. Igneous dike acts as dam to prevent migration of groundwater with resultant spring on uphill side of dike. Waterholes which result are common in arid areas.

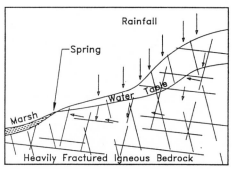

5. Groundwater migrates along fractures in bedrock breaking ground as spring where surface dips below water table.

6. Groundwater trapped above or between level impervious strata results in seeping springs where top edge of strata meet sloping surface.

Figure 5.5 Geologic Formations That Can Result in the Creation of Springs

will dissolve only 20 parts per million (ppm) of calcium carbonate and 28 ppm of magnesium carbonate. However, as noted above, water entering the groundwater system as rainfall will be acidic. Such water can dissolve hundreds of parts per million of sodium, calcium, magnesium, and iron minerals.

One of the main criteria for the acceptability of drinking water is its salinity. Below about 400 ppm sodium chloride imparts no taste to water. By about 500 ppm the water begins to taste brackish and by 4,000 ppm, water is undrinkable. The salinity of groundwater depends on the composition of the local rock formations, the depth from which the water is drawn, and the climate. Water also plays a primary role in chemical weathering and alteration by dissolution phenomena and frost action.

The accessibility of groundwater is critical if it is to be exploited economically. The structure, porosity, and permeability of the near-surface rock strata in large part govern the accessibility. Most important is how the pervious and impervious beds alternate. If impervious strata lie at the surface, no water will penetrate to the groundwater system. If an impervious layer lies somewhat beneath the surface, it will be a barrier to vertical flow. When pervious and impervious strata lie at an angle to the surface, springs may develop as groundwater moves down because of the pull of gravity. Because both geologic and climatic conditions remain stable for long periods, most springs have a continuous flow. Figure 5.5 illustrates the geologic conditions that lead to the formation of springs. For a comprehensive discussion of springs, see Chapter 9.

CHAPTER 6

Provenance Studies

Provenience is a common archaeological term referring to the precise location at which an artifact was recovered (from a survey or excavation). Without provenience data, artifacts have little archaeological value. By *provenance*, however, geoarchaeologists mean something quite different. The provenance of an artifact is the location, site, mine that is the origin of the artifact *material*. In geoarchaeological terms, this means the geographic-geologic source of the raw material from which the artifact was made, that is, a specific geologic deposit—usually a quarry, mine, geologic formation, outcrop, or other coherent and bounded geologic feature. Geoarchaeological provenance studies do not address the question of where the artifact was manufactured but only the source of the raw material. A large number of chemical, physical, and biologic parameters can be used to determine the source of natural materials. Use of DNA has received wide attention in forensics, archaeology, and paleontology, but it is not geologically based. Geologists use trace elements, isotopes, diagnostic minerals or assemblages, microfossils, geophysical parameters, and many other distinguishing characteristics to determine the source or origin of geologic materials. Space permits us to consider only a few of the geologic techniques that are useful to archaeologists.

The underlying assumption for provenance studies is that there is a demonstrable set of physical, chemical, or mineral characteristics in raw-material source deposits that is retained in the final artifact. This assumption can be justified only through empirical work, which requires large data sets of high analytic accuracy.

The archaeological significance of information

concerning the location of the origin of an object, as opposed to where it was found, is considerable. Provenance studies can provide evidence for the reconstruction of the patterns of exchange systems and trade routes, as well as giving the territory, location, and size of resources that may relate to social stratification and organization of crafts and industries.

One of the earliest attempts to source archaeological remains by geologic analysis was the effort to trace the origin of the megaliths at Stonehenge (figure 6.1), an undertaking that was begun in the mid-eighteenth century. Early observers realized that two types of rock had been used in the construction of Stonehenge. The circle is dominated by large "sarsens," quartzose rocks of local origin, which were also used in the great circle of Avebury. The other stones, termed "blue stones," are doleritic igneous rocks. In the nineteenth century the first careful petrographic descriptions of the rocks were made, and by the early twentieth century H. H. Thomas was able to trace the exotic blue stones by petrologic and petrographic analyses to the Preseli Mountains in Wales.[1] In the late twentieth century, studies using X-ray fluorescence analysis showed that the dolerites came from three sources in the eastern Preseli Mountains, and the rhyolitic rocks from four sources in the northern Preseli Mountains.[2] The altar stone came from southwestern Wales. This variety of sources suggests that the monoliths may have been taken from a glacially mixed deposit, rather than from an in-situ quarry. In other words, the long transport of these large stones to the Salisbury Plain may have been accomplished by a glacier, not by humans.

Provenance determinations have three major

components: 1) locating and sampling for analysis all potential source geologic deposits for the artifact material in question; 2) choosing an analytic method that has the sensitivity and scope to provide diagnostic signatures for each geologic deposit as well as for the artifacts; and 3) choosing a statistical- or data-analysis technique that can evaluate the data and then assign artifacts to source deposits.

Only the first part of this process is geologic, so we shall concentrate on it. Students interested in exploring the second and third steps in provenance determination should consult the journal *Archaeometry*, which since the 1960s has published many excellent articles on the analytical and statistical problems involved.

Attempts to assign artifactual materials to a particular geologic deposit have two inherent problems: 1) it must be established that the artifact has not undergone any chemical or physical alteration that would invalidate direct comparison of it with the same component material from known deposits, and 2) all potential source deposits must be adequately represented in the database for a confident assignment of provenance on the basis of chemical or physical patterning.

Item 1 has many aspects. First, artifacts fall into three groups, depending on the nature of the processing needed to transform the raw material into a useful object. Second, it must be determined whether significant chemical changes occurred to the object (artifact) during use or after burial. Only chemical characterizations unaffected by processing, manufacturing, use, or postburial diagenesis can be used for provenance determination. Minor and trace-element patterns in lithics and ceramics are not usually altered by use or post-use (burial) conditions.

There is a large group of rock and mineral raw materials that require no chemical or physical processing during the manufacture of the object that will alter the chemical characterization found in the raw-material deposit. These include various lithic materials like obsidian, chert, jade, quartzite, serpentinite, and marble, as well as native copper, gold, and amber. For a second group of raw materials, the production of an object is more complex. The most important members of this group are clay and temper for the making of pottery. Clay, water, and frequently temper must be selected, prepared, and mixed in appropriate proportions before being shaped, dried, and fired. The final object is a new material that is not found in nature.

A third group of materials requires even more advanced processing and change on the way to becoming a manufactured object. The best example of this group is the complex ores of copper. After mining, the ores must be smelted with fuel and usually a **flux**. With copper sulfide ores an intermediate stage, **matte**, is produced. In smelting to produce copper metal, the complex of materials in the furnace splits into metallic and slag phases. Hence, it is impossible to track the trace elements in an original copper mineral once they have been mixed with fuel and flux and divided between metal and slag during the processing. Throughout most of its metallurgical history, smelted copper was then alloyed with tin (usually tin and lead in ancient China) to make bronze or with zinc to make brass. This alloying of metals, plus the use of scrap metal and remelting, also obscures the trace-element content of the original copper. The chemical reactions in smelting do not alter the lead isotope composition of an ore mineral, however—copper minerals contain small amounts of lead—and so may provide provenance data on smelted ores.

Determining the chemical characteristics of geologic deposits and artifacts requires careful location or selection of sites or objects, statistical sampling of deposits or objects, selection of the most appropriate analytical techniques, standardization of analytical procedures, establishment of databases, and evaluation of large sets of data. The quantitative requirements for sampling, chemical analysis, and statistical analysis are much smaller for many archaeological problems if the researcher is merely trying to determine that the raw material in an artifact did *not* come from a specific deposit rather than figure out the specific deposit where the material originated.

Geologic Deposits

To establish and define a potential geologic source through trace-element concentrations, it is nec-

Figure 6.1 Stonehenge
(Drawing by Elaine Nissen)

essary to do two things: establish the geologic uniqueness and boundaries of the deposit; and collect and analyze ten or more samples that are widely dispersed statistically throughout the deposit. In practice, both these tasks range from difficult to impossible to accomplish. The first condition appears clear: What is the geologic deposit being sampled? Some primary and secondary native copper deposits are quite large (both in terms of kilometers in extent and hundreds of meters in depth). Others are small, perhaps no more than 100 meters. Our work has shown that good, nonoverlapping fingerprints are common for small deposits and for smaller parts of large deposits, such as individual mines (for example, in the Keweenaw Peninsula of northern Michigan). The larger the deposit or the larger the area or volume represented, the more diffuse the trace-element fingerprint.

In practice, defining the three-dimensional geometry of an ore deposit when only the surface outcrop is available is impossible. This ordinarily does not matter because the prehistoric miners did not penetrate to any great depth (usually they went only a few meters). It is necessary, however, to establish the areal integrity of the deposit. The samples should be collected as widely as possible from the extent of the outcrop to ensure coverage and provide the complete variation in trace-element concentrations. If a well-defined ancient quarry is being investigated, one problem is traded for another. The boundaries of the quarry can be adequately established, but, unlike most ancient mines, in quarries most or all of the material that ought to be sampled has been

removed. Researchers also need to determine whether modern, large-scale mining or quarrying techniques have obliterated a deposit exploited in ancient times.

The number of samples needed to characterize a deposit will increase with the trace-element variation in the deposit and the number of trace elements needed for the provenance determination. Our work on native copper has shown that it takes more than ten samples to characterize a deposit even minimally, assuming that eight or more trace elements are used in the characterization. Working with trace-element data on archaeological ceramics, Harbottle proved mathematically that when fewer than ten elements are used, serious overlaps in source characterizations occur.[3] With discriminant analysis it is assumed a priori that each trace element has equal weight in the classification scheme. The greater the number of trace elements used, the more reliable the classification will be, if the number of samples analyzed is greater than the number of elements used in the discrimination. It should be emphasized that although concentration data on two or three elements may allow sourcing in some local situations, for example, with obsidian (which generally needs fewer elements for characterization), reliance on too few elements will defeat the provenancing effort.

An excellent example of how to trace the source of stone objects is the work that was done on the origin of the rock used to construct the Colossi of Memnon on the plain near Thebes in Egypt. The statues were made of a very hard, ferruginous quartzite. Based on macroscopic examination, the quartzite blocks could have come from at least six sites. Using instrumental neutron activation analysis (INAA) for trace-element characterization, it was shown that the Gebel el Ahmar quarry, lying 676 kilometers downstream on the Nile, was the likely source, rather than the quarries at Aswan (only 200 kilometers upstream) which would have provided much easier transport, since the rocks would have been traveling downriver.[4]

Finally, for an understanding of the regional geology and the location of specific deposits, both the technical literature and the appropriate geologic survey personnel need to be consulted. We have worked in nearly a dozen countries and have always found the government geologic surveys— at all levels of government—extremely helpful. Only a small part of geologic knowledge finds its way into the published literature, however. Most of it resides in unpublished reports, maps, field notes, and the brains of field geologists. Go to where the knowledge is.

Materials Used in Geologic Sourcing

Obsidian

Throughout the Neolithic of the Old World and the prehistoric of the New World, the main material traded widely over long distances was obsidian. Some of the most successful trace-element sourcing has been accomplished for this material. Obsidian is not common in most regions of the world, and the number of possible sources is limited. A good knowledge of the bedrock geology of a region will allow a quick determination of the location of any potential obsidian sources. Obsidian is formed in lava flows and as blocks in **tuff** from explosive volcanic eruptions. Obsidian flows do not have the same appearance as normal basaltic flows. Owing to its higher silica content and the resulting viscosity of the lava, obsidian flows are often dome shaped. The result of rapid cooling, obsidian often occurs on the outside of flows. In regions of silicic volcanic rocks a significant amount of fieldwork may be necessary to locate all possible sources of workable obsidian, including transported material in river beds.

Nearly all obsidian originates in volcanic arcs

or chains. Volcanic arcs extend from Alaska to Oregon, over much of Mesoamerica, down the west coast of South America, across the island chains of southeast Asia, in the Caribbean, in East Africa, and in the Aegean. Similar volcanoes are found in the mountain belt extending from the Alps to the Himalayas, including archaeologically important deposits in the Carpathians and in central and eastern Anatolia.

In common with other lithic artifacts, the chemical composition of obsidian objects does not alter during manufacture. There are now large databases of chemical analyses of the major obsidian deposits for most of the world, and publications of successful sourcing of obsidian are abundant. Both instrumental neutron activation analysis and X-ray fluorescence analysis (XRF) techniques are commonly employed in obsidian provenance studies. Some obsidian deposits can also be sourced by means of ^{87}strontium/^{86}strontium isotope ratios plotted against rubidium trace-element concentrations, by thermoluminescence (TL) analyses, or using magnetic properties.

Concentrations of such elements as manganese, barium, scandium, rubidium, lanthanum, and zirconium vary by as much as three orders of magnitude among obsidian flows, while varying by less than 50 percent within a single flow or **pyroclastic** deposit. The precise suite of discriminating elements must be determined empirically for each regional situation. In at least some regions, obsidian deposits may be distinguished by means of major-element (such as calcium and magnesium) ratios rather than trace-element concentrations. Atomic absorption (AA) techniques can determine calcium and magnesium. This instrumentation is more readily available to most archaeologists than XRF or INAA.

Since the early 1960s considerable research has been devoted to locating Anatolian obsidian sources and determining chemical fingerprints for them. Archaeologists have developed reconstructions of early trade and cultural exchange from this database. However, as of 1996 this database may be misleading for two reasons: not all potential source deposits have been sampled, and many deposits were not sampled systematically—

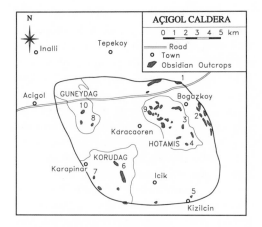

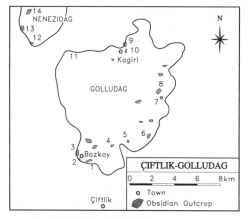

Figure 6.2 Açigol and Çiftlik
Açigol and Çiftlik volcanic areas in central Turkey, showing caldera rims, interior domes, obsidian outcrops, and (numbered) collection sites for a provenance project by Rapp.

with full knowledge and coverage of the geology of the site. Some deposits have obsidian flows covering a span of two to four million years. Flows two million years apart in age are unlikely to have the same trace-element composition.

The two major central Anatolian deposits of Açigol and Çiftlik have up to a dozen distinct flows varying in age by as much as two million years. Figure 6.2 illustrates this phenomenon. Using INAA to determine twenty-five major and trace elements, Rapp and his colleagues have defined eight separate signatures, not simply one for Açigol and one for Çiftlik. In the eastern part of

the Açigol **caldera** three separate flow signatures can be defined. In the western part of the caldera there is only one distinct signature—from the youngest of the obsidians in central Anatolia. In the Çiftlik area three separate sources can be distinguished. The eighth source is from the obsidians at Nenezi Dag, about halfway between Açigol and Çiftlik.

Obsidian sourcing using trace-element characterizations is now routinely performed in many parts of the world. Until the 1990s it was assumed that obsidian found in prehistoric American Southwest contexts derived from the Government Mountain source in northern Arizona, the Picketpost Mountain source in central Arizona, one of the obsidian deposits in northern New Mexico, or Mesoamerica. This assumption was based on lack of archaeometric studies of the obsidian in this region. Now studies have expanded the number of potential sources and assembled a quantitative trace-element database, which allows much better obsidian artifact sourcing for this important archaeological region.[5]

A review article by Williams-Thorpe covering obsidian provenance studies in the Mediterranean and the Near East should be consulted for a summary of recent findings. It includes data from Carpathian northeastern Hungary and eastern Slovakian sources, as well as the well-known Italian, Aegean, Anatolian, and Armenian deposits. An extensive bibliography is provided.[6]

The development of new research techniques has moved the sourcing of obsidians beyond dependence on trace-element and related compositional analyses. Back-scattered electron petrography has proven a valuable technique for obsidian provenance studies in the southwestern United States and the Mediterranean.[7] It relies on the ability to distinguish the different cooling histories of the originally molten obsidian. Back-scattered imaging, energy-dispersive X-ray analysis, and image analysis with a scanning electron microscope, in conjunction with one another, provide a petrographic method to investigate geologic and archaeological materials that are difficult or impossible to analyze by optical thin-section microscopy.

Granite and Related Igneous and Metamorphic Rocks

Coarse-grained igneous and high-grade metamorphic rocks have served as building and monumental stone for more than five millennia. Sometimes these rocks were quarried hundreds of kilometers distant from the place they were found. Many granites have **jointing** patterns which aid in quarrying. Quality granites widely used for building stone occur throughout most of the British Isles, in northwestern France, in much of Scandinavia, in Italy, and in Russia. Perhaps the most famous granitic rock is the syenite outcropping between Aswan and the first cataract of the Nile River. This rock has been used since the First Dynasty for tombs, temples, and sarcophagi. It was exported to other parts of the Mediterranean for obelisks and statues. At Aswan there is also a gray granite that was used for buildings in Egypt and exported. The red porphyry quarried near the first cataract of the Nile in Egypt has been used for sphinxes and statues in Egypt and was shipped by the Romans to Pompeii and other cities of the Roman Empire.

Another popular rock used in antiquity is diorite. Unfortunately, many of the igneous rocks from archaeological contexts have been erroneously identified by nonspecialists, and these errors have been compounded and perpetuated by archaeological tradition. Once in the literature, incorrect names are hard to correct. Diorite is a good example. Some true diorites were quarried in Egypt for statues and bowls, but many Egyptian monumental and statuary rocks have been misnamed "diorite."

The identification and classification of fine-grained lithics of volcanic origin present special problems for the archaeologist. Petrographic and geochemical analyses can overcome these problems and provide the data for firm identification, classification, and sorting. Petrography and/or major-element geochemistry is required for rock classification, and trace-element geochemistry can be used for discriminating among potential source deposits.

Lithic debitage from the British Camp shell midden on San Juan Island, Washington, had been classified for the past hundred years as basalt, with a local source predicted. Petrographic and geochemical analyses have shown that these lithics are dacite rather than basalt and that the source is in the High Cascades, about 200 kilometers from the site.[8]

Thin-section petrography (see below) has often been used to characterize and determine the provenance of coarse-grained igneous rocks, especially Roman millstones in the British Isles. **Magnetic susceptibility** provides a rapid, nondestructive method of in situ characterization and sourcing for rocks containing magnetic minerals. Although corrections must be made for object size, surface relief, and curvature, more than 350 Roman granite columns were measured with this method. Results showed clear groupings and similarities with potential sources in Italy, Turkey, and Egypt.

Chert

Chert (including flint and other varieties—see Chapter 5) is microcrystalline quartz with few trace chemical impurities in the quartz crystals but abundant impurities as micro-inclusions. Chert from even a single deposit can have considerable visual variability, particularly in color. Trace elements within source deposits vary in complex ways, but with adequate sampling, trace-element fingerprints of chert sources can be established. Trace-element variation may be great, but the variation usually involves stratigraphic position and horizontal distance between samples. In some cases chert may be sourced by petrographic features. Some chert deposits have diagnostic fossil impurities or microstructures that can easily be seen under the petrographic microscope.

Knife River Flint is a high-quality lithic material that was used by indigenous cultures of the northern Great Plains of North America from Paleo-Indian to historic periods. It has been reported at archaeological sites up to 1,000 kilometers from its geologic source. In the past, identification has been made on the basis of visual criteria—hence, many misidentifications were likely. Some regional brown cherts called

Hudson Bay Lowland cherts are visually similar to Knife River Flint but have been shown by INAA to be chemically distinct from it.[9] Rapp has undertaken a major study of INAA sourcing of western Great Lakes lithic materials.

An underlying problem with chert provenance studies is that there may be hundreds—or possibly thousands—of potential sources for chert throughout the world. As with other geologic materials, it is first necessary to determine the geology of the chert sources in a region, not forgetting glacial or alluvial sources. The fact that not all chert is workable into objects mitigates this problem. As with other geologic materials, local museums and academic departments will have collections of cherts from the region. However, it is unwise to rely completely on such collections, because the full range in variability of each deposit must be analyzed to obtain an adequate fingerprint.

Marble

Attempts to source classical marble in the Mediterranean and Anatolia go back at least to the times of Theophrastus and Pliny. Geologists in the nineteenth century tried (unsuccessfully) to distinguish marble quarries by petrographic methods. Scientific efforts in the second half of the twentieth century using XRF, emission spectroscopy, INAA, and TL were also unsuccessful. Finally, stable ratios of carbon and oxygen isotopes, sometimes augmented by strontium isotope analyses, proved to be the key to sourcing marble.

The geologic history of the rock, including its sedimentary origin and subsequent metamorphism, governs the carbon and oxygen isotope composition of marble. For isotope provenance to work, the isotope fingerprint must be uniform over the volume of the quarry, and preferably over the entire geologic district. Uniform isotopic compositions will be attained over a broad area if isotopic equilibrium was attained during original formation and metamorphism, the metamorphic gradient was not too steep, and the marble rock body is relatively pure and thick. Because only the purest white marble was quarried, accessory minerals and other impurities do not generally occur.

Since Roman times the principal marble quarries of Italy have been those of Carrara, which are located about 50 kilometers northwest of Pisa in the Apuane Alps. This marble is noted for its purity, grain size, and color, which make it a coveted ornamental and statuary stone. Carrara marble was first quarried under Julius Caesar in the first century B.C. Both Julius Caesar and Augustus used Carrara marble to replace older brick buildings. In addition, the Romans exported Carrara marble throughout the ancient world.

Greeks and Romans of the classical period preferred pure white marble for statuary and monuments bearing inscriptions. Therefore classical lands have extensive remains of buildings, monuments, and statuary composed of pure white marble. In the Aegean area much of this marble came from Proconnesus on the island of Marmara in Turkey, while some came from Carrara, and some from quarries in Greece. Proconnesus marble was perhaps the commonest for use in buildings throughout the classical world. It was also used for large sarcophagi. An extensive database of isotope analyses from all the major marble quarries in the classical lands of the eastern Mediterranean (Italy, Greece, Turkey, and Tunisia) has been assembled by Herz, among others.[10] These data allow sourcing of Mediterranean area marbles in most cases. In addition to sourcing, these databases can be used to detect forgeries, and for associating broken and separated pieces of statues, epigraphy, and monuments.

Clay

For a discussion of clay minerals used in ceramics, see Chapter 5. Although clay sources are needed for tile, brick, adobe, and related materials, the most important archaeological questions have centered on sourcing pottery clays. In fact, the greatest amount of time and money spent in archaeological provenance studies may have been for attempts to source pottery clays. Provenancing the clay component of pottery to a local deposit has been successful in only a few cases. This is in part because minor and trace elements are not distributed homogeneously in clay beds (particularly in comparison with obsidian and native copper deposits) and in part because potters selected clays from heterogeneous clay deposits. They then prepared the material, often removing undesirable impurities which may have affected the ratio of clay minerals; sometimes they mixed the clays to achieve a better product. We can have no direct knowledge of the pottery-making practices of prehistoric potters, so we cannot correct for or evaluate the chemical alterations inherent in the pottery manufacture. Consequently, provenancing of ceramic artifacts is most frequently performed on the basis of a comparison between the trace-element composition of the unprovenanced ceramic object and the composition of a group of ceramic objects of known provenance.

Provenancing pottery raw materials takes two forms: minor and trace-element analysis and petrographic analysis. For Anatolian pottery and clays, cesium, thorium, scandium, hafnium, tantalum, and cobalt have proven good discriminating elements. Similarly, in the nearby Aegean area, hafnium, manganese, cerium, and scandium have high discriminating power. Sourcing ceramic raw materials has at least one advantage. It can reasonably be assumed that local sources (not more than a half-day's journey away, and usually less) were used. Contrast this with copper, obsidian, and especially tin, where the nearest source could be hundreds of kilometers away. Examples of the use of petrography to source pottery raw materials are given below in the section on petrographic analysis.

Microfossils have been used as indicators of provenance in Sub-Neolithic pottery from Finland. The glacial clays of Finland formed during different stages in the history of the Baltic Sea, and fossil diatom flora are important in the study of this period. The diatoms in the clay are related to the sedimentary environments of the ancestral Baltic. Siliceous valves of diatoms can withstand the firing temperatures of pottery. Prehistoric peoples used clays deposited during two stages of Baltic history, ignoring clays found nearer the settlements. In one study, changes in diatom composition mirrored changes in pottery decoration style.

Temper

Grains much larger than clay particles can become incorporated in pottery either by being a constituent in the source clay bed or by being added as temper by the potter to modify the properties of the clay. Mineral tempers include crushed rock (of many types), shell material, quartz sand, and volcanic ash. For provenance studies, the critical question is whether the coarse-grained material was present naturally or was added by the potter. One way to approach this problem is to characterize the material carefully: in terms of mineral identification, particle shape, size distribution, and amount. This will give some indication of whether the material is a likely constituent of a clay bed or more typical of a local stream deposit or, in the case of angular crushed rock, unlikely to be derived from a natural geologic source. Provenancing temper is best accomplished with petrographic techniques (see below).

The source of the volcanic temper sands in prehistoric pottery from the South Pacific island of Tonga has been a major provenance problem. The scarcity of noncalcareous sand on most of the inhabited islands in the Tongan group has prompted the suggestion that either temper was imported from a volcanic island to the west or the pottery was imported from Fiji. Although the mineralogy of the tempers is compatible with that of Tongan volcanic rocks, Tonga lacks deposits of the rounded and well-sorted sands found in the tempers. Recent discovery of beach placer sands derived from the geologic reworking of **tephra** deposits provides a satisfactory source. Using petrographic techniques, compositional analyses of temper sands in many ancient sherds from throughout the island group indicate that pottery making using local raw materials was once widespread.[11]

One of the most thorough and inclusive case studies of the provenance of ceramic and metal raw materials is focused on the Bronze Age of the island of Cyprus.[12] This study originated in efforts to reconstruct prehistoric production and exchange systems. The monograph assesses the various analytical techniques used in sourcing Cypriot metals, pottery, and clays, as well as the geochemical, archaeological, and statistical prerequisites for any provenance study. In this assessment, the authors point out that unlike the highly successful provenancing of metals, sourcing pottery raw materials has proven exceedingly difficult. Patterns in trace-element data on ceramics may relate to ware rather than location. This study also emphasizes the problems that arise when analytical data sets are obtained by different techniques or by the same technique from different laboratories.

Amber

Establishing the provenance of European amber artifacts by infrared spectroscopy has been successful in many studies. The reliability of this technique rests on the fact that Baltic amber has a highly characteristic infrared spectrum. Assignments for known material are about 97.5 percent correct. Limitations of this method became apparent in source studies of artifact amber which was badly weathered. Research on this problem resulted in the creation of a special method for studying weathered amber that uses gas chromatography to determine the diagnostic amount of succinic acid.

Soft Stone, Other Rock, and Semiprecious Minerals

Using trace-element analyses, many other lithic materials have been successfully sourced to their geologic deposit of origin. These rock and mineral materials include steatite (soapstone), serpentinite, turquoise, and, from Japan, sanukite (an andesite with orthopyroxene, garnet, and andesine in a glassy groundmass). For nonarchaeological purposes, geologists have used a wide variety of techniques to source geologic deposits, formations, and minerals, including isotopic provenancing of sandstones from the Eocene Type Formation in the Oregon coast range, correlation of North American Ordovician bentonites using apatite chemistry, and trace-element sourcing of detrital quartz in a sedimentary formation to the granite where the quartz originated.

Soapstone artifacts dating to the first millennium B.C. from the James River drainage in Virginia have been successfully traced to their quarries of origin by **rare-earth element** concentrations using INAA. Many soapstone bowls from habitation sites in Virginia have rare-earth trace-element patterns that match outcrops and quarries in Albemarle and Nelson counties. Artifacts from five North Carolina habitation sites also had rare-earth trace-element patterns that matched the Virginia soapstone sources. Three of sixteen soapstone artifacts from as far away as northwestern Mississippi were also traced to the Virginia deposits.

Native Copper

In North America, north of the Rio Grande River, utilitarian copper artifacts appear initially in the archaeological record about 5500 B.P. Use of native copper flourished in the western Great Lakes area because of the wealth of available copper in the form of nuggets and lode deposits outcropping at the surface. Early uses of copper include tools and ornaments, but by the time of the first European contact, the indigenous peoples used copper primarily for decorative purposes. Since the only technology available to North American indigenous societies was hammering and annealing, the size of a piece of copper governed its usefulness. There was not even a technology available to retrieve usable sizes of copper from an oversized mass. The famous Ontonogan (Michigan) copper boulder is a good example: it weighed about one-and-a-half metric tons. Such masses could not be chiseled, sawed, broken, or otherwise comminuted and so remained unavailable to prehistoric miners.

In the eastern Mediterranean and Near East, copper has been in use since early in the ninth millennium B.C. Until about 4000 B.C., the copper used was probably native copper. In Anatolia, where the earliest extensive use of native copper is known from Neolithic Çayonu, it is assumed that copper was native copper from the large deposits at Ergani Maden, located just 20 kilometers from Çayonu. However, extensive modern openpit mining has removed all or most of the evidence, including the native copper portion of the deposits, thus limiting the opportunity for trace-element sourcing studies. Compared to work on North American native copper sourcing, little research has been done on the specific sources of native copper from this, the region where copper metallurgy developed.[13]

Native copper occurs primarily in three geologic environments: in **mafic** lavas and mafic and **ultramafic** intrusives; in the oxidized zone of copper-sulfide deposits; and deposited in clastic sediments associated with mafic igneous rocks. We refer to deposits of the first type as *primary*, deposits of the second type as *secondary*, and deposits of the third type as *sedimentary*. In North America large deposits of native copper occur in basaltic lavas (and related sedimentary rocks) of the Lake Superior region. Most of the native copper available to pre-Columbian North Americans at or near the surface was derived from mafic igneous rocks. The opposite is true of Old World native copper deposits. There most of the native copper has come from secondary deposits, where it occurs as a secondary alteration mineral within the oxidized zones of copper-sulfide deposits. Strong oxidation takes place in these deposits because of the abundance of pyrite, which dissolves in water to form sulfuric acid and ferric sulfate. The associated chemical reactions are quite different from those in native copper formation in basaltic lavas. This oxidized zone is always closer to the surface than the remainder of the deposit and often outcrops at the surface. In the sulfide copper ores of western North America, native copper is a common but minor constituent of the oxidized zone.

Chemical characterization of native copper is performed on the basis of trace-element concentrations. Several analytic methods are available to determine the chemical elements in the low parts per million–parts per billion range. By far the most commonly used is INAA. Because trace elements may vary by orders of magnitude among deposits and by more than 100 percent in a single nugget, absolute values are not as critical as the overall pattern of element concentrations.

Rapp and his colleagues have been trace-element fingerprinting North American native copper deposits for more than two decades. The principal finding of our research indicates that the chemical fingerprint of an individual native copper source, coming from a single, well-defined deposit, can be firmly established. This is true in cases where the deposits are geographically close, as well as where they are distant.[14] Although our neutron activation analysis procedures automatically determine forty-seven elements, only about seventeen have any discriminating value, and only thirteen (iron, cobalt, arsenic, mercury, scandium, silver, iridium, lanthanum, europium, gold, antimony, nickel, and zinc) provide nearly all the discrimination.

Two examples can illustrate sourcing of native copper. The first concerns the creation of a database of trace-element signatures for native copper deposits; it illustrates the problem of adequate sampling. In 1988 we chose three precisely defined native copper sources: Michipicoten Island (Ontario), with thirty-five samples; Isle Royale–Minong Mine (Michigan), with nine samples; and the Wisconsin Weyerhauser Number 3 Mine (Wisconsin), with seventeen samples, all of which belong to the same Lake Superior volcanic region. We wished to show that sources can be clearly identified on the basis of their trace-element composition. These deposits are a few hundred kilometers apart. We successfully assigned 100 percent of the samples to their known source.

In 1992 a second expedition to the Weyerhauser mine was successful in collecting an additional suite of fifteen samples from a greater percentage of the deposit (the first set of seventeen samples was collected from a far more restricted rock mass). The addition of the trace-element analyses of these additional samples to the database and the rerunning of the sourcing calculations dropped the percentage of samples correctly assigned from 100 to 91. This demonstrates that considerable care and effort must be invested in sampling deposits adequately to obtain a representative trace-element definition of a source.

The second example illustrates the value of the database in the sourcing of artifact copper. Twenty-two copper artifacts from three archaeological sites in northern Minnesota were analyzed for trace-element concentrations and sources calculated. Overall, sixteen of the twenty-two artifacts (72.7 percent) had trace-element patterns that indicated a source in western Wisconsin, specifically the Weyerhauser mine mentioned above.

Four artifacts were traced to nearby Isle Royale. The rest were traced to other possible sources.

Complex Copper Minerals

The smelting of copper goes back six millennia to the smelting of malachite and perhaps azurite. Malachite, azurite, and other oxide copper minerals occur in the upper, oxidized zone of copper sulfide deposits. These oxide-zone deposits are not as rich or as extensive as the sulfide-zone copper deposits. As the oxide-zone copper was depleted by ancient miners and metalsmiths, increasing pyrotechnical skills were required to smelt sulfide copper; this would have had a profound effect on economies and trade relations in early phases of the Bronze Age. The ability to determine whether a copper or copper alloy artifact was derived from native copper, oxide copper, or sulfide copper thus provides archaeologists with important information on the development of ancient technologies and economies. Research has shown that analyses of artifacts for a suite of diagnostic elements (antimony, arsenic, iron, lead, silver, and sulfur) can, in a majority of cases, trace the origin of the copper to ore type, though not to specific deposit.[15]

Myth has influenced ideas concerning the sources of Old World copper, and not all myths are ancient. Modern commentaries on the Old Testament contain references to King Solomon's mines, supposed to be located at the head of the Gulf of Aqabah. Copper from this area was said to have been one of the mainstays of Solomon's wealth. This myth was added to by an American archaeologist named Nelson Glueck. From 1938 to 1940, Glueck excavated a tell near the head of the Gulf of Aqabah. Although there is no specific reference in the Old Testament to King Solomon's mines, Glueck reported that during the earliest phase of occupation, the tell had been the site of a copper refinery for the nearby "King Solomon's mines." But later research showed that during the early mining operations at Timna, the local copper deposits were under Egyptian control—long before Solomon was born. And later mining activity took place long after Solomon died. Absolutely no evidence of mining activity during Solomon's time exists. Myths and archae-

ology come together only when there is sufficient evidence to support oral tradition or myth.

Tin

Tin has been far more important to metal-using societies than is commonly understood. Tin is an essential component of bronze and pewter, from which many artifacts were made. (Bronze is approximately 90 percent copper and 10 percent tin.) One mineral, cassiterite, accounts for virtually all of the tin that has ever been exploited. Fortunately, cassiterite is a stable oxide that remains unaltered when weathered out of lodes to form placer deposits; this makes it easier to source.

Perhaps the most perplexing provenance problem in geoarchaeology is where the tin came from for the bronze in the Mediterranean and Near East during the Bronze Age. To understand the problem let us first contrast the abundances of iron, copper, and tin. Iron makes up approximately 5 percent (50,000 ppm) of the earth's crust, and deposits of iron oxide are ubiquitous. The abundance of copper in the earth's crust is about 50 ppm, and copper deposits are widespread. Tin, on the other hand, makes up only 5 ppm in the earth's crust, and exploitable concentrations of tin occur only in a few metalliferous zones.

In the Old World, where tin bronze originated, the only significant known deposits are in Cornwall, Brittany, Iberia, the Erzgebirge Mountains of the northwest Czech Republic, and Tadjikistan (figure 6.3). Minor deposits are found in the eastern desert of Egypt, Tuscany, Sardinia, and a few other locations. There is no evidence that humans used the tin areas of the Erzgebirge until about the twelfth century A.D. and no evidence of contact between Anatolia, where the first tin bronzes occur in the late fourth millennium B.C., and Cornwall, Brittany, or Iberia.

For most of history, Europe's largest producer of tin has been Cornwall, where tin mineralization is linked to the intrusion of granites more than 250 million years ago. During Roman times there was more tin mined in the Iberian Peninsula, and during the fifteenth century the mines at Erzgebirge outstripped Cornwall. The tin deposits of Iberia are similar in most respects to those of

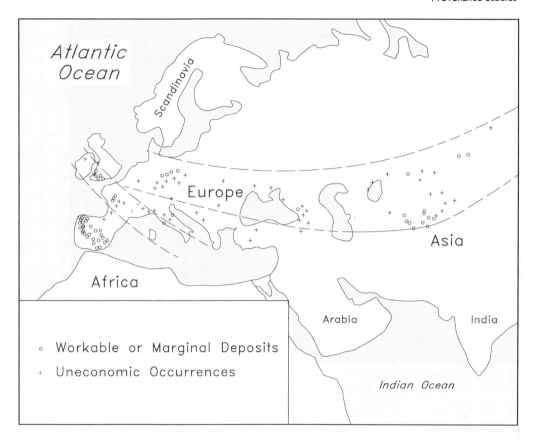

Figure 6.3 Tin Belts in Europe and Asia

Cornwall. The Iberian tin belt extends more than 480 kilometers, from Galacia in the northwest to Extremadura in the south central region, with the whole of northwest Iberia dotted with abandoned mines, including the heavily worked alluvial (placer) deposits. Iberian deposits were exploited in the Bronze Age, but there is no evidence of trade with the eastern Mediterranean. However, the popular myth persists that the Phoenicians went to Cornwall to trade for tin, which they used to supply the ancient civilizations of the eastern Mediterranean and Near East.

In the Near East, ancient texts indicate trade in tin at least back to the middle of the third millennium B.C. from an eastern source, perhaps beyond the Indus Valley of Pakistan. Malaysia and Thailand have been the largest producers of tin in recent times, but there is as yet no scientific

evidence that Southeast Asian tin was imported into the West before the first millennium B.C. There is no textual or archaeological evidence of tin coming from the west to the Aegean and Near East in the Bronze Age. Archaeological evidence for the tin trade, from a shipwreck off the coast of Anatolia, takes us back only to the latter half of the second millennium B.C., and that evidence indicates an eastern source.

There are four cassiterite deposits in the eastern desert of Egypt. Although it had previously been believed that Egypt came relatively late to bronze making, one of the tin deposits, at Mueilha, has hieroglyphic evidence on nearby outcrops that ancient activity of some sort goes back at least to the Sixth Dynasty, 2200 B.C. On a Fifth Dynasty tomb at Giza a scene shows molten metal being poured from what may be a smelting crucible. This indicates that metal technology existed in Egypt from at least sometime in the mid-third millennium B.C.

Rapp and colleagues have collected and analyzed cassiterite from Cornwall, Erzgebirge, Egypt, and a few other locations and have demonstrated that cassiterite can be sourced using trace-element signatures. However, as with smelted copper, smelted tin has an altered trace-element chemistry, and so far, archaeologists have failed to locate eastern Mediterranean or Near Eastern Bronze Age tin mining or smelting sites (where some cassiterite should be found). They have also failed to identify or recover any cassiterite in the excavated material.[16]

Lead, Silver, and Gold

Lead objects, all of which must be derived from the smelting of lead minerals, appear in the late seventh millennium B.C. in Turkey. Because of lead's low melting point (327° C) and the ease of smelting galena (lead sulfide), which is metallic in appearance (at below 800° C), lead was easy for early metalsmiths to exploit. Galena deposits are fairly abundant throughout the area in the Near East where metalsmithing originated. In the earliest Chinese bronzes, lead was already serving as an alloying element, perhaps providing the castability desired by Chinese metalsmiths. Lead ores, especially galena and cerussite (lead carbonate), often contain a substantial amount of silver and were probably the chief source of silver in antiquity.

We can source most lead and silver artifacts from regions, such as the Mediterranean area, where the geologic deposits have been analyzed for their lead isotope ratios. Lead has four isotopes: ^{204}Pb, ^{206}Pb, ^{207}Pb, ^{208}Pb. Each has the same chemical properties. Therefore, in the process of smelting, the isotope ratios derived from the ores are not altered. This means that any isotopic signature in a lead or copper ore will be retained intact in the finished artifact (unlike trace-element signatures, which alter during smelting). Lead isotope ratios of ore minerals vary from deposit to deposit, depending on the geologic age of the deposit. This is because the radioactive decay of ^{238}U, ^{235}U, and ^{232}Th (thorium)

is constantly producing ^{206}Pb, ^{207}Pb, and ^{208}Pb, respectively. Over geologic time the constant decay of uranium and thorium leads to changing ratios of ^{206}Pb, ^{207}Pb, and ^{208}Pb to ^{204}Pb, because the latter has not changed throughout geologic time. However, two geologic conditions can complicate this situation. A serious problem can arise when initial lead isotope ratios in a deposit are altered by subsequent episodes of metamorphism, which may introduce lead from surrounding rocks. A second problem stems from the fact that deeper parts of the earth's crust and outer mantle have different ratios of lead to uranium and thorium than rocks in the upper crust. This can lead to isotope variations within a particular ore deposit, especially in the extensive lead-zinc deposits in sedimentary rocks. Because of early difficulties in measuring the abundance of the least-abundant isotope, ^{204}Pb, scientists routinely use the ratios $^{207}Pb/^{206}Pb$ and $^{208}Pb/^{206}Pb$, which can be plotted graphically (figure 6.4).

Lead-isotope measurements have been used to determine the source of ores used in lead smelting, providing confirmation that in the early eighteenth century, people in central North America used local ores to produce metallic lead objects. Smelting appears not to alter the isotope ratios of source materials, and the lead ores frequently display different isotope compositions. The Guebert site, near the Mississippi River in southwest Illinois, contained a crude lead smelting operation associated with a village occupied between 1719 and 1765. Several other sites from about this time period also contained lead objects, ceramics, musket balls, and lead scrap. Isotope analysis identified the local sources of lead and also lead smelted in Europe. The European objects found were finished products like bale seals and musket balls.

Lead-isotope analyses have also been used to determine the ore sources for lead-rich metallic artifacts from the Bronze Age, for Roman age lead objects from Africa, and for lead in glazes on ceramics from the New World.[17]

Lead provenancing shows that ancient miners did not always locate and exploit the nearest ore deposits. For example, the Romans at Carthage imported substantial amounts of lead from mines in Spain and Britain. In North America, where in-

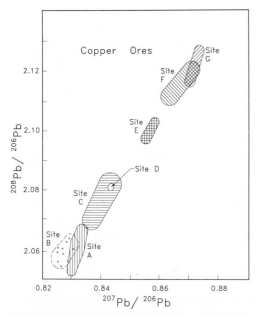

Figure 6.4 Typical Lead Isotope Fields for Copper Deposits in the Mediterranean Area
At site B the actual plots for the ten samples that make up the field are shown. Except for site D, which is completely contained within the field for site C, the overlaps typically disappear when the third ratio ($^{207}Pb/^{206}Pb$) is factored in.

Methods Used in Geologic Sourcing

Trace-Element Analyses

The rapid growth of accurate, automated techniques for trace-element chemical analysis has made the modern development of provenance studies possible. Some of the new techniques are nondestructive, and most require only small samples, which makes sampling more acceptable to museum curators and excavators. These newer techniques can be used economically on large numbers of samples under standardized conditions so that statistically valid results can be obtained.

The most common analytic techniques for provenance have used trace-element patterns or isotopic compositions to fingerprint geologic deposits. Each trace-element technique has its own set of problems with establishing standards; techniques have differing sensitivities and interferences for various elements; and the results often cannot be compared between laboratories. All techniques have the problem of inhomogeneities in the samples, and all require that care be taken to prevent postsampling contamination at trace levels. Each technique has either advantages for certain types of materials or cost benefits. Optical-emission spectroscopy, for example, which was the first instrumental technique used in provenance studies, did not have the sensitivity or precision necessary for trace-element fingerprinting.

Modern instrumental techniques are all capable of multi-element analysis. These techniques can be used to identify more than half the elements in the periodic table. They provide high precision and accuracy over a range of element concentrations. However, each technique has its limitations, so geoarchaeologists must evaluate the relative merits of the competing systems in terms of the provenance problem at hand. The dominant techniques used by geologists for multi-element analyses are atomic absorption spectrometry (AA), inductively coupled plasma spectrometry (ICP), X-ray fluorescence spectrometry (XRF), and instrumental neutron activation analysis (INAA). Analysts doing archaeological provenance studies favor INAA; laboratories that lack access to a

digenous peoples did not smelt or melt metals, the silvery metallic mineral galena was used as a ceremonial object. Lead-isotope analyses have been used successfully to source galena in artifacts.[18]

Since the early 1970s, studies attempting to evaluate the trace-element sourcing of ancient gold objects have been inconclusive. Some research has indicated that major trace impurities in gold complicate the process of characterizing or identifying its source. Other investigations have been able to correlate these trace impurities with metallogenic provinces rather than specific deposits. Still other research has shown that some trace elements, such as indium, can be diagnostic. Tin and platinum have been shown to occur as minor impurities in secondary (alluvial) gold but not in primary (lode) gold deposits from European sources. However, no universal method has yet been established for provenancing gold.

nuclear reactor generally use XRF: geoarchae-ologists should have some familiarity with both. In AA and ICP, the sample must be dissolved before it is introduced into the instrument. When dealing with trace concentrations, this requirement adds significantly to the problems of accuracy.

Instrumental Neutron Activation Analysis

Neutron activation analysis is a physical method of determining trace-element concentrations with high precision and sensitivity. Many chemical elements can be detected at the low parts-per-million level and some can be detected well into the parts-per-billion range. In addition, a wide range of elements can be measured simultaneously with no loss in precision. Finally, INAA requires only a small sample (50 mg for metals, 200 mg for silicates); there is no complex sample preparation, and there are no extraction techniques. In this technique, the sample is subjected to irradiation by slow (thermal) neutrons in a nuclear reactor. Various constituent atoms capture these neutrons, producing unstable daughter elements. These unstable isotopes emit gamma rays characteristic of the original element present in the sample, and the gamma-ray intensity is a measure of the concentration of each original element present. The gamma-ray spectrum from the decay is measured in a multichannel gamma-ray spectrometer.

Neutron activation methods can achieve high accuracy and precision for some elements but only moderate or poor results for others. As a technique, INAA has a different sensitivity (detection limit) for each chemical element. Sensitivities vary with irradiation time and intensity, delay time, counting conditions, and composition of the sample. Where a reactor is accessible and set up for automated INAA, the per-sample cost is low. A major advantage of INAA is the lack of a matrix interference, a problem with AA and ICP. The principal disadvantage for most investigators is the difficulty of gaining access to a reactor. Other disadvantages include the need for compromises when setting the counting routine and the need to monitor the neutron flux. Neutron activation analysis is one of the commonest tech-niques for determining the geologic sources of raw materials used by prehistoric human groups. It has often been employed by geoarchaeologists interested in trading patterns, population territories, and migration. The basic steps involved are the same as those of all other raw-material sourcing techniques: both the artifact and the potential raw material used to produce it need to be analyzed to determine their compositional characteristics and whether there is a statistical match between the artifact and its potential source.

As an example, INAA was used to characterize the rocks from two prehistoric quarries that both contained varieties of the Chadron Formation chalcedony (or the White River Group Silicates, which may be either from the Chadron or Brule Formations). After the two sources were studied, stone artifacts from a Clovis archaeological site in Kansas (the Eckles site) were analyzed by INAA. Because the sources of the Chadron Formation chalcedony apparently lay some distance from the site, locating a likely source gave the researcher a way to evaluate the long-distance movement associated with Clovis stone tool use. The two source areas studied were in Colorado and South Dakota. Element analysis was used to distinguish them. Using multivariate statistics, the artifacts from the Clovis site were found to match the Colorado source most closely. Based on INAA, it was possible to demonstrate that the materials at the Kansas Clovis site probably derived from the Colorado source.[19]

Instrumental neutron activation analysis was also used to obtain trace-element composition data for chipped stone artifacts from the Mayan site of Colha in Belize. The major human occupations occurred between 1000 B.C. and 1250 A.D. Studies were undertaken to investigate chert sources and to trace the exchange and distribution patterns of objects made of chert. First, researchers ascertained that there were compositional differences among cherts from different regions. Using discriminant analysis, archaeological chert samples from Colha and other Mayan centers were characterized according to geologic chert samples. Two chert types found at Colha were local, indicating that the people of Colha procured their chert from outcrops surrounding the site. Colhalike chert was also found at other Mayan centers, discoveries that have implications for our understanding of chert exchange within the region.[20]

X-Ray Fluorescence Spectrometry

This technique achieved prominence in the 1960s and has been used widely ever since. In XRF, a sample irradiated by an X-ray beam emits a secondary X-ray fluorescence spectrum characteristic of the elements in the sample. The principal advantage of XRF for provenance studies is that it is a bulk technique and, like INAA, can be applied to the raw sample. This answers concerns about sample homogeneity and resistance to dissolution. It is possible to automate XRF systems, and they provide high-precision analyses for many elements. One can also design XRF systems to be both nondestructive and portable—highly desirable when dealing with museum artifacts. The principal disadvantages of XRF are matrix and interference problems, an instrument cost that is perhaps four times as great as that of AA, and lack of sensitivity in the parts-per-billion range compared to INAA. This has led to its use in those provenance investigations, such as with obsidian, where discrimination can be achieved even at the high parts-per-million and percent levels for diagnostic elements.

Isotope Analysis/Mass Spectrometry

As the various isotopes of an element vary from one another only in their mass, the determination of isotope abundances or ratios is made with a mass spectrometer. In a mass spectrometer, the sample is positively ionized, then accelerated through a magnetic field. On leaving the magnetic field, ions of specific masses are collected separately and counted electronically.

Accelerator Mass Spectrometry (AMS) is commonly used in archaeology because it can determine accurately $^{14}C/^{12}C$ ratios on as little as one milligram of carbon for purposes of dating. In provenance studies the major use of the technique has been determining marble sources by means of ratios of carbon, oxygen, and strontium-stable isotopes and determining lead, silver, and copper sources with stable lead isotopes.

Petrographic Analysis

This brief introduction to optical petrography is designed to present only a general picture of the usefulness of the polarizing microscope in geoarchaeology. Books and articles abound that cover all aspects of these methods in great depth. In our view such microscopic methods are woefully underused in archaeological investigations.

Most lithic and ceramic materials and products are composed of minerals (obsidian—a volcanic glass—is an exception). Because minerals are crystalline, petrography is based on crystal symmetry and crystal chemistry. In its coarsest categorization, crystal symmetry classifies minerals into seven crystal systems: isometric, hexagonal, tetragonal, trigonal, orthorhombic, monoclinic, and triclinic. For petrographic analysis, it is the optical symmetry and optical parameters of minerals that allow identification and interpretation.

Isometric minerals are optically isotropic: they have only one index of refraction. Hexagonal, tetragonal, and trigonal minerals are uniaxial—they have one optic axis and two indices of refraction. Orthorhombic, monoclinic, and triclinic minerals are biaxial. They have two optic axes and three indices of refraction. Uniaxial and biaxial crystals are said to be *anisotropic* (not isotropic). Mineral grains can be immersed in oils with known indices of refraction to measure the refractive indices and other optical characteristics that help identify them. Clay minerals are too fine-grained to be studied by the methods of optical mineralogy.

The most important technique for petrologic and petrographic analysis is thin-section petrography. Thin sections are thirty-micron-thick slices of rock or ceramic that under polarized light reveal textures and chemical alteration as well as mineral identification. (A note on nomenclature: petrology is the study of the origin of rocks, petrography is the description of rocks. American usage follows the strict definition. The description of rocks or ceramics in thin section is *petrography*. British usage is to call thin-section analysis *petrology*.)

Thin-section petrography requires a polarizing microscope (figure 6.5). The polarizing microscope is the most important instrument for deter-

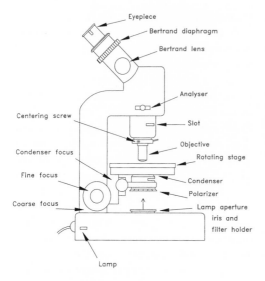

Figure 6.5 Polarizing Microscope

mining the optical properties of minerals because with it information can be obtained easily and quickly. The polarizing microscope has two functions: it provides an enlarged image of the object placed on the microscope stage, and it provides plane- and crossed-polarized light and convergent light. The polarizing lens below the rotating microscope stage forces light to vibrate in a front-back (north-south) direction. A converging lens is also mounted in the substage. Above the microscope stage (and above the object under study) is a second polarizer, called an analyzing lens, which forces light to vibrate left-right (east-west). The substage polarizing lens is fixed in place, but the analyzer can be moved in or out of position. Minerals exhibit a host of distinguishing characteristics in plane- and crossed- (both lenses in position) polarized light and in convergent polarized light. As with other compound microscopes, polarizing microscopes contain a variety of other lenses and devices that can modify the transmission of light for specialized studies.

Thin sections of pottery allow identification of mineral constituents and their relative abundance, associations, and states of alteration; grain orientations and related fabric features; the size, shape, and orientation of voids; cracking; and

post-use (diagenetic) recrystallization. The mineral grains will exhibit distinct size, shape, sorting, roundness, and sphericity characteristics. All these parameters can provide provenance data. Most thin sections are cut parallel to the vertical axis of the ceramic vessel, but different orientations may be useful for some studies.

The aims of petrographic study of pottery are understanding the manufacturing technology and characterization. For example, one can usually determine how the clay paste was mixed from observing the types and distribution of inclusions. Also, whether the vessel was made by hand or a wheel can be inferred from observing the orientation of long inclusions. The chief disadvantage of thin-section petrography in ceramic characterization is that it does not permit study of the fired clay mineral particles. The extreme fine-grained nature of clays requires that clay mineralogy be studied by X-ray analysis because X rays have much shorter wavelengths than visible light. Another drawback is that for many ceramics the only inclusions are quartz. Determining provenance from this ubiquitous geologic material is difficult.

Two of the pioneers in the application of ceramic technology to archaeology, Anna O. Shepard, who worked on prehistoric pottery of the American southwest, and Frederick R. Matson, who worked on ceramics from the Near East, depended on thin-section petrography for their analyses. Shepard's first success was her demonstration that much of the pottery found at Pecos, New Mexico, was not made locally but was imported from adjacent regions. This finding established petrography as an effective tool for the study of cultural interaction. Shepard's *Ceramics for the Archaeologist* and Matson's *Ceramics and Man* formed the basis for most of the later work in this field.

Two examples of the use of petrographic methods in ceramic provenance will serve to illustrate the value of this method. The first example concerns Early Bronze Age pottery from the site of Akrotiri on the Aegean island of Thera. Because one rarely finds whole vessels, ceramic analysis depended on ascertaining diagnostic features of sherds. The sherds at Akrotiri came from the first and second destruction levels.[21] Fourteen ware groups were identified, representing coarse local storage vessels and finer decorated wares thought to have been imported. The mineral composition and manufacturing technology of the fabrics were established in order to determine the existence of multiple workshops and/or sources of raw materials for each ware group. The composition of the coarse fraction of the assemblage included a wide range of lithic material including discrete carbonate microfossils, angular quartz, mica, black iron oxide, argillaceous clasts, quartzite, talc, amphibole, and feldspar—a generous suite with which to work.

The pottery fabrics represented a variety of raw materials and sources, including clays derived from volcanic pyroclastic sediments, lavas, micaceous clays derived from schistose rocks, and siliceous sediments. Although the origins of some of the raw materials remain problematic because of the lack of compounds or undiagnostic clays, the petrographic analyses identified local fabrics and imported wares which pointed to specific contact with other Aegean islands, such as Naxos, Syros, and Crete. The microfossils in one of the fabrics suggested a possible source in the island of Melos. Chemical analysis further supported some of the petrographic data, particularly the presence or absence of fine-grained calcium oxide to distinguish one of the fabrics.

For the second example we turn to work from the Upper Mississippi Valley of the United States. The issue addressed was the extent to which petrographic analysis of ceramics can shed light on culture contact among prehistoric communities—specifically, two late-prehistoric villages 80 kilometers apart.[22] From a total of 331 vessels at one site, 10 were suspected on stylistic grounds of coming from the other site. The thin-section petrographic analysis consisted of a two-step procedure. The first step involved observing the mineral inclusions and compiling a list of those that were natural as opposed to those that had been introduced as temper. The second step consisted of a point-count analysis (in which the frequency of occurrence of an object in a sample is determined by counting the number of times the object occurs at specified intervals throughout the sample), using a 1-mm counting interval over the entire area of the thin section. Between 100 and 350 nonvoid points were counted for each slide. The petrography characterized each thin section in terms of: kind of temper, temper grain size, temper amount, and relative proportions of natural materials (excluding temper).

The petrographic data strongly suggest that the sixteen Late Woodland vessels from one site were all of local manufacture. They constitute discrete groupings and have a close similarity in composition to the B horizon soil within the loess that blankets the terrace at the site. The primary temper added to these vessels was hematite, which occurs as natural concretions in the local sandstone bedrock. The petrographic data also established that the fired paste and body materials from the vessels that were thought to be imported from the other site had been.

Statistics and Data Analysis

Many statistical methods have been used in provenance studies. The most common and most powerful are multivariate discriminate analysis and various systems using cluster analysis, such as K-means cluster analysis. The mathematical methods employed in provenance studies must be able to evaluate the statistical characteristics of the large, multivariate chemical databases now available and to characterize groups and assign unknowns with precision. Most multivariate statistical procedures assume that the variables (for example, trace concentrations of chemical elements) follow multivariate normal distributions. Therefore, the distribution properties of the data must be analyzed. In addition, the researcher must determine whether the data should be standardized. The standard statistical computer software packages used in discriminant analysis Statistical Package for the Social Sciences (SPSS) and Statistical Analysis Systems (SAS) have such features built in. This is not always the case with cluster programs.

The use of discrimination procedures or clustering procedures depends on whether there is prior knowledge of the existence of groups. If groups are known to exist, discrimination procedures should be chosen; otherwise, use cluster procedures. In other words, discriminant analysis seeks to discover and use those attributes which discriminate between known groups in order to assign unknowns to one of the groups. Cluster analysis is useful for identifying completely separate groups but less helpful for identifying groups that overlap. In most geoarchaeological provenance studies, one should first locate and characterize potential source deposits chemically. This means that the existence of groups (deposits) is known and that their trace-element concentrations will have some overlap. Therefore, discriminant methods are preferable. The SPSS^X Discriminant Analysis package computes both linear discriminant and classification functions and has a thorough stepwise procedure that offers five different selection criteria.

In using SPSS^X one must determine which elements are discriminating, based on the results of the trace-element analyses from the geologic deposits. It should be noted that a number of factors must be considered in interpreting discriminant-analysis results. The computer assignment of an artifact to a source deposit as the most probable source does not ensure that the artifact raw material did indeed come from that deposit. It is possible that other sources exist that are not represented in the database. It is also possible for two deposits to have similar trace-element fingerprints; both will thus have strong assignment potential, although only one can be assigned. Probability must also be considered in the assignment of a source. The SPSS^X package will assign as a source that deposit whose centroid of points in multidimensional (equal to the number of elements used) space lies closest to the point defined by the trace-element concentrations in the unknown. However, if the location of the unknown in the multidimensional space does not indicate that it belongs to this source, the probability will be reported as zero.

It must be borne in mind that data analysis cannot improve on the original data. If potential source deposits are inadequately sampled, or there are errors in the analyses, no amount of statistical power will correct for these faults. Finally, remember that when archaeologists puzzle over the source of a new object, the question is, "What has moved? People (artisans), ideas, the object itself, or the raw material from which it was made?" Geoarchaeological provenance methods address only the source of the raw materials.

CHAPTER 7

Estimating Age in the Archaeological Record

Estimating the age of archaeological materials and Quaternary strata is one of geoarchaeology's primary tasks. Chronology provides the temporal dimension that distinguishes the historic natural-science disciplines of geology, paleontology, and archaeology from sciences like ethnography and ethology that focus on present-day processes. An understanding of the methods used to date the past is critical to an interpretation of the archaeological record. Before the development of chronometric techniques, temporal control depended either on relative age estimates that were based upon intrinsic features of artifacts or on the correlation of artifacts with evidence for environmental or climatic change. Although these methods are still fundamental, the application of chronometric techniques has considerably affected our understanding of the prehistoric record. Increasingly better-defined age estimates have played a critical role in the development and testing of ideas about past human behavior.

"Relative" methods of dating have been employed throughout the history of prehistoric research. Most "absolute" methods of dating were developed during the second half of the twentieth century. Relative dating can be used to determine the temporal order or sequence of events associated with artifacts. In contrast, absolute dating provides age estimates that can be expressed in standard time increments (usually years). Absolute-dating techniques are based on physical or chemical properties or processes that can be measured. Although some techniques described below can be used to date artifactual and fossil materials directly, often one dates the geoarchaeological context—the deposits associated

with specific archaeological materials—thus providing an indirect estimate of the age of past human events.

In all types of dating that can be applied to archaeological situations, the most critical factors are the existence of a time-dependent quantity that can be documented or measured and that the event or episode being dated have a direct association with artifacts or archaeological features. The geoarchaeologist must determine that the methods employed can translate a temporal signal into a reliable estimate of age and that this age has a firm relation to the archaeological context. Too often dates are discarded because they do not fit a working model of the archaeological context. Although the reliability of an age estimate should be reconsidered if it does not accord with other independent chronological criteria, the researcher is well advised to consider possible explanations for dates that do not "fit" a model, unless there are other reasons to question a date.

The choice of dating techniques in a particular situation is limited by the materials available for analysis and the age constraints of the archaeological phenomena. Figure 7.1 shows some materials that can be dated by various techniques and presents the typical age limits. These limits vary according to sample character and technical circumstances.

Stratigraphy

Stratigraphic relations have always been the primary method for inferring the age of artifacts. Some stratigraphic techniques, which use varves

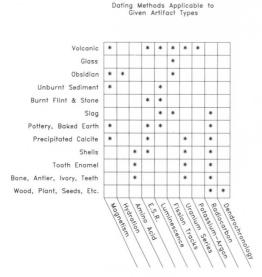

Dating Methods Applicable to Given Artifact Types

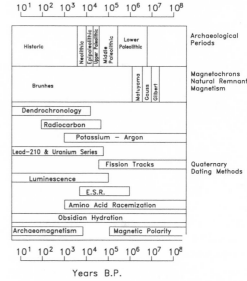

Age Range Applicable to Specific Dating Methods

Years B.P.

Figure 7.1 Archaeological Materials Dating Chart Dating methods, the materials that can be dated, and the general age ranges for these methods. Both organic and inorganic materials can be dated. Different methods are used to date specific ages of the archaeological record.

or other annual laminae, can provide absolute ages directly, while others rely on independent dating—for example, dating paleosols in loess or volcanic ash deposits (tephrochronology).

Rhythmites (Varves)

Rhythmic accumulations of sediments forming distinctive laminae (see Chapter 2) are a common occurrence in the geologic record. The geologic term for such sequences is *rhythmites*. When the laminations arise because of annual variations in supply and type of sediment they are called *varves*. The potential of annually laminated sediments as a means of dating was first exploited by the Swedish geologist Gerard de Geer in the late nineteenth century. Along with tree rings, varves provide absolute ages when even a single varve date is known. The top layer of sediment at the bottom of a still-active lake belongs to the year just past, a fact that can anchor the chronology. Varves have also provided an absolute calibration of the radiocarbon timescale and can be directly applied to pollen stratigraphies in varved sequences.

Varve dating technique is based on variation in sediment deposition during an annual cycle. Commonly, finer particles or chemical precipitates may be deposited during the winter months, while coarser particles are deposited during other periods. The two layers combined represent an annual cycle of deposition. In Scandinavia varve sequences go as far back as 13,000 years. De Geer initially developed the technique in the Baltic region,[1] while in North America the work of Ernest Antevs represents an early effort to use varve chronologies.[2]

In northern lakes that freeze over in the winter, deposition of coarser particles (sand and silt) in the summer is followed in the winter by deposition of finer material (clay and organics). The resulting laminations are easy to distinguish because the light-colored summer sediment alternates with the much darker winter laminae. Unfortunately, bioturbation and other phenomena

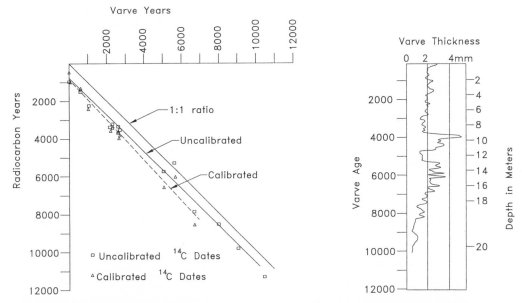

Figure 7.2 Varves and Radiocarbon Years
Varve years are usually younger than radiocarbon

years because the radiocarbon chronology is measuring older carbon within the system.

often disturb the laminations in all but the deepest lakes. Nevertheless, varve chronologies have long provided a calibration for late Quaternary events. Approximately 10,000 laminations have been recorded in a five-meter core from Elk Lake, Minnesota, thus extending varve chronology back to the onset of the Holocene in central North America.[3]

As can be seen in figure 7.2, varve years (which should represent actual calendar years) differ from ^{14}C years, because of the reservoir effect (see radiocarbon, below). The differences may be as great as 1,950 years. The varve dates at Elk Lake are consistently more recent than radiocarbon dates because of older carbon in the carbon reservoir of the lake. The varve chronology was also compared with the pollen stratigraphy and a chronology based on other nearby pollen records. Rapid and distinctive changes in vegetative patterns occurred several times over the past 11,000 years, including a decrease in spruce around 11,000 B.P., a rise in sagebrush around 8560 B.P., a rise in birch around 3390 B.P., and an increase in white pine around 2700 B.P. Based on

the regional pollen records, the uncalibrated ages for the spruce decline and sagebrush rise seem too old, but if the change in spruce in the Elk Lake area can be calibrated to about 10,000 B.P., it would agree with the varve chronology.

Varves can also occur in more temperate climates. Sediment load, biomass accumulation, and chemical precipitation all vary seasonally. If bioturbation or current action does not rework the resulting sediments, annual layering will be recorded. The resulting laminations are visible in some lakes. In others they are apparent only through analytical and microscopic study. In limestone regions, light-colored summer layers of calcium carbonate alternate with dark winter layers rich in humus. When one layer is rich in organic material, radiocarbon dating by accelerator mass spectrometry is possible.

Paleosols in Loess and Alluvium
Loess deposition interrupted by periods of stabilization and soil formation has led to stratigraphic sequences that can be dated. In North America, Europe, and China the substantial progress made

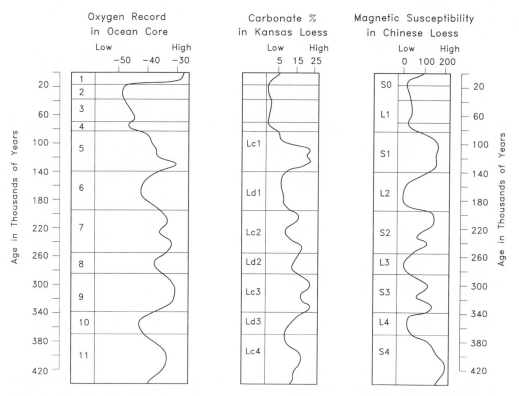

Figure 7.3 Three Analytic Tools That Show Similar Curves and Reversals

The similar patterns of climate change recorded in these stratigraphic sequences are interpreted as reflecting major global warming and cooling events during the past 400,000 years and can be related to the human prehistoric record. The oxygen-isotope record from layers of ocean sediment shows changes associated with glacial and interglacial intervals. Conditions were somewhat similar to the present-day interglacial during oxygen isotope stages 5, 7, and 9. Similar patterns in the carbonate content of loess deposits in central North America have been correlated with the ocean isotope record. Intervals associated with higher amounts of carbonate accumulation in the loess coincide with the interglacial intervals. In the windblown loess deposits of China, a similar correlation has been made. There, sediments with high magnetic susceptibility are thought to coincide with interglacial or warmer climatic episodes.

in dating loess deposits and the soils developed within them have considerable value for archaeology.[4] These loess-paleosol sequences need to be anchored by independent dating correlations before they can be used as time indicators. Figure 7.3 shows a correlation of the North American and China loess sequences with the marine oxygen isotope curve (see the appendix for chronological charts). In this way, a timescale can be superimposed on the loess sequences. Other criteria have been used to prove such correlations. For example, the China sequence has been dated with magnetic reversal chronology and potassium-argon (K-Ar) dating, while parts of the North American sequences have been dated with thermoluminescence (TL) methods (described below). The loess sequence in Europe has been dated using radiocarbon, TL, and stable-isotope series techniques (see figure 7.4).

Johnson and Logan present an excellent example of the use of loess-soil chronostratigraphy.[5] The Peoria loess of the Kansas River basin dates from about 23,000 B.P. and is overlain by the Brady soil, dated to about 11,000 B.P. The younger

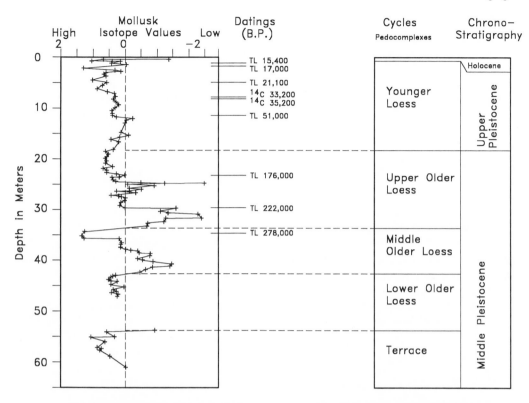

Figure 7.4 Thermoluminescence and Radiocarbon Dating of Microfauna Within Loess Deposits
Comparison of isotopic variation in mollusk shells with time. In this example, chronological control of the isotopic signal is based on TL and radiocarbon measurements. The Middle Pleistocene older loess sediments generally have lower isotopic values than the Upper Pleistocene younger loess mollusks. In this instance, the use of TL measurements was crucial to the discovery of the presence of Middle Pleistocene age strata, since radiocarbon techniques cannot date this interval.

Bignell loess overlies the Brady soil. Both the Peoria loess and the Holocene loess fall within the interval of prehistoric occupation on the American Plains. The Lindsay mammoth location in eastern Montana provides another North American instance of loess dating. At this site archaeologists recovered the remains of a mammoth overlain by silts containing buried soils. The silts have been interpreted as loess that began to accumulate around 13,000–12,000 B.P. Using radiocarbon, the bone bed was dated to between 12,000 and 9500 B.P.; it may be the result of Paleo-Indian activities during that time. The silt and soil sequence over the mammoth bones may correlate with a wide-ranging Terminal Pleistocene and Early Holocene loess and soil sequence on the

Great Plains (the Aggie Brown Member and the Leonard Paleosol).

Sedimentary sequences composed primarily of alluvial deposits containing buried soils have been extremely useful in dating archaeological accumulations, especially in areas like the American Midwest. As with paleosols in loess deposits, the chronological framework is based either on the relative stratigraphic order of buried soils within a sequence or on independent dating methods (such as ^{14}C dating of soil humates or bones in the paleosol). Studies by Rolfe Mandel in Kansas, Arthur Bettis in Iowa, and Edward Hajic in Illinois show how useful soil chronologies can be in interpreting the temporal context of artifact-bearing sediments. Based on detailed studies of the characteristics of buried soils and radiocarbon determinations of charcoal, wood, bone, and soil humates, Mandel was able to use paleosols to correlate regional alluvial sequences containing artifacts.[6] Late Archaic and Plains Woodland archaeological sites in Kansas are likely to be associated with two buried soils that are valuable stratigraphic markers of valley fill dating to the Late Holocene. The oldest of the buried soils, called the Hackberry Creek Paleosol, is associated with Late Archaic artifacts. The soil started to form at about 2800 B.P. and continued to develop until at least 2000 B.P. The Hackberry Creek Paleosol is buried by alluvium. The Buckner Creek Paleosol developed within this alluvium and contains Plains Woodland artifacts. The Buckner Creek Paleosol began to develop around 1350 B.P. and continued to form until at least 1000 B.P.

In the Upper Midwest it is possible to separate Holocene alluvial deposits into three groups. Each group is of a different age, so each is potentially related to a different archaeological interval and has a unique set of associated soils. Sediments deposited from about 10,500 to 4000 B.P. are designated Early to Middle Holocene (EMH) alluvium. They are characterized by oxidized colors and mottling, and have surface soils with well-developed horizons, especially the subsurface argillic, or Bt, horizons typically formed in Mollisols or Alfisols. Because of organic carbon, Late Holocene (LH) alluvium deposited after 3500 B.P. is generally darker than EMH and does not have argillic horizons developed in the surface soils. The youngest deposits are mostly historic-age sediments. They are characteristically lighter in color than LH deposits, exhibit distinct bedding in their lower sections, are oxidized, and show a slight pedogenic alteration. These three alluvial groups have different weathering zone features and different surface soils developed on them, and they can be found throughout the Upper Midwest. Bettis used these distinctive features to help determine the age of artifacts associated with them. Paleo-Indian and Archaic artifacts have been associated with EMH deposits, while LH deposits are likely to contain Late Archaic and Woodland components.

At the Koster site in western Illinois there are twenty-three distinct archaeological zones within a Holocene sedimentary and paleosol sequence. The zones are defined by laterally continuous accumulations of artifacts. These artifact accumulations represent a succession from the Early Archaic through the Mississippian periods of human prehistory. Hajic showed that the sequence consists mostly of colluvium and alluvial fan sediments composed of loess that was redeposited as sheetwash and of stream-related deposits. During some intervals, surface processes at Koster became stable enough for soils to form. On the basis of soil morphology and the degree of horizon development, Hajic was able to discern two groups of soils. Soils that formed over relatively short intervals of time did not have distinct B horizons. Often these soils had distinctive, thick A horizons that had formed during intervals of continuing sedimentation. The time necessary for a **cummulic** soil horizon to form was roughly several hundred years. The second group of paleosols formed over a longer time on more stable slope and fan surfaces. They have more developed B horizons that may have taken from 500 to 1,500 years to form. The first soil with a developed B horizon appears to have started forming around 9800 B.P. The second major soil formed after about 4100 and before 2500 B.P., since it is older than Early Woodland Black Sand pottery. The third soil with a well-developed B horizon formed sometime between about 2600 and 1150 B.P. Interpretation of the timing of depositional and soil-forming events at Koster related the deposits to diagnostic artifacts (used as time markers) and radiocarbon measurements.

Tephrochronology

Volcanic ash deposits have proven effective for relative dating of archaeological sites—and for absolute-age correlations when their ages can be determined through such chronometric techniques as potassium-argon dating (see below). To be useful dating tools, ash deposits need to have been widely dispersed, have a chemical signature that is unique, and be able to fit into a chronology.

A major challenge in geoarchaeology involves dating the Bronze Age volcanic eruption on the

Aegean island of Thera. In the Bronze Age, Thera was the site of an extensive Minoan culture of sea traders. In the middle of the second millennium B.C. two-thirds of the island was blown away in a catastrophic eruption. The whole center of the island, once a mountain, became a great caldera, open to the sea. A once-thriving seaport on the southern tip of the island was buried under volcanic ash. The Archaeological Society of Greece, under the auspices of the Greek Archaeological Service, is currently excavating the ancient town now called Akrotiri that is situated on one of its remnant islands. This site and its history have tremendous importance in their own right but in addition have received worldwide attention because the cataclysmic eruption and attendant destruction might have been the inspiration for Plato's legend of Atlantis.

Volcanic eruptions eject large quantities of fine particles and sulfur compounds into the upper atmosphere circulation system. These materials return slowly to earth in rain and snow. A significant increase in acidity from this sulfur is found in distinct layers in glacier ice cores. A Greenland ice core has a strong acidity peak at 1,644 ± 20 B.C. This has been interpreted as recording the eruption of Thera. Artifacts from Akrotiri, linked to the Egyptian calendar, put the Thera eruption at more than a hundred years later. While the controversy remains open, it is our view that the volcanic activity recorded in the Greenland ice core more likely came from nearby Iceland than from the eastern Mediterranean (this may be testable by comparing chemical signatures).

In western North America three postglacial volcanic ash deposits are useful marker beds for the Latest Pleistocene and Lower Holocene. Glacier Peaks G and B and Mount Saint Helens' J ashes date to Late Pleistocene. The Glacier Peak ashes are from a volcano in north central Washington and date to 11,200 B.P. The Mount Saint Helens J ash comes from southern Washington and consists of ash layers from eruptions that occurred between about 11,500 and 10,800 B.P. The most widespread Holocene ash in western North America, the Mazama ash, came from the volcano at Crater Lake, Oregon, in an eruption dated to approximately 6845 B.P. The ages of these ashes

have been determined primarily by radiocarbon dating, although TL and other techniques were also used.[7]

Tephrochronology has helped to date many archaeological contexts and stratigraphic sequences in western North America.[8] The Clovis cache at the Wenatchee site in Washington was dated by eruptions from the Glacier Peak volcano. At this site, pumice-rich sediments derived from the Glacier Peak tephra were found directly underlying the Clovis artifacts. A nearby stratigraphic sequence contained the Mazama tephra. Glacier Peak Layer G ashfall was identified at the Indian Creek Site in western Montana. The ash was dated by radiocarbon to about 11,125 B.P. and underlies an assemblage of Folsom-related artifacts dated to about 10,980 B.P. The Mazama ash was also found within the Indian Creek sequence. Because these two ash deposits have dates, they can be used as time markers once they have been identified. Identification can sometimes be made on the basis of thickness or color, but field identification needs to be checked against mineralogic or geochemical signatures that distinguish the volcanic ashes.

Dating Techniques Based on Animal and Plant Remains

Paleontology

Principles of biostratigraphy have been useful in indicating relative age, although, as with the use of artifacts as "index" fossils, the problems of contemporaneity, time transgression, and habitat differences need to be considered. The most useful indicators of specific age intervals are the remains of organisms with two characteristics: they have a wide geographic distribution, and they appear and then become extinct over a short time. In North America, the presence of the remains of extinct animals associated with artifact-bearing deposits has been decisive for determining the antiquity of humans in the Americas. Although earlier discoveries of extinct fauna near artifacts had occurred, their contextual associations were questioned. It was the substantiation of the association of extinct bison with undisputed artifacts in a gully near Folsom, New Mexico, that led to the consensus that humans had been in North America for thousands of years. At the time of the discovery, the age of the extinct animals was a matter of extrapolation based on nonabsolute methods of dating. In another example, the first appearance and the evolutionary development of fossil rodents in Europe have been used as paleontologic markers in Quaternary stratigraphic sequences. In Africa the remains of horses, pigs, and elephants have been used as relative time markers for Plio-Pleistocene strata containing hominid remains and Lower Paleolithic artifacts.

In addition to their use in evaluating environmental and climatic change, pollen-stratigraphic sequences can also be used as temporal indicators. To be an age indicator, a pollen sequence must be correlated with a previously determined chronology. In turn, this environmental-temporal framework can be correlated with archaeological events. For example, pollen sequences in France from the La Grande Pile and Les Echets peat bogs have been correlated with a chronology derived from a radio-isotope timescale and can be used as a starting point for evaluating environmental change throughout the Paleolithic of Europe. High pollen abundances correspond to warm climates, associated with interglacials and interstadials. The oldest major peak is attributed to the beginning of isotope stage 5 (interglacial), about 130,000 years ago. Changes in arboreal pollen frequency occur throughout the rest of the sequence and can be related to Paleolithic occurrences in the region that were dated independently.

Over a wide area, the time-transgressive nature of vegetative change is reflected in pollen-stratigraphic sequences. Before radiocarbon dating, pollen zones in northern Europe were dated using varve chronology. In an archaeological context, the presence of a particular pollen zone within a site's stratigraphic sequence allows it to be correlated to regional chronozones dated by radiocarbon.

Dendrochronology

A. E. Douglass developed tree-ring dating.[9] It is based on the observation that in many trees a new ring or row of wood cells grows each year.

The basic requirement for tree-ring dating is the presence of clearly defined annual rings, while the major problem is that rings may be missing because of situations like extreme climatic conditions. Along with varves, tree-ring dating has proven extremely useful as an independent check on the radiocarbon chronology. The two major tree-ring chronologies come from North America and Europe, although other areas of the world continue to push back the beginning date of the regional sequences.

Tree-ring chronologies have been created that extend throughout the Holocene in North America, Europe, and the Near East. The dendrochronological calibration currently goes back to about 10,000 radiocarbon years B.P. Once a reliable tree-ring series has been obtained, it can be applied to archaeological sites where parts of the series have been preserved. Keep in mind that archaeological application of tree-ring dating generally provides maximum age limits for an archaeological feature; trees older than the archaeological feature that contains the tree remains may have been used or reused.

Tree-ring dating provided convincing evidence that the Viking period in northern Europe extended back as early as the eighth century.[10] Three Viking ship-burial mounds were dated using dendrochronology. The tree-rings were measured from the sapwood structure of the grave chambers of the ships. Dendrochronology is not by nature geologic, but the wood being dated is often found in sedimentary contexts, and tree-ring analysis provides data for paleoclimatology.

Dating Techniques Based on Chemical Accumulation

Chemical Analysis

Dating based on chemical content can be either relative or absolute. In relative dating, the principle is straightforward and based on the concept that certain chemical constituents will accumulate in (or on) an object over time: the greater amount of the chemical present, the older the material. The chemical composition of buried bone can change through time, so chemical analysis of bone has been employed to test the validity of human remains and extinct fauna. Human skeletal remains recovered from near Midland, Texas, had a chemical content within the range found in extinct faunal materials, but it differed from the chemical content found in Late Holocene bones. U-series dates (see below) have independently confirmed the Terminal Pleistocene age of the Midland human remains, although the radiocarbon and U-series dates are not strictly comparable. One of the criteria that led to the conclusion that the human remains from Midland were "as much a Pleistocene fossil as any of the extinct vertebrates discovered at this site" was a comparison of chemical properties.[11] Rabbit bones from modern sediments had low levels of fluorine, while those of horse and human remains had higher fluorine values. Some caution needs to be used in interpretations based on relative amounts of elements in bones, because more than one set of postdepositional circumstances can result in bones having the same chemical content.

Chemical dating was also used to confirm that the bones from the infamous Piltdown assemblage did not come from a single animal and were not contemporary. The hominid remains were attributed to gravels that contained Pleistocene fauna. Chemical tests demonstrated that jawbone and teeth had essentially modern concentrations of fluorine, while the Piltdown skull bones were Pleistocene.

Patination and Desert Varnish

The use of weathering and chemical alteration of artifacts to estimate their age is based on the principle that the thickness of an alteration rind provides an estimate of age. Chemical accumulation on materials is known as *patina*, and it is produced by weathering.

Desert varnish (cation ratio) dating provides another method of directly dating artifact surfaces. The basis of cation ratio dating is that certain elements (cations) leach out from lithic material faster during weathering than others. For instance, potassium and calcium are more easily leached than titanium. The ratio of K and Ca to Ti provides an indication of relative age. The lower the ratio of K and Ca relative to Ti, the older the sample. Absolute ages for these lithics can sometimes be determined from correlations and extrapolations based on other dating techniques.

Varnish dating using the cation ratio technique has been cited by proponents of human occupation in the Americas before the Clovis Complex.[12] Whitley and Dorn used cation ratio varnish dating as supporting evidence for radiocarbon dates to propose dates earlier than 11,500 B.P. for petroglyphs and stone artifacts. In this instance, the dates obtained from radiocarbon and cation ratio dating provide limiting ages for older artifacts.

Temperature-Affected Dating

Amino Acid Racemization and Epimerization

Amino acid geochronology relies on the fact that through time L-amino acids (left-handed) convert to a D-amino acid (a right-handed configuration). This conversion is termed *racemization*. The D/L ratio moves from being wholly L to being an equal mixture of D and L. Early research concentrated on the use of bone (including human remains) and mollusk shells, but wood, organic sediments, and ostrich eggshell have also been used. Major problems with the application of amino acid geochronology to fossil bone include the potential of geochemical contamination because of the porous nature of the material and complications that may arise from the degradation of collagen in the osteological material. Although relative age estimates have been obtained using mollusks, nonlinear kinetic reactions complicate the conversion of the ratios to absolute ages.

The three primary controls in amino acid dating are time, ambient temperature, and moisture. Conversion from one type of amino acid form to another strongly depends on temperature. One method of obtaining current temperature conditions, which provide a way to estimate past temperatures, is to place sensors into the sediments surrounding the object being dated.

High moisture promotes the racemization process; therefore, samples subjected to extremely dry conditions may have lower D/L ratios. The ostrich eggshell amino acid *isoleucine* has been used to estimate the age of deposits that contain artifacts.[13] In contrast to mollusks, there is less potential for leaching because the amino acids are within the calcite crystals of the eggshell. Conversion of D/L ratios into absolute ages can be done when the effective ambient temperature and the D/L ratio are available. Calibration can be accomplished with other dating techniques.

Hydration (Obsidian)

The rhyolitic volcanic glass obsidian, extensively used as the raw material for making stone tools, can be useful for relative dating. A hydration "rind" can develop on obsidian as a result of its absorbing water: the thicker the hydration rind, the older the sample. A fundamental assumption is that obsidian hydrates at a given rate. Hydration in obsidian follows the diffusion equation $x^2 = kt$, where x = hydration thickness, k = hydration rate, and t = time. Several variables influence the rate of the hydration, including the chemical composition of the obsidian, the available water, and the temperature associated with the environmental context of the artifact. When the geologic source of the sample is known, a hydration constant for that source plus an estimate of the temperature during hydration will provide a hydration rate for that material at that location. To obtain relative age estimates, the thickness of the hydration rind needs to be compared with local hydration rate. Where there is reason to believe artifacts have undergone uniform thermal histories, it is possible to construct relative chronologies. Attempts have also been made to construct more absolute timescales using hydration rates.

When a piece of obsidian acquires a fresh surface, as when it is fractured during sediment transport or flaked to make a stone tool, it begins to absorb water. If the fresh exposure of the obsidian surface can be related to a specific prehistoric event (like the flaking), the thickness of the hydration rind provides an indication of the time elapsed since that event.

Many factors affect the hydration rate in a specific location, including the site-specific microclimate, the orientation of the site, the burial depth of the artifact, and past changes in the environmental context. These factors affect the temperature and relative-humidity history of the artifact. Heating caused by forest fires, by fires that destroy occupations, or by ritual activity (like cremation) may alter the hydration rind thickness through dehydration. It has been shown that the hydration rind can be completely eliminated with no change in surface appearance if obsidian is heated to > 430° C. Hydration rims can apparently also undergo spalling. When this happens, a fresh hydration rim forms, giving what appears to be a more recent date for the artifact.

Hydration measurements can help infer the presence of mixed components in an artifact accumulation if one knows the variation within a component of a single age. Clark and McFadyen Clark used the example of specimens collected from a single sealed dwelling floor that were all part of the same occupational event.[14] Even in this situation the hydration measurements may not be tightly clustered. To accommodate natural variation within a single age set, an average rind thickness can be used.

The traditional method used to measure the thickness of the hydration rind is optical microscopy. However, tests conducted among different hydration-measurement laboratories indicate that measurements are subject to operator variables. To reduce this, some laboratories use computer-assisted imaging technology to digitize and measure hydration rims.

An effort has been made to use the thicknesses of hydration rims on artifacts to provide absolute-age determinations. The hydration thickness can be calibrated by experimental determination of the hydration rate. Once a temperature-dependent rate constant has been obtained for a given obsidian source, it can be used for all artifacts made from that source. Where the site is already dated by other means, it should be possible to use the thickness of the hydration rind to estimate the temperatures associated with the site. In this way, hydration measurements are potentially a useful paleoclimatic proxy.

The depth of burial of an artifact can have

a major influence on the degree of hydration. Artifacts nearer the surface may be subjected to higher variations in temperature, and relative humidity varies with depth. At depth, relative humidity can be 100 percent, but nearer the surface it may be much less.

Reported ages in obsidian dating range from greater than 100,000 to about 200 years old. Hydration measurements have also been used to date glacial moraines. Rocks fractured during glacial transport have fresh surfaces that can develop a hydration rind. This allows us to date the moraine and the timing of the glacial advance. In the same way, cobbles and boulders made of obsidian that were fractured during transport as part of glacial outwash can be dated. This helps us determine the time since the glacier melted. Archaeologists can use the age of glacial melting to evaluate the possible timing and duration of human occupations of glaciated regions.

One potential use of the obsidian hydration is in dating archaeological site formation. Joe Michels used hydration measurements to test the chronological integrity of midden deposits and to evaluate the stratigraphic implications of artifact mixing and reuse at the Mammoth Junction site in California.[15] After measuring the hydration rim on obsidian artifacts from each unit of deposition, a three-dimensional plot of the distribution of hydration-rim values and depositional units was constructed. Based on the premise that artifacts of the same age would have the same rind thickness despite their depth, significant differences in hydration measurements for artifacts in the same depositional units were interpreted as indicating the presence of mixing. To obtain an average age for artifacts within a depositional unit, the median hydration rim value for each unit was calculated. Although the artifacts were extensively mixed, the slope of the trend line showed that they conformed to the principle of superposition.

Michels dated artifacts from Kenya as far back as about 120,000 B.P. using experimentally derived hydration rates for a particular obsidian.[16] First he determined experimentally the hydration rate for two different obsidians. Then he determined the source of the obsidians by comparing compositional characteristics of artifacts with those of quarry sites. Obsidian artifacts from the Prospect Farm site were recovered from four main episodes of occupation. The oldest artifacts were related to the Middle Stone Age, followed by artifacts from the early Later Stone Age, and by the youngest, from the Pastoral Neolithic. Because of spalling, many artifacts from the Middle Stone Age were calculated to have ages that are probably younger than the actual age of the artifacts. The calculated age for unspalled surfaces of Middle Stone Age artifacts was about 120,000 to 50,000 years old. Hydration rates from the early Later Stone Age put the artifacts in the age range of 33,000–22,000 years old, while artifacts from the Later Stone Age have hydration ages of around 10,000 years old. Neolithic artifacts were dated to about 3,000 years ago. In this study, the hydration rates used to calculate the dates from the Prospect Farm site were calibrated from the ^{14}C chronology.

Obsidian hydration measurements were used to help date a Tecep phase burial at the Mayan site of Nohmul in Belize.[17] Obsidian artifacts, some freshly struck, were found in a sealed burial. This provided a chance to date the burial and evaluate whether it was the same age as the structure or a later intrusion. First the obsidian source was determined. All of the material matched the El Chayal source near Guatemala City, Guatemala. Based on the source and estimated effective hydration temperatures, hydration dates were calculated. The different ways of estimating effective hydration temperature change the calculated age by about a thousand years. Using the thermal-cell estimate of temperature, the dates mostly fell around 950 A.D., while using the mean-temperature estimates they tended to fall around 1050. Timbers of the building containing the burial were radiocarbon-dated to about 700. Hence the obsidian-hydration dates were interpreted as indicating that the burial was intrusive.

Radiometric Dating

Potassium-Argon and Argon-Argon Dating
Potassium is a major element in many rocks. One of its isotopes, ^{40}K, decays naturally to argon (^{40}Ar).[18] In such minerals as mica and potas-

sium feldspars, and in volcanic glass, this decay can be used to date igneous and metamorphic rocks. The half-life for ^{40}K decay is around 1.25 billion years. The latest published dates for this method are around 35,000 B.P., although it works best when applied to igneous rocks that are more than 100,000 years old. In determining ages of artifacts younger than that, the atmospheric concentration of Ar disguises the age signal.

Minerals containing K are produced in volcanic activity. The technique can thus be employed when there is a direct relation between volcanic rocks and archaeological phenomena. The amount of trapped ^{40}Ar that has accumulated relative to the amount of remaining ^{40}K provides an estimate of the age of the volcanic event. Minerals in igneous rocks can be eroded and redeposited. The K-Ar measurements of the minerals in the sediments measure the age of the original igneous event, not the time of redeposition and formation of the sedimentary strata.

When using K-Ar dating, it is assumed that: 1) the argon contained in the mineral was produced solely as a result of the decay of ^{40}K; 2) no argon has been lost since the mineral was formed; and 3) no argon was added at the time of formation or during some later event. Similarly, the potassium content of the mineral must be part of a closed system with no changes except for decay of ^{40}K.

Later recrystallization caused by a subsequent metamorphic igneous or melting event may cause loss of argon. Weathering and alteration can cause loss of both potassium and argon and can introduce ^{40}K. Older dates can result from the incorporation of potassium from older volcanics.

Dates based on the decay of potassium to argon have been especially useful in delineating a timescale for the Pliocene and Pleistocene. This chronology has been extremely important to paleoanthropology and Paleolithic archaeology. The research by Brunhes and Matuyama in the early part of the twentieth century led to the discovery that the earth's magnetic field had reversed polarity several times during the Quaternary. The timescale for these polarity reversals is based on potassium-argon dates of volcanic rocks.

Potassium-argon dating has been especially successful for the Pliocene and Pleistocene strata in East Africa, where volcanism has been common. Important archaeological findings that have been dated include the sequence at Olduvai Gorge in Tanzania and the Lucy remains in Ethiopia. Among the earliest applications of K-Ar dating was the work by Evernden and Curtis on tuff (volcanic ash) beds at Olduvai Gorge. Potassium-argon dates from Olduvai Gorge were at first considered surprising; they were much earlier than expected. The application of a related technique, ^{40}Ar/^{39}Ar, during the early 1990s provided even more precise ages.[19] Bed I at Olduvai Gorge contains some of the world's best-known hominid fossils and is associated with an interval of major biologic and climatic change. Using ^{40}Ar/^{39}Ar analyses, single mineral grains from the middle and upper part of Bed I were found to be about 1.8–1.75 million years old. Dates from the lower part of Bed I may be about 100,000 years later than previously proposed. In Ethiopia, J. D. Clark and an interdisciplinary research team have used Ar-Ar dating of tephra deposits to determine the age of Paleolithic artifacts and vertebrate remains.

Uranium-Series Dating

The element uranium is radioactive, and it decays to a sequence of other elements at a known rate. This decay sequence, terminating with lead, is known as the U series. This chain of decay is the foundation for several ways of estimating age. Two isotopes of uranium, ^{235}U and ^{238}U, decay through different routes and at different time rates to produce different isotopes of lead. Methods of uranium-series dating are based on these two decay series. Uranium-series dating is possible only under the following conditions: 1) at the time the uranium-containing mineral is formed, the daughter isotopes were either absent or their concentration can be determined; 2) the activity of the daughter product must reach equilibrium—that is, daughter products have a constant concentration; and 3) the sample has not been chemically disturbed since formation. Usually uranium-series dating relies on the solubility of uranium in water, while the decay products precipitate from hydrous solution.[20]

Within the decay series of U two isotopes

have been used extensively in dating. The isotope ^{230}Th is within the ^{238}U sequence, and ^{231}Pa lies within the ^{235}U series. In a closed system, where there was no initial ^{230}Th and ^{231}Pa and no U or decay products have entered or left, the ratios of ^{230}Th/^{238}U or ^{231}Pa/^{235}U can be used to estimate the age of a material less than 200,000 years old. The ratio of ^{230}Th/^{238}U was first used to date corals and later shells and carbonate deposits.

Uranium-series dating has a range of about 1,000 to 800,000 years. For comparison, radiocarbon is most useful for ages up to about 40,000 years, and potassium-argon is best used for ages greater than about 750,000 years. Uranium-series methods have been useful in dating organic carbonates, corals, and shells (mollusks), and successful attempts have been made to date tooth enamel. Inorganic carbonates such as limestones, speleothems, and travertines from cave, spring, and lake deposits have been dated using uranium series. The uranium-series method has been used to date archaeological materials embedded in or encrusted with calcium carbonate. It is especially useful for dating Paleolithic sites. Spring-deposited travertine (tufa) deposits are useful chronostratigraphic markers. The ^{230}Th/^{234}U method has been used to date travertine deposits within the interval between 171,000 and 149,000 B.P.

At El Castillo Cave in Spain (discussed in Chapter 3; see figure 3.9), the U-series method was used to evaluate the age of artifacts designated Acheulian and Mousterian.[21] A massive flowstone layer separates two types of artifact assemblages. Beneath the flowstone are artifacts traditionally labeled Acheulian and above the flowstone are artifacts designated Mousterian. The flowstone is mainly composed of a solid travertine with a spongy breccia for the upper part. The base of the unit is a dripstone or stalagmite that was dated to about 89,000 B.P. Dates calculated directly from the daughter-parent ratio of ^{230}Th/^{234}U gave ages that were too old because of the detrital addition of ^{230}Th. Since ^{232}Th is not part of the ^{238}U/^{235}U decay series, it can be used as an indicator of the degree of detrital contamination. A date of 89,000 B.P. would correspond to the cool oscillation related to oxygen isotope stage 5b, al-

though at one standard deviation the flowstone could also be associated with either stage 5c or 5a. If this is a reasonable estimate for the flowstone, it shows that Acheulian assemblages were in existence before the flowstone's deposition and that Mousterian artifacts were deposited some time after about 90,000 B.P.

For historic archaeology, ^{210}Pb provides an important dating technique. The isotope occurs naturally in lake sediments as one of the radio-isotopes of the ^{238}U decay series. It has a half-life of 22.26 years. Because of its short half-life, ^{210}Pb works only for artifacts dating from the middle of the nineteenth century to the present.

Radiocarbon Dating

Carbon-14 is a radioactive isotope of carbon that was initially used by Libby to date organic materials.[22] The bombardment of nitrogen atoms by cosmic rays in the upper atmosphere produces the ^{14}C isotope (figure 7.5). The ^{14}C isotopes are incorporated in all geochemical and biochemical systems that are in equilibrium with atmospheric carbon dioxide. The half-life for ^{14}C is about 5,730 years. Dates determined before 1970 were calculated with a half-life of 5,568 $\pm$ 30; the more accurate half-life is 5,730 $\pm$ 40. Radiocarbon dating beyond about forty thousand years is possible but it is not as reliable as shorter spans because of contamination problems and diminishing concentrations of ^{14}C.

There are two methods of obtaining a radiocarbon date. The conventional technique relies on measuring beta rays from the radioactive decay. The second method uses an accelerator mass spectrometer to measure the number of atoms of ^{14}C remaining in a sample. The AMS method directly measures the concentration of ^{14}C relative to the amount of ^{12}C or ^{13}C. In the conventional method, 1 gram of present-day carbon would have approximately fifteen disintegrations per minute, but a 22,000-year-old sample would have only about one disintegration per minute. With AMS dating, the speed of counting is faster, much smaller samples can be used (down to less than 1 milligram), and it may be possible to extend the age range to 60,000 or more years.

Several aspects of the carbon system directly

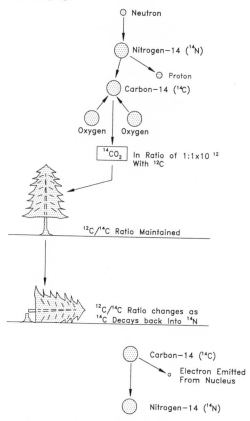

Figure 7.5 The Carbon-14 Cycle
This diagram illustrates the formation of ^{14}C in the upper atmosphere, the incorporation of the ^{14}C as part of the CO molecule into living matter, and finally the radioactive decay of ^{14}C back to ^{14}N.

influence radiocarbon measurements, including the carbon reservoir, isotopic fractionation, the earth's magnetic field, sunspot activity, and fossil fuels and nuclear testing. Scientists assume that ^{14}C is evenly spread within the carbon reservoir. Carbon-14 production varies with cosmic-ray intensity, magnetic-shield intensity, and atomic explosions. If ^{14}C production is low for a given period, less of the isotope can be found in samples from that period, and any measurement would indicate a date earlier than the actual age.

Several phenomena have influenced the production of ^{14}C in the past. Because cosmic rays result in the production of ^{14}C, any change in their intensity alters the natural concentration of ^{14}C.

When the magnetic field is weak, more cosmic rays are present, and the production of ^{14}C would therefore increase, while the opposite would happen when the magnetic field was stronger, and more cosmic-ray particles were deflected away from earth's atmosphere. Similarly, during geomagnetic reversals, there is higher production of ^{14}C. Calibrations based on tree-ring, varve, and U-series chronologies have been used to correct ^{14}C dating (see figures 7.6 and 7.7).

The geochemical context of radiocarbon dating includes reservoir effects. For ^{14}C to provide comparable dates for organic materials, worldwide atmospheric ^{14}C must be mixed rapidly throughout the world's carbon-containing reservoirs. This is known not to be the case. One potential influence is called the *hard water effect*, where old or "dead" carbon containing no ^{14}C becomes mixed with the carbon in an organic substance, thus making the sample appear older than it is. This is a special problem in areas saturated with groundwater that has been influenced by bedrock limestone. This problem is critical where old carbon has been incorporated into the carbonate in shells. Living samples from a freshwater lake on limestone terrain have been known to give a radiocarbon date of up to 1600 B.P. The atmospheric ^{14}C concentrations can be modified by the lack of any ^{14}C in the carbon contribution emanating from the limestone. In a similar way, the present-day combustion of coal and oil has diluted the concentration of ^{14}C because of the addition of dead carbon from these sources. On the other hand, detonation of nuclear devices has introduced large amounts of ^{14}C into the system.

The geochemical fractionation of the stable carbon isotopes ^{12}C and ^{13}C in geologic processes is another source of error in radiocarbon dating. In isotope fractionation, ^{14}C is used at a slower rate than ^{12}C, creating differences in the ratios of the two isotopes within different organic materials. Figure 7.6 shows some typical differences in isotope fractions. The enrichment or depletion in ^{14}C because of natural fractionation is twice the δ ^{13}C values in the same sample. To eliminate this problem, all ^{14}C values are now normalized to a common δ.

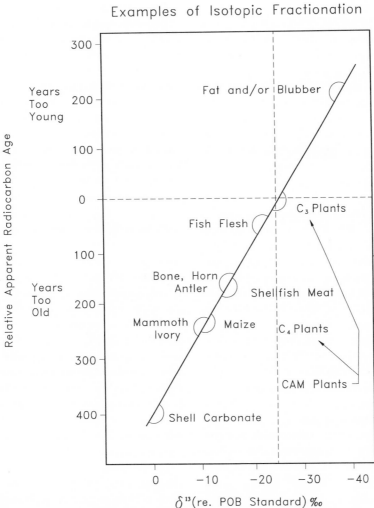

Figure 7.6 Variation in the Apparent Radiocarbon Age of Different Types of Samples Because of Carbon Isotope Fractionation

Because of carbon-isotope fractionation, the radiocarbon content in specimens of the same age can vary. This figure demonstrates that, depending on the relative amount of ^{13}C, which is a measurement of isotopic fractionation, the radiocarbon measurement of artifactual materials can provide an age estimate that is either too old or too young. Because of the relatively low amounts of ^{13}C in fat and blubber, these types of materials appear younger than they are. On the other hand, shells made of carbonate or mammoth ivory have high ^{13}C values and appear older. Because the isotopic-fractionation values of different materials can be measured, corrections can be applied to the radiocarbon measurement. This provides a closer estimate of the age of the artifact and allows the radiocarbon ages derived from isotopically different materials to be compared.

Datable Materials and Geoarchaeological Applications

Datable archaeological materials include wood charcoal, wood, peat, shell, dung, bone, iron, and parchment. Although good chronologies have been developed using shells and soil organics, potential problems need to be considered. Shells of land snails are thought to be poorly suited for radiocarbon dating because ^{14}C activities in the sources of carbon incorporated into these shells are not always in equilibrium with atmospheric ^{14}C. Radiocarbon ages from soil-organic fractions may also be poorly suited because the ^{14}C activities may not be known for the carbon sources in the soil. In addition, the organics in soils may represent an accumulation over a long time, perhaps even several generations of pedogenesis. Potentially the same problem of unknown ^{14}C activities is there for carbonate incrustation on artifacts and for geologic deposits like caliche and tufa. Reservoir effects can also occur when volcanic (fumarole) gas emissions containing only dead carbon are incorporated into plants growing within approximately 100 meters of the fumarole. The major laboratories undertaking radiocarbon dating have developed sophisticated approaches to these problems, so geoarchaeologists should discuss sample type and sample origin with the senior laboratory personnel responsible for the analyses.

Geoarchaeologists must evaluate the geologic and geochemical contexts that relate a carbon sample to a specific geologic or archaeological feature. The integrity of the association of the carbon sample with an event is of primary importance. Potential geochemical contamination from the environmental matrix where the sample was taken is of nearly equal importance. Geoarchaeological problems in sample collection include: samples taken from eroded or reworked deposits, samples taken from deposits mixed by bioturbation or cryoturbation, geochemical contamination from a fossil-carbon source (e.g., limestone or coal), and geochemical contamination from nearby organic-decay products like humus. It is critical to ascertain that no recycled older carbon is in the sample.

Three methods of calibration relate radiocarbon years to real years, or relate radiocarbon chronologies to calendar dates. Radiocarbon chronologies covering the past 10,000 years or so have been calibrated by tree-ring and varve chronologies. Radiocarbon ages of about 30,000 years have been calibrated by chronologies based on U-series dates (figure 7.7). Tree-ring derived calibration curves are applicable only to samples formed in equilibrium with atmospheric CO_2. Deep ocean water is not in equilibrium with the atmosphere. Upwelling of deep water occurs near many coastlines, causing disequilibrium in surface waters and in the shells of mollusks and marine microfauna that derive their carbonate from these waters. Upwelling is affected by the shape of the coastline and the bottom topography, local climate, and wind and current patterns. Hence correcting for this disequilibrium is a local problem. For maximum accuracy, each coastal environment (e.g., estuary) must be evaluated to determine the magnitude and variability of marine-shell carbonates of equivalent age. For a generalized calibration of samples of marine origin a curve has been developed by the University of Washington at Seattle, and published in the journal *Radiocarbon* (a computer program is also available), derived from the tree-ring information but modified by carbon-reservoir modeling.

Uranium-series calibration of the radiocarbon timescale has been used to investigate the differences between calendar years and radiocarbon years for the final part of the Upper Pleistocene, where varve and tree-ring calibrations are not available.[23] Before 9000 B.P., ^{14}C ages are consistently younger than true ages. Comparisons between U-Th ages and ^{14}C, as reflected in figure 7.7, indicate this divergence. Figure 7.7 also shows that there is reasonable agreement between the Lake of the Clouds, Minnesota, varve sequence and dendrochronological ages. The extension of the radiocarbon-calibration curve indicates that the deglaciation dated to about 18,000 radiocarbon years B.P. is associated with a calibrated date of 22,000–21,000 B.P.

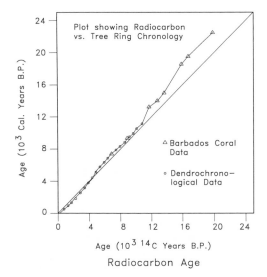

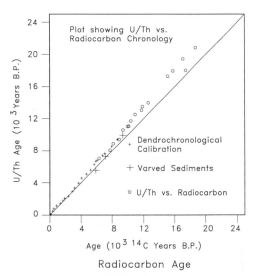

Figure 7.7 Dendrochronology Versus Various Other Dating Methods

Tree-ring dating, varves, and uranium-series dating can be used to obtain a more reliable radiocarbon time-scale. In both plots, radiocarbon measurements be- come progressively younger in the interval between 4,000 and 20,000 years ago. For samples younger than about 12,000 years, tree-ring and varve data are used to compare the radiocarbon chronology. The uranium-series method is used for older materials.

Radiation Dating

Fission-Track Dating

Fission-tracks are produced when alpha particles created by spontaneous fission (of ^{238}U) leave a trail of damage across minerals (including mica, apatite, and zircon) and glass.[24] To examine these, the researcher polishes and etches a previously unexposed surface of a sample. This enlarges the size of tracks; the researcher then counts the fis- sion tracks, which can be seen through a micro- scope. The age of the sample is determined by the number of tracks per unit area: the higher the number of tracks, the older the sample. Fission- track dates are a measure of the time elapsed since the substance was solid enough to retain tracks. The age range amenable to fission-track dating is from about 20 years to 1.5 million years.

The major problem in fission-track dates is that there may be thermal annealing, which causes the tracks to fade. In addition, the concentration of uranium in a sample must be high enough to pro- duce a high-track density, and the uranium dis- tribution must be sufficiently uniform. Materials that can be dated include obsidian, minerals, ar- chaeological glasses, and ceramics.

Fission-track dating has been used as an inde- pendent check on K-Ar dates in east Africa at Olduvai Gorge and Koobi Fora. One well-known example is the dating of the KBS tuff in Kenya. The first published date for the KBS tuff was about 2.37 million years B.P. After this, dates of around 1.80 and 1.88 million years B.P. were ob- tained. A fission-track date was used to strengthen the argument that the tuff was about 1.87 million years old.

Paleomagnetic and Archaeomagnetic Dating

Both paleomagnetic and archaeomagnetic dating techniques rely on the phenomenon of the earth's magnetic poles changing in space and time.[25] Paleomagnetism relates to geologic deposits and archaeomagnetism to archaeological materials or features. The basis of the dating techniques is

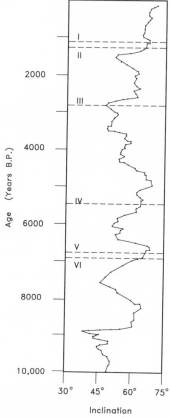

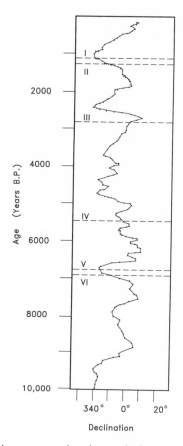

Inclination

Declination

Figure 7.8 Typical Magnetic Inclination and Declination Compared Through Roughly Opposite Reversals
Two patterns of change can be used to study inclination and declination of the magnetic field. This sequence has been proposed as the standard curve recording magnetic secular variation during the Holocene in western North America. The roman numerals denote volcanic-ash deposits within the sequence.

that the earth's magnetic poles "wander" (show secular variation) and "flip" (reverse direction).

Iron dipoles in minerals in crystallizing igneous rocks align with the earth's magnetic field at the time of their formation or deposition. The earth's magnetic field also affects magnetic particles during sedimentation, influencing them to become oriented parallel to the field. This creates detrital remnant magnetism, whose direction and intensity mimic the earth's magnetic field at the time of deposition. By establishing a chronology for the change in the earth's magnetic field, it is possible to date rocks by matching their magnetic orientation against the master record. There is now a master curve recording secular change of the geomagnetic field for the past 10,000 years (figure 7.8).

Archaeomagnetism has been useful in resolving the problem of dating Hohokam canals in North America.[26] The detrital remnant magnetism in the sediments demonstrated that most of the dates clustered around A.D. 900–1000. At one site, from La Lomita, detrital remnant magnetism results could be compared with diagnostic ceramics. Archaeomagnetic dating indicated that the oldest canal dated to 910–1025. A slightly younger canal, dated to 1000–1100, was associated with late Sacaton phase artifacts and was used around the time of the Sedentary to Classic transition (see the appendix for archaeological chronologies). The youngest canal contained Soho phase (Classic period) artifacts. Archaeomagnetic results of clay deposits associated with the Soho-phase feature suggested a date of between 1165 and 1350.

In addition to the standard set of techniques for obtaining information on magnetic variation through time, archaeological structures may be of use. In a unique study, Barmore used the orientation of Turkish structures (which, by Islamic law, must be aligned toward Mecca) built from the late eleventh century onward to see whether they contained information on the earth's secular magnetic variation. The study indicated that some of the mosques were no longer so oriented. Some of the builders' mistakes seem to have resulted from using a magnetic compass without correcting for magnetic declination. It may thus be possible to use this type of error to study magnetic variation in the past.[27]

Electron Spin Resonance and Thermoluminescence Dating

Both electron spin resonance (ESR) and thermoluminescence (TL) dating are based on the accumulation of trapped electrons in minerals; the more trapped electrons present, the older the age of the sample. The ongoing formation of electron traps in minerals results from the bombardment of the crystal structure by radiation from radioactive elements within and adjacent to the mineral. The increase in **paramagnetic** defects with time in crystalline solids is the basis of ESR dating, which provides an age estimate by directly measuring the number of trapped electrons in minerals within artifacts or sediments. The ESR signal of a crystal is proportional to the number of paramagnetic radiation-induced defects. Where a constant or known level of past radiation can be assumed or determined, the ESR signal should be proportional to the age of the crystalline sample (figure 7.9).

Two parameters need to be determined to obtain an ESR date: the Total Dose (TD; also called the accumulated dose, or AD) and the annual radiation dose rate that a sample has received. The TD is the total radiation dose that a specimen has received since its formation or its last

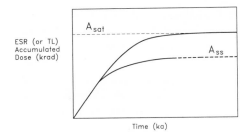

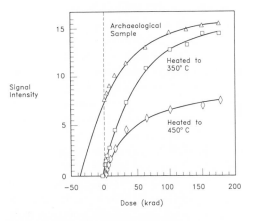

Figure 7.9 Growth Curves for ESR Dating
Curves demonstrating changes in ESR with increased time or dose. The accumulated dose or signal intensity increases until it reaches a plateau or point of saturation.

effective heating (which would drive the electrons from the traps). The ESR age is equivalent to the Total Dose divided by the annual dose. An estimate of TD is back extrapolation to zero ESR intensity, which corresponds to the time of the formation of the sample. The TD is generally not difficult to determine using the additive-dose method, but several possible interference factors need to be considered. These include changes that are due to grinding, bleaching, humic acid radicals, pressure effects, and the thermal stability of the trapped electrons. The major application of ESR has been to Quaternary carbonates. Fossil bone, teeth, and shells have also been dated using ESR. The application of ESR to the dating of spring-deposited travertines is more difficult if the content of manganese is high. Variation in the geochemical content of water associated with lacustrine sediments makes it difficult to evaluate the annual dose and, consequently, to determine ESR ages on lacustrine carbonates.

Travertine samples from the El Kown archaeological site in Syria have been dated using ESR. The ages were then compared with uranium-series ages. The oldest of the travertine deposits from this open-air site gave ESR ages of 216,000 years and uranium-series ages of 245,000 years. Some uranium-series and ESR dates did not correlate well, but most fell in the range of 160,000–80,000 B.P. An unexpectedly young sample of about 18,000 years old provided by ESR was confirmed by a uranium-series age of about 17,000–15,000 years. It is possible that the disconjunctive dates were the result of postdepositional changes.

Dating spring-deposited travertines has been attempted at several sites in Hungary. External dose rates had to be assumed for all the sites, and internal dose rates were calculated using U and Th contents and U-series dating. When these were compared with U-series dates, the ages were generally close. Travertine spring deposits above and below the "Paleolithic stratum" at the site of Tata, Hungary, gave U-series ages of 98,000 and 101,000 years, and ESR ages of 81,000 and 127,000 years, respectively. The other dates did not match.

Eolian quartz grains and gypsum may be used to obtain ESR signals. Eolian and stream-sedimented quartz grains have been studied from the site of Arago, France, and gypsum has been analyzed from the Mammoth Cave, Kentucky, area.

Thermoluminescence is the light given out of a crystal as it is heated. The light emitted by the heating is proportional to the age of the sample: it increases with older samples. The release of electrons from the traps at defects in the crystal structure produces the light. It is necessary to measure the background radioactivity of a sample to obtain an age estimate with the TL technique. The TL produced by past exposure to radiation can be compared with induced TL in the laboratory. This allows the past radiation dose to be determined (figure 7.10). The upper age limit for TL dating is about 250,000 years for quartz and 500,000 years for feldspars. It is important to note

that exposure to sunlight can free trapped electrons and thus "reset the clock."

Thermoluminescence has been applied to the dating of pottery, continental and marine sediments, burnt rock, igneous rocks, loess and eolian sands, alluvial and lacustrine deposits, calcitic formations, and shells.[28] It has been especially useful when dating igneous rocks too young to be dated by the potassium-argon method. Continental volcanics have been dated with TL measurements of feldspars.

At the important Lower and Middle Paleolithic site of Tabun Cave in Israel, flint artifacts were selected that had been recovered near a sedimentary sequence that could be analyzed through **dosimetry**. To obtain a measurement of the cave's external dose rate forty-six dosimeters were placed as close to the locations of the flint artifacts as possible. To measure the paleodose, the outer 2 mm of each artifact was removed, and the remaining fragments were analyzed after treatment to remove carbonate. The paleodose was measured according to the second TL growth curve. The internal dose rate was calculated using INAA for concentrations of ^{238}U, ^{232}Th and ^{40}K. Radiation doses of sediments that surrounded the artifacts were also measured. Based on the TL rates on flints a new chronological timescale was proposed for the site, which was older than it had seemed in earlier chronologies, one of which was based on ESR. Units XIII to II were assumed to date from 330,000 to 210,000 B.P. (correlated with isotope stages 9 and 8). The lower units, XIII–XI, are associated with Acheulian and Yabrudian artifacts, while IX–II contain Mousterian artifacts, indicating a possible transition to the Middle Paleolithic around 300,000 B.P. Unit I, which also contained Mousterian artifacts, was probably deposited around 171,000 B.P. (correlated with either the end of isotope stage 7 or the early part of stage 6). One of the important consequences of these TL dates is that they place the beginning of the Mousterian back to about 270,000–250,000 B.P., which is similar to the earliest known Middle Paleolithic in the Saharan Desert. Another archaeological consequence is that Neanderthals may have been in

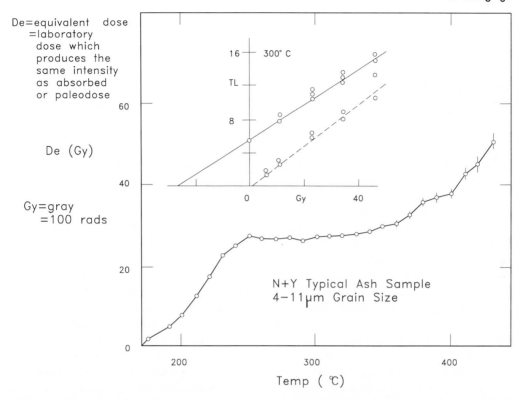

De=equivalent dose
=laboratory
dose which
produces the
same intensity
as absorbed
or paleodose

De (Gy)

Gy=gray
=100 rads

N+Y Typical Ash Sample
4-11 μm Grain Size

Temp (°C)

**Figure 7.10 Additive Dose Technique in Thermolumi-
nescence Dating**
Dating an ash fall using thermally stimulated luminescence, or thermoluminescence. The lower graph shows
the presence of a plateau for the equivalent dose. The
empty circles that form this plateau are the result of
using the additive-dose technique. The upper graph
shows a TL build-up curve. The estimated age of this
ash is 7,800 years.

the Levant about 170,000 years ago (oxygen isotope stage 6). There is also the possibility that
the burnt-flint TL chronology indicates the existence of archaic forms of *Homo sapiens* more than
250,000 years ago.[29]

A loess sequence in northern Pakistan dated
by TL helped to assign a site to the Paleolithic.
The archaeological remains included conjoinable
blade tools, associated debitage, and a structure
that was probably a small shelter.[30] The site contained no hearths or charcoal, so TL dating of the
loess was the only available method. Because the
loess overlies the artifact accumulation, it provides a minimum age for the site. It was found
that TL dates from the site could be grouped
into three sets. The youngest (uppermost) loess

was deposited between 27,000 and 24,000 B.P., or
just before the last glacial maximum. Older dates
in the range of 47,000–42,000 B.P. and 64,000–
59,000 B.P. were obtained from loess overlying
the archaeological zone. The older dates may
represent sediments that were redeposited and
not entirely zeroed-out before their redeposition.
Because of this, they may have "inherited" TL
associated with an earlier depositional event. It
was concluded that the Paleolithic artifacts dated
to around 45,000–42,000 B.P. and that the loess
cover dated to the last glacial. Before the use of
TL dating, an age assignment for these materials
would have been based on stone-tool typology or
the tenuous association of sites with river terraces.

Thermoluminescence has been extensively

used for dating loess deposits containing paleosols.[31] Thermoluminescence measurements were used to estimate the age of soils developed within a loess sequence in western Europe. The loess correlated with **stadial** events and soil formation associated with interglacials and interstadials. The TL dates ranged in age from about 140,000 to 13,000 years.

There are two other ways luminescence has been used to derive archaeological chronologies. Whereas TL is stimulated by heat, optical stimulated luminescence (OSL) is stimulated by visible light, and infrared stimulated luminescence (IRSL) by infrared light. An example of IRSL dating of sediments that are directly related to ancient human activity is the work on the Neolithic site of Bruchsal Aue in Germany.[32] Exposure to daylight appears to wash out any previous IRSL signal. This resets the luminescence clock, even in redeposited colluvium exposed to light for as little as thirty minutes. The amount of new luminescence energy stored after resetting was used to date colluvial sediments deposited as a result of erosion. The erosion was thought to have been initiated by human activities like forest clearing and agriculture. The archaeological site of Bruchsal Aue contained traces of both an Early and a Late Neolithic settlement. During the time Bruchsal Aue was occupied, defensive trenches were dug into a late-glacial loess. Later, after the settlement was abandoned, colluvial sediments accumulated in the trenches. Some trenches show periodic episodes of colluvial fill separated by intervals of erosion. Sediment samples were collected and analyzed from the late-glacial loess, the three stratified colluvial layers, and trench and pit fill (dug either into the loess or into one of the colluvial deposits). The IRSL dates on loess ranged from 14.7 to 10.9 thousand years ago (ka). Pit fill and the earliest colluvial layer dated around 7–6 ka. Less luminescence had accumulated in the stratigraphically higher samples, and the IRSL ages of these sediments were consequently younger. The luminescence dates from the site of Bruchsal Aue have been used to argue that colluvial deposition in Germany was related to high population density and intensive land use starting in the Neolithic and continuing through the medieval period.

Because the IRSL method dates a sedimentary deposit's last exposure to light, it is a direct method of dating the accumulation event. It is thus a potentially valuable tool to understanding human-landscape interactions. Furthermore, IRSL is based on feldspars, a common mineral in the earth's crust, not on rare constituents or charcoal or bone fragments.

Dating Exposed Surfaces

Dating erosional or depositional surfaces, as opposed to the material or deposits underlying those surfaces, is a burgeoning field of study of great importance in geoarchaeology. The investigation of weathering rinds has been particularly useful. The critical *rate of weathering* must be established by other, independent dating methods.

Weathering rinds can be used to date artifacts (see obsidian hydration dating, above), deposits, and landscape surfaces. All landscape surfaces are subject to weathering processes that result in physical and chemical alteration. Once a geomorphic surface has been stabilized, soil formation and weathering begin immediately. Exposed surfaces of rock outcrops and clasts eroded from the outcrops will exhibit increasing surface alteration with time. Rind-dating is particularly successful in regions where a single rock type is widely distributed.

Another landscape dating method is based on the accumulation of cosmogenic chlorine-36 (^{36}Cl) on exposed rock surfaces. Because of its half-life of 100,000 years, the ^{36}Cl method can be used to date landforms constructed during the past two million years. Intense chemical weathering can complicate the matter by mixing ^{36}Cl that comes from the rock with ^{36}Cl from the atmosphere, so appropriate corrections need to be made. Chlorine-36 has been used to date meteorite craters, glacial deposits, and lava flows.[33]

CHAPTER 8

Geologic Mapping, Remote Sensing, and Surveying

Geologic Maps and Mapping

Classification is central to mapping. Information selected for mapping or display on a map has already been grouped into a small number of categories. Consequently, map makers begin with information which has already been classified. Classification, then, reflects the point of view of those gathering the data and making the maps more than it does the underlying physical reality. Classification schemes are designed to be functional. When they aren't, they are altered or abandoned. Maps always reflect a simplification of the variables displayed.

Many kinds of maps are available to the archaeologist. Two of these, topographic maps and surficial-geology maps, sometimes called Quaternary maps (first introduced by the Geological Survey of England in 1863), are of major importance in geoarchaeology. Maps of the bedrock geology (the map they give you when you ask for a geologic map), mineral deposits, hydrology, or seismicity are important for some studies. Quaternary maps are quite distinct from soil maps. The former show deposits that are about 0.5 meters below the ground and do not take topsoil into consideration. The colors on a Quaternary map represent genetically and lithologically different deposits. Soil scientists make similar maps, on various scales. Their field methods are nearly identical to those used in geology, but there is an added emphasis on close examination using coring and trenching (because soils vary more rapidly laterally than do geologic features or materials).

A topographic map, as distinct from other kinds of maps, portrays the shape and elevation of the terrain. Most topographic maps represent elevations by contour lines. Contour intervals vary with the relief of the terrain. On quadrangle maps made by the U.S. Geological Survey and similar organizations, small irregularities of the ground surface are omitted from the map: the contours are drawn as smooth lines through areas of irregularity. Thus small mounds and other features that are of interest to archaeologists may not be represented on topographic maps.

Topographic maps contain a great deal of information other than contours of elevations. Surface-water features (including swamps and springs); modern or abandoned quarries and mines; buildings, roads, and other cultural features; and areas of vegetation are all recorded on topographic maps. Major geomorphic features like escarpments, terraces, dunes, and waterfalls can easily be seen, which makes it possible to reconstruct landscapes. When geologists do their field mapping, they use topographic maps as base maps on which to record their observational data about geologic materials and features. However, the contours on topographic maps (and even less on elevation maps) do not adequately express the details of roughness and steepness of landscapes.

When the scale is appropriate, geoarchaeologists use topographic maps as base maps on which to plot special features or information. That is, they construct a thematic map, such as one that portrays slope stability. In the United States, the largest-scale topographic maps are 1:24,000. One should be aware that maps compiled before the

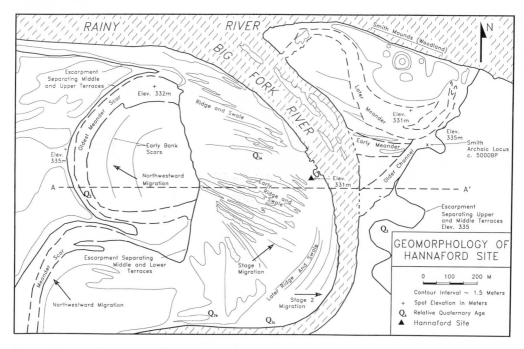

Figure 8.1 Geomorphology of the Hannaford Site

second half of the twentieth century, particularly those from the nineteenth century, are less accurate than current maps.

Topographic maps also record the important landscape features that are the first level of geomorphic interpretation. Erosional features like stream valleys, gullies, and washes can easily be identified. In the contours outlining a hill, the shape of the contour lines will show the courses of streams too small to be drawn in with blue lines. Residual features that have resisted erosion, like mesas and terraces, can also be easily identified on topographic maps. Depositional features like alluvial fans and sand dunes have clear topographic expression. In addition, topographic maps locate benchmarks that are critical in establishing vertical control in an excavation.

A good example of what can be learned from a topographic map can be seen in figure 8.1. Supplemented by aerial photography, limited drilling, excavation, and ^{14}C dating, the geomorphic context and paleographic history of a Woodland site called Hannaford was compiled from the Delvin Quadrangle topographic map. The Rainy River

is the boundary between the state of Minnesota and Canada. The stratigraphy and geomorphology of the region are the result of geologic events that have affected all of northern Minnesota over the past 15,000 years.

The ridge and swale topography, easily seen in figure 8.1, is the geomorphic expression of an eastward movement of the Big Fork River channel before about 2500 B.P. This was later overlain by sediments deposited in a floodplain regime. The meander scar pattern to the west/southwest of the Hannaford site is clearly older than the ridge and swale topography on which the Hannaford site strata lie. The Hannaford site itself has a **point-bar** setting. The geoarchaeological interpretation of the site-geomorphic context is shown in figure 8.2. This figure is a generalized cross-section of the A-A' line of figure 8.1.

A good general picture of the hydrosphere is also displayed on topographic maps. Because potable water resources, water transportation routes, barriers to transportation (large marshes or peat bogs, rivers), and food resources derived from water bodies are vital, topographic maps are

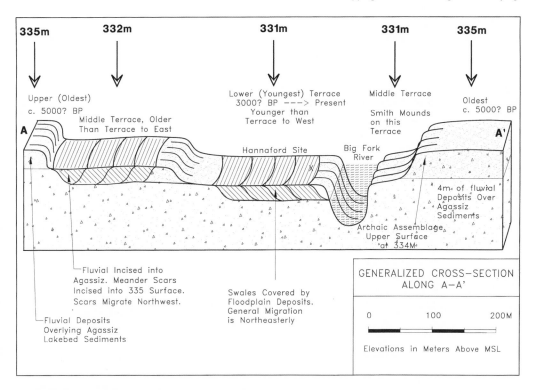

Figure 8.2 Generalized Cross Section of the A–A' Line
in Figure 8.1

central to understanding sites and settlement patterns. Field archaeologists and geoarchaeologists are strongly advised to become expert in interpreting topographic maps. Manuals at all levels of expertise are readily available.[1] Geoarchaeological interpretation of fossil-plant records requires assembling information on the broad ecological conditions prevailing and their variation in different parts of the landscape. This is vital in reconstructing human activity across ancient landscapes. Most multidisciplinary archaeological projects now begin by mapping the present vegetation. In a landscape with a natural or seminatural vegetation, a map of the present vegetation will reflect the natural **edaphic** conditions—the soil and water regimes. When combined with soil maps and geologic, paleoecologic, and paleopedogenic studies from drill cores, the pattern of ecological change and land use should emerge. In combination with archaeological survey, the human rationale for past land use, settlement patterns, and exploitation of flora and fauna can be determined. Enhanced detail can be added by geochemical surveys tracking phosphate concentrations immediately below the topsoil.

Terrain mapping may include many surface and remote survey techniques including coring, test pits, geophysical and geochemical surveys, and laboratory analyses. The terrain, as it exists at present, will have been modified since the period of archaeological interest. Terrain features of interest, such as slopes, soil, vegetation, hydrology, and outcrops, can be mapped at a scale appropriate to the study. Terrain patterns—areas of recurring topographic, soil, and vegetative associations will emerge. Terrain evaluation supplements site evaluation and places a site in its environmental context. The slope of the ground, for example, with its frequent connection to actual or potential human occupation of an area, is a fundamental aspect of terrain that can be measured from a contoured topographic map. Slopes must always be measured at right angles to the contours. Between contours the measurement will show only average slope, but this should suffice.

Hammond has devised a system of terrain classes using local relief and the percentage of smooth slopes.[2] Specifically, Hammond uses four geomorphic properties to define terrain classes: 1) an inclination index—the percentage of an area occupied by slopes with an inclination of less than 8 percent; 2) maximum difference in elevation within the area—commonly called *relief*; 3) the general profile character—the percentage of slope of less than 8 percent that falls in the upper and lower halves of the elevation range; and 4) character of the surface materials. Terrain classes directly affect the distribution of large herbivores, the possibility for various types of agriculture, and the like. Specialized maps, in our view, are too sparingly used in archaeology.

The concept of landscape as a cultural artifact is being increasingly addressed by anthropologists, archaeologists, geographers, and historians, as well as by geoarchaeologists.[3] Geographers, in particular, have long recognized that landscapes represent the interactions of humans with the environment. In contrast, until recently, archaeologists have focused on architectural features and settlement plans, rather than on the space between communities.

Because bedrock and surficial geology maps are two-dimensional representations of three-dimensional structures, they often contain cross sections printed along map borders. Geologic maps, by means of graphic devices indicating, for example, the inclination of nonhorizontal strata, present a great deal of information in concise form. Geologic maps contain the information about natural resources—metal deposits, building stone, some types of clay deposits—as well as the information necessary to gauge the present and past suitability of an area for construction of canals or dams.

A geologic map provides the basis for preparing second-order maps like isopach maps, which show the variation in thickness of a rock unit; structure-contour maps, which show the variation in altitude of the upper surface of a rock unit; and landslide-susceptibility maps, which show, in addition to bedrock, geomorphic and climatic factors. With additional data, second-order maps can be constructed for almost any physical (e.g., aquifers), chemical (e.g., variation in phosphate content), or cultural (e.g., quarries) feature that varies systematically with the geology.

From geologic mapping and from surface observations, the geologist can predict the subsurface geology. The archaeologist is not as fortunate. The geoarchaeologist should be able to gather the maximum amount of subsurface information from geologic techniques available. For example, if a site is on a ridge composed of a gently dipping sequence of sands, silts, and gravels, the geoarchaeologist can project the depths of a given geologic layer from one part of the site to another. Hydrogeologic conditions, including water-table depth and springs, can also be predicted. The U.S. Geological Survey publishes *Hydrologic Investigation Atlas* maps, overprinted on the 7.5 minute, 1:24,000 topographic map base.

Soil maps show the distribution of soils on the landscape. This distribution is related to active surface and near-surface processes. The age of a soil can be no greater than that of the land surface upon which it has developed. Geologic maps, by contrast, represent in a given area the history of the earth's outer crust for a considerable length of time. A lithostratigraphic unit depicted on a geologic map may or may not be related to geologic processes currently active in the area.

In the United States the main source of soil-related information is the Soil Conservation Service, which can provide soil maps and soil data forms. The latter contain a soil description, soil properties like permeability and pH, and interpretations of land-use limitations. Land-use limitation maps can be constructed for geoarchaeological reconstruction of paleoenvironmental contexts.

Special maps of great significance for geoarchaeological investigations have often been made for very different purposes. A good example is shown in figure 8.3. The U.S. Army Corps of Engineers and other government bodies responsible for waterways investigations compile and often publish data and maps that relate directly to paleogeomorphic change. Figure 8.3 details the

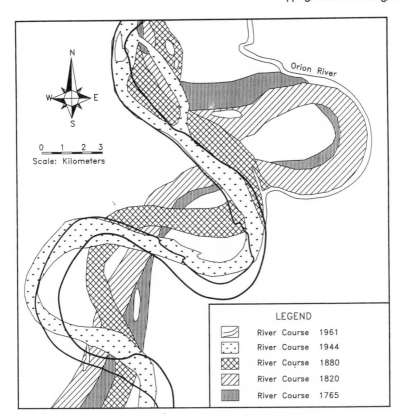

Figure 8.3 The Course of the Mississippi River, 1765–1961

(Reconstructed from data and maps published by the U.S. Army Corps of Engineers)

wide meandering of the Mississippi River from 1765 to 1961. Using coring techniques, geoarchaeologists can follow meandering river courses back through a considerable amount of time.

Every human activity has its own scale: that is, scales differ according to activity area, habitation site, or site-catchment area. Maps of these activities have scales that range from 1:50 to 1:2,500. Geologic phenomena are mapped at vastly different scales—1:25,000 or 1:50,000—and are not made for archaeological purposes. In mapping, the concept of scale is really one of resolution. *Small scale* means low resolution, and *large scale* means high resolution.

Reading the Landscape from Topographic Maps

If a topographic map shows an isolated prominent hill, there is no single probable explanation for this distinctive feature. It may represent an isolated outcrop of rock, more resistant to weathering than surrounding rocks. Commonly these will be outcrops of igneous rocks—for example, a volcanic neck like Devil's Tower, Wyoming. A second possibility is that the hill is not formed from more resistant rock but is merely capped by a more resistant layer. This cap rock can be either igneous or sedimentary. A third explanation is that the hill is merely a residual feature of the landscape, not associated with a resistant lithology.

There are many linear hill features that find expression on a topographic map. Asymmetrical hills with one steep face and one gently sloping face may well be caused by the outcrop of a resistant, gently dipping bed. More symmetrical ridges, with both sides steeply sloping (known as hogbacks), are often formed by an outcrop of a resistant bed that dips steeply or is even near vertical. Flat-topped hills bounded by steep slopes, sometimes called mesas, are most often caused by resistant cap rocks that are nearly horizontal.

Very flat coastal plains often represent land that has emerged because of regression of the sea. Large, very flat areas inland may be either the floodplain of a large river or the bottom of a former lake.

The pattern of rivers and streams exhibited on a topographic map will indicate their nature and origin, as well as aspects of the bedrock and climate. A detailed analysis of river drainage patterns, valley forms, and coastal geomorphologies is beyond the scope of this book. The reader is referred to the many excellent geomorphology books available. Suffice it to say that geoarchaeologists responsible for terrain analysis will need to become competent geomorphologists.

Settlement Patterns

Understanding landscape change is crucial to geoarchaeological analysis of settlement patterns. Landscape preservation can vary greatly over small areas, depending on conditions: weathering, erosion, cultivation, downslope creep, burial, and even geomorphic stability. A site that lies on open ground for long periods of time will suffer destructive effects. The dating of events and deposits—crucial to any analysis of landscape change—can be quite complex and requires a thorough understanding of the regional geomorphology. One can often date the establishment and abandonment of sites archaeologically. When landscape factors affect these processes, geoarchaeologists need to relate rapid (e.g., earthquakes) or slow (e.g., sediment infilling of harbors) geomorphic changes to the human chronology. An example of this kind of change is when a site is missing because of erosion.

Such landscape features as availability of potable water or communication routes may undergo marked change in relatively short periods of time, which also affects habitation sites. The changes that occurred to the coast of Greece near Thermopylae had a marked effect on the human habitation (see Chapter 3).[4]

Settlement patterns are a mixture of two basic forms: nucleated and dispersed. An available water supply may be the most important of the landscape features that can explain nucleation and/or siting. Where surface water or water from shallow wells is widely available, it is unlikely to be an important factor. In desert areas or areas underlain by wide expanses of chalk, limestone, or loose and permeable sand, lack of available surface water can be key.

Other landscape features that affect settlement patterns that are readily apparent from good topographic maps include areas offering flood protection and defensive advantages. The floodplains of major rivers are all subject to periodic inundation. A major difficulty in using topographic maps to assess the possible importance of the flood factor is that the contour interval may be too large to show relevant altitude differences. During periods of danger, settlements have been concentrated on tops of steep-sided hills or, in the case of danger from the sea, away from observation by passing ships.

Habitation sites are more numerous on coasts and large rivers. Rivers provide water, transport, food, an element of defense, and, at crossing points, an element of control of communication. Coastal sites offer some of the same advantages. *We stress here that modern topographic maps are likely to misinform concerning ancient sites. Coastal harbors on estuaries can rapidly become landlocked as sediment fills the estuary. In broad flat floodplains, the major rivers meander rapidly—as much as 20 kilometers in two hundred years for the lower Mississippi.*

Finally, there may be bedrock geology or pedological features that influence settlement patterns. At different sides of a boundary of bedrock or soil types, different settlement patterns may result from the different exploitable potentials. Around the peripheries of the larger **poljes** in the Yugoslavian karst topography are settlements that combine freedom from flooding on the polje floor with the ability to exploit the deeper soils which accumulate along the break in the slope.

Geoarchaeologists need to be aware of the data available on "prehistoric" maps from the Old World. The earliest maps grew out of prehistoric art. Picture maps from Çatal Höyük, a major Neolithic site in Anatolia, and from Maikop,

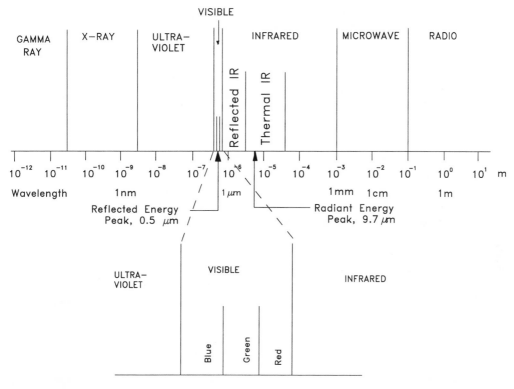

**Figure 8.4 Electromagnetic Spectrum
(Detail: The Visible Spectrum)**

Russia (ca. 3000 B.C.) are two striking examples. Both the Babylonians and the Pharaonic Egyptians made maps. A diagrammatic map of the late second millennium B.C. from Nippur shows nine settlements with canals and a road between them but no indication of distances. A complete history of ancient maps is provided by Harley and Woodward.[5] This volume should be consulted by anyone working in Old World prehistory.

Remote Sensing

The term *remote sensing* was introduced in the 1960s to describe any method of deriving information about an object (or a stratum) from measurements made at a distance—that is, without contact. The advent of computer digital processing and data-analysis techniques have greatly increased our remote-sensing capabilities, for they

have given us new pattern-recognition methodologies that help us derive information about materials at or near the earth's surface from spatial and spectral distributions of energy emanating or reflecting from these materials. An important step is the analysis of the data: through analysis, data become information.

Pattern recognition is a two-step process. First, the classes (objects, strata, rock types, vegetation types) are characterized through the analysis of data that are representative of them. In remote sensing, ground truthing is the process of verifying "on the ground" the correspondence of remotely sensed data with classes of materials. Second, all new data are then classified by means of numerical rules that make use of these class characterizations.

Remote-sensing systems can be passive or active. In passive systems the sensor receives energy from a target that has been illuminated by an external radiation source—the sun, for example. An active remote sensing system, like radar, generates the radiation. Most remote sensing devices use the electromagnetic spectrum. Electromagnetic energy spans the spectrum of wavelengths from 10^{-10} micrometers (cosmic rays) to 10^{10} micrometers of broadcast wavelengths (figure 8.4).

There are many prospecting techniques available for locating deeply buried archaeological sites: geophysical, geochemical, core drilling, and aerial satellite remote sensing. Because each method has its special strengths, they must be applied in an ordered and efficient way. The geoarchaeologist should try to confirm results at every step. A map of geophysical anomalies remains only an ordered set of possibilities until drilling or excavation can provide confirmation.

Geophysical Prospecting

As excavation becomes increasingly expensive, permits become more difficult to attain (at least in some parts of the world), and scientists seek the least destructive methods of gaining information, archaeology turns more and more to methodologies like geophysical prospecting that can resolve these problems. Geophysical methods can detail the location, extent, and character of modified terrain. Surface geophysical surveys can be combined with magnetic analysis of soil and geochemical prospecting to give a good picture of the extent of the anthropogenic context of a buried site or feature. With the addition of more extensive core drilling and sediment analysis, the pre-occupational topography and landscape history of a site can be determined (figure 8.5).

Until the 1970s, magnetic susceptibility and related techniques were not viewed as tools capable of investigating cultural landscapes. A notable exception was a study at Maiden Castle, an Iron Age hill fort near Bickerton, England. Magnetic analyses were used to determine whether charred wood within the ramparts had been burned before emplacement or in situ during or after construction.[6] Magnetic analyses of soils and archaeological sediments can be used to examine variations in soil-forming processes, including past weathering and climatic regimes; correlate stratigraphic

levels, sequences, and paleosols; and determine sediment sources.

The approach to any geophysical survey depends on the surficial geology and the presence or absence of interfering systems. The choice of methods should be matched to both archaeological goals and geologic conditions. A geophysical survey can be one of the main techniques of site evaluation, not just a guide to where to dig. A note of caution: the complexity of most urban stratigraphy, combined with interfering materials, structures, and powerlines, presents a nearly insuperable deterrent to geophysical surveying in intensely urbanized areas. Geophysical prospecting is both a broad and a specialized topic that goes well beyond its geologic aspects. For a fuller introduction to geophysical methods, see the sources in the notes to this chapter.[7]

Surface geophysical methods depend on the presence of contrasting physical properties of target features and their surroundings, which enable scientists to interpret subsurface deposits. Once the local subsurface geology is understood, any deviation in geophysical response is considered an anomaly. Anomalies can be the result of archaeological features, unexpected geologic features, or postoccupation intrusions. To date, geophysical surveys have been used primarily to locate discrete features before excavation rather than to assist in landscape reconstruction. Exceptions include the work on the mound builders of the Amazon and the reconstruction of landscape modification at the Cahokia Mounds site in Illinois.[8] Geophysical methods have become so diverse and pervasive in archaeology that it is impossible to review the field in any depth. Readers should consult the voluminous literature. Following are brief introductions to geoarchaeological aspects of four geophysical prospecting techniques that have been successful in archaeological contexts.

Magnetometry and Magnetic Properties of Soils and Sediments

The magnetometer is the survey instrument that has the widest possible application. However, depending on the relative magnetic susceptibility of the subsurface materials, small or poorly magne-

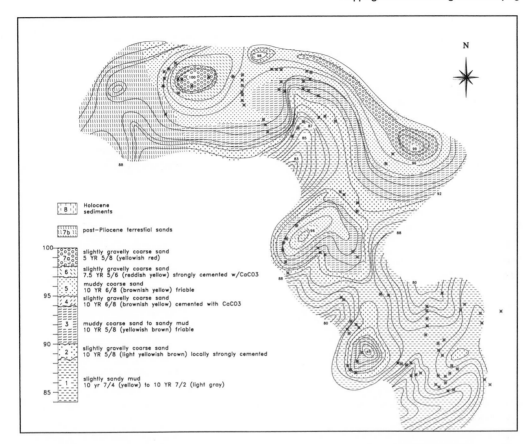

Figure 8.5 Paleotopography of Nichoria
Even in areas of moderate relief, the pre-occupation and occupation topography of a site are likely to be quite different from that of the present because of human activities and erosion/deposition. This figure illustrates the paleotopography of a large site in south-western Greece that was heavily modified during and subsequent to its occupation. (Data from Rapp and Aschenbrenner, *Excavations at Nichoria*)

tized features are not likely to be resolved if they are buried more than a meter deep. Magnetic anomalies show a tendency to broaden as they become more deeply buried by soils and alluvium. The problems of depth of burial are accentuated by waterlogging.

Magnetic methods are based on the magnetic field of the earth, which can be measured at any geographic location. The earth's magnetic field strength varies from about 50,000 to 70,000 **gamma** and is increased locally by magnetic materials. Baked clays, kiln walls, and other materials containing iron become magnetized when heated to a few hundred degrees Celsius. In North America the use of magnetic methods in archaeology goes back more than thirty years, to the survey at Angel Mounds in Indiana.[9] Magnetometry surveys are usually employed to locate specific archaeological features on sites that have been identified by other means, such as a scatter of sherds on the surface. Positive magnetic anomalies result from such features as iron objects, fire pits, kilns, forges, storage pits with high humic content, burned features, bricks, and the foundations of historic buildings. Negative magnetic anomalies are usually associated with graves, middens, wells, and various prehistoric structures. Many anomalies may be dipolar. Magnetic contrast is the key to locating buried archaeological features. Rapp was successful in locating buried (iron-free) limestone walls in a typical clayey soil matrix that had 5 percent or more iron, but he could not locate buried limestone walls that were resting on bedrock limestone in a high-lime soil.

The most commonly used magnetometer in archaeological prospecting uses the precession of spinning protons in a fluid (usually kerosene, alcohol, or water) to measure magnetic field strength. Spinning protons create magnetic dipoles which align in a uniform magnetic field. In the absence of other fields, protons align with the earth's field. The magnetometer first realigns the protons perpendicular to the earth's field then allows them to realign parallel to the earth's field. The protons precess with a frequency proportional to the total local magnetic field, providing a measurement of the field.

Magnetic surveying cannot be undertaken in areas where the bedrock is volcanic or where there are extensive powerlines or modern construction because these geologic or industrial materials have strong magnetic properties that will swamp out the weaker contrasts found in archaeological sites. A metal detector may be used to check for interferences produced by modern metallic waste. A distinct advantage of magnetic surveying is that it is not affected by the moisture content of the ground.

The magnetic properties of minerals have been used in conjunction with magnetometry to determine the magnetic properties of site sediments, soils, and features and have been used with core drilling and sediment analysis to investigate anthropogenic soil-forming processes and landscape change at archaeological sites. The minerals that contribute most to the magnetic character of typical soils are hematite (alpha-Fe_2O_3), maghemite (gamma-Fe_2O_3), and magnetite (Fe_3O_4). Many human activities can alter the magnetic character of soils. For example, hematite can be reduced to magnetite during heating in a reducing environment, which can occur in a hearth, resulting in a greater magnetic susceptibility. Offsite magnetic studies can also contribute key information. For example, the magnetic character of lake sediments can reflect local land use, climate, and fire frequency.

Magnetic susceptibility (MS) is a measure of the ability of a substance to be magnetized. Two factors determine magnetic susceptibility in a soil/sediment context: the presence of iron oxides inherited from parent rocks; and the degree to which these oxides have become enhanced by processes associated with anthropogenic activity, particularly burning.

Magnetic-susceptibility studies contribute to a geophysical survey by providing information in support of the interpretation of magnetometer data. They may also be used as a separate prospecting technique. Magnetic-susceptibility surveys can detect features of landscape change, anthropogenic disturbances like those resulting from agriculture, and bioturbation. These surveys are not usually adequate to pinpoint individual features but rather can provide a broader pattern that can be used in combination with other survey techniques. An MS survey should be conducted at a 10-meter sampling interval followed by a magnetometer or resistivity survey of areas of magnetic enhancement.

Magnetometers are particularly useful in historic sites, where shallow remains can be easily detected. Magnetometry can be an important technique for assessing the archaeological content of protected sites for cultural resource management. For prehistoric North America the most common targets of magnetic prospecting have been hearths, fired rock, and pottery. Magnetic prospecting is more successful when the archaeological features are large. Hearths are theoretically easy to detect but may be missed if they are too small.

Two examples, one from the New World, one from the Old World, will serve to illustrate the use of magnetometer surveying in archaeology. At the junction of the Knife and Missouri rivers north of Bismarck, North Dakota, is the Knife River Indian Villages National Historic Site. Magnetometer surveys revealed the remains of earth lodges that did not appear as depressions in the topography (figure 8.6).[10] The magnetic record is due in part to differences in soil mag-

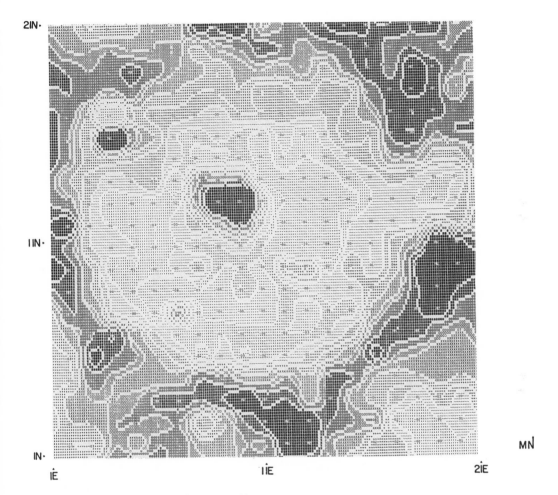

GRADIOMETER SIMULATION EXPERIMENT
HOUSE 6, SAKAKAWEA VILLAGE
ORIGINAL DATA
SENSOR HEIGHT ▪ ·6m

Figure 8.6 Gradiometer Simulation Experiment, House 6, Sakakawea Village

netic susceptibility inside and outside the lodges. The characteristic anomaly of these lodges is their central fire hearths, which lie at a depth of 40 to 120 cm and produce anomalies of 20 to 50 gamma. Anomalies associated with smaller interior or exterior hearths and with midden areas are also visible. These identifications have been established by coring and test excavations.

In the Old World, Rapp performed a magnetometer survey at the site of Nichoria in south-western Greece at a time before computers were used to record and display data. Figure 8.7 shows a contoured magnetometer grid that was hard to interpret precisely. The numbers represent the last two numbers from magnetometer readings on a 6 × 10–meter grid at 1-meter spacings. In an attempt to interpret the data the magnetic field values were contoured. Since the underlying geology was flat-lying Pliocene silts and sands, this magnetic record seemed to indicate the presence

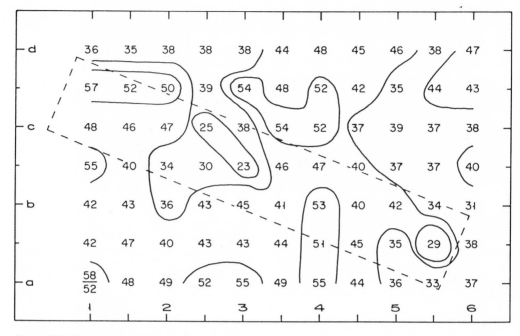

Figure 8.7 Magnetometer Record from Nichoria, Greece

of archaeological features, although it is hard to interpret. A test excavation was then laid out along the area marked by the dashed-line rectangle. The photograph in figure 8.8 was taken from a hydrogen-filled balloon. It reveals the results of the rectangular test trench. The correspondence between the circular feature in the lower right from the contouring and in the actual situation is probably fortuitous. The wall at 4 a-b was accurately reflected in the magnetic data, but the other two walls to the left at about 2.5 and 1.5 were not revealed in the contouring.

Electrical Resistivity

Electrical resistivity techniques that could be applied to archaeology were mainly developed in England during the 1950s. In resistivity surveying, a series of metal probes is inserted into the ground at measured intervals along a surveyed traverse. A voltage is applied to outer probes, and the inner probes record the resultant current flow in the earth. The depth to which the current will penetrate the earth is one to one-and-a-half times the

probe spacing. Resistivity measurements are suitable where there are soil or sediment contrasts involving differing water retention or dissolved ion concentrations—for example, ditches and pits. Historic architectural features like building foundations and house floors usually provide good electrical contrast. Resistivity methods have been successful in locating features that range from Roman walls to a paleolithic flint mine in Hungary.

Electrical resistivity is not an efficient method for broad surveys. Resistivity surveying should be favored where a strong electrical contrast with the enclosing soil/sediment matrix is provided, such as building foundations, ditches, and defensive works. A resistivity survey presumes that such features exist in the survey area. Magnetometry and electrical-resistivity survey methods complement each other. It is usually best to try magnetometry first, followed by a selected resistivity survey of significant magnetic anomalies.

Electrical resistivity surveying allows the researcher to control the depth of the investiga-

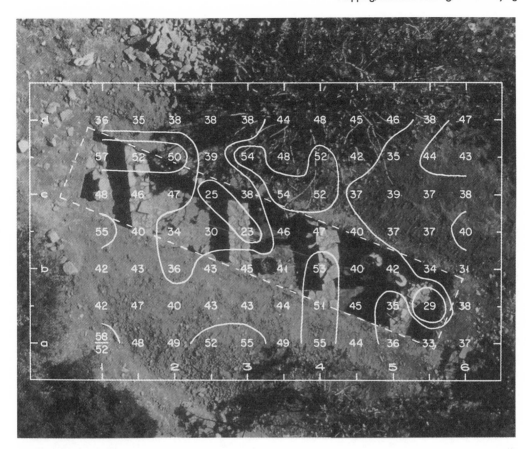

Figure 8.8 Photograph of a Test Trench at the Site of Nichoria, Greece, with the Magnetometer Record in Figure 8.7 Superimposed

tion because it varies the distance between the electrodes. Geoarchaeologists should have previous knowledge (e.g., by core drilling) of the approximate depth of archaeological features which generate the anomalies as well as the depth of the undisturbed geologic strata. Geologic strata display strong electrical conductivity contrasts among clays, silts, sands, and gravels and between weathered and unweathered rock. If the archaeological sediments are thick enough, one can set the probes close enough together to be free of the underlying geologic effects. This is important because geologic anomalies are most often one or more orders of magnitude stronger than archaeological anomalies and easily wash out the latter.

Buried walls, tombs, and related features that restrict the flow of electrons result in resistivity maxima. Ancient pits, ditches, and the like that were later filled, even with sediment or soil from the surrounding area, will result in resistivity minima because the material of the fill is more loosely packed and consequently retains more moisture. In most geoarchaeological situations, porosity, soil/sediment moisture, and the concentration of ions will govern both conductivity and resistivity in the subsurface.

Uneven terrain presents serious difficulties to the prospector. In a depression the current density is constrained to rise and, conversely, over a mound the current can spread out, which causes the the current density to fall. Because electrical currents in the ground are largely controlled by

187

moisture content, current agricultural practices, which are designed to retain soil moisture, may have a strong effect on electrical resistivity measurements. Electrical resistivity profiles that run parallel to or close to sharp boundaries—for example, where flat hilltops fall off into steep valley sides or where parallel excavation trenches exist—will be subject to "edge effects" because the open air of the hillside or trench represents an infinitely resistant volume.

Electromagnetic Conductivity

Electromagnetic methods were introduced in archaeology at the end of the World War II, when surplus mine detectors became available. The later development of specialized electromagnetic methods was prompted by the desire to replace the electrical-resistivity method, which required good contact between the ground and the electrode system—a major source of problems. The electromagnetic (EM) conductivity method induces current flow in the ground without actual electrical contact, thus providing a means of traversing an area rapidly to determine changes in the conductivity of the terrain. The chief disadvantage of EM is that if there is only one instrument (with a given frequency range), the vertical resolution is limited.

The Geonics EM-31 has an effective penetration of about 6 meters, while their EM-38 has an effective penetration of 1.5 meters. In contrast, with the electrical-resistivity method the desired penetration can be obtained by varying the configuration and spacing of the electrodes. The Geonics EM-38 can measure both terrain conductivity and magnetic susceptibility. The EM-31 has the ability to reveal stratigraphy and structure (e.g., pits). Profiles obtained by EM-38 are often noisier than EM-31 profiles and record generally lower conductivity values. Variations in soil moisture and temperature can affect the conductivity to the point that one must correct for the effects of weather-related survey conditions when comparing results from various EM surveys.

Ground Penetrating Radar

Magnetic and electromagnetic instruments rely on the presence of magnetic and conductive materials to produce anomalous responses. Ground-penetrating radar (GPR) records variations in the dielectric (nonconducting) properties of near-surface sediments and soils, which are usually caused by variation in moisture content. Ground-penetrating radar can be used on frozen or snow-covered sites.

In GPR, a short pulse of radio energy is generated from an antenna on or near the ground. The downward moving pulse is partially reflected by any change in the bulk electrical properties of the ground. This change usually correlates with a change in volumetric water content and may indicate a change in bulk density.

Ground-penetrating radar has successfully located buried structures at many archaeological sites. The instruments are more costly than magnetometers, instruments for EM conductivity, or electrical-resistivity instruments, but its unique, high-resolution capabilities make it an important tool in geoarchaeology.

First used in the United States in the early 1970s, GPR is finding increasing use in archaeological prospecting. It works well where sharp dielectric discontinuities exist at buried walls, foundations, and floors. Concentrations of metals and bricks produce strong radar echoes. One advantage of the GPR method is that it provides fairly direct information on depth. Another advantage is that the results are relatively easy to interpret. One disadvantage is that conductive soils cause a strong attenuation of radar echoes. In dry, sandy soils or sediments, 100 MHz GPR can penetrate 15 meters, whereas in wet, clayey soils the depth can be as little as 1 meter. Increasing the frequency improves the resolution but decreases the penetration.

On the positive side, such buried landscape features as river channels, as well as the depth of alluvium, can be determined using GPR. Traditionally, GPR has been successful at locating tombs, mine tunnels, and other voids. The extent to which walls or foundations can be detected depends on contrast with the enclosing matrix.

On the negative side, waterlogged soils and sediments present a problem for GPR, owing to signal attenuation. In clay-rich horizons the useful penetration of GPR can be less than half a meter. The use of longer pulses or lower frequencies can overcome this difficulty to some extent, but these tactics result in a trade-off between depth of penetration and resolution.

Similarly, higher frequency signals are required to resolve small features. Since higher frequencies are more rapidly attenuated, as the depth explored increases so does the size of objects that can be detected. Therefore the choice of frequencies is dictated by the size and depth of the target and the nature of the subsurface matrix. Ground-penetrating radar is most effective when applied to specific and localized problems. It is not efficient as a broad exploratory tool.

Ground-penetrating radar has been successful in intrasite investigations, locating shallow graves, mapping historic-period fortifications, defining the outlines of features, and providing an immediate picture of the site stratigraphy. As the price of GPR instrumentation continues to decrease, this technique will become more commonplace in geophysical surveying.

Seismic Profiling

Seismology takes its name from the Greek words for the study of earthquakes, and it is from such studies that much of the instrumentation evolved. Seismic instruments record two types of seismic waves that reveal subsurface structures. One vibrates parallel to the direction of propagation, and the other vibrates perpendicular to it. The seismic disturbance of the ground in prospecting is produced either by controlled explosions or by impacting the earth with a heavy hammer hitting a steel plate. Seismic waves generated by such devices are reflected and/or refracted from subsurface layers with contrasting properties. When these reflected or refracted waves return to the surface, they can be recorded to provide an account of subsurface stratigraphy.

Although seismic reflection methods are commonly used in geology for shallow depth prospecting, they have not been successful in archaeological feature location. However, seismic methods can be used to evaluate offshore archaeological site potential and to reconstruct the offshore paleogeomorphology of coastal areas. For example, archaeological sites dating to between 12,000 and 6000 B.P. are likely to be found on the portion of the Gulf of Mexico's continental shelf that was subaerially exposed during that period. Although current methods in high-resolution seismic profiling cannot locate archaeological sites themselves, related geomorphic features such as river channels, bays, and lakes are easily detected. Regional studies have dated these geomorphic features to the period when human presence in the Gulf Coast is well documented. Possible habitation areas can be authenticated by analysis of drill cores.

Marine geophysical techniques can be more broadly applied. The study of the location and evolution of ancient harbors is receiving increasing attention. Because Early Holocene coastlines shifted so rapidly and are now offshore, marine geophysical techniques are required for investigations of these transgressions. High-resolution seismic-reflection profiling has been used to reconstruct the postglacial transgressive shorelines in southwestern Greece.[11] The shorelines of the Late Pleistocene and Holocene and their coastal environments were mapped. The sea-level rise from approximately −115 meters to its current level covered a former geomorphic landscape of scarps, beaches, river channels, and lagoons. These are now buried under a few meters of post-transgression deposits. Some features can be roughly dated by reference to known sea-level rise curves; after 6000 B.P. sparse archaeological data can provide a local sea-level rise curve.

In a related study, sub-bottom seismic-reflection profiling was used to determine the position and nature of the Holocene embayment at Franchthi Cave in the Argolid, Greece.[12] Franchthi Cave is an impressive karstic feature of about 150 meters in length whose mouth lies approximately 15 meters above the present shoreline. Excavation at the front of the cave revealed a succession of human occupations down to a depth of 10 meters and covering a time span of more than 20,000 years—from the Upper Paleolithic through the Mesolithic to the Neolithic. A second site lies along the shore below the mouth of the cave. A number of Neolithic structures have been uncovered there. Offshore seismic investigations revealed that the site was probably much larger originally. This information, along with the related landscape reconstruction, indicates the extent to which marine geophysical techniques can be applied in geoarchaeology.

Aerial Photography

Photography from tethered balloons predates the American Civil War. Civil engineers and soil scientists have used remote sensing for mapping since the 1930s. In fact, aerial photography for detecting buried features or features not visible from the ground was the earliest remote-sensing technique. Unfortunately, most of the aerial photographs available to archaeologists were made for other purposes and therefore have a limited usefulness in detecting archaeological features. Because a camera records everything it sees, the inventory of features of the earth's surface found in an aerial photograph is far more complete than that presented on even the largest-scale map. This has its disadvantages as well as advantages. Maps are selective and explicit—therefore clear and easy to understand. However, in many areas aerial photographs have replaced topographic maps as base maps for both geologic and archaeological fieldwork. The use of aerial photography in archaeology has had striking successes; the shadows cast by a low sun can highlight faint bands, ditches, and mounds that are difficult to observe in a ground-level survey. The results have been even more spectacular in cases where all traces are invisible to the ground observer.

Most aerial photographs are taken vertically (the camera aims straight down, perpendicular to the earth's surface, rather than at an oblique angle). For many archaeological features, oblique photographs that are taken when the sun and shadows are at an optimal angle are more revealing. Archaeological aerial photographs may be used either for prospecting or for mapping. The two often require different techniques and different geometric accuracy.

For most geologic and archaeological purposes, stereoscopic aerial photographs are preferable because the topographic variables stand out in contrast. Most features of archaeological interest have simple geometric shapes that are well known to archaeologists and geoarchaeologists. However, buried features may have shapes that differ significantly from those surface expressions that result from secondary differences in soil, vegetation, or plowing patterns. It takes some skill to differentiate among geologic, pedologic, modern agricultural, modern cultural, and archaeological features in an aerial photograph. In fact, although aerial photography can be an important exploration technique, one would not want to publish a site distribution map based solely on it. Repeated flights under varying conditions (e.g., differences in season and time of day), combined with field surveys, are necessary to determine the efficiency of aerial photography as an exploration tool for a given area.

Usually in aerial photography only black-and-white or infrared-sensitive film that makes use of the visible light spectrum is used. Because visible light has little penetrating power, surface materials, particularly soils, account for most of the variations in the imagery. Even for long-abandoned sites the disturbance of the soil is likely to have long-term effects that are observable in textural variations (which affect water retention—loosely packed soil retains more water) and color variation. The process of new soil formation can make these variations permanent. Many of them are not reflected in an archaeological section which exhibits differences through depth rather than surface patterns.

Soil color is a function of the spectral reflectance of the material components of the soil. This reflectance is primarily a function of the moisture content, iron oxide content, organic matter, major soil minerals, and texture. Organic matter darkens the soil, iron oxide reddens it, and reflectance increases with decreasing particle size. Soil scientists have found that spectral-reflectance curves follow the standard soil classifications. Variations in Munsell soil colors are sometimes enhanced in black-and-white aerial photographs. The greatest contrasts are caused by differences in soil moisture, which is affected by grain size and grain-size distribution.

Different types of buried features will result in different crop markings (figure 8.9). Basically,

Advanced Growth
Green

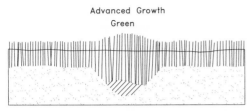

Ditch or pit allows higher water retention and availability.

Retarded Growth
Yellow

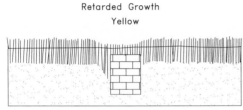

Solid structure lowers moisture availability.

Figure 8.9 Effects of Buried Structures on Overlying Crops

a buried structure will either enhance or retard crop growth. The starkness of the contrast in crop growth depends on the plants under cultivation. Plants with deeper roots may be less affected by differences in near-surface moisture content. Crop markings are more common over buried ditches and pits than over buried walls. It should be noted that agricultural treatments like spraying for weed control will make artificial patterns that show up on aerial photographs.

Most of the United States has been mapped on large-scale aerial photograph maps, sometimes called *photomaps*. For many regions the coverage has been repeated several times since aerial photomapping began in the 1930s. Thus, not only can landscape features be identified and measured, but short-term landscape change can be quantified. Photomaps are usually made directly from photographs, although electronic scanner images are becoming more important. The researcher should bear in mind, however, that scanner images are not identical to photographs.

Satellite and Airborne Remote Sensing

Imaging spectrometry is now practiced from spacecraft as well as aircraft. The wavelengths of the greatest interest in satellite remote sensing are the optical wavelengths from 0.30 to 1.5 micrometers. At these wavelengths, electromagnetic energy can be reflected and refracted from solid materials. Effective use of remote-sensing data requires a thorough knowledge of the spatial characteristics of the various earth-surface features and the factors that influence these spatial characteristics. Landsat data can provide the information for predictive models in archaeology.[13] Geologic and ecological variables form the basis for such models.

Aside from spatial features, spectral data can reveal the chemical nature of earth-surface materials. Spectral data from satellites now monitor crop growth throughout the world as each growing season progresses. Spectral-reflectance curves from soil are less complex than those from vegetation. One of the major reflectance characteristics of dry soil is a generally increasing level of reflectance with increasing wavelength, particularly in the visible and near-infrared portions of the spectrum. The moisture content, percentage of organic matter, percentage of iron oxide, and ratio of clay/silt/sand all influence the spectral reflectance of soils. The increase of moisture will cause a decreased reflectance. The percentage of organics will have the opposite effect.

Thermal infrared images depict the pattern of heat that is emitted or reflected by target materials. The thermal characteristics of earth-surface materials yield information that is not detectable in other regions of the electromagnetic spectrum. Thermal contrasts are indirect indicators of moisture content or heat capacity and direct indicators of heat radiating from volcanic or geothermal phenomena. The strong, solar-induced diurnal temperature flux must be taken into account in projects using thermal infrared imagery. Water has the highest heat capacity of all earth-surface materials, so it is easily detected in postsunset imagery.

The best resolution available to geoarchaeologists from satellite sensors comes from the 10-

meter Satellite Positioning and Tracking (SPOT) imagery. This is too coarse for most site-specific archaeological applications, but it is valuable for assessing current and past landscape features. Much finer resolution, down to 2 meters or less, can be obtained from sensors mounted on aircraft. Until the early 1980s the main limitation with satellite remote sensing was that no subsurface information could be acquired. Orbital imaging radar can now provide subsurface data in arid regions. The buried river valleys of the southeastern Sahara are systems of aggraded valleys that were first formed in the Middle Tertiary, containing inset drainage channels that have been entirely obscured by windblown sand. These features, first recorded as radar images, are remnants of a moister landscape in the Pleistocene and Early Holocene. Acheulian artifacts can be found in the alluvium that fills these old valleys. The imaging radar carried on the space shuttle *Columbia* in 1981 penetrated the extremely dry sands of the eastern Sahara, revealing previously unknown buried valleys.[14] Sand-filled and alluvium-filled valleys, some nearly as wide as the Nile, were brought to light by radar images. Wadis superimposed on the large valleys provided sites for episodic early human occupation. These ancient drainage networks offer a geologic explanation for the location of current oases.

An airborne radar survey in 1978 and 1979 over the dense rain forest of Guatemala led to the discovery of an elaborate network of Mayan canals from the Classic period, dug apparently between 250 B.C. and A.D. 900. The canals extend over a vast region of swampy jungle and are thought to be the basis for extensive lowland Mayan agriculture. The Maya were known to have dug canals in the arid highlands, but this was the first evidence of an extensive canal network in the lowlands.

A technique related to orbital imaging radar is Side-Looking Airborne Radar (SLAR) imagery, available from the U.S. Geological Survey. SLAR is applicable to land-use, cartographic, and groundwater studies. The SLAR system has an active sensor, providing its own microwave energy. It also has cloud-penetration capability, which allows it to collect imagery in situations where the conventional aerial photograph is inadequate, such as in the rain forests of Brazil. SLAR imagery presents an obliquely illuminated view of the terrain that enhances subtle surface features. More than 25 million square kilometers of SLAR data have been gathered in the Western Hemisphere.

Core Drilling

Core drilling has many facets in geoarchaeology. In regional environmental reconstruction, especially in areas subject to rapid change like coastal and riverine environments, core drilling is a critical technique for recovering data. Archaeological excavation is slow and costly. To determine the nature, depth, and extent of habitation, drilling, along with sediment/soil analysis and perhaps geophysical prospecting methods, can be quick, minimally destructive, and cost-effective. It is too little used in archaeological studies, but it is becoming more popular.[15]

There is some confusion about the terms *drilling*, *coring*, and *augering*. A distinction should be made between methods that recover a continuous (or nearly continuous) core and methods that merely bring up sediments in the sequence encountered. Although there is some distortion, especially compaction, core-recovery methods give far more comprehensive and undisturbed information than augers, which propel the material to the surface by means of an Archimedes screw. In the latter technique there is general mixing of the sediments, although gross stratigraphic relations are retained. Core recovery uses a hollow cylinder to bring a relatively undisturbed section of the subsurface stratigraphy to the surface.

In much of the world the water table is within a few meters of the surface. Trenching beneath the water table is impractical at best (requiring massive pumping to lower the water table in the area of the site). But core recovery is not materially affected by the water table, although well-sorted wet sand is difficult to recover without special equipment. Many types of instruments are available for coring, ranging from hand corers (figure 8.10) to vibracorers, truck- or trailer-mounted Giddings corers and large rotary drill rigs. Each has its place, depending on the nature

Figure 8.10 Core Drilling Equipment

of the problem and the resources available. As the environmental and geomorphic components of cultural-resource management increase, the use of coring techniques to recover subsurface information will become mandatory.

Core drilling was employed by Jing and his colleagues to reconstruct landscape change in relation to a sequence of archaeological habitation levels and soil development in the Yellow River Plain in China.[16] On the basis of stratigraphy and sedimentology, a Holocene landscape-evolution model was constructed (figure 8.11). The prolonged landscape stability from the very Late Pleistocene or Early Holocene to about 2000 B.P. provided Neolithic and Bronze Age human occupation with a favorable environment. After 2000 B.P., the hydrologic regime changed, and the floodplain experienced 2–3 meters of gradual vertical accretion during the next millennium. In response to a dramatic change in hydrologic regime after the early twelfth century A.D., overbank

deposition covered the floodplain by as much as 10 meters of younger alluvium. This had a pronounced effect on the preservation, visibility, and discovery of the ancient dynastic sites.

Although we occasionally use the term *landscape stability* when we are referring to a period of very slow change that allows good soil formation, landscapes are forever changing. Geoarchaeologists, even when they are dealing entirely with Holocene sites, must understand the entire Late Quaternary geomorphic history of the region where they work. Many geologic processes throughout the entire Pleistocene have contributed to the relevant geomorphic and sedimentary record.

The Thames River, currently flowing through the center of London, has provided a generous sequence of alluvial terraces in response to the succession of Pleistocene climatic events. In southern England, the Thames meandered across a wide area.[17] Studies of the pebble lithology of

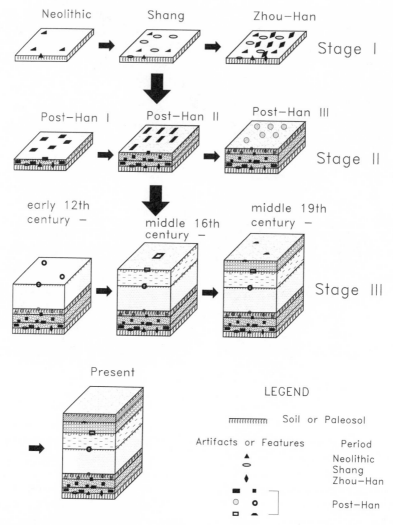

Figure 8.11 Holocene Landscape Evolution Model of the Yellow River Plain, China

gravel pits and of heavy mineral content in the sediments help us determine the former courses of the Thames. With the wealth of Paleolithic activity in the Thames drainage, the roving course of the river was a major determinant in settlement patterning.

Geochemical Prospecting and Analysis

Geochemical prospecting in archaeology is generally analogous to geophysical prospecting.

Based on a grid system and samples recovered from coring, a three-dimensional picture of the anthropogenic biogeochemistry can be developed. More focused studies can also be undertaken to locate and delineate graves, refuse areas, and agricultural plots. To understand the human-induced biogeochemical impact, similar analyses must be made of nearby (offsite) profiles for comparison.

Most chemical nutrients required for life on land are supplied from the soil. Nitrogen, oxygen, and carbon dioxide come from the atmosphere,

194

and water is taken from the hydrosphere. Human activities, even in nonagricultural settlements, alter the levels of micro and macro plant nutrients. Macronutrients are the chemical elements nitrogen, phosphorus, potassium, calcium, magnesium, and sulfur. Because all plants use these elements, the removal of vegetation by human activities depletes their concentration in soils and underlying sediments. Substantial amounts of nitrogen, phosphorus, and calcium are added to the soil by food wastes and human and animal wastes. Wood burning raises the amount of magnesium in the soil, and a high pH may be related to fire.

Of special interest in archaeology is the biogeochemistry of phosphorus. Separate analytical techniques can distinguish three distinct phosphate fractions: 1) easily extractable, mainly aluminum and iron phosphate, associated with growing plants (including crops); 2) more tightly bound phosphate, commonly associated with human activity; and 3) natural geologic phosphate.[18] A total phosphate concentration of more than 2,000 ppm indicates a burial.

Chemical prospecting to locate sites, as distinct from burials, is inefficient but useful in determining horizontal and vertical boundaries of known sites and features within sites. A detailed look at the use of biogeochemical analysis as applied to the study of abandoned settlements is given by Eidt for prehistoric **anthrosols** in Colombia.[19] Eidt was able to delineate dwellings, gardens, work and storage areas, field types, and agricultural potential using soil analysis and biogeochemistry.

Eight chemical elements are considered important micronutrients (nutrients that are required in smaller amounts than macronutrients). These are: iron, manganese, zinc, copper, boron, molybdenum, cobalt, and chlorine. One of the ways human activities alter the soil environment is by adding trace amounts of metals and hydrocarbons. These chemicals can depress some nutrients to the point of deficiency or augment others to the point of toxicity. Most of these chemical activities leave clear records in archaeological sediments because trace elements released from anthropogenic sources become part of normal biogeochemical processes. Toxicities are recorded

in human paleopathologies. Examples can be seen in the processing and use of lead and arsenic. In historic archaeology the burning of coal and the smelting of iron and nonferrous metals have contributed a heavy load of trace-metal contaminants like mercury and cadmium to the environment. Soils are geochemical sinks for contaminants, and this contamination is often permanent, providing a geoarchaeological record of human activities.

Pollution aside, there have always been geographic patterns in deaths that are related to the toxic elements in local bedrock that find their way into soil and water. The trace-metal content of soils and plants varies widely in different geologic provinces. A well-known historic example is the selenium poisoning that has occurred over the past 150 years in parts of Wyoming and South Dakota. Selenium deficiency in soils and the plants growing on them can pose an equal danger to grazing animals like cattle. Unfortunately, only a few of these toxic and/or nutrient elements are retained in bone, teeth, and hair, where they would be recoverable in archaeological contexts. As recovery methods in archaeology improve, and as biochemical and geochemical analyses become possible on smaller and smaller quantities of material, additional information on ancient geochemical environments and their impact on human society will become available.

In addition to nutrient elements, geochemical analyses that are helpful for understanding site stratigraphy, sedimentology, and anthropogenic impacts include studies of organic matter and carbonates as well as pH measurements. Organic matter and carbonate analyses provide indications of activity and refuse areas and site boundaries. Total organic carbon and carbonate can be measured together in a simple loss-on-ignition method.[20] When plotted in conjunction with stratigraphic profiles, these data can help us understand mixed layers, define features and boundaries, display changes through time, and unravel soil horizons and processes.

Although they are beyond the scope of this book, stable-isotope analyses of soils and sediments also provide evidence of human activities. Physical and biologic processes, as distinct from strictly chemical processes, fractionate isotopes. Where human activities interact with and alter physical or biologic processes, there will be a record for geoarchaeologists. An example would be sulfur-isotope fractionation in coal burning and copper smelting. Sulfur has four stable isotopes: ^{32}S, ^{33}S, ^{34}S, and ^{36}S. These have natural abundances of approximately 95 percent, 0.75 percent, 4.21 percent, and 0.02 percent, respectively. When humans bring raw materials that formed deep within the earth and process them by burning or smelting, they alter the existing sulfur-isotope ratios, particularly the $^{34}S/^{32}S$ ratio, depending on the source of the raw material.

Geographic Information Systems

The variety, nature, and volume of geologic data have increased markedly over the past few decades. It has become essential to use databases and geographic information systems to turn these data into usable information. In developing geoarchaeological databases and modeling, it is necessary to separate the recording of descriptive features (empirical data) from processes (concepts). Geoarchaeological databases are four-dimensional—they can involve variations in shape and the relations and distribution of spatial objects through time.

A traditional geologic map conveyed an understanding of the geology of an area. In like fashion, a topographic map conveyed geomorphic features. With the advent of Geographic Information Systems (GIS) and digital databases, a range of new possibilities for data analysis emerges. Many of the data from drill cores that do not find direct expression on the traditional geologic map can be stored and used in regional analyses, taking advantage of GIS and database-analysis software.

This book cannot focus on the development of geologic databases and GIS, but the reader needs to be aware of the rapidly changing possibilities in the analysis and presentation of geoarchaeological data. Geologic, paleontologic, ecological, pedologic, hydrologic, climatic, geographic, topographic, and archaeological data can all be integrated within one GIS set.[21]

Software for GIS analysis manipulates data in either a raster or vector format. Rasters are grid cells of a specified dimension, and raster-based software (e.g., GRASS) is particularly useful in manipulating spatial data. Vector-based software (e.g., ARC/INFO) is mainly used for linear data, such as drainage networks.

Implementing an appropriate Geographic Information System should be one of the first undertakings in any archaeological project. Archaeology is concerned with the spatial arrangement of features and their relation to other parameters (time, climate, soils, land use). The display and manipulation of such data sets are the function of GIS, which evolved as a means of assembling and analyzing diverse spatial data. Current GIS methods had to await the recent developments in digital computer systems.

Geographic Information Systems can integrate spatial data acquired at different scales, at different times, and in different formats. These systems can accept raster and vector data structures. The systems are particularly valuable for data structures dealing with mapping, measuring environmental parameters, determining change through time, and modeling. These are fundamental to archaeology. Data acquisition for GIS follows procedures that have long been in use in geology and archaeology. The accuracy of the final GIS product will reflect the quality and quantity of the raw data. Most archaeological and geoarchaeological data will require a certain amount of preprocessing so that they can be entered into GIS. Once in the systems, the data can be manipulated and analyzed. Geographic Information Systems offer a wide range of final graphic products, including thematic maps, bar and pie charts, and scatter plots, as well as numerical products.

Most remote-sensing data are fed directly into GIS. Digital image-processing techniques are an integral component of GIS. Powerful pattern-recognition techniques are also available in GIS, but these usually require previous knowledge (ground truth) of the basic elements used in the image analysis. A key application of remotely sensed data is for classification: organizing data into discrete categories in terms of land use or vegetation types, for example.

The Complexities of Scale

Geologists and archaeologists operate on quite different scales of time and space. Archaeologists work in human timescales of years, decades, or centuries, whereas even those geologists who work exclusively in the Quaternary are dealing with more than two million years. Geographically, archaeologists usually focus on a few square meters in an excavation or a few square kilometers in a survey. Most field geologic problems encompass a much larger area. Similarly, in stratigraphy, archaeologists need higher resolution than most geologists require. Geoarchaeologists must bridge these gaps. When studying artifacts, archaeologists are usually measuring objects in centimeters. Geochemists investigating the same artifacts are generally making measurements at the scale of atoms. How chemically homogeneous or inhomogeneous an artifact is can be critical in determining the technology of its manufacture. Geoarchaeologists must work with both scales.

The scale of a map controls what features it can adequately represent. Few geologic features would need to be shown at scale of 1:20—a common scale for representing archaeological features. The detail, accuracy, and method of mapping will all change with the scale at which the mapping is carried out. The smaller the scale, the greater the amount of interpretive, as opposed to factual, information on the map. The relation between scale, content, and clarity is fundamental. Each separate geoarchaeological problem requires a careful consideration of scale for maximum clarity.

For topographic maps, the landscape to be represented may dictate the scale. Depending on which detail is being shown, areas with rugged or broken relief will require a larger scale than a featureless plain. The same applies to contour interval. Scale on an aerial photograph is not as explicit as scale on a map. The scale on an aerial photograph will differ from place to place on the photograph.

As historic sciences, archaeology and geology must deal with resolution in timescales. Again, archaeologists typically deal with fairly high-resolution timescales. Specialists in the Late Bronze Age pottery of Greece believe that the ceramic chronologies they have created are correct to plus or minus thirty years. For the same period, ^{14}C dating would be on the order of plus or minus ninety years. Purely geologic dating for this period would be much less precise (see Chapter 7).

Soil scientists and archaeologists use similar temporal and spatial scales. In most cases soils develop and stabilize on a scale similar to that of evolutionary and cultural changes in the human sphere. Anthrosols, in particular, are keyed to the human timescale.

Integration of archaeological and geologic perspectives in temporal and spatial scales and resolution is vital for geoarchaeological investigations. A 1993 study by the Archaeological Geology Division of the Geological Society of America presents a good review of some of the effects of scale in geoarchaeology, paying particular attention to the problems inherent in archaeo-chronological scales.[22]

CHAPTER 9

Construction, Destruction, Site Preservation, and Conservation

This chapter will concentrate on what happens when humans and nature interact, as well as on how archaeologists use geologic methods and knowledge to try to mitigate the effects of that interaction and preserve what is left.

Ancient Geotechnology

From the first selection of appropriate lithologies for chipped stone implements through prehistoric techniques for exploiting various metal ores to make complex alloys, early societies have struggled to develop geotechnologies to accommodate their increasingly complex societies.

The early societies of Mesopotamia had developed geotechnologies by the third millennium B.C. to cope with problems of building in places where stone was difficult to procure and where the local soils and sediments had poor load-bearing capacity. Even with these handicaps the Sumerians managed to build massive ziggurats. They used sun-dried bricks, the materials of which must have initially flowed outward at the base of the large structure. Compaction would slowly have increased the load strength of the material. At some stage they learned to place woven reed mats at regular intervals to absorb some of the horizontal thrust.

Another example of the development of geotechnical knowledge can be seen in the evolution of pyramid construction in Egypt. The first stone pyramids were built in step fashion of carefully dressed hard rock, to resist the horizontal thrusting. Pharaoh Snefru (reigned 2575–2551 B.C.) had to give up his plan of building a 140-meter true

pyramid with a slope angle of 60° because the marly soil on which it stood could not support it. He reduced the slope angle twice and was finally obliged to add an outer casing to make the structure a true pyramid.

The "bent" shape of the southern stone pyramid at Dashur owes its success to Snefru's earlier problem. During the construction of the Bent Pyramid, the slope angle was reduced from 54.5° to 43.5° to increase stability, shortening the pyramid from approximately 130 meters to 100 meters. By the time of the construction of the three great pyramids at Giza (ca. 2591–2536 B.C.), the major geotechnical problems of pyramid-building had been overcome.

The greatest difficulty faced by the ancient Mayans was the destructive nature of their tropical climate. They, too, built large pyramids. However, unlike Egyptian pyramids, their large structures must have required a great deal of repair and upkeep because of climatic and geotechnical problems. Except for their recognition that large structures could not be built on swampy ground, the Mayans do not seem to have developed a geotechnical understanding of either rock-foundation stability or management of water run-off. The underlying soils included hydroscopic clays and tropical forest humus with high absorption capabilities, which expanded and contracted significantly during the wet-dry cycle and led to the displacement of masonry facing and the cracking of internal plastered surfaces. The technical response of the Mayans to these problems seems to have been to continually rebuild damaged structures.

Much of the Mayan civilization was established on karst terrain. Little surface water exists in karst, so the Mayans had to develop groundwater resources in caves and from springs. Karst soils are typically thin and easily depleted of nutrients. In addition, karst soils are easily lost to the subsurface, a condition that not only affects agriculture but leads to the contamination of the potable water supply. The inability of the Mayans to solve their geotechnical problems may have contributed to their downfall.

Construction

Archaeologists tend to focus on habitation, ceremonial, or burial sites. However, archaeology has become increasingly concerned with other large-scale construction that has modified the landscape. Modern construction has also had a major impact on archaeological sites. Salvage archaeology has thus become one of the the largest archaeological enterprises in many countries.

Dams

The construction of dams to impound or divert water causes more interference with natural conditions than any other civil construction. From the geoarchaeological perspective, earth and rock dams of any age require materials with suitable strength and deformation characteristics, durable rock or earth, and minimal leakage through the foundations or materials from which the dam is constructed. Dams are probably the least well-known of ancient structures but they have a long history. A cut-stone masonry dam, whose ruins are still in existence, was built in Egypt about 3000 B.C. to divert the waters of the Nile into a canal. It was still in use in Roman times. In the second millennium B.C. the Marduk Dam was built across the Tigris River to control flooding. This dam was maintained for thousands of years, finally falling into ruin in about 1400. A dam was built near Tiryns in Greece to divert water into another river system as a flood-prevention measure.[1] The Romans built many dams of massive cut-stone masonry set in lime mortar. Ancient dams, their geologic settings, and the construc-

tion materials used have received too little attention by archaeological scientists.

Dams built to impound water impound sediment as well and thus have a finite life. Earth dams may wash away, often catastrophically, along with the impounded sediments. However, careful geologic study should reveal erosion and/or deposition impacts on the landscape. Evidence of ancient masonry dams should last many millennia. The various causes of dam failure are only tangentially relevant here, but because catastrophic dam failures have dramatic effects on humans, geoarchaeologists should be aware of the array of geologic evidence available about ancient dam construction.

Dam construction has a number of harmful effects on the landscape, including siltation (a heavy silt load can cause sediment or soil liquefaction), reservoir bank erosion from wave action, leaching (owing to elevation of the water table), oxidation and other changes resulting from alternating wet and dry cycles, subaqueous slope failures, and biogeochemical alteration of archaeological contexts.

Finally, freshwater inundation is overwhelmingly detrimental to archaeological remains. In the United States the Reservoir Salvage Act of 1960 (amended in 1974) requires that any federal agency undertaking dam construction and reservoir impoundment must provide written notice to the Secretary of the Interior, who shall cause an archaeological survey to be conducted. If significant cultural resources are found, a salvage excavation or protective burial must be undertaken. The latter is basically a geoarchaeological problem, which will be discussed later in this chapter.

Canals

Humans have been extending or connecting inland waterways, and penetrating narrow land barriers between seas, by canals for more than three millennia. In building canals without locks, the main problem is that the canal bed and banks must be impermeable to attain a consistent water level. The banks must also be stable. If there are locks, they need to be anchored to solid foundations. Local geology is of fundamental importance in all these concerns.

A canal connecting the Nile and the Red Sea was begun in the fourteenth century B.C. but was not completed until the time of Ptolemy II (reigned 285–246 B.C.). It was rebuilt four times between the seventh century B.C. and the second century A.D., and rehabilitated again in the middle of the seventh century. In the time of Strabo it boasted locks with movable gates. Surviving remains indicate that it was approximately 97 kilometers long, 46 meters wide, and up to 5 meters deep. This considerable depth was due to varying flood and low-water conditions of the Nile. At the Cairo end of the canal, silting would have been a constant problem.

Many canals were also built in ancient Mesopotamia, while the Romans built canals to link their rivers. In the first century B.C. a canal traversed 26 kilometers across the Pontine marshes near Rome, parallel to the Appian Way, and carried passengers when the local road was damaged by floods.

In China, large-scale building of navigational canals began in the first millennium B.C. The rivers traversed the great North China Plain in parallel fashion on the way from the western mountains to the sea. Thus, north-south transport links were needed. In 219 B.C., the oldest contour transport canal was built in Guangxi Province. One of the world's great inland waterways was built in China during the Sui dynasty (A.D. 581–617), by rebuilding and extending an earlier canal. The waterway began near Hangzhou, ran north across the Yangtze and Yellow Rivers, and ended near Beijing. Part of the route lay along rivers and part near lateral canals.

Irrigation canals for water management in agriculture have been with us for millennia. Irrigation canals probably developed out of floodwater farming. The level of technology or geologic knowledge required for simple irrigation canals is not high. Over time, technology improved, populations grew, and a greater sense of geologic concepts was needed to develop earthworks adequate to provide the water for sustainable agriculture. For example, by the fourteenth century in the Basin of Mexico, the need for food was so great that even marginal lands were cultivated intensely, and every geologic source of water was

exploited. Irrigation canals ranged from poor and inefficient canals dug in local porous earth to those lined with stone or stucco.

Although most ancient irrigation canals were cut into soil and surface sediment, a few were chiseled into bedrock. Because ancient irrigation proceeded by gravity flow, determining the precise orientation of irrigation canals provides a three-dimensional marker on the former landscape. Canals in floodplain sediments would have needed regular attention. Erosional deterioration of canal walls and bottoms as well as sedimentation would have altered the profile of canals that were not well maintained. As indicated in Chapter 8, ancient ditches and canals are often easy to trace through geophysical methods.

The oldest known features in Mexico that could be a canal irrigation system are Olmec, dating to perhaps 1400 B.C. Sometime before 1000 B.C. a storage dam of uncut stone and masonry blocks was built across the natural drainage. A canal lined with unfinished rock slabs led away from the dam to agricultural fields. The Olmec also used similar conduits constructed of U-shaped basalt troughs as drains. Sometime in the early first millennium B.C. riprap (rock placed on embankments to protect against erosion and increase stability) was used in this region to prevent lateral erosion in a meandering stream. Stone slabs are available throughout Mexico. In contrast, they are scarce throughout much of the lower Mesopotamian plain, another area of early irrigation.

An interesting canal phenomenon occurred in prehistoric Oaxaca in Mexico. Spring-fed irrigation water at a canal system was so high in calcium carbonate that travertine accumulated along the canals, thereby fossilizing them over the centuries. Doolittle has summarized the sequence of technological change in canal building at Oaxaca and the Valley of Mexico.[2] He presents the following sequence (dates are approximate): 1400 B.C. —relocation of rivers; 800 B.C.—advanced relocation of ephemeral streams; 400 B.C.—rock diversion dams; A.D. 200—use of valley bottoms, advanced channelization; A.D. 350—use of permanent springs; 550—masonry storage dams with floodgates; 750—earthen dams.

Ancient societies also built canals for flood control, to keep excess water away from fields and to protect habitation sites and roadways. They also channeled streams to increase runoff in times of flooding. Careful investigation of the sediment composition, textures, and stratigraphy can reveal the nature of these ancient constructions.

Great Britain is laced with historic-period canals. Perhaps the first canals date to the Roman period, but efforts in the 1600s to make rivers navigable led to the construction of a vast network of canals, which had a major effect on the landscape, on river and terrigenous hydrology, and on the local ecology and microclimatology. Effects of this construction left records in the sediments of ponds and lakes.

An example of a historic-period canal in the United States is the Erie Canal, constructed to link New York and Albany on the Hudson River through the Mohawk River Valley to Buffalo on Lake Erie. This canal, begun in 1817, had to rise 198 meters on its way to Buffalo. It had ample water, and a local muck called "the blue mud of the meadows" served as a lining to prevent seepage. A high grade of limestone found near Medina, New York, provided excellent facing for locks and other structures. A special variety of limestone provided the raw material for the underwater cements. Geoarchaeologists in the future seeking to understand the construction of the canal, which has few comprehensive written records, need to keep in mind not only the geologic aspects of excavation but the whole range of raw materials involved.

Roads

There are three geologic aspects to consider in studying land transportation networks: 1) the topography (relief); 2) the surficial geology — the need of a roadbed capable of carrying the intended traffic and with reasonable permanent stability; and 3) the availability of geologic materials needed in road building. Roman road construction marked a significant break from the earlier practice of following the easiest path. Roman engineers laid out their roads as straight as possible (possibly because their wheeled vehicles were not good at taking corners). This approach required an understanding of the engineering geology. At the height of the Roman Empire, Roman engineers with geologic insight built more than 75,000 kilometers of high-quality roads. Archaeologists can trace most of this network today.

The oldest road in the archaeological record runs between Van and Elazig in eastern Anatolia. It can be traced on foot for 100 kilometers. This road predates the Persian Empire and was probably built by the Urartians in the late ninth or early eighth century B.C. It had a width of greater than 5 meters and included bridges over small streams.

It was in South America, however, that we find perhaps the greatest skills in road building under difficult geologic conditions. The Incas constructed more than 6,000 kilometers of mountainous roadway, stretching from Quito in Ecuador to Tucuman in central Chile. The road was more than 7 meters wide, and some of it was paved with bitumen. It traversed the pathless sierras, crossed rivers and deep ravines, and scaled precipices, using stairways cut into the rock face. Deep ravines were filled with solid masonry to make bridges. The roadbed was often composed of flagstones.

A second Inca road, stretching nearly 3,000 kilometers along the coast, paralleled the main road. Here the geology and topography dictated a different construction. Much of the route was sandy, sometimes requiring an elevated causeway, other times the use of piling. Nevertheless, with simple tools and a good sense for engineering geology, the Incas were able to forge an empire in a land that would inspire only small enclaves.

Excavation

Except for the construction of dams, the major earth-moving activities in ancient times were stone quarrying and mining. In some cases, such as for the exploitation of coal, open-pit mining was essentially a quarrying operation. Conversely, some quarrying was done in underground caverns, so quarrying and mining overlap.

In ancient Egypt, methods of quarrying and

working stone were developed early in the third millennium B.C. By the time of the construction of the first large pyramids (the Step Pyramid of Djoser) more than a million tons of limestone were needed. The grand pyramids at Giza each contain about 700,000 limestone blocks weighing roughly 2.5 tons apiece as well as about 200,000 square meters of casing blocks of Tura limestone. The Tura limestone came from underground quarries in the Mokattam hills on the east bank of the Nile.

As discussed in Chapter 5, there are many references by classical authors to the rock types used by the ancient Greeks, Romans, and Egyptians for their buildings and monuments. Despite these sources, we are just beginning to understand the technical side of ancient quarrying. Unless a later quarry obliterates an ancient quarry, the latter may remain a major topographic feature. However, modern quarrying, coastal erosion, and the steady onslaught of rock weathering can remove even large ancient quarries from the landscape.

Preliminary shaping of monumental forms, frequently carried out in situ, is a well-known feature of ancient quarry practices. In their quarries at Aswan, the Pharaonic Egyptians created massive obelisks (up to 75 meters in length) that they removed in one piece. Hence, a knowledgeable geoarchaeologist can use the scraps of rock sculpting as a guide to the location of ancient quarries. The broken tools of early mining, chert, and hard igneous rocks are also evidence of ancient quarrying sites.[3]

The catacombs of Rome, which extend more than 850 kilometers, developed as stone quarries. The catacombs of Paris required the excavation of more than 16 million cubic meters of rock. The disposal of so much earth probably presented a greater challenge than the excavation.

Natural Burial of Sites

Site burial results from two conditions: sediment input from fluvial, eolian, or downslope processes and lack of erosion. Sediment derived from upstream erosion has many sources: cultivated areas, grass and forest land, habitation sites, valleys and gullies, and the stream channel. The amount of sediment deposited on a site is due not only to upstream erosion but also to the carrying capacity of the stream and whether topographic conditions are favorable to deposition. The important factors influencing sediment movement are watershed size, land use, topography, bedrock and surficial geology, soil and vegetation cover, and precipitation patterns. Erosion, transport, and deposition are complex processes; the site geoarchaeologist needs to understand the interplay of these factors during site occupation and burial.

Eolian deposition varies tremendously from region to region. Both extremes (deposit and removal of sediment) can be found in deserts. In sand deserts, such as the Sahara, eolian processes keep surface particles in near-constant motion, whereas some rock deserts have no particles fine enough to be carried by the wind. Although there are no wholly reliable criteria by which to identify ancient eolian deposits, the scarcity or absence of clay or gravel, the predominance of fine-to-medium-grained sand, thick cross-bedding, and the presence of **ventifacts** indicate eolian deposits. Windblown dune sands are unimodal in size distribution with a mean size that is rarely less than 0.20 mm and rarely greater than 0.45 mm.

When rock debris moves downslope under the influence of gravity rather than water, mass-wasting deposits are created. They are common terrestrial sediments—although obviously, there are few of them on broad, flat plains. Mass-wasting transport can take the form of falling, sliding, flowing, creeping, or subsidence. Sedimentary features, including structures, grain size, and sorting, may indicate the mode of transport. Seasonal creep produces a distinctive deposit with a stratified sequence that becomes attenuated downslope and passes into trails of debris (figure 9.1). Geoarchaeologists can use this property to assess mass-wasting-driven geomorphic change for help in locating buried sites and in paleogeomorphic reconstruction.

A much rarer geologic process that has buried places that are now famous archaeological sites (Pompeii, Akrotiri) is ash flow or ash fall from a volcanic eruption. Most deposits of volcanic ash

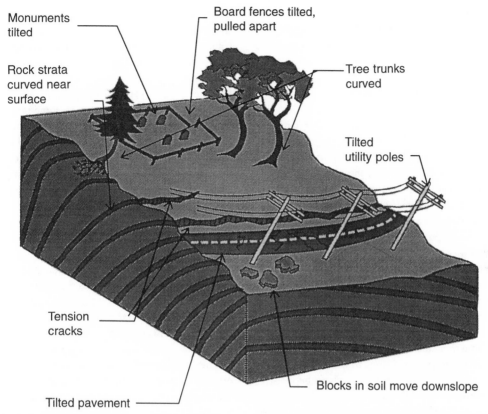

Monuments tilted

Board fences tilted, pulled apart

Rock strata curved near surface

Tree trunks curved

Tilted utility poles

Tension cracks

Blocks in soil move downslope

Tilted pavement

Figure 9.1 Composite Diagram of Typical Effects of Downslope Creep
Under the influence of gravity there is constant if exceedingly slow movement of the earth's surface ma-terial downslope (creep). Rigid monuments tilt; growing trees overcome the tilt by bending back skyward. This slow creep can be contrasted with such rapid downslope movements as landslides.

are elongate in plan, with the long axis of the deposit extending downwind. The horizontal distance the volcanic ash is transported depends on the maximum height the ash column attains in the atmosphere, the direction and velocity of the wind, the size-distribution of the ash particles, and whether there is rainfall in the path of the ash plume.

Finally, in addition to depositional forces, the lack of erosional forces—that is, a stable land-scape—at a site can allow burial. Erosion is the norm in landscape development. It must be noted that erosion by water or wind varies according to time and place. A cultivated field may be in the process of eroding while the next field, under pasture or forest, may not. Each soil and surficial sediment is characterized by a particular topog-raphy and land use and consequently has its own erosion regime, which changes with time. Slope stability and effective ground cover (vegetation) are the keys to understanding local erosional processes that take place away from meandering rivers and wave-pounded coasts. Geoarchaeologists should be able to detect at least the general form and intensity of current and past erosion at a site.

Destruction

The deterioration of stone artifacts and monuments proceeds from: chemical attack and dissolution; mechanical disintegration caused by water freezing in pores and cracks; abrasion from wind-driven particles; exfoliation from rapid heating and cooling; disintegration because of the activities of organisms; crystal-formation on surfaces; and damage from poor conservation or restoration procedures.

Rock Properties

Geoarchaeologists should be familiar with the properties of rocks that affect their suitability as building stone. The most important of these are compressive strength, shear strength, tensile strength, porosity, permeability, moisture content, and durability. Most sedimentary and metamorphic rocks are layered, with each layer differing in composition, texture, and fabric from the adjoining layers. Marble and some quartzites are exceptions. Compositional and textural inhomogeneities, along with joints and fractures, lead to structural weakness.

In some cases shape is also important. In order to be effective, riprap should have a shape that produces a stable interlocking and must be durable under the conditions to which it will be exposed. In particular, riprap needs to be resistive to alternate wetting and drying.

Rocks weather in two main ways: physical disintegration, and chemical decomposition. The processes involved in decomposition are oxidation, reduction, hydration, hydrolysis, carbonation, and solution. Rock weathering leads to gradual and gradational alterations that are marked by a deterioration in the mechanical and durability properties of the rock.

Weathering

All materials have a stable state for the environment in which they exist. A significant change in environment, however, may force the material to transform into a material with a new stable state. Water, ice, and steam are each a stable state of H_2O, under different temperature and pressure environments. Rocks formed at high temperatures under anhydrous conditions weather rapidly under moist conditions at the earth's surface. The chemical breakdown of feldspars provides a good example of the weathering process. Feldspars make up nearly 60 percent of the earth's crust. Feldspar weathering proceeds by the re-

moval of potassium, calcium, and sodium and the formation of clay minerals. Because of its high solubility, most of the released sodium finds its way to the oceans. Most of the potassium remains in the soil in new minerals like illite. Some becomes part of growing plants. Calcium does both: some ends up in the oceans, some remains in groundwater systems to precipitate in such terrigenous processes as the formation of carbonate and sulfate minerals. Calcium is the most common cation in fresh water, and the precipitation of calcium carbonate crusts on sherds is common.

After burial an object enters a new environment with which it will eventually come to equilibrium. When it is excavated, the object is exposed to yet another set of physical, chemical, and biologic contexts that may cause it to change quickly to a new stable state—a process that may destroy the object. How much alteration is brought about by the processes of burial or excavation depends on the structure and composition of the material and the severity of the contrast between the old and new environments. Bone survives fairly well in a neutral or somewhat alkaline earth matrix but disintegrates in acidic soils. The oxidizing potential, acidity (pH), moisture, and soluble-salt content are all environmental parameters affecting the stability of an object.

Masonry in the presence of chlorides, sulfates, and nitrates of calcium, magnesium, and sodium suffers serious damage because these salts, by repeated solution, crystallization, and hydration, generate sufficient pressure to cause fragmentation and spalling. Although these salts commonly occur as efflorescences on buildings in all climatic conditions, they are far more deleterious in arid regions, where the lack of precipitation results in their accumulation. (In wetter climates they are washed away by rain.) Night-time condensation on stone surfaces in arid regions followed by its evaporation at sunrise, leaves behind a small but significant amount of the harmful salts, which crystallize as the evaporation proceeds.

In damp conditions, underfired or low-fired earthenware will gradually rehydrate to clay, which crumbles. This is especially true where the fabric is coarse and porous. Crumbling will be exacerbated in acidic conditions by loss of calcite or other carbonate components. High-fired ceramics are reasonably stable under most burial conditions, although even well-fired ceramics may become softened under alkaline conditions by dissolution of the glassy phase.

Deposits of both soluble and insoluble salts readily form on buried ceramics. Porous pottery is prone to staining, particularly by iron oxides. Iron oxide encrustation may form if there is a high, localized pH caused by calcium carbonate within the pottery.

Such soluble salts as chlorides, sulfates, and carbonates are ubiquitous in groundwater and are absorbed by any porous object in the ground. After excavation, moisture in an object will begin to evaporate, and dissolved salts will crystallize. The wall paintings of the tomb of Nefertari in the Valley of the Queens at the Theban necropolis in Egypt present a classic example of this geoarchaeological conservation problem. The tomb was hewn to a depth of about 12 meters in poor-quality, fractured, clayey limestone. Layers of plaster were placed on the tomb walls. The exquisite tomb paintings were then painted over the plaster. Salts, especially gypsum and halite, have crystallized behind the plaster layer, pushing it outward. These dissolved salts were brought to the site by groundwater and seeping surface water during rainfall. A significant part of the conservation program must be control of microdrainages to the tomb.[4]

In Venice, building stone is subject to the severe saltwater environment from the marine lagoon (exacerbated by modern air pollution). Only one of the materials, Istrian stone, used in building the city has successfully resisted rapid deterioration. Istrian stone is a compact microcrystalline limestone with few natural planes where dissolution can proceed. Exposure to atmospheric sulfuric acid causes the formation of white gypsum powder on its surface, but its low porosity and impermeability protect it from rapid deterioration.

The famous Carrara marble, used throughout the eastern Mediterranean since ancient times, has been especially beleaguered by the corrosive environment. Differential thermal expansion and contraction of the megascopic calcite crystals, which are oriented in multiple directions in the marble, cause microcracks along the edges of the crystals and allow pollutants to penetrate.

All materials expand and contract with temperature change. These changes in dimensions are not in themselves harmful. It is the combination of dissimilar expansions, or contractions where two different materials are combined, that produces mechanical disintegration. For example, lime mortar has a coefficient of linear thermal expansion that is approximately 50 percent greater than that for bricks. In making ceramics, it is necessary to ensure that any additives, like temper, have similar coefficients of expansion to that of the clay matrix.

The amount of water vapor absorbed by a porous rock depends on the relative humidity and porosity of the rock. Most rock damage occurs during the process of drying out, not during the absorption. Moisture in a porous rock causes dissolution and recrystallization of mineral salts, which results in structural damage and often discoloration.

Frost damage in building stone is common where temperature variations around the freezing point cause cycles of freezing and thawing. The influence of frost action on dry stone is limited, but it can be substantial on wet stone: when water freezes, it expands by about 10 percent. When this freezing occurs in a confined or limited space, the pressures on the confining material are enormous. Building stone with high porosity is thus more vulnerable than compact stone.

A related process that occurs during drying is the crystallization of soluble salts. During evaporation these salts can crystallize, with consequences similar to those of frost action. The salts can also form crusts on the exterior of the material. The most common salts occurring in walls are $CaSO_4 \cdot 2H_2O$ (gypsum) and Na_2SO_4 in various hydration states. Dry deposits of $CaSO_4$ are difficult to remove. Sulfates cause damage because they exist in different hydration states. Under varying moisture conditions, one hydration state will convert to another. Transformation to more hydrated states leads to expansion and pressure on the walls of the pores in the stone.

The general resistance to deterioration of sandstone building materials is affected by their chemi-

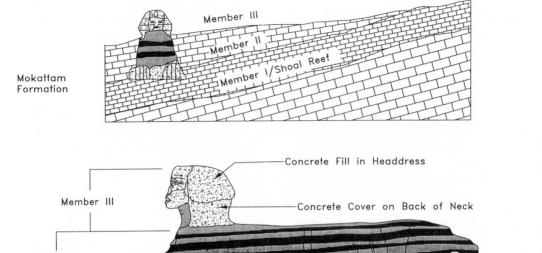

Figure 9.2 Geological Composition of the Sphinx
(After Hawass and Lehner, "The Sphinx: Who Built It,
and Why?")

cal composition. Those which contain carbonate as the natural cementing agent are susceptible to attack by acid rain. The loss of just a small amount of the carbonate, depriving sand grains of their adhesion, results in those grains being loosened and removed. As with other rock types, moisture is a major disruptive agent as well as a means of transporting salts. Coarse-grained and porous sandstones usually withstand freezing and frost action better than fine-grained ones because water escapes more readily.

The historical buildings in Upper Egypt were built largely of local sandstone. The Horus temple at Edfu was completely constructed of local sandstone, while the Abu Simbel temples were cut in the Nubian sandstone quarry in South Aswan. These sandstones mainly consist of quartz grains cemented by ferruginous, siliceous, carbonaceous, and clay cements. Diurnal and seasonal changes in temperature and relative humidity are the principal threats to monuments made of these rocks. The result of these temperature and hu-

midity variations is the growth of halite and gypsum crystals, which cause cracking and structural failure.

A dramatic change in environment occurred when large obelisks were taken from Egypt. Sculpted in the middle of the second millennium B.C., these monuments stood in Egypt for 3,000 years with little surficial damage. Then, three were exported, one to Paris in about 1840, one to London in about 1870, and one to New York in about 1890. In the more humid and polluted atmospheres of these cities, the three obelisks have suffered major deterioration. Sulfur and nitrogen acids in the atmosphere have done most of the damage. The recent increase of vehicle emissions in Cairo, however, does not augur well for the preservation of the obelisks left in Egypt.

An important part of our culture is chiseled in stone, and these stones are slowly weathering away. Although low rainfall has retarded the rate the limestone has weathered in the great pyramids of Egypt (now close to 5,000 years old), the recent dramatic increase in the acidity of the rain could reduce their projected survival time from 100,000 years to substantially less than 10,000 years. Their companion structure, the Sphinx, is even more threatened. In recent years the Sphinx has deteriorated rapidly. Carved from the natural limestone of the Giza Plateau, the Sphinx is composed of varying rock types with different weathering abilities. The lowest stratum of the Sphinx consists of member I hard rock of a reef (figure 9.2). This rock has not weathered appreciably. Most of the body of the Sphinx is carved from much softer layers of member II, lying above the reef limestone. The head is carved from member III, a more durable rock than member II. Without intensive conservation, the Sphinx could crumble in less than a hundred years.

Water

Water is the most aggressive weathering agent there is, and it acts as the vehicle for most chemical weathering processes. The property of water that gives it its critical role in weathering derives from its molecular structure: the two hydrogen atoms lie not on opposite sides of the oxygen to which they are linked but on the same side (figure 9.3). This structural arrangement makes the water molecule a dipole and allows water to dissolve many natural materials. A water molecule can electrically wedge its way between surface ions in a mineral and "float" the ions away.

Water molecules themselves aggregate into a structure. In effect, a water molecule has four electrically charged "arms" extending from the nucleus. Two extend from the positively charged hydrogen atoms and two from the double negativity (to balance the positive charges on the hydrogen) of the oxygen. When H_2O molecules are packed together, as in water, each negative arm attracts a positive (hydrogen) arm in a neighboring molecule. The hydrogen atoms then join the molecules in what is called a hydrogen bond (figure 9.4), which is very strong.

No other substance absorbs or releases more heat than water. In order for water to evaporate, these strong bonds must be broken. It thus requires a great deal of energy to boil or evaporate water. Approximately five times as much heat

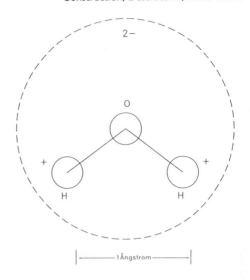

Figure 9.3 Structure of the Water Molecule
The hemisphere with the two hydrogens carries a net positive charge; the opposite hemisphere carries a net negative charge.

energy is needed to change a given volume of water from liquid to vapor as is needed to raise its temperature from freezing to the boiling point. The world's climate is made more temperate by water's ability to soak up and store heat from the sun and then release it slowly. Without large bodies of water, the earth's surface would be an inhospitable place: the daily variation of temperatures would be far more extreme.

Most materials contract when cooled. Over a wide range of temperatures, water is no exception. However, close to its freezing point water behaves very differently. As the temperature falls below 4° C, water expands. A rapid expansion occurs at the freezing point during the transformation to ice, which is about 9 percent greater in volume than the water that froze. The consequences of this abnormality control many geologic phenomena at the earth's surface. As we have seen, a common change is mechanical breakdown of rocks because of frost action. If ice were denser than water, rather than vice versa, lakes in high latitudes would freeze from the bottom up, and most would remain partially frozen through-

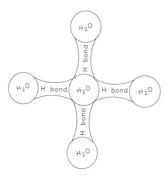

Figure 9.4 The Hydrogen Bond
In the liquid state, each water molecule establishes hydrogen bonds with its four nearest neighbors. These bonds give water many of its unique qualities.

out the summer. Climates in temperate regions would therefore be much harsher.

Oxidation and reduction reactions in groundwater are geochemically important in determining the preservation of buried materials. In many reactions micro-organisms are involved. The presence or absence of free oxygen in groundwater essentially determines whether oxidizing or reducing conditions will prevail. Dissolved oxygen in atmospheric, surface, and underground waters acts as a powerful weathering agent. Oxidation processes proceed more rapidly in warm climates than in cold and more rapidly in humid or alternating humid and dry climates than in arid climates. In the past few hundred years human-induced pollution in atmospheric, surface, and underground water has had serious consequences for buried materials. Even simple cultivation of the soil stimulates microbial activity, which raises the carbon dioxide content and causes additional carbonic acid to form.

Water moves freely through the soil and sediments because of gravity flow, capillary action, and, in some situations, osmotic pressure. Groundwater chemistry is the chief agent in dissolution, diagenesis, and such changes as the uptake of uranium in bone. Dissolution and precipitation are controlled chiefly by the hydrogen-ion concentration (pH) and the oxidation-reduction potential (Eh). Bone can last more than 100,000 years in some burial contexts but will survive only

10,000 years when the groundwater is neutral (has a pH of 7) and only 100 years or less if the groundwater-soil matrix has an acidic pH of 5.

Archaeological excavations are expected to be dry enough to maintain the stability of the baulks and to protect the important finds and features. Occasionally, water flowing above the water table saturates the sediment and soil. This condition obstructs recording and leads to instability. In most cases the water flow is seasonal and may force the excavation to be postponed. If the sediment or soil is permeable, pumping may be fruitless.

Many buried sites lie below the water table. In small excavations, in low-to-medium permeability materials, adequate drainage may be achieved with a sump pump. For larger excavations, below the water table in permeable materials, the water table will have to be lowered. This is achieved by drilling to a level below the lowest level of the projected excavation and pumping from each bore hole. The pumping must continue until the excavation is completed.

When acid groundwater is able to flow, the process of dissolution of carbonate rock is accelerated. A spring at Silver Springs, Florida, flows at the rate of 15 cubic meters per second, carrying 274 ppm of dissolved solid. This represents about 400 tons of dissolved rock per day. The result of this dissolution is the formation of caves and sinkholes.

Caves have played a major role in human evolution. Caves in northern France along the Seine River were formed in chalk strata and have been used by humans for millennia. One of the greatest of the Norman chiefs made his home there in a group of caves, one of which contained a room more than 100 meters long. The Romans used the great caves at Pommeroy Park to quarry building stone. Today these caves provide storage for the maturing of champagne.

Erosion

In the past four billion years whole mountain chains have come and gone. Mountains are formed largely by tectonic forces; today, all but the cores of very ancient mountain systems have been obliterated by the powerful forces of weathering and erosion. In Quaternary times continental glaciers have come and gone with dramatic effects on weathering, erosion, and climates. An extensive review of the destructive potential of erosion is not warranted here. However, it is necessary to understand such erosional phenomena as those that accompany meandering rivers. Rivers, meandering across broad floodplains, move down, up, and—primarily—laterally over time. Thus, although they provide the resources for development of habitation sites, they often turn destructive and devour these sites with lateral erosion.

Land Subsidence

Ground subsidence that is not part of the main earth movement (along a fault) may accompany earthquakes. The likelihood of earthquake-induced subsidence is governed by the geology of the surficial rocks and soils. Subsidence and elevation occur with the loading and unloading of the earth's upper crust by glaciers, deltaic deposits, and marine transgression. Dramatic subsidence may occur in carbonate rock terrain through the development of sinkholes. These phenomena are not tied directly to human activity, but geoarchaeologists need to understand all phenomena that may be encountered in the field assessment of an archaeological problem.

In the past 150 years serious land subsidences have been created by the removal of oil and water from the ground and from underground mining. Almost 2 meters of ground subsided in Santa Clara Valley south of San Francisco as a result of withdrawal of groundwater. Historic archaeologists should also note that falling groundwater tables have led to the decay of wooden pilings for buildings in Boston, San Francisco, and Milwaukee. In addition, the load-bearing capacity of clayey sediments, soils, and fill is changed appreciably by alteration of their moisture content. The troubles experienced with the foundations of St. Paul's Cathedral in London appear to be related to the nearby excavation for a deep sewer that began in 1831. The Tower of London rises and falls with the tide in the Thames River. Subsidence of more than 3 meters has occurred in the city of Long Beach, California, because of oil

Figure 9.5 The Leaning Tower of Pisa
Perhaps the most famous example of foundation problems is the Leaning Tower of Pisa. Construction of the tower began in 1174 but was not completed until 1350. It has continued to tilt since then, with a displacement of 5 meters in a total height of 55 meters. Foundation strata consist of a bed of clayey sand 4 meters thick underlain by 6 meters of sand. Attempts over the past two hundred years to stop the progressive leaning have not only been futile; most or all have increased the rate of leaning. A thorough knowledge of both the underlying geology and the principles of soil mechanics must be applied to correct the problem. (Drawing by Elaine Nissen)

wells. Subsidence has long been recognized as the aftermath of mining in soft ground.

Most subsidence problems in urban areas stem from poor geologic conditions for bearing the heavy loads that buildings impose. Subsoil conditions in Mexico City consist of 50 meters of saturated sandy clays with interbedded sand layers that are dangerous in earthquakes and provide little support for heavy buildings. The Palace of Fine Arts there, completed in 1934, has already sunk more than 3 meters. Such subsidence problems plague many famous archaeological sites. Venice has been sinking for centuries, and the Leaning Tower of Pisa was closed to tourists because of its increasingly dangerous tilt, the result of differential subsidence (figure 9.5).

Seismic Disturbance

Historic records chronicle earthquakes of tragic cultural consequences. Catastrophic seismic disturbances are also recorded in geologic and archaeological strata. Archaeologists define chronological horizons by stratigraphic and/or cultural discontinuities. Stratigraphic discontinuities are sometimes defined by "destruction layers" that may be accompanied by a cultural change evident in ceramic or other artifact typologies. In the earthquake-prone eastern Mediterranean region these layers are often attributed to seismic destruction. In one excavation volume for the site of Knossos, Crete, Evans uses subheadings that include phrases like "seismic catastrophe," "seismic deposit" and "fresh earthquake shock."[5] However, although his observations were consistent with seismic destruction, they cannot, without a set of diagnostic criteria, confirm seismic destruction as a single cause. It is necessary to consider multiple working hypotheses.

From the geophysical point of view, one must be cautious about attributing structural damage to seismic violence. For example, structures built on slopes underlain by shale, unconsolidated sediments, or fill can topple or come apart because of uncommonly heavy rainfall that saturates new parts of the underlying ground, causing major downslope earth movements. Careful analysis of the geologic and geophysical setting of the archaeological strata is necessary before any attribution to seismic events can be made.

The size of an earthquake is defined in two distinct ways. Because the energy released by an earthquake is the most precise measure of its size, seismologists have adopted a related measure, the Richter magnitude scale. Major earthquakes have magnitudes of 5.5 to 8.9. Each increase of one unit in magnitude corresponds to a tenfold increase in the amplitude of the seismic waves and to roughly a thirtyfold increase in energy.

A second scale of earthquake size is based on earthquake intensities, which are defined by the observed destruction. The most commonly used intensity scale is the Modified Mercalli Scale. Table 9.1 presents the characteristic effects of earthquakes of designated intensities in the Modified Mercalli Scale. This scale is particularly useful for interpreting seismic damage to sites in the archaeological record. It must be noted that seismic effects at the earth's surface reflect not only the strength of the seismic vibrations but also differences in the character of the local bedrock and overlying unconsolidated sediments and soil. Water-saturated alluvium can shake like jelly, causing destruction at great distances from the quake. Table 9.1 indicates that an intensity rating of X can result in large landslides. However, landslides are common in nonseismic areas as well. The poorest supporting ground is unconsolidated earth, particularly recent fill; this is the kind of ground on which many ancient sites developed.

Structures contain many separate parts (walls, roofs, pillars). Often these parts are made of different materials with different vibrational characteristics. Mud brick has very different vibrational characteristics from cut stone. In an earthquake of intensity VII, mud-brick superstructures on top of stone walls or foundations will topple, with only moderate damage to the stone structure. Mud-brick and undressed-stone construction with no mortar or with mud mortar are the materials least resistant to seismic events. Mud brick and adobe dwellings will usually be destroyed at intensity VIII. Wooden structures will flex under the stress of strong earth vibrations. Low, rigid masonry structures can withstand strong vibrations if the structure moves with the ground as a single unit.

The most common rock materials at the surface of the earth are unconsolidated sediment and soil. These materials provide the base on which structures are built: ancient societies did not carry their foundations to bedrock. The ability of

Table 9.1 Modified Mercalli Earthquake Intensity Scale
with Approximate Richter Magnitude

Intensity	Characteristic effects	Approximate Richter magnitude
I	Detected only by seismographs.	2.2–2.5
II	Delicately suspended objects may swing.	2.5–3.1
III	Standing automobiles may rock slightly. Hanging objects swing. Vibrations resemble those caused by the passing of a light truck. Duration can be estimated.	3.1–3.7
IV	Vibrations resemble those caused by the passing of a heavy truck or by a heavy object striking the building. Walls, windows, and doors creak. Hanging objects swing, and standing automobiles rock noticeably.	3.7–4.3
V	Some windows broken; some cracked plaster. Unstable objects overturned. Liquids may be spilled. Doors swing, pictures move, motion of tall objects may be noticed. Pendulum clocks may stop or change rate.	4.3–4.9
VI	People walk unsteadily. Objects fall off shelves, and pictures fall off walls. Windows and glassware broken. Some heavy furniture moves. A few instances of fallen plaster or damaged chimneys. Overall damage slight.	4.9–5.5
VII	Difficult to stand. Furniture broken. Poorly built structures damaged. Weak chimneys break at roof line. Waves form on ponds. Sand and gravel banks cave in. Damage slight in well-constructed buildings.	5.5–6.1
VIII	Difficult to steer automobiles. Considerable damage in ordinary, substantial buildings, partial collapse, great damage to poorly built structures. Some masonry walls fall. Fall of chimneys, factory stacks, monuments, towers. Heavy furniture overturned. Branches broken from trees. Wells change water level. Cracking in wet ground and on steep slopes.	6.1–6.6
IX	Poor masonry destroyed; good masonry damaged seriously. Foundations damaged generally. Buildings shifted off foundations. Reservoirs seriously damaged. Conspicuous cracks in ground. In areas of loose sediment, sand, mud, and water ejected. Underground pipes broken.	6.6–7.1
X	Most masonry and frame structures destroyed. Foundations and some bridges destroyed. Serious damage to dams, dikes, embankments. Large landslides occur. Water splashes over banks of rivers, lakes, and canals. Flat areas of mud and sand shift horizontally.	7.1–7.6
XI	Few, if any masonry structures remain standing. Bridges destroyed. Broad fissures in ground. Extensive landslides on slopes. Underground pipes completely out of service.	7.6–8.1
XII	Damage to humanmade structures nearly total. Waves seen on ground surface. Large rock masses displaced. Lines of sight and level distorted. Objects thrown into air.	8.1 or greater

unconsolidated sediments to bear a load, maintain a slope, or transmit a stress varies widely with mineral composition, grain-size distribution, water content, density, and compaction. The clay minerals in these sediments have varying properties, depending on their chemical composition and structure, that dictate their response to seismic phenomena. For example, montmorillonite clays swell because they absorb water readily, which affects the lubrication of the sediment, and wet sediments, especially saturated sediments, are more intensely affected by seismic phenomena than dry sediments. Bedrock geology, surficial deposits, and the nature of the soil all affect the intensity of the shaking and the resulting damage. Bolt illustrates the close relation between rock type and the intensity of the 1906 San Francisco earthquake.[6] Harder rock underlay areas of small damage, whereas high damage occurred on filled lands and unconsolidated sediments. Unfortunately, standard geologic maps do not contain sufficient data on the nature and depth of unconsolidated sedimentary deposits. Data are needed on thickness, bedding, bulk density, cohesiveness, porosity, texture, and water content.

Major seismic events leave clear impressions in the surficial geologic record. The 1964 Good Friday earthquake in Alaska left secondary structures as indelible marks on the sediments of the Copper River Delta.[7] A relatively dense pattern of geologic structures, including **sand dikes, sand pipes,** slumps, faults, and joints, was formed in the sediments. These structures sometimes terminated in an unconformity. Earthquake-generated **seiches** planed off the upper 2 meters of tidal flats; this led to deposits of clam shells, which resulted from the instantaneous destruction of the clam's habitat. Unless eroded, such evidence remains in the geologic record. The problem for geoarchaeology is to achieve a sufficiently extensive cross-sectional view of the regional picture to reconstruct the detailed sequence of geologic events responsible for the stratigraphy.

Sims has shown that the seismic history of an artificial lake can be correlated with deformational structures in the lake sediments.[8] His articles contain good illustrations of seismic-induced sedimentary structures. Doig interprets silt layers in organic-rich lake sediments as representing five historic earthquakes dating from 1638 to 1925 in eastern Canada.[9] The silt layers were presumably caused by landslides on tributary streams and resuspension of the sediment. Palynologists seeking to reconstruct the paleoenvironment of an archaeological site or region most often take their cores from nearby lakes or lagoons. Niemi and Ben-Avraham have found evidence for earthquakes in Jericho from slumped sediments of the Jordan River Delta in the Dead Sea.[10] They used seismic-reflection data to show that a long-term record of ancient earthquakes in Jericho can be found in the sedimentary record. Geoarchaeologists working to reconstruct the seismic history of a site or region must often turn to analogous offsite sedimentary records.

The strongest earthquake in the contiguous United States during historic times occurred near New Madrid, Missouri. During the winter of 1811–1812, there was a series of four quakes with estimated surface-wave magnitudes greater than eight. Modified Mercalli intensities near the epicenter ranged from X to XII, indicating almost complete destruction of structures.[11] Because of the low attenuation of seismic waves in the central United States, these earthquakes were felt over an area of 5,000,000 square kilometers. Roughly 50,000 square kilometers were affected by ground failure, including fissures, **sandblows,** landslides, and subsidence. Liquefaction of subsurface sand deposits ejected sand, water, and other materials through fissures, some of which were kilometers in length and tens of meters wide. Massive bank failure along the Mississippi River sent large tracts of land into the river channel. Although the river quickly eroded and obliterated these soft sediments, the seismic events left a huge footprint on the local geology.

Saucier has detailed the geoarchaeological evidence for strong prehistoric earthquakes in the New Madrid seismic zone.[12] Archaeological excavations at the Towosahgy State Archaeological Site (23M12) revealed a village dating to A.D. 400–1500 constructed on a Late Holocene natural levee ridge that overlay sandy point-bar deposits on the inner side of a large abandoned channel of the Mississippi River. The site lies on the northeastern periphery of the seismic-induced blows and fissures. Excavation showed that although part of this site was occupied, an earthquake-induced fissure of 18 cm in width had formed and broken through a midden deposit. That the site continued to be occupied after the earthquake can be deduced from trash pits dug into the sandblow. Evidence at the Towosahgy site indicates that a seismic event capable of producing liquefaction occurred less than a hundred years before A.D. 539, based on a calibrated radiocarbon date.

Holocene archaeological deposits usually provide more material suitable for dating (radiometric or typological) than geologic deposits. Thompson has dated Holocene tectonic activity in West Africa by archaeological methods.[13] Movements on a local fault amounted to more than 10 meters of vertical displacement in the past 3,000 years. The time of the major offsetting was dated by the discovery of an inscription carved in hard quartzite at a depth of 10 meters.

One of the effects of major earthquakes is the disruption and alteration of the groundwater system of springs. Hough records tribal movements in the American southwest as a response to the suppression of old springs and the generation of new ones.[14] No greater environmental misfortune can befall a population than the loss of its water supply.

The largest earthquake felt in historic Europe was the one that destroyed Lisbon in 1755. Martinez Solarez and colleagues have drawn valuable intensity maps from the data available. They were able to map the geographic distribution of such effects as changes in wells, springs, and rivers; surface cracks; and liquefaction landslides.[15] They note that ground effects do not always provide a reliable measure of the severity of shaking. Their data support the proposition that seismic intensity, as a measure of earthquake damage, is different for buildings of different frequency response.

A good example of historic study coupled with field observation can be seen in the work of Ambraseys and Melville.[16] These authors contend that landslides, rockfalls, soil failures, and faulting are often of limited value in assessing seismic intensity. Destruction of a village built on

a slope frequently occurs from ground deformation unaided by seismic activity. They note that many adobe houses and public buildings collapse every year without the assistance of an earthquake. They also record that the earthquake of 26 February 1894 in Shiraz, Iran, caused no damage but that the heavy rainfall that followed soon after destroyed two thousand houses.

Assessing seismic damage in archaeological contexts is difficult. The examination of field evidence cited in support of ancient seismicity has shown that individual features are difficult to distinguish from the features of damage that result from poor construction and adverse geotechnical effects. Tilting and other severe distortions of walls are cited frequently by archaeologists as evidence of archaeoseismic damage. But such damage can also be caused by ground conditions beneath the wall, including ground stresses imposed by the construction of the wall or by earth movements unrelated to earthquakes. Karcz and Kafri provide a good summary of the problems and propose a general scheme for determining suspected archaeoseismic damage.[17]

Much conjecture about seismic damage may be correct. But a much firmer evidential base is necessary to consider such conjecture likely. Much of this can come from studies of the effects of modern tremors on structures similar to those that existed in ancient times. For best results, detailed intensity maps must be constructed for the local area. Local geology and geomorphology will affect intensity, so specialized geologic maps should also be made where appropriate.

Floods and Flood Legends

Floodplains are where the world's best agricultural land, and the large populations that go with it, are found. Floodplains develop in the lower reaches of large river systems as rivers meander back and forth and periodically overflow their banks, depositing fertile sediment. These floodplains are extensive and flat, which allows flooding over a very wide area. Each time a river overflows its banks, the current velocity decreases at the channel margin, and the coarsest fraction of the sediment load is deposited there. Over time, this builds up to create a natural levee. Beyond the levee the ground slopes down. When rivers are also depositing sediment in the channel, increasing the elevation of the river, this can be catastrophic. When large floods occur, the river, which has been flowing well above the elevation of the surrounding floodplain, destroys the levee and flows unhindered across the land. When the flood abates, a new channel forms in a different location.

The Yellow River flows from the easily eroded loess plateau, carrying vast quantities of silt and clay onto the North China Plain. Its riverbed has been elevated as much as 15 meters above the floodplain, rising up to 5 centimeters a year. This great river has had catastrophic floods at least once every two hundred years during recorded history, resulting in millions of deaths and the destruction of thousands of villages and cities. A new course is established after each major flood. Sometimes the Yellow River flows northeast to the Bohai Sea, at other times southeast to the South China Sea. The distance from the farthest north to the farthest south of its mouths is nearly 500 kilometers. The archaeology of the North China Plain is dominated by the deposition and the destruction from the Yellow River.

Of all the myths in the world none seems to have attracted more attention than that of Noah's flood. The development of geology in the early nineteenth century played a critical role in our recognition of the lack of historicity in this legend. By the late nineteenth century, scholars had translated a cuneiform tablet excavated at Nineveh. On this tablet was an account of the flood that was written much earlier than the biblical account. This flood took place in Mesopotamia, not ancient Palestine. Even a quick look at the landscape shows that Mesopotamia is a flat land dominated by two great river systems—a land subject to flooding—whereas mountainous Palestine would require more water than was around to incur a deluge of the biblical proportions.

Prehistoric flooding is easily identified in the geologic record and should be clear in most archaeological sediments. Yet no less an archaeological light than Leonard Woolley was led astray. In reporting on his excavations at Ur, Woolley stated that evidence of a flood was associated

with the "Flood Story of Genesis."[18] One of the crew at these excavations was Max Mallowan, who later published an article, "Noah's Flood Reconsidered," that backed away from Woolley's contention and provided a worthwhile table of Mesopotamian floods discovered in archaeological sequences.[19] Dundes has provided a detailed look at the flood myth that includes annotated reprints of important contributions from scholars representing many disciplines.[20]

Volcanoes

Volcanoes have played a greater role in human misery than is commonly understood. The destructive capacity of volcanism can be seen in the 1883 eruption on the Indonesian island of Krakatoa. The eruption occurred after the volcano had been dormant for more than two hundred years. On 27 August 1883, two-thirds of the island (about 20 square kilometers) blew away, forming a caldera 250 meters deep and creating three huge tsunamis that reached heights of more than 30 meters. A Dutch warship was washed nearly a kilometer inland, coming to rest 10 meters above sea level. Thirty-six thousand people were killed, mostly by drowning; 165 coastal villages were destroyed. Thick rafts of floating pumice, some crossing the Indian Ocean and others reaching Melanesia, were still afloat two years later. The explosion was heard 4,500 kilometers away, and the quantity of ash was so great that for the surrounding 450 kilometers, "day was turned to night."[21] The ash circumnavigated the earth, lowering global temperatures by as much as .5° C in the year after the eruption. Temperatures did not return to normal until 1888.

The great Mount Mazama eruption (more than 6500 B.P.) led to the formation of Crater Lake (Oregon). The surrounding region was blanketed by more than 40 cubic kilometers of volcanic ash from the eruption. The Klamath Indians were living in the area at the time. Their sandals and other artifacts have been recovered from the ash.

In the middle of the second millennium B.C. the Aegean island of Thera witnessed an even larger volcanic cataclysm. The resulting caldera is 83 square kilometers and 350 meters deep, about five times the size of the Krakatoa caldera. The ash layer covering the remnants of the island is

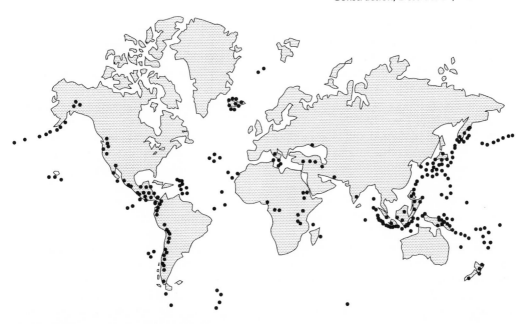

Figure 9.6 Major Volcanic Eruptions of the World
(Reported by the Center for Short-Lived Phenomena,
1968–1974)

more than 30 meters thick. Pumice floated all over the Aegean and eastern Mediterranean. Ash fell on settlements in Crete and Aegean Turkey. Geoarchaeologists have sought evidence of the destructive force of associated seismic and tsunami events but have so far been unsuccessful.

Early peoples living in volcanic areas attributed the destructive eruptions of volcanoes to malign deities. The Aztecs and Mayans offered human sacrifices to volcanoes. The Hawaiian volcano goddess Pele is well known in Western lore. The legend of Pele, however, clearly shows that the Hawaiians understood the geologic fact that volcanic activity in the islands is progressively younger from northwest to southeast.

Figure 9.6 shows the zones of high volcanic activity. Many of these zones coincide with areas of intense current and past human settlement. Humans evolved in east Africa in the context of intensive periods of volcanism. Volcanic ash layers provide both good preservation of sites and a datable stratigraphic sequence. As all human societies possess adaptive mechanisms for coping with environmental fluctuations, Sheets and McKee and others have used the natural hazards of vol-

canic destruction to provide a framework for exploring the dynamic relations between human societies and their changing environments.[22]

Site Preservation

The three main aspects of site preservation are the geologic/geotechnical, those concerned with materials science, and the architectural. Geoarchaeologists must deal with the first group, in addition to paying attention to the second. *Geologic* problems in site preservation include: 1) erosion, including the action of waves, meandering rivers, rising sea level, wind, and ice; 2) freshwater inundation from dam construction; 3) land subsidence because of mining or the withdrawal of water, oil, or gas; 4) landslides, mass wasting, and soil creep; 5) sediment and soil compaction; 6) earthquakes, tsunamis, and movement along faults; 7) diagenesis, bioturbation, and frost action; and 8) volcanic hazards.

Geotechnical responses to ameliorate these problems include: 1) draining; 2) waterproofing; 3) chemical stabilization; 4) structural stabilization; 5) channeling; 6) riprapping; and 7) reduction in biologic activity. (There is no geotechnical response to volcanoes.) In terms of geotechnical responses geoarchaeologists should adopt their own Hippocratic oath: "First, do no harm." There is a long history of attempts at building and monument preservation that did more harm than good—unfortunately, most of these well-meaning preservers had little or no geologic knowledge.

Site Preservation Problems

River, lake, reservoir, and coastal erosion present an ever-present threat to archaeological sites. Bank erosion, its causes and effects, were the subject of a classic study by G. K. Gilbert in the nineteenth century.[23] This pioneering geomorphologist explained the forms lake-shore landforms take and the processes that give rise to them.

Geoarchaeologists can help with site preservation in the face of natural erosion by understanding the dynamics of the erosion processes. Although the processes are well known, the rates of erosion vary dramatically with time and with landscape parameters unique to each site. Once the local geology is understood, a variety of techniques can be used to establish baselines for rates of erosion. Historical, sequential aerial photographs provide one of the most accurate records. Aerial photographs provide a record that covers a considerable length of time in the United States and some other developed countries. Most of these photographs offer stereo coverage. The U.S. Geological Survey has a systematic and repetitive aerial mapping program. The U.S. Army Corps of Engineers has large-scale metric aerial photographs that were taken with a calibrated camera for engineering mapping of its project areas—projects that often affect potential erosion at archaeological sites.

A geologic framework is essential for any site-protection plan. It is particularly necessary in river floodplain situations, where the river course can change in response to individual floods, and in coastal situations, where one storm can cause more beach recession than a hundred years of normal erosion.

Each site presents a special set of circumstances that depend on such factors as: whether there was instantaneous abandonment rather than slow decrease of human activity (a more complex situation); the rate and depth of burial; and the age of the site. Natural geomorphic and climatic changes over time will result in some stress in the preservational aspects of archaeological remains. Once a site is abandoned, geologic processes are the primary agents responsible for site destruction or burial. These geologic processes include both the physical (compaction and cryoturbation) and chemical (weathering and a host of dissolution phenomena). Until the 1980s, little research was done on the effects of burial and diagenesis. For sites residing in the soil zone, the complex pedologic activity will have an impact on cultural resources. Although burial may decrease weathering and leaching, sites buried beneath the active soil zone are still affected by one or more of the following: pH and changes in pH; physical movement of materials; compression; wet-dry and freeze-thaw phenomena; wet aerobic and anaerobic reactions; other diagenetic changes; and organisms.

An example of special geologic conditions can be seen at Thebes in Egypt. The New Kingdom pharaohs built their tombs in the rock cliffs on the west bank of the Nile. Figure 9.7 illustrates in cross section the geologic stratigraphy and lithology of a typical tomb placement. Three marine sedimentary formations outcrop in the area: the Theban limestone, the Esna shale, and the Dakhla chalk. The Esna shale is composed of montmorillonite clay, silt, and fine sand. Most of the royal tombs were cut into the Theban limestone on a descending slope. Those tombs that descended into the Esna shale (as in figure 9.7) encountered a geologic "time bomb." The high montmorillonite content of the Esna shale makes it highly expansive when moistened. Such expansions exert tremendous pressures on rock columns and partitions in the tombs. Preservation efforts must concentrate on keeping the tombs dry.

Reservoirs

When new reservoirs are filled, engineers frequently must deal with bank conditions where there are flat terraces, and the banks against which

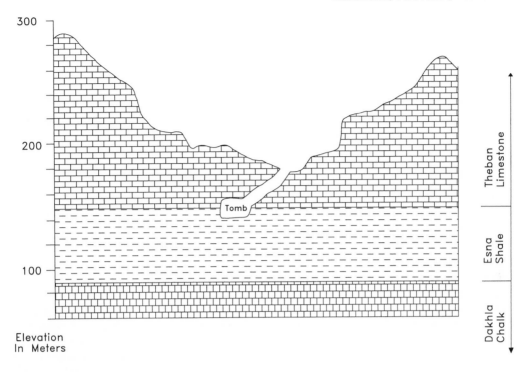

Figure 9.7 Generalized Cross Section of the Valley of the Kings, Egypt

the waters lap have steep gradients composed of incompetent silt, sand, or gravels. When these reservoirs are filled, erosional forces are directed against new shorelines that have not previously been affected. Until equilibrium is reached, the reservoir bank may suffer extremely rapid erosion. River-bank terraces throughout the world have been preferred by prehistoric peoples for habitation sites, fishing sites, and places for related activities. Gatto and Doe cite at least thirty-four processes that influence the nature and rate of bank erosion in reservoirs.[24] These researchers used ten northern U.S. reservoirs for historical bank-recession analysis covering periods of twenty to thirty years. They found that bank erosion was extremely variable even within small areas and that recession measurements along two or three transects may not adequately characterize recession for a given area. In their work on reservoirs from the middle stretch of the Missouri River, they calculated rates of recession between 0 and 12 meters per year.

From a geomorphic perspective, not only the erosional feature itself but those landscape features bounding it must be part of the study and interpretation. With stereo aerial-photograph coverage, an exposed erosional bank and its immediate geomorphic context is usually apparent. However, ground-truth investigation of bank sediment types and vegetative cover is necessary for building an adequate model for site-protection schemes.

The factors that influence reservoir-bank erosion operate in several timescales. Water levels change as often as every few days: floods can raise water levels dramatically. Climatic parameters, such as droughts, operate on a scale of years.

Reservoirs are deepest near dams, whereas lakes are deepest near their centers. The tendency of sediments to erode along the extended shorelines of reservoirs and large lakes varies. The shores of new reservoirs are in disequilibrium with their new "lacustrine" environment. The time they take to reach equilibrium will vary, but in some

217

reservoirs along the Missouri River, equilibrium has not been achieved in more than thirty years.

Hilltops or Slopes

From the Bronze Age to medieval times, generally for defensive reasons, Mediterranean area habitation sites and fortifications were often built on flat-topped hills delimited on all sides by steep escarpments. This makes rocky hills highly susceptible to erosion. Stabilization attempts on unstable cliffs or steep slopes were carried out as far back as the Renaissance in Italy. Prominent slopes are especially sensitive to wind and water erosion. The eroded profile may show an irregular shape because of the differential resistance of clay, sand, carbonate, or igneous rock layers. Wind can be erosive on steep slopes or cliffs formed by poorly cemented sediments. Wind velocities increase with height, and sand grains entrained by the wind can be abrasive. Geotechnical preservation techniques to inhibit erosion include filling voids with concrete under cantilevered rock, filling open joints and cracks with cement grout, treating with pigmented **shotcrete**, building protective walls of rock similar to those of the cliff or slope, treating rock formations with durable, water-repellent coatings like silicone compounds, consolidating friable rock, and impregnating porous rock with silicates.

Major rockfalls of large blocks are usually contained by bolting or otherwise anchoring the rocks. A special case of instability arises when ancient walls stand at the edge of, or on, steep slopes. The problem is compounded by the fact that such walls are often located on fill—a notoriously poor foundation material. When rainwater accumulates inside a wall that lacks adequate drainage and saturates the foundations, a slide is likely to develop. Ensuring proper drainage will help relieve this stress. A good knowledge of rock properties and local stratigraphy is necessary for any of these techniques.

Pueblo Bonito in Chaco Canyon, northwest New Mexico, was built and occupied between about 900 and 1130. The early inhabitants built their village near the north canyon wall, over and between great blocks of sandstone. They may have been unaware of the significance of these

fallen blocks. Later inhabitants, recognizing the instability of the nearby canyon wall, braced the cliff during Pueblo III time (1050–1060) with timber posts embedded in stone rubble and protected by masonry. The whole structure was supported by a vast buttress of adobe and rubble. The ancient mitigation efforts were successful—the sandstone cliff that had long menaced Pueblo Bonito did not collapse until January 1941.

Seismicity

Seismicity problems in geoarchaeology go beyond assessing seismic damage at archaeological sites. They extend to monument preservation. The maximum seismic hazard in high-risk areas needs to be determined. Paleoseismic maps are a starting point in assessing future seismic load, but the evaluation of seismic hazard owing to earthquakes originating from a fault requires a quantitative description of fault activity. Additional information is needed concerning the possible ground acceleration at a site if at-risk monuments are to be protected.

Seismic risk analysis is an advanced science in countries like Japan and the United States. Hence, the data may already be available for assessing the role of paleoseismic activity and seismic hazards in site protection. Such data, combined with engineering geology investigations common in many geologic hazard areas, can provide the geoarchaeological framework for site-preservation analysis. Engineering geology studies typically reconstruct the morphologic transformations undergone by a site over many centuries or millennia. Geologic time horizons are typically much larger than those in archaeology.

Site Stabilization

Although archaeological sites are susceptible to natural aging processes, erosion and related mass movements can often be predicted and mitigated. Site-stabilization efforts have a much longer history than the relatively recent archaeological interests. Thus, mature geotechnical sciences concerned with site stabilization are available. Geomorphology, engineering geology, hydrology, soil mechanics, and related sciences all come to bear on site-protection problems. However, archaeological site protection often has a unique set of problems associated with the preservation of buried features. Although some surface sites may be protected by heavy riprap, the application of the same material to a site buried in soft sediments may result in differential compaction that all but destroys the spatial integrity of the features it was designed to preserve. Prestabilization site testing should be considered in every geoarchaeological project of site preservation.

The objective of site preservation is to strike a balance between systematic recovery of data and artifacts and the long-term protection of cultural resources that can be preserved in situ.

Earth Burial

Although burying archaeological sites under a mantle of earth has often been used for site protection, there are few studies that assess long-term effects. There are some basic geologic considerations involved. Among them:

- Fill should be sterile and of a composition that does not retard vegetation.
- Sand fill may be unstable and easily eroded. Fine sand and silt may be subject to deflation.
- Heavy stone (riprap), though durable and resistant to erosion, may compact the site sediments to an unacceptable degree.
- The sediments and soils at the site must be investigated for soil mechanical and hydrologic properties. Similarly, a knowledge of artifacts and features to be protected is essential.
- Fill material must be chemically compatible with site matrix, artifacts, and biofacts. The term "chemically compatible" includes the acid-base character of the site, and pH levels of the fill, and the site earth matrix should be similar. Bone deteriorates rapidly in an acid environment and may be damaged by salt-crystal formation if soluble salts are available in a fill material.
- Deep burial may lead to undesirable compaction and other diagenetic effects.
- A coarse sand or pea gravel layer may be an appropriate marker between fill and artifact-bearing matrix.

- When rock berms are appropriate for exposed banks of streams, lakes, and reservoirs, determination of the ground surface preparation and expedient slope angle must include the nature of the site matrix, artifacts, and features. The toes of rock berms may be subject to erosion and catastrophic failure if water levels drop below the base of the berm.
- Where soils are involved, easily altered soil properties like organic matter, pH, nitrogen, and soluble salts will move toward a new equilibrium. Laboratory analysis will help to characterize site soils and matrix.
- Shallow cores can be used to characterize the site sediments and soils and to evaluate the continuity and extent of site strata.

Burial has the potential for limiting erosion, weathering, and biotic damage to archaeological sites, but increased loading, increased moisture, and incompatible chemistries may limit its usefulness. The most successful uses of site burial will be those where the original chemical characteristics of the site matrix are retained and where the deleterious effects of freeze-thaw and wet-dry cycles are reduced or eliminated. The approximate relative significance of decay factors for buried sites is:

Most Severe	Wet-dry/freeze-thaw
	Wet aerobic conditions
	Compression
	Micro-organisms
	Freezing
	Wet anaerobic conditions
	Low pH conditions
	Micro-organisms
	Movement
	High pH conditions
Least Severe	Thawing

Historic Cultural Resource Preservation

The geologic aspects of historic property protection differ somewhat from those of most prehistoric (buried) sites. Although lateral river migration, coastal erosion, and related destructive natural forces are common to both historic and prehistoric sites, natural processes like major floods and acid rain have a far greater impact on historic sites where there are standing structures. An elevation of the groundwater table that could serve to preserve buried sites from alternating wet and dry conditions could well be damaging to a historic structure.

In general, preservation of historic sites will have fewer geoarchaeological considerations than are attendant at prehistoric sites. The major geologic aspects of many historic site–preservation problems revolve around the weathering of stone structures under adverse atmospheric conditions. On other sites such geotechnical mitigation procedures as berm walls, earth burial, and riprap revetment are indicated.

Conservation

Materials Preservation

The first commandment of conservation is: "Any preservation or restoration treatment must be preceded by an exhaustive study of the deterioration process." The remedial action usually includes the following sequential steps: diagnosis; cleaning; consolidation. Cleaning and consolidation employ standardized treatments that are well known to conservators. Diagnosis is where geologic knowledge is necessary, for it cannot proceed without a detailed knowledge of the material. For earth materials, this means the mineralogy and geochemistry of the material and its previous and current environments. For example, limestone and marble are exceedingly and immediately vulnerable to acids in the atmosphere—and the typical outdoor atmosphere is fairly acidic—whereas fresh granite will weather slowly. (But weather it does.) The standard carbonic acid in the atmosphere simply dissolves the calcite (the chief component in limestone and marble), while the sulfuric acid in the atmosphere turns the surface layers of the calcium carbonate to calcium sulfate, which causes the material to crumble. Marly limestone (a common building stone in Italy) also suffers from its heterogeneity. The physical process of a dissolution of the carbonate

component is further accelerated by the penetration of acidic solutions along the clay layers.

In sandstones where the clastic particles are composed of quartz—a highly resistant mineral—the cementing agent is likely to be the vulnerable component. Calcite cement suffers from the same chemical problems as limestone and marble. If the cementing is weak, abrasion caused by particles in wind can generate rapid mechanical disintegration. Even quarrying methods can affect stone deterioration. Ancient manual-quarrying methods will have done less mechanical damage than modern methods that rely on a pneumatic hammer whose vibrations cause microcracks. All worked surfaces acquire adhering carbonaceous particles more easily that are good catalysts for the hydration of atmospheric sulfur dioxide to sulfuric acid, promoting dissolution.

An attempt to quantify the relation of shaping processes to the physical characteristics of building stone has been made on *Pietraforte*—a sandstone widely used as a building stone in Florence. The clastic particles of this sandstone are derived from metamorphic and sedimentary rocks. The rock is a roughly equal mixture of silicate and carbonate components. Decay of this material is principally caused by absorbed water in pores and discontinuities, combined with sudden temperature changes. The porosity appears to be affected by working processes, particularly when the worked surface is parallel or perpendicular to the stratification in the rock.

Mineralogic (including X-ray) and petrographic analyses, along with chemical analysis, are necessary to characterize rocks and understand rock weathering. Many geologists can identify upward of two hundred minerals with the aid of a hand lens. Petrographic analysis allows the geologist to determine porosity and permeability, two important parameters in judging the susceptibility of rocks to chemical weathering.

The chemical treatments of stone undergoing conservation or restoration are beyond the scope of a book on geoarchaeology.[25] What the geoarchaeologist contributes to materials conservation is the knowledge of the stability or instability of rock and other building materials in various environments. It is largely because of insufficient knowledge of materials in given chemical environments that there has been a century of failures in conservation treatment of stone sculpture, monuments, and buildings.

Corrosion

Fundamental to the deterioration and weathering of metals is the phenomenon of corrosion. Most metals are not stable under the conditions prevailing at the earth's surface. The resulting corrosion has two important, contradictory aspects: it leads to deterioration and disfigurement, but, depending on the metal or alloy, a thin layer of corrosion may form a protective film on the surface, inhibiting further deterioration.

The characteristic weathering phenomenon associated with copper and such high-copper alloys as bronze is the formation of a green patina on the surface of the metal. The patina consists of copper hydroxide salts of sulfate, carbonate, or chloride, as well as salts of lead and tin, where these have been alloying elements. It should be emphasized that more than a dozen minerals have been found as corrosion products on bronze. The rate of corrosion will depend upon environmental factors, especially the acidity that comes from sulfuric and carbonic acids in the atmosphere and in soils. From wet sites, including undersea locations, where oxygen is relatively scarce, the excavated copper or copper alloy is often virtually uncorroded. In reducing environments, bluish-black copper sulfides may form on the surface of objects. Copper in solution is toxic to marine life, so the presence of encrusting marine creatures probably indicates that the metal is free from active corrosion.

Ancient iron is not pure iron but an alloy with about 0.1 percent carbon, called wrought iron. A later alloy was developed which we call cast iron, with a carbon content of more than 2 percent. Steel is also an alloy of iron and carbon, but it is a very different material. Iron corrodes easily to a porous and inhomogeneous iron oxide rust. Highly corroded iron artifacts are fragile and require special conservation techniques. They should be stored in as dry a place as possible.

Iron excavated from damp, aerated sites usually appears to be a nondescript, reddish-brown mass. The shape of the mass frequently bears no resemblance to that of the original object. The mass is composed of iron oxides, oxyhydroxides, and carbonates. Iron objects from wet, oxygen-free deposits may appear black because of the formation of ferrous iron sulfide by the action of sulfur-reducing bacteria.

From marine sites, ferrous concretions of iron oxides and oxyhydroxides, calcium carbonate and debris, form around the corroding iron. As these concretions form, they can spread across a site, trapping everything in their way. Where oxygen is relatively scarce, lepidocrocite (gamma $FeO.OH$), magnetite (Fe_3O_4), and pyrrhotite (FeS) may be present.

As a noble metal, gold is not affected by normal geochemical processes at or near the earth's surface. However, in the natural and artificial alloy of gold and silver (electrum), the silver can be subject to corrosion. In gold and copper alloys, especially the Central and South American alloy *tumbaga*, the copper can corrode so severely that the artifact is covered with the typical green copper-alteration products. Gold alloys are also subject to cracking—a phenomenon not found in pure gold.

By Roman times lead was in common use in Europe. Fresh lead has a bright metallic bluish-gray color. Corrosion first dulls this color then produces a gray and finally a grayish-white surface. Most excavated lead is covered with this grayish-white alteration product This is usually cerussite ($PbCO_3$) and/or hydrocerussite ($2\,PbCO_3.Pb(OH)_2$). These corrosion products are found on lead from damp, calcareous soils and on lead from the sea. In both cases they protect the metal from greater corrosion. Because lead is so soft, the corrosion products have a higher Mohs hardness than the underlying metal. The tin-lead alloy pewter will have a similar dull, grayish-white corroded surface when excavated.

The Future

Archaeologists are trained to recover data through carefully orchestrated procedures of excavation that destroy the site being examined. For many reasons, including costs, the twenty-first century is likely to see a shift toward the in situ preservation of sites and the preservation of entire cultural and natural landscapes.

Geologists and geoarchaeologists frequently focus on larger areas than sites and site-catchment areas and therefore employ different methodologies from archaeologists. This focus also colors their research and preservation strategies. Recent archaeological survey research has tended more toward the recording of "find spots" and other "nonsite" data. Humans wandered and worked across, and made an impact on, a continuous landscape. It is with the continuous landscape that geoarchaeologists must deal. The concentration of archaeological efforts at "sites" ensures that these areas remain important, but the continuum rather than the isolation will attain greater attention in the future.

Somewhat the same thing can be said for the approach to time. Archaeologists have always focused on the specific strata in archaeological sediments where artifacts and features occur. They considered time between the deposition of these strata dead time, largely out of bounds for archaeological work. Geoarchaeologists need to see time as a continuum. Life went on whether the deposits recorded it or not. Landscape changes, the climate, gross impacts of human activities, soil development, change in vegetative cover—all are continuous features in our earth's surface environment. Paleoecologists have added much to archaeological thought with their careful reconstruction of environmental change.

Often data from paleoecology or geomorphology are at a much coarser scale than desired by site-oriented archaeologists. This can and is being remedied with multidisciplinary, archaeology-centered projects in specific areas. The regional orientation of geomorphology and geoarchaeology is well suited to these future needs.

Because archaeological site preservation is largely a post–World War II phenomenon, and because few follow-up studies have been undertaken concerning the effectiveness of site-preservation methodologies, site preservation is a fertile field for future research. Short-term protection of a resource, though often expedient, does little to ensure long-term preservation. Until we evaluate long-term effectiveness, we cannot begin the appropriate cultural-resource management planning. With their broad training in archaeological science, geoarchaeologists can play a major role in the preservation, monitoring, and evaluation of our past.

Appendix: Geologic Time Divisions

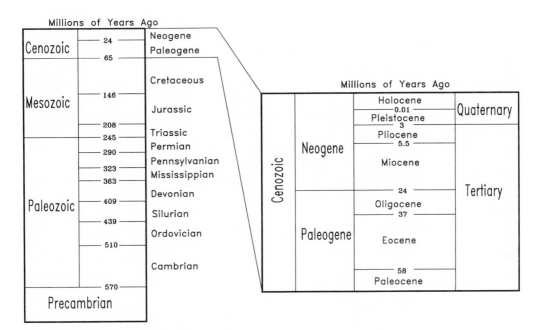

Appendix A.1 Geologic Time Divisions

Appendix

Appendix A.2 Geologic and Archaeological Time Divisions for the Past Three Million Years

Years BC/AD — 1500 AD · 1000 AD · AD/BC · 1000 BC

Eastern United States	Southwest United States	Mesoamerica
Mississippian	Mogollon — Western Pueblo · Hohokam (Classic, Sedentary) · Anasazi — Pueblo	Aztec · Late Post Classic · Toltec/Tula · Early Post Classic · Terminal Classic · Late Classic · Middle Classic · Early Classic
Woodland · Hopewell · Adena	Mogollon (Colonial) · Mogollon (Frontier) · Basket Maker	Proto-Classic
Late Archaic	Late Archaic	Olmec

Years BP — 1000 · 2000 · 3000

General Geologic Time Divisions	Years BP (Approx)	Geo-Paleoclimatic Divisions	Generalized Archaeological Sequence
Late Holocene	100	Present	Historic
	400	Neo-Boreal	
	850	Pacific (hypothermal)	Late Prehistoric
	1300	Neo-Atlantic (Medithermal)	
	1700	Scandic	
	2800	Sub-Atlantic	
Middle Holocene	5000	Sub-Boreal (Altithermal)	Archaic
Early Holocene	8000	Atlantic (Hypsothermal)	Late Paleo-Indian
	9000	Boreal (Anathermal)	
Terminal Pleistocene	10,000	Pre-Boreal / Late Glacial	Folsom Clovis (Paleo-Indian)

Appendix A.3 Relation Between Geologic Time Divisions, Paleoclimate Terms, and Archaeological Sequences for North America from About 10,000 B.P.

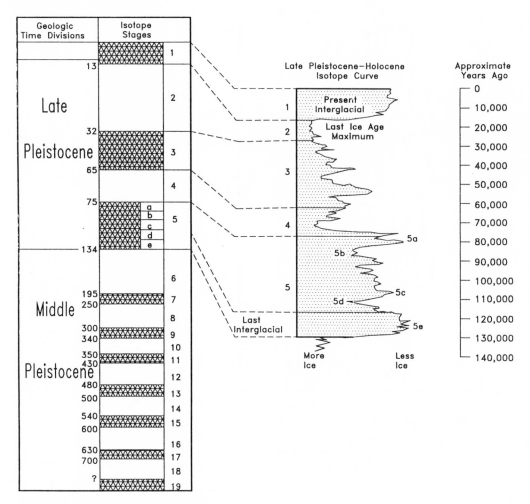

Appendix A.4 Oxygen Isotope Stages for the Middle
and Late Pleistocene

Notes

Chapter 1: Theoretical and Historical Overview

1. Konigsson, "Pollen Analysis in Archaeogeology and Geoarchaeology."

2. Ferring, Review of *Principles of Geoarchaeology: A North American Perspective*, 218.

3. Gladfelter, "Developments and Directions in Geoarchaeology," 343; Butzer, *Archaeology as Human Ecology*, 35.

4. We refer to the contextual archaeology of Butzer, *Archaeology as Human Ecology*, not to be confused with the postprocessual contextual archaeology described by Willey and Sabloff, *History of American Archaeology*, 306, or Trigger, *History of Archaeological Thought*, 348.

5. Graubau, *Principles of Stratigraphy*, 19.

6. West, "Archaeological Geology," 9.

7. Thorson, "Archaeological Geology."

8. For example, by Binford, in *Debating Archaeology*.

9. Leach, "On the Definition of Geoarchaeology."

10. Renfrew, "Archaeology and the Earth Sciences"; Gladfelter, "Geoarchaeology: The Geomorphologist and Archaeology"; Butzer, *Archaeology as Human Ecology*; Schoenwetter, "Prologue to a Contextual Archaeology"; Rapp and Gifford, "Archaeological Geology"; Rapp, "Archaeological Geology"; Rapp, "Geoarchaeology."

11. Butzer, *Archaeology as Human Ecology*, 11; see also Butzer, *Environment and Archaeology*; Butzer, "Ecological Approach to Archaeology"; Butzer, "Toward an Integrated Contextual Approach in Archaeology"; Butzer, "Response to Presentation of the Archaeological Geology Division Award."

12. Wheeler, *Archaeology from the Earth*, 2.

13. Gladfelter, "Geoarchaeology"; Waters, *Principles of Geoarchaeology*.

14. Hassan, review of *Formation Processes in Archaeologic Context*.

15. Daniel, *Hundred and Fifty Years of Archaeology*; Butzer, *Environment and Archaeology*; Butzer, *Archaeology as Human Ecology*; Rapp and Gifford, "Archaeological Geology"; Gifford and Rapp, "Early Development of Archaeological Geology in North America"; Gifford and Rapp, "History, Philosophy, and Perspectives"; Rapp, "Geoarchaeology"; Grayson, *Establishment of Human Antiquity*; Grayson, "Eoliths, Archaeological Ambiguity and the Generation of 'Middle-Range' Research"; Grayson, "Provision of Time Depth for Paleoanthropology"; Meltzer, "Antiquity of Man and the Development of American Archaeology"; Stein and Farrand, "Context and Geoarchaeology"; Stein, "Deposits for Archaeologists"; Daniel and Renfrew, *Idea of Prehistory*.

16. Schiffer, *Behavioral Archaeology*; Stein and Farrand, "Context and Geoarchaeology."

17. Gifford and Rapp, "Early Development of Archaeological Geology in North America"; succinct reviews of the history of interaction between geology and archaeology are provided by Rapp, "Archaeological Geology"; Rapp, "Geoarchaeology."

18. Daniel, *Hundred and Fifty Years of Archaeology*, 189, 236.

19. Harris, *Principles of Archaeological Stratigraphy*, 96.

20. Frere, "Account of Flint Weapons Discovered at Hoxne in Suffolk," 204–05.

21. Prestwich, "On the Occurrence of Flint Implements, Associated with the Remains of Extinct Mammalia, in Undisturbed Beds of a Late Geological Period in France at Amien and Abbeville, and in England at Hoxne"; Gruber, "Brixham Cave and the Antiquity of Man."

22. Lyell, *Geological Evidences of the Antiquity of Man*; Lubbock, *Prehistoric Times*; and Geikie, *Great Ice Age and Its Relation to the Antiquity of Man*.

23. Daniel, *Hundred and Fifty Years of Archaeology*, 24.

24. Squier and Davis, *Ancient Monuments of the Mississippi Valley*.

25. Trigger, *History of Archaeological Thought*, 121.

26. Meltzer, "Antiquity of Man and the Development of American Archaeology."

27. Foster and Whitney, *Report on the Geology and Topography of a Portion of the Lake Superior Land District in the State of Michigan, Copper Lands;* Whittlesey, "Ancient Miners of Lake Superior."

28. Meltzer, "Antiquity of Man and the Development of American Archaeology," 22; and Gifford and Rapp, "Early Development of Archaeological Geology in North America," 413.

29. Holmes, "Modern Quarry Refuse and the Paleolithic Theory," 297.

30. Powell, "Prehistoric Man in America," 638.

31. Abbott, "Paleolithic Man: The Last Word," 345.

32. Haynes, *Man and the Glacial Period*, 540.

33. Salisbury, "Man and the Glacial Period," 19.

34. Wright, *Man and the Glacial Period*.

35. Meltzer, "Antiquity of Man and the Development of American Archaeology," 22.

36. Pumpelly et al., *Explorations in Turkestan: Expedition of 1904;* Pumpelly, *Explorations in Turkestan: Expedition of 1903*.

37. Daniel, *Hundred and Fifty Years of Archaeology*, 254.

38. Stein and Farrand, "Context and Geoarchaeology."

39. Zeuner, *The Pleistocene Period;* Zeuner, *Dating the Past;* Zeuner, *The Pleistocene Period: Its Climate, Chronology, and Faunal Successions*.

40. Daniel and Renfrew, *Idea of Prehistory*, 188.

41. De Morgan, *Prehistoric Man*, 10–11.

42. See Capper, *Archaeologia* 60, plates 69 and 70, for photographs of Stonehenge from a military balloon; Beazeley, "Surveys in Mesopotamia During the War"; Crawford, "Air Survey and Archaeology"; Crawford, *Air-Photography for Archaeologists;* Judd, *Prehistoric Canals from the Air*.

43. Atkinson, "Resistivity Surveying and Archaeology"; see also for South America, Shippee, "Great Wall of Peru," and other studies by the Shippee-Johnson Peruvian expedition.

44. See for example, Piggott, *Ancient Europe from the Beginnings of Agriculture to Classical Antiquity*, 175.

45. Gifford and Rapp, "Early Development of Archaeological Geology in North America"; Meltzer, "North American Archaeology and Archaeologists."

46. Kidder, "Pottery of the Pajarito Plateau and Some Adjacent Regions in New Mexico"; Meltzer, "North American Archaeology and Archaeologists," 256.

47. Gifford and Rapp, "Early Development of Archaeological Geology in North America."

48. Howard, "Evidence of Early Man in North America."

49. Antevs, "Occurrence of Flints and Extinct Animals in Pluvial Deposits near Clovis, New Mexico," Part 2, "Age of Clovis Lake Beds"; Antevs, "Climate and Early Man in the Southwest"; Antevs, "Great Basin, with Emphasis on Glacial and Postglacial Times"; Antevs, "Geologic Climate Dating in the West."

50. Holliday, *Guidebook to the Archaeological Geology of Classic Paleoindian Sites*.

51. Haynes, "Antevs-Bryan Years and the Legacy for Paleoindian Geochronology."

52. Gifford and Rapp, "Early Development of Archaeological Geology in North America," 418.

53. MacCurdy, *Early Man*.

54. Stein and Farrand, "Context and Geoarchaeology."

55. Movius, "Old-World Paleolithic Archaeology," 1444; Movius, "Old World Paleolithic"; Braidwood, "Means Towards an Understanding of Human Behavior Before the Present"; Braidwood, "Old-World: Post Paleolithic"; Wright, "Geology"; Cornwall, *Soils for the Archaeologist;* Clark, "Human Ecology During the Pleistocene and Later Times in Africa South of the Sahara."

56. Taylor, *Identification of Non-Artifactual Archaeological Materials*.

57. Butzer, *Archaeology as Human Ecology*, 36.

58. Pyddoke, *Stratification for the Archaeologist*, 116.

59. Butzer, *Environment and Archaeology*, 4.

60. Haynes, "Geologist's Role in Pleistocene Paleoecology and Archaeology."

61. Binford, "Consideration of Archaeological Research Design," 431.

62. Isaac, "Towards the Interpretation of Occupation Debris."

63. Acher, "Time's Arrow and the Archaeology of Contemporary Community."

64. McDonald and Rapp, *Minnesota Messenia Expedition*.

65. Wendorf, *Prehistory of Nubia*.

66. Caldwell, "New American Archaeology."

67. Binford, "Consideration of Archaeological Research Design"; Binford, *Theory Building in Archaeology*; Binford, *Bones: Ancient Men and Modern Myths*; Binford, *In Pursuit of the Past*; Schiffer, "Archaeological Context and Systemic Context"; Schiffer, *Behavioral Archaeology*; Schiffer, "Towards the Identification of Formation Processes"; and Schiffer, *Formation Processes of the Archaeological Record*.

68. Binford, *In Pursuit of the Past*, 21; Binford, *Bones*, 18–19.

69. Raab and Goodyear, "Middle Range Theory in Archaeology."

70. Hassan, "Sediments in Archaeology," 197.

71. Butzer, *Archaeology as Human Ecology*; Gladfelter, "Developments and Directions in Geoarchaeology," 355; Waters, *Principles of Geoarchaeology*.

72. Fedele, "Sediments as Paleo-land Segments."

73. Stein and Farrand, "Context and Geoarchaeology," 2; Schick, *Stone Age Sites in the Making*, 9; Dincauze, "Strategies for Paleoenvironmental Reconstruction in Archaeology," 256; Potts, *Early Hominid Activities at Olduvai*; Kolb, Lasca, and Goldstein, "Soil-Geomorphic Analysis of the Midden Deposits at Aztalan Site, Wisconsin," 200; Johnson and Logan, "Geoarchaeology of the Kansas River Basin, Central Great Plains," 267; Thorson, "Geologic Context of Archaeological Sites in Beringia," 399; Waters, "Geoarchaeology of Gullies and Arroyos in Southern Arizona"; Waters, *Principles of Geoarchaeology*.

74. Clarke, *Analytical Archaeology*, 100.

75. Dunnell, *Systematics in Prehistory*, 120–21; Leroi-Gourhan, *Art of Prehistoric Man in Western Europe*.

76. North, "Geology for Archaeologists," 114–15.

Chapter 2: Sediments and Soils

1. Bettis, "Soil Morphologic Properties and Weathering Zone Characteristics as Age Indicators in Holocene Alluvium in the Upper Midwest." As Bettis has written: "Archaeological remains, being deposits, are subject to the same natural processes of burial, weathering, and erosion that affect the preservation and distribution of noncultural deposits," 119.

2. Shlemon and Budinger, "Archaeological Geology of the Calico Site, Mojave Desert, California."

3. Gleeson and Grosso, "Ozette Site."

4. Stockton, "Shaws's Creek Shelter: Human Displacement of Artifacts and Its Significance."

5. Stein, "Earthworm Activity."

6. Gladfelter, "On the Interpretation of Archaeologic Sites in Alluvial Settings," 43.

7. For an example, see Haynes, "Calico Site."

8. Peacock, "Distinguishing Between Artifacts and Geofacts."

9. Meltzer, Adovasio, and Dillehay, "On a Pleistocene Human Occupation at Pedra Furada, Brazil."

10. Fladmark, "Microdebitage Analysis."

11. Rapp, "Archaeological Field Staff"; Aschenbrenner and Cooke, "Screening and Gravity Concentration," 164.

12. Eidt, "Theoretical and Practical Considerations in the Analysis of Anthrosols."

13. Dincauze, *Neville Site*.

14. Clark, *Excavations at Starr Carr*.

15. See for example, chapter 7, in Coles and Coles, *People of the Wetlands*.

16. Holliday, "Soil Formation, Time and Archaeology" 102.

17. Soil Survey Staff, *Soil Taxonomy*.

18. Kapp, "Background."

19. Kamilli and Steinberg, "New Approaches to Mineral Analysis of Ancient Ceramics."

20. Ferring, "Alluvial Pedology and Geoarchaeological Research."

21. Birkeland, *Soils and Geomorphology*.

22. U.S. Department of Agriculture, *Keys to Soil Taxonomy*.

23. Kraus and Brown, *Pedofacies Analysis*.

24. Mack and James, *Paleosols for Sedimentologists*; see also the later article by Mack, James, and Monger, "Classification of Paleosols."

25. Alexander, "Color Chart for Organic Matter."

26. Schulze et al., "Significance of Organic Matter in Determining Soil Colors."

27. Schick, "Geoarchaeological Analysis of an Acheulian Site at Kalambo Falls, Zambia."

28. Allen, "Quantitative Technique for Assessing the Roundness of Pottery Shards in Water Currents."

29. Shackley, "Stream Abrasion of Flint Implements."

30. Schick, *Stone Age Sites in the Making*.

Chapter 3: Contexts of Archaeological Record Formation

1. See, for example, Behrensmeyer and Hill, *Fossils in the Making*; Lyman, *Vertebrate Taphonomy*.

2. Todd and Frison, "Taphonomic Study of the Colby Site Mammoth Bones."

3. Schiffer, "Archaeological Context and Systemic Context"; Schiffer, *Formation Processes of the Archaeological Record*.

4. Kolb and Van Lopik, "Depositional Environments of the Mississippi River Deltaic Plain, Southeastern Louisiana"; Coleman, "Deltaic Evolution."

5. Stanley and Warne, "Nile Delta."

6. See, for example, Davis and Greiser, "Indian Creek Paleoindians."

7. Wendorf, Schild, and Close, *Prehistory of Wadi Kubbaniya*.

8. Gibbard, *Pleistocene History of the Lower Thames Valley*.

9. Joyce and Mueller, "Social Impact of Anthropogenic Landscape Modification in the Rio Verde Drainage Basin, Oaxaca, Mexico."

10. Kempe, *Living Underground*.

11. Butzer, "Cave Sediments, Upper Pleistocene Stratigraphy and Mousterian Facies in Cantabrian Spain."

12. Brady and Veni, "Man-Made and Pseudo-Karst Caves."

13. See Liu, "Paleoclimatic Changes as Indicated by the Quaternary Karstic Cave Deposits in China."

14. Phillipson, *African Archaeology*.

15. Barton and Clark, "Cultural and Natural Formation Processes in Late Quaternary Cave and Rockshelters."

16. Moss, "Geology of Mummy Cave."

17. Sutcliff et al., "Cave Paleontology and Archaeology."

18. Wymer, *Paleolithic Sites of East Anglia*; Roe, *Lower and Middle Paleolithic Periods in Britain*.

19. Ashton, Cook, Lewis, and Rose, *High Lodge*; see also Roe, "Landmark Sites of the British Paleolithic."

20. In 1995 D. J. Stanley revived the possibility of determining a global sea-level rise curve (Stanley, "Global Sea-Level Curve for the Late Quaternary").

21. Reinhardt, "Hydrologic Artifact Dispersals at Pingasagruk, North Coast, Alaska."

22. Kraft et al., "Pass at Thermopylae, Greece."

23. Julig, McAndrews, and Mahaney, "Geoarchaeology of the Cummins Site on the Beach of Proglacial Lake Minong, Lake Superior Basin, Canada"; Larsen, "Geoarchaeological Interpretation of Great Lakes Coastal Environments"; Farrand, *Former Shorelines in Western and Northern Lake Superior Basin*; and Farrand and Dexler, "Late Wisconsin Man and Holocene History of the Lake Superior Basin."

24. A detailed treatment of the problems in deciphering a shell midden is available in Stein, *Deciphering a Shell Midden*.

25. An often-cited summary is Wood and Johnson, "Survey of Disturbance Processes in Archaeological Site Formation."

26. Rick, "Downslope Movement and Archaeologic Intrasite Spatial Analysis"; Culling, "Soil Creep and the Development of Hillside Slopes"; Young, "Soil Movement by Denudational Processes on Slopes"; Moeyerson, "Behavior of Stones and Stone Implements, Buried in Consolidating and Creeping Kalahari Sands"; Taber, "The Mechanics of Frost Heaving"; Wasburn, *Geocryology*; Johnson and Hansen, "Effects of Frost-Heaving on Objects in Soils"; Johnson, Muhs, and Barnhardt, "Effects of Frost Heaving on Objects in Soils, II: Laboratory Experiments"; Reid, "Fire and Ice"; Schweger, "Geoarchaeology of Northern Regions"; Thorson, "Geologic Contexts of Archaeologic Sites in Beringia"; Thorson and Hamilton, "Geology of the Dry Creek Site."

27. Johnson, "Frost Action in Roads and Airfields."

28. Corte, "Vertical Migration of Particles in Front of a Freezing Plane"; Corte, "Particle Sorting by Repeated Freezing and Thawing"; Inglis, "Particle Sorting and Stone Migration by Freezing and Thawing"; Jackson and Uhlmann, "Particle Sorting and Stone Migration Due to Frost Heave"; Schweger, "Geoarchaeology of Northern Regions"; Bowers, Bonnichsen, and Hoch, "Flake Dispersal Experiments."

Chapter 4: Paleoenvironmental Reconstructions

1. Gifford, "Taphonomy and Paleoecology."

2. Betancourt, Van Defender, and Martin, *Packrat Middens*; Reinhard and Bryant, "Coprolite Analysis."

3. Faegri, Kaland, and Krzywinski, *Textbook of Pollen Analysis*; Moore, Webb, and Collinson, *Pollen Analysis*.

4. See Wright, "Environmental Setting for Plant Domestication in the Near East." See also Roberts and Wright, "Vegetational, Lake-Level, and Climatic History of the Near East and Southwest Asia."

5. Shay, *Itasca Bison Kill Site;* see also Bradbury, Platt, and Dean, *Elk Lake, Minnesota: Evidence for Rapid Climate Change in the North-Central United States.*

6. See Aikens, "Environmental Archaeology in the Western United States"; Stoltman and Baerreis, "Evolution of Human Ecosystems in the Eastern United States."

7. Solecki, "Prehistory in the Shanidar Valley, Northern Iraq"; Solecki, "Shanidar IV: A Neanderthal Flower Burial in Northern Iraq."

8. Rowley-Conwy, "Was There a Neanderthal Religion?"

9. Dimbleby, *Palynology of Archaeological Sites.*

10. Finlayson, Byrne, and McAndrews, "Iroquoian Settlement and Subsistence Patterns near Crawford Lake, Ontario"; Byrne and McAndrews, "Precolumbine Purslane (*Portulaca oleracea* L.) in the New World."

11. Hebda and Mathewes, "Holocene History of Cedar and Native Indians of the North American Pacific Coast."

12. Wendorf et al., "New Radiocarbon Dates on the Cereals from Wadi Kubbaniya." See also Wendorf and Schild, *Prehistory of Wadi Kubbaniya,* vol. 2.

13. LaMarch, "Paleoclimatic Inferences from Long Tree-Ring Record"; Fritts, *Tree-Rings and Climate,*; Fritts, Lofgren, and Gordon, "Variations in Climate Since 1602 as Reconstructed from Tree-Rings"; Pilcher and Hughes, "Potential of Dendrochronology for the Study of Climate Change."

14. Schwengruber, *Tree Rings.*

15. Rapp and Mulholland, *Phytolith Systematics;* Piperno and Pearsall, *Current Research in Phytolith Analysis.*

16. Pearsall, Gilbert, and Martin, "Late Pleistocene Fossils of Natural Trap Cave, Wyoming, and the Climate Model of Extinction."

17. Rovner, "Floral History by the Back Door."

18. Fox, Perez-Perez, and Juan, "Dietary Information Through the Examination of Plant Phytoliths on the Enamel Surface of Human Dentition."

19. Hohn and Hellerman, "Diatoms."

20. Blinn, Hevly, and Davis, "Continuous Holocene Record of Diatom Stratigraphy, Paleohydrology, and Anthropogenic Activity in a Spring-Mound in the Southwestern United States."

21. Bradbury, "Diatom Stratigraphy and Human Settlement."

22. Palacios-Fest, "Nonmarine Ostracod Shell Chemistry from Ancient Hohokam Irrigation Canals in Central Arizona."

23. Mergard, "Late Quaternary Cladocera of Lake Zeribar, Western Iran."

24. Evans, *Land Snails in Archaeology.*

25. Jones and Fisher, "Environmental Factors Affecting Prehistoric Shellfish Utilization."

26. Elias, *Insects and Their Environments.*

27. Buckland and Kenward, "Thorne Moor."

28. Elias, "Timing and Intensity of Environmental Changes During the Paleoindian Period in Western North America."

29. Steadman and Miller, "California Condor Associated with Spruce-Pine Woodland in the Late Pleistocene in New York."

30. Pregill, "Body Size of Insular Lizards."

31. Casteel, "On the Remains of Fish Scales from Archaeological Sites"; and Casteel, *Fish Remains in Archaeology and Paleoenvironmental Studies.*

32. Van Neer, "Fish Remains from the Last Interglacial at Bir Tarfawi."

33. Wells and Jorgensen, "Pleistocene Wood Rat Middens and Climate Change in Mojave Desert"; see also Betancourt, Van Defender, and Martin, *Packrat Middens.*

34. Shackleton, "Stratigraphy and Chronology of the KRM Deposits."

35. For age estimates of the marine isotope record, see Martinson et al., "Age Dating and the Orbital Theory of the Ice Ages."

36. Ortloff and Kolata, "Climate and Collapse."

37. Wright, "Environmental Determinism in Near Eastern Prehistory"; Willey and Phillips, *Method and Theory in American Archaeology.*

38. Clark, *Excavations at Starr Carr.*

39. Langbein and Schumm, "Yield of Sediment in Relation to Mean Annual Precipitation."

40. Bettis, *Archaeological Geology of the Archaic Period in North America.* The volume contains the following articles: J. P. Albanese and G. C. Frison, "Cultural and Landscape Change During the Middle Holocene, Rocky Mountain Area, Wyoming and Montana"; C. R. Ferring, "Middle Holocene Environments, Geology, and Archaeology in the Southern Plains"; R. D. Mandel, "Geomorphic Controls of the Archaic Record in the Central Plains of the United States"; J. A. Artz, "Geological Contexts of the Early and Middle Holo-

cene Archaeological Record in North Dakota and Adjoining Areas of the Northern Plains"; E. A. Bettis III and E. R. Hajic, "Landscape Development and the Location of Evidence of Archaic Cultures in the Upper Midwest"; C. Chapdelaine and P. LaSalle, "Physical Environments and Cultural Systems in the Saint Lawrence Valley, 8000 to 3000 B.P."; and M. J. Stright, "Archaic Period Sites on the Continental Shelf of North America."

Chapter 5: Raw Materials and Resources

1. For a detailed summary of the use of minerals and rocks in ancient Egypt, see Lucas, *Ancient Egyptian Materials and Industries.*

2. Luedtke, *An Archaeologist's Guide to Chert and Flint.*

3. Wen and Jing, "Chinese Neolithic Jade."

4. Harlow, "The Maya Rediscovered Hard Rock" (contains an insert by Hammond, "Precious Stone of Grace," 8).

5. Desautels, *The Jade Kingdom.*

6. Francis, "Simojovel, Mexico"; Poinar, "The Amber Ark"; Mustoe, "Eocene Amber from the Pacific Coast of North America."

7. Ferguson provides an annotated list of prehistoric mica mines in the southern Appalachians in "Prehistoric Mica Mines in the Southern Appalachians."

8. Aufderheide et al., "Lead Exposure in Italy."

9. Pendergast, "Ancient Maya Mercury."

10. Walthall, *Galena and Aboriginal Trade in Eastern North America.*

11. Kaeser, "Fossils and Concretions from Coastal New York Sites."

12. Dittert, "Minerals and Rocks at Archaeological Sites."

13. Ball, *The Mining of Gems and Ornamental Stones by American Indians.*

14. Heizer and Treganza, "Mines and Quarries of the Indians of California."

Chapter 6: Provenance Studies

1. Thomas, "The Source of the Stones of Stonehenge."

2. Thorpe, Williams-Thorpe, Jenkins and Watson, "The Geological Sources and Transport of the Bluestones of Stonehenge, Wiltshire, UK."

3. Harbottle, "Neutron Activation Analysis in Archaeological Chemistry."

4. Heizer et al., "The Colossi of Memnon Revisited."

5. Shackley, "Sources of Archaeological Obsidian in the Greater American Southwest."

6. Williams-Thorpe, "Obsidian in the Mediterranean and the Near East."

7. Burton and Krinsley, "Obsidian Provenance Determination by Back-Scattered Electron Imaging"; see also Kayani and McDonnell, "The Potential of Scanning Electron Microscope Techniques for Non-Destructive Obsidian Characterization and Hydration-Rim Research."

8. Bakewell, "Petrographic and Geochemical Source-Modeling of Volcanic Lithics from Archaeological Contexts."

9. Julig, Pavlish, and Hancock, "INAA Provenance Studies of Lithic Materials from the Western Great Lakes Region of North America."

10. Herz, "Isotopic Analysis of Marble."

11. Dye and Dickinson, "Sources of Sand Tempers in Prehistoric Tongan Pottery."

12. Knapp and Cherry, *Provenience Studies and Bronze Age Cyprus.*

13. Rapp, Henrickson, and Allert, "Native Copper Sources of Artifact Copper in Pre-Columbian North America"; see also Rapp, Allert, and Peters, "The Origins of Copper in Three Northern Minnesota Sites."

14. G. Rapp, Jr., J. Allert, V. Vitali, and E. Henrickson, "The Determination of Sources of North American Artifact Copper Using Trace-Element Patterns." Unpublished manuscript.

15. Rapp, "On the Origins of Copper and Bronze Alloying"; Rapp, "Determining the Origins of Sulfide Smelting."

16. A thorough history of tin in antiquity is available in Penhallurick, *Tin in Antiquity.*

17. Farquhar, Walthall, and Hancock, "Eighteenth Century Lead Smelting in Central North America."

18. Farquhar and Fletcher, "The Provenience of Galena from Archaic/Woodland Sites in Northeastern North America."

19. Hoard et al., "Neutron Activation Analysis of Stone from the Chadron Formation and a Clovis Site on the Great Plains"; Church, "Comment on 'Neutron Activation Analysis of Stone from the Chadron Formation and a Clovis Site on the Great Plains' by Hoard et al."; Hoard, Holen, Glascock, and Neff, "Additional Com-

ments on Neutron Activation Analysis of Stone from the Great Plains: Reply to Church."

20. Tobey, *Trace Element Investigations of Maya Chert from Belize.*

21. Vaughn, "Petrographic Analysis of the Early Cycladic Wares from Akrotiri, Thera."

22. Stoltman, "Ceramic Petrography as a Technique for Documenting Cultural Interaction."

Chapter 7: Estimating Age in the Archaeological Record

1. De Geer, "Early Man and Geochronology"; de Geer, *Geochronology Suecica Principles.*

2. Antevs, *Retreat of the Last Ice Sheet in Eastern Canada;* Antevs, "Telerrelation of Varves, Radiocarbon Chronology, and Geology"; Antevs, "Varve and Radiocarbon Chronologies Appraised by Pollen Data."

3. An excellent presentation is provided in Bradbury, Platt, and Dean, *Elk Lake, Minnesota.*

4. For North America, see Feng, Johnson, Sprowl, and Lu, "Loess Accumulation and Soil Formation in Central Kansas, United States, During the Past 400,000 Years"; for Europe, see Rousseau and Puisseguir, "350,000 Year Climatic Record from the Loess Sequence of Achenheim, Alsace, France"; for China, see Kukla, "Loess Stratigraphy in Central China," and Kukla and An, "Loess Stratigraphy in Central China."

5. Johnson and Logan, "Geoarchaeology of the Kansas River Basin, Central Great Plains."

6. Mandel, "Soils and Holocene Landscape Evolution on Central and Southwestern Kansas"; Bettis, "Soil Morphologic Properties and Weathering Zone Characteristics as Age Indicators in Holocene Alluvium in the Upper Midwest"; Hajic, *Koster Site Archaeology I.*

7. For example, Foit, Mehringer, and Sheppard, "Age, Distribution, and Stratigraphy of Glacier Peak Tephra in Eastern Washington and Western Montana, United States."

8. Some examples are: Mehringer and Foit, "Volcanic Ash Dating of the Clovis Cache at East Wenatchee, Washington"; Davis and Greiser, "Indian Creek Paleoindians"; Davis, "Late Pleistocene to Mid-Holocene Adaptations at Indian Creek, West-Central Montana Rockies."

9. Douglass, "Climate Cycles and Tree Growth"; Douglass, "Dating Pueblo Bonito and Other Ruins in the Southwest."

10. Bonde and Christensen, "Dendrochronological Dating of the Viking Age Ship Burials in Oseberg, Gokstad and Tune, Norway."

11. Wendorf, Krieger, Albritton, and Stewart, *The Midland Discovery*, 100.

12. Whitley and Dorn, "New Perspectives on the Clovis vs. Pre-Clovis Controversy."

13. Brooks et al., "Dating Pleistocene Archaeological Sites by Protein Diagenesis in Ostrich Eggshell"; Miller, "Chronology of Hominid Occupation at Bir Tarfawi and Bir Sahara East, Based on the Epimerization of Isoleucine in Ostrich Eggshells."

14. Clark and McFadyen Clark, *Batza Tena.*

15. Michels, "Testing Stratigraphy and Artifact Reuse through Obsidian Hydration Dating."

16. Michels, "Obsidian Dating and East African Archaeology."

17. Hammond, "Obsidian Hydration Dating of Tecep Phase Occupation at Nohmul, Belize."

18. Hall and York, "Applicability of $^{40}Ar/^{39}Ar$ Dating to Younger Volcanics."

19. Walter et al., "Laser-Fusion $^{40}Ar/^{39}Ar$ Dating of Bed I, Olduvai Gorge, Tanzania."

20. Schwarcz, "Absolute Age Determination of Archaeological Sites by Uranium Series Dating of Travertines"; Schwarcz and Gascoyne, "Uranium-series Dating of Quaternary Sediments"; Schwarcz, "Site of Vertesszollos, Hungary"; Schwarcz and Morawska, "Uranium Series Dating of Carbonates from Bir Tarfawi and Bir Sahara East"; Stearns, "Uranium-Series Dating and the History of Sea Level"; Hennig, Grun, and Brunnacker, "Speleothems, Travertines and Paleoclimates."

21. Bischoff, Garcia, and Straus, "Uranium-Series Isochron Dating at El Castillo Cave."

22. Libby, *Radiocarbon Dating;* Terasmae, "Radiocarbon Dating"; Rucklidge, "Radioisotope Detection and Dating with Particle Accelerators"; Hester, "Significance of Accelerator Dating."

23. Himalayan, Fairbanks, and Zindler, "Calibration of the ^{14}C Timescale over the Past 30,000 Years Using Mass Spectrometric U/Th Ages from Barbados Corals." The relevance of this difference is addressed in Tushingham and Peltier, "Implications of the Radiocarbon Timescale for Ice-Sheet Chronology and Sea-Level Change."

24. Gleadow, "Fission Track Age of the KBS Tuff and Associated Hominids in Northern Kenya"; Naeser, "Fission-Track Dating."

25. See Eighmy and Sternberg, *Archaeomagnetic Dating.*

26. Eighmy and Howard, "Direct Dating of Prehistoric Canal Sediments Using Archaeomagnetism."

27. Barmore, "Turkish Mosque Orientation and the Secular Variation of the Magnetic Declination."

28. For comprehensive reviews of TL methodology, see Berger, *Dating Quaternary Events by Luminescence*; Aitken, *Thermoluminescence Dating*; Lamothe, Driemanis, Morency, and Raukas, "Thermoluminescence Dating of Quaternary Sediments"; Wintle and Aitken, "Thermoluminescence Dating of Burnt Flint"; Balescu, Pacman, and Wintle, "Chronological Separation of Interglacial Raised Beaches from Northwestern Europe Using Thermoluminescence"; Balescu, Dupuis, and Quinlif, "TL Stratigraphy of Pre-Weichselian Loess from NW Europe Using Feldspar Grains"; Wintle, Shackleton, and Lautridou, "Thermoluminescence Dating of Loess Deposition and Soil Formation in Normandy"; Ningawa et al., "Thermoluminescence Measurements of a Calcite Shell for Dating."

29. Mercier et al., "TL Dates of Burnt Flints from Jelinek's Excavations at Tabun and Their Implications."

30. Rendell and Dennell, "Thermoluminescence Dating of an Upper Pleistocene Site, Northern Pakistan."

31. See, for example, Wintle, Shackleton, and Lautridou, "Thermoluminescence Dating of Periods of Loess Deposition and Soil Formation in Normandy."

32. Lang and Wagner, "Infrared Stimulated Luminescence Dating of Archaeosediments."

33. A review of techniques is presented in Wintle, "Archaeologically Relevant Dating Techniques for the Next Century."

Chapter 8: Geologic Mapping, Remote Sensing, and Surveying

1. Miller and Westerback, *Interpretation of Topographic Maps*; Upton, *Landforms and Topographic Maps.*

2. Hammond, "Analysis of Properties in Landform Geography."

3. Wagstaff, *Landscape and Culture.*

4. Kraft et al., "Pass at Thermopylae, Greece."

5. Harley and Woodward, *History of Cartography*, vol. 1.

6. Oldfield et al., "Role of Mineral Magnetic Measurements in Archaeology."

7. Aspinall, "New Developments in Geophysical Prospection"; Aitken and Milligan, "Ground-Probing

Radar in Archaeology—Practicalities and Problems"; Bevan, "Search for Graves"; Clark, "Archaeogeophysical Prospecting on Alluvium"; Scollar, Tabbaugh, Hesse, and Herzog, *Archaeological Prospecting and Remote Sensing*; Tite and Mullins, "Enhancement of the Magnetic Susceptibility of Soils on Archaeological Sites"; Vaughn, "Ground-Penetrating Radar Surveys Used in Archaeological Investigations"; Wynn, "Archaeological Prospection."

8. Roosevelt, *Mound Builders of the Amazon*; Dalan, *Landscape Modification at the Cahokia Mounds Site.*

9. Black and Johnston, "Test of Magnetometry as an Aid to Archaeology."

10. Weymouth and Huggins, "Geophysical Surveying of Archaeological Sites."

11. Van Andel and Lianos, "High-Resolution Seismic Reflection Profiles for the Reconstruction of Postglacial Transgressive Shorelines."

12. Van Andel and Sutton, *Landscape and People of the Franchthi Region.*

13. Custer, Eveleigh, Klemas, and Wells, "Application of Landsat Data and Synoptic Remote Sensing to Predictive Models for Prehistoric Archaeological Sites."

14. McCauley et al., "Subsurface Valleys and Geoarchaeology of the Eastern Sahara Revealed by Shuttle Radar."

15. A thorough history of archaeological coring in North America and an introduction to techniques and procedures are presented by Stein, "Coring Archaeological Sites." See also Stein, "Coring in CRM and Archaeology," and Schuldenrein, "Coring and the Identity of Cultural-Resource Environments."

16. Jing, Rapp, and Gao, "Holocene Landscape Evolution and Its Impact on the Neolithic and Bronze Age Sites in the Shangqiu Area, Northern China."

17. Bridgeland, *Quaternary of the Thames*; see also Gibbard, *Pleistocene History of the Lower Thames Valley.*

18. Eidt, "Theoretical and Practical Considerations in the Analysis of Anthrosols." For the analysis of phosphate fractions, see pp. 183–85; Walker, "Phosphate Survey."

19. Eidt, *Advances in Abandoned Settlement Analysis.*

20. Dean, "Determination of Carbonate and Organic Matter in Calcareous Sediments and Sedimentary Rocks by Loss-on-Ignition."

21. For extensive coverage of the archaeological uses of GIS the reader is referred to Lock and Stancic, *Archaeology and Geographical Information Systems.*

22. Stein and Linse, *Effects of Scale on Archaeological and Geoscientific Perspectives.*

Chapter 9: Construction, Destruction, Site Preservation, and Conservation

1. Zangger, "Prehistoric Coastal Environments in Greece."

2. Doolittle, *Canal Irrigation in Prehistoric Mexico.*

3. In his *Ancient Mining*, Shepherd presents details on ancient mining practices throughout the Old World.

4. *Wall Paintings of the Tomb of Nefertari: Scientific Studies for Their Conservation.*

5. Evans, *Palace of Minos at Knossos*, Vol. IV, Part II.

6. Bolt, *Earthquakes.*

7. Reimnitz and Marshall, "Effects of the Alaska Earthquake and Tsunami on Recent Deltaic Sediments."

8. Sims, "Earthquake-Induced Structures in Sediments of Van Normsan Lake, San Fernando, California"; Sims, "Records of Prehistoric Earthquakes in Sedimentary Deposits in Lakes."

9. Doig, "2300-Year History of Seismicity from Silting Events in Lake Tadoussac, Charlevoix, Quebec."

10. Niemi and Ben-Avraham, "Evidence for Jericho Earthquakes from Slumped Sediments of the Jordan River Delta in the Dead Sea."

11. Street and Nuttli, "Central Mississippi Earthquakes of 1811–1812."

12. Saucier, "Effects of the New Madrid Earthquake Series in the Mississippi Alluvial Valley"; Saucier, "Evidence for Episodic Sand-Blow Activity During the 1811–1812 New Madrid (Missouri) Earthquake Series"; Saucier, "Geoarchaeological Evidence of Strong Prehistoric Earthquakes in the New Madrid (Missouri) Seismic Zone."

13. Thompson, "Holocene Tectonic Activity in West Africa Dated by Archaeological Methods."

14. Hough, "Earthquakes and Tribal Movements in the Southwest."

15. Martinez Solarez, Lopez Arroyo, and Mezcua, "Isoseismal Map of the 1755 Lisbon Earthquake Obtained from Spanish Data."

16. Ambraseys and Melville, *History of Persian Earthquakes.*

17. Karcz and Kafri, "Evaluation of Supposed Archaeoseismic Damage in Israel."

18. Woolley, "Excavations at Ur, 1928–1929."

19. Mallowan, "Noah's Flood Reconsidered," in *Early Mesopotamia and Iran.*

20. Dundes, *Flood Myth.*

21. Quoted in Simkin and Fiske, *Krakatau 1883*, 91.

22. Sheets and McKee, *Archaeology, Volcanism, and Remote Sensing in the Arenal Region, Costa Rica.*

23. Gilbert, "Topographic Features of Lake Shores."

24. Gatto and Doe, *Historical Bank Recession at Selected Sites Along Corps of Engineers Reservoirs.*

25. Readers are referred to Amoroso and Fassina, *Stone Decay and Conservation.*

Glossary

aggradation The process of building up a surface by deposition of sediment

alkaline earth Sediments and/or soils containing a high proportion of alkaline cations like sodium and potassium

amphibole An important rock-forming mineral group of ferromagnesian silicates found in granitic rocks

anoxic Lacking oxygen

anthrosol A soil whose main characteristics are the result of human activity

aragonite A carbonate mineral with the same composition ($CaCO_3$) as calcite

arroyo Steep-sided, flat-bottomed gully in an arid region through which a stream flows only after very heavy rainfall (usually seasonally)

articlasts Objects once used by humans that are found in sedimentologic situations far removed from their original context. Artifacts that are not in primary or behavioral context.

authigenic Formed or generated in place. Rock constituents and minerals that have not been transported or that were formed on the spot where they are found.

bajada The surface of a system of coalesced alluvial fans

bases (chemical) Any of a large class of compounds, including the hydroxides and oxides of metals, with the ability to react with acids to form salts

bioturbation The churning and mixing of a sediment by organisms

caldera A large, basin-shaped depression resulting from the explosion or collapse of the center of a volcano

calcrete A conglomerate consisting of surficial sand and gravel cemented into a hard mass by calcium carbonate precipitated from solution and redeposited through the agency of infiltrating waters

capillary rise The tendency of a fluid to rise within narrow passages because of surface tension

cation A positively charged ion

clastic Fragmental rock material that has been mechanically transported and deposited in a sedimentary environment

colloidal Pertaining to a suspension of finely divided particles in a continuous medium

crevasse splay A deep fissure or crack in a valley glacier that runs parallel to the direction of flow in the center of the glacier but curves toward the margin downstream

crinoid An echinoderm with a disk-shaped or globular body, characterized by the presence of a stem (more common in fossils than in living forms).

cross bedding Creation through deposition of inclined beds in a sedimentary rock. Formed by currents of wind or water in the direction in which the bed slopes downward.

cryoturbation Stirring, churning, and related disturbances of soil and surficial sediment created by frost action

cummulic Describes a soil that accumulates laterally as the landform moves

deflation Removal by strong winds

deposition The accumulation of sediments by either physical or chemical processes

diagenesis The physical and chemical change undergone by a sediment during lithification and compaction

diatom A microscopic one-celled plant that grows in both marine and fresh waters. It secretes walls of silica in a variety of geometric forms, depending on the species. These silica forms accumulate in sediments in great numbers.

diatomite A siliceous chertlike sediment formed from the hard parts of diatoms

distal Anatomically located far from the origin or line of attachment, as an end of a bone

dosimetry The process of measuring the dosage of radiation

edaphic Relating to any soil characteristic that affects plant growth, like acidity or alkalinity

eluvial Deposited by the action of wind

eluviation Internal movement of soil particles when rainfall exceeds evaporation

endogenic Derived from within; deposits originating from within the rocks that contain them

epipedon A soil horizon that forms at the upper end of the soil profile. An epipedon can include the dark *A* horizon as well as the illuvial *B* horizon when organic matter extends from the surface through the *B* horizon.

eustatic Relating to a worldwide change of sea level

exogenic, exogenetic Pertaining to materials or processes that originate at or near the surface of the earth

facies A portion of a rock unit with a distinctive group of characteristics (mineral assemblage or fossil assemblage, for example) that differs from other parts of the same rock unit

fen carr A pool in a waterlogged or marshy ground containing decaying alkaline vegetation

ferric Pertains to iron with a +3 valence; Fe^{3+}

ferrous Pertains to iron with a +2 valence; Fe^{2+}

flux In metallurgy, material added in smelting to form a fluid slag

fractionated Pertains to a homogenous chemical material that has been separated into its components

gamma A unit of magnetic field strength, symbolized by γ

geofacts Geologic objects that have the appearance of artifacts

glaciofluvial Deposited by glacial meltwater

gleyed, gleying Mottled: in soils, caused by partial oxidation and reduction of the soil's ferric iron compounds

gossan An iron oxide product created by weathering that overlies a sulfide deposit

hardpan A layer of hard subsoil or clay, produced when precipitation of insoluble materials like silica, iron oxide, or calcium carbonate cements the particles

humification The process of development of humus or humic acids, essentially by slow oxidation

illuvial Pertains to a soil horizon that has been subjected to illuviation

illuviation The deposition in an underlaying soil layer of colloids, soluble salts, and mineral particles that are transported from an overlying soil layer

isotropic Pertaining to a substance in which the magnitude of a physical property does not vary with direction within the substance

jointing Creation of a fracture in a rock body where no movement has occurred

lag Coarse sediment left behind the surface by wind action

limonite A general term for brown hydrous iron oxides, chiefly the mineral goethite

lithification The process by which unconsolidated sediments are converted to rock

lithofacies A lateral subdivision of a stratigraphic unit, distinguished from other adjacent subdivisions on the basis of lithologic characteristics

loess Fine-grained, loosely consolidated sediments, usually formed from wind-deposited silts

mafic Pertaining to low-silica igneous rocks that contain an abundance of iron-magnesium silicates

magma Molten silicate originating within the earth from which igneous rocks crystallize

magnetic susceptibility The magnetic permeability of a medium relative to that of a vacuum; it will be positive for a paramagnetic or ferromagnetic medium and negative for a diamagnetic medium

marker horizons Easily recognized strata whose distinctive characteristics allow them to serve as a reference or datum

matrix Relatively fine-grained material in which coarser materials are embedded

matte In metallurgy, an intermediate-stage product in the smelting of copper-sulfide ores composed of iron and copper sulfides

moraine Landform produced by an accumulation of glacial till

outwash A sediment deposited by meltwater streams from a glacier

oxbow lake Geographic feature created when erosion on the outside of a meander loop causes a river to meet itself, and it abandons the water-filled meander, which becomes the oxbow lake

oxidation A chemical reaction in which one or more electrons are removed from an atom, making its charge more positive

oxidized The result when an element combines with oxygen or in some other way gives up electrons

paramagnetic Denoting a substance in which an induced magnetic field is in the same direction as and greater in strength than the magnetizing field but weaker than in ferromagnetic materials

pediment A planar, sloping rock surface forming a ramp up to the front of a mountain range in an arid region, which may be covered by local alluvium

perched The condition in which the upper surface of a local zone of saturation lies above the regional water table

periglacial Processes, climates, and topographic features that are either on the immediate margins of former or existing glaciers or are influenced by cold temperatures

pH A measure of the alkalinity or acidity of a solution, numerically equal to 7 for neutral solutions. Alkalinity is indicated by numbers above 7, acidity by numbers below 7.

phenocryst A large crystal surrounded by a finer matrix in a porphyry

phylogenetic Pertaining to the evolutionary development of a species of plant or animal

pisé Rammed earth: a building material made by ramming or pounding earth with a high clay or silt content into a durable structure

playa The flat floor of a closed basin in an arid region. It may be occupied by an intermittent lake.

pluvial Caused by, or pertaining to rain. A period of increased rainfall and decreased evaporation.

point bars Deposits of sediment on the inner banks of meanders; formed because the stream velocity is lower against the inner bank

polje An interior valley; an elongated basin with a flat floor and steep enclosing walls found in karst regions

proglacial Features produced by glacier ice immediately in front of the glacier or ice sheet

progradational sequence A sequence that shows prograding or regression of sediments, a process that results in an upward-fining sequence of sediments

prograding When a deposit is being built forward or outward by deposition and accumulation

pyroclastic Formed by the accumulation of fragments of volcanic rock scattered by volcanic explosions

pyroxene An iron and magnesium silicate mineral that occurs primarily in mafic igneous rocks

rare-earth elements Chemical elements with the atomic numbers 57 through 71; they were discovered as oxides (earths) in rare minerals

reducing atmosphere (1) In soils, an atmosphere that promotes chemical elements to lose electrons; (2) In ceramics, a firing atmosphere that is oxygen poor

refractory Having the ability to withstand high temperatures without melting. In ceramics, refractory materials are usually high in alumina and silica.

regression The retreat or withdrawal of water from a land area

retrograding When a coastline is being eroded by wave action

sandblow A patch of coarse sandy sediment or soil denuded of vegetation by wind action

sand dike A sedimentary dike consisting of sand that has been squeezed or injected upward into a fissure

sand pipe A tubular cavity in sedimentary rocks filled with sand and gravel

scarp A steep slope; cliff

seiche A wave that oscillates in lakes, bays, or gulfs

septarian Pertaining to an irregular polygonal system of cracks occurring in some rock concretions

sheet flood A broad expanse of moving storm water that spreads as a continuous sheet over a large area rather than being concentrated into well-defined channels

shotcrete A mixture of portland cement, sand, and water applied by pneumatic pressure as a sealing agent

slag The vitreous mass formed as a part of the smelting process

slickensides A smoothly striated rock surface that results from friction during movement along a fault plane

slip A suspension of clay in water that has the consistency of cream; it is applied to the surface of pottery as a decoration

slumping A collapse of unlithified sediments or soils caused by gravity

spall A fragment removed from the surface of a rock by weathering, in particular, a relatively thin piece of rock produced by exfoliation

stadial Pertaining to or formed during a glacial substage that is marked by glacial readvance

taiga Subarctic evergreen forest of Siberia and similar regions elsewhere in Eurasia and North America

talus A pile or sheet of loose rock fragments accumulated at the base of a steep slope

taphonomic, taphonomy Pertaining to a branch of paleoecology concerned with the manner of burial and preservation of plant and animal remains. Artifact taphonomy is the study of archaeological site formation processes.

tectonism The regional or global deformation of the earth's crust

tell A mound site formed by successive human occupations over a considerable period of time

tephra Rock material expelled by a volcanic explosion

terrigenous Pertaining to, or derived from the land (as opposed to marine)

till Unstratified and relatively unsorted glacial deposits

transgressive, transgression Spread or extension of the sea over land areas

tuff A general term for all consolidated pyroclastic rocks, that is, rocks formed of particles originating from a volcanic explosion

turbation Stirring, mixing, or other modifications of a sediment or soil by unspecified agents

ultramafic Pertaining to igneous rocks composed mainly of iron-magnesium silicates

uniformitarianism The concept that ancient rocks can be understood in terms of the processes presently operating on the earth; sometimes summed up as "the present is the key to the past"

ventifacts Rocks that exhibit the effects of sandblasting or "snowblasting" on their surfaces

vesicular A rock texture characterized by abundant vesicles (voids) caused by gas bubbles that occurred when the rock was fluid

wadi A valley, gully, or river bed that remains dry except in the rainy season

Bibliography

Abbott, C. C. "Paleolithic Man: The Last Word." *Science* 20 (1892): 344–45.

Acher, R. "Time's Arrow and the Archaeology of Contemporary Community." In *Settlement Archaeology*, ed. K. C. Chang, 43–53. Palo Alto, Calif.: National Press Books, 1968.

Aikens, C. M. "Environmental Archaeology in the Western United States." In *Late-Quaternary Environments of the United States. Volume 2: The Holocene*, ed. H. E. Wright, Jr., 239–51. London: Longman, 1983.

Aitken, M. J. *Thermoluminescence Dating*. New York: Academic Press, 1985.

Aitken, M. J., and R. Milligan. "Ground-Probing Radar in Archaeology: Practicalities and Problems." *Field Archaeologist* 16 (1992): 288–91.

Alexander, J. "A Color Chart for Organic Matter." *Crop Soils* 21 (1969): 15–17.

Allen, J. R. L. "A Quantitative Technique for Assessing the Roundness of Pottery Shards in Water Currents." *Geoarchaeology* 4(2) (1987): 143–55.

Ambraseys, N. N., and C. P. Melville. *A History of Persian Earthquakes*. Cambridge: Cambridge University Press, 1982.

Amoroso, G. G., and V. Fassina. *Stone Decay and Conservation: Atmospheric Pollution, Cleaning, Consolidation and Protection*. Materials Science Monographs 11. New York: Elsevier, 1983.

Antevs, E. "Climate and Early Man in the Southwest." In *Early Man*, ed. G. G. MacCurdy, Philadelphia: Lippincott, 1937.

Antevs, E. "Geologic Climate Dating in the West." *American Antiquity* 20 (1955): 317–35.

Antevs, E. "The Great Basin, with Emphasis on Glacial and Postglacial Times." *University of Utah Bulletin* 38 (1948): 20.

Antevs, E. "The Occurrence of Flints and Extinct Animals in Pluvial Deposits near Clovis, New Mexico." Part 2: "Age of Clovis Lake Beds." *Proceedings of the Philadelphia Academy of Natural Science* 87 (1935): 304–11.

Antevs, E. *Retreat of the Last Ice Sheet in Eastern Canada*. Canada Department of Mines, Geological Survey Memoir 146. Ottawa: F. A. Acland, 1925.

Antevs, E. "Telerrelation of Varves, Radiocarbon Chronology, and Geology." *Journal of Geology* 62 (1954): 516–21.

Antevs, E. "Varve and Radiocarbon Chronologies Appraised by Pollen Data." *Journal of Geology* 63 (1955): 495–99.

Aschenbrenner, S., and S. R. B. Cooke. "Screening and Gravity Concentration; Recovery of Small-Scale Remains." In *Excavations at Nichoria in Southwest Greece. Volume 1: Site, Environs and Techniques*, ed. G. R. Rapp, Jr., and S. E. Aschenbrenner. Minneapolis: University of Minnesota Press, 1978.

Ashton, N. M., J. Cook, S. G. Lewis, and J. Rose, eds. *High Lodge: Excavations by G. De G. Sieveking, 1962–68, and J. Cook, 1988*. London: British Museum Press, 1992.

Aspinall, A. "New Developments in Geophysical Prospection." In *New Developments in Archaeological Science*, ed. A. M. Pollard. *Proceedings of the British Academy* 77 (1992): 233–44.

Atkinson, R. J. C. "Resistivity Surveying and Archaeology." In *The Scientist and Archaeology*, ed. E. Pyddoke. London: Phoenix House, 1963.

Aufderheide, A. C., et al. "Lead Exposure in Italy: 800 B.C.–700 A.D." *International Journal of Anthropology* 7 (1992): 9–15.

Bakewell, E. F. "Petrographic and Geochemical Source-Modeling of Volcanic Lithics from Archaeological Contexts: A Case Study from British Camp, San Juan Island, Washington." *Geoarchaeology* 11(2) (1996): 119–40.

Balescu, S., Ch. Dupuis, and Y. Quinlif. "TL Stratigraphy of Pre-Weichselian Loess from NW Europe

Using Feldspar Grains." *Quaternary Science Reviews* 7 (1988): 309–13.

Balescu S., S. C. Pacman, and A. G. Wintle. "Chronological Separation of Interglacial Raised Beaches from Northwestern Europe Using Thermoluminescence." *Quaternary Research* 35 (1991): 91–102.

Ball, S. H. "The Mining of Gems and Ornamental Stones by American Indians." Anthropological Papers 13. *Bureau of American Ethnology Bulletin* 128 (1941): 1–77.

Barmore, F. "Turkish Mosque Orientation and the Secular Variation of the Magnetic Declination." *Journal of Near Eastern Studies* 44(2) (1985): 81–98.

Barton, C. M., and G. A. Clark. "Cultural and Natural Formation Processes in Late Quaternary Cave and Rockshelters of Western Europe and the Near East." In *Formation Processes in Archaeological Context*, ed. P. Goldberg, D. T. Nash, and M. D. Petraglia, 33–52. Monographs in World Archaeology 17. Madison, Wis.: Prehistory Press, 1993.

Beazeley, A. "Surveys in Mesopotamia During the War." *Geographical Journal* 55(2) (1920): 109–12.

Behrensmeyer, A. K., and A. P. Hill. *Fossils in the Making: Vertebrate Taphonomy and Paleoecology*. Chicago: University of Chicago Press, 1980.

Berger, G. W. *Dating Quaternary Events by Luminescence*. Special Paper 227. Boulder, Colo.: Geological Society of America, 1988.

Betancourt, J. L., T. R. Van Devender, and P. S. Martin. *Packrat Middens: The Last 40,000 Years of Biotic Change*. Tucson: University of Arizona Press, 1990.

Bettis, E. A. III. "Soil Morphologic Properties and Weathering Zone Characteristics as Age Indicators in Holocene Alluvium in the Upper Midwest." In *Soils in Archaeology: Landscape Evolution and Human Occupation*, ed. V. T. Holliday, 119–44. Washington, D.C.: Smithsonian Institution Press, 1992.

Bettis, E. A. III, ed. *Archaeological Geology of the Archaic Period in North America*. Special Paper 297. Boulder, Colo.: Geological Society of America, 1995.

Bevan, B. "The Search for Graves." *Geophysics* 56(9) (1991): 1310–19.

Binford, L. *Bones: Ancient Men and Modern Myths*. New York: Academic Press, 1981.

Binford, L. "A Consideration of Archaeological Research Design." *American Antiquity* 29(4) (1964): 425–41.

Binford, L. *Debating Archaeology*. New York: Academic Press, 1989.

Binford, L. *In Pursuit of the Past: Decoding the Archaeological Record*. New York: Thames and Hudson, 1983.

Binford, L. *Theory Building in Archaeology*. New York: Academic Press, 1977.

Birkeland, P. W. *Soils and Geomorphology*. New York: Oxford University Press, 1984.

Bischoff, J. L., J. F. Garcia, and L. G. Straus. "Uranium-Series Isochron Dating at El Castillo Cave (Cantabria, Spain): The "Acheulian"/"Mousterian" Question." *Journal of Archaeological Science* 19 (1992): 49–62.

Black, G. A., and R. B. Johnston. "A Test of Magnetometry as an Aid to Archaeology." *American Antiquity* 28 (1962): 199–205.

Blinn, D. W., R. H. Hevly, and O. K. Davis. "Continuous Holocene Record of Diatom Stratigraphy, Paleohydrology, and Anthropogenic Activity in a Spring-Mound in the Southwestern United States." *Quaternary Research* 42 (1994): 197–205.

Bolt, B. *Earthquakes: A Primer*. San Francisco: Freeman, 1978.

Bonde, N., and A. E. Christensen. "Dendrochronological Dating of the Viking Age Ship Burials in Oseberg, Gokstad, and Tune, Norway." *Antiquity* 67 (1993): 575–84.

Bowers, P. M., R. Bonnichsen, and D. M. Hoch. "Flake Dispersal Experiments: Noncultural Transformation of the Archaeologic Record." *American Antiquity* 48 (1983): 553–72.

Bradbury, J. P. "Diatom Stratigraphy and Human Settlement." *Geological Society of America Special Paper* 171 (1975): 1–74.

Bradbury, J. P., J. Platt, and W. E. Dean, eds. *Elk Lake, Minnesota: Evidence for Rapid Climate Change in the North-Central United States*. Special Paper 276. Boulder, Colo.: Geological Society of America, 1993.

Brady, J. E., and G. Veni. "Man-Made and Pseudo-Karst Caves: The Implications of Subsurface Features Within Maya Centers." *Geoarchaeology* 7(2) (1992): 149–67.

Braidwood, R. J. "Means Towards an Understanding of Human Behavior Before the Present," and "The Old World: Post Paleolithic." In *The Identification of Non-Artifactual Archaeological Materials*, ed. W. W. Taylor, 14–15 and 26–27. National Academy of Sciences Publication 565. Washington, D.C.: National Academy of Sciences—National Research Council, 1957.

Bridgeland, D. R. *Quaternary of the Thames*. London: Chapman and Hall, 1994.

Brooks, A., et al. "Dating Pleistocene Archaeological Sites by Protein Diagenesis in Ostrich Eggshell." *Science* 247 (1990): 60–64.

Buckland, P. C., and H. K. Kenward. "Thorne Moor: A

Paleo-Ecological Study of a Bronze Age Site." *Nature* 241 (1973): 405–06.

Burton, J. H., and Krinsley, D. H. "Obsidian Provenance Determination by Back-Scattered Electron Imaging." *Nature* 326 (1987): 585–87.

Butzer, K. W. *Archaeology as Human Ecology.* New York: Cambridge University Press, 1982.

Butzer, K. W. "Cave Sediments, Upper Pleistocene Stratigraphy and Mousterian Facies in Cantabrian Spain." *Journal of Archaeological Science* 8 (1981): 133–83.

Butzer, K. W. "The Ecological Approach to Archaeology: Are We Really Trying?" *American Antiquity* 40 (1975): 106–11.

Butzer, K. W. *Environment and Archaeology: An Introduction to Pleistocene Geography.* Chicago: Aldine, 1964.

Butzer, K. W. "Holocene Alluvial Sequences: Problems of Dating and Correlation." In *Timescales in Geomorphology*, ed. J. Lewin, D. Davidson, and R. Cullingford. New York: John Wiley and Sons, 1980: 131–41.

Butzer, K. W. "Response to Presentation of the Archaeological Geology Division Award." *Bulletin of the Geological Society of America* 97 (1985): 1397–98.

Butzer, K. W. "Toward an Integrated Contextual Approach in Archaeology: A Personal View." *Journal of Archaeological Science* 5 (1978): 191–93.

Byrne, R., and J. H. McAndrews. "Precolumbian Purslane (*Portulaca oleracea* L.) in the New World." *Nature* 253 (1975): 726–27.

Caldwell, J. "The New American Archaeology." *Science* 129 (1959): 303–07.

Capper, J. E. *Archaeologia* 60 (1907), photographic plates 69 and 70.

Casteel, R. W. *Fish Remains in Archaeology and Paleoenvironmental Studies.* London: Academic Press, 1976.

Casteel, R. W. "On the Remains of Fish Scales from Archaeological Sites." *American Antiquity* 39 (1974): 557–59.

Childe, V. G. *The Most Ancient Near East: The Oriental Prelude to European Prehistory.* London: Kegan Paul, 1928.

Church, T. "Comment on 'Neutron Activation Analysis of Stone from the Chadron Formation and a Clovis Site on the Great Plains,' by Hoard et al. (1992)." *Journal of Archaeological Science* 22 (1995): 1–5.

Clark, A. J. "Archaeogeophysical Prospecting on Alluvium." In *Alluvial Archaeology in Britain*, ed. S. Needham and M. G. Macklin, 43–49. Oxbow Monographs 27. Oxford: Oxbow, 1992.

Clark, D. W., and A. McFadyen Clark. *Batza Tena, Trail to Obsidian: Archaeology at an Alaskan Obsidian Source.* Archaeological Survey of Canada, Mercury Series Paper 147. Hull, Quebec: Canadian Museum of Civilization, 1993.

Clark, J. D. "Human Ecology During the Pleistocene and Later Times in Africa South of the Sahara." *Current Anthropology* 1 (1960): 307–24.

Clark, G. *Excavations at Starr Carr.* 1952. Rpt. Cambridge: Cambridge University Press, 1954.

Clarke, D. *Analytical Archaeology.* New York: Academic Press, 1979.

Coleman, J. M. "Deltaic Evolution." In *Encyclopedia of Geomorphology*, ed. R. W. Fairbridge, 255–60. New York: Reinhold, 1968.

Coles, B., and J. Coles. *People of the Wetlands.* New York: Thames and Hudson, 1989.

Cornwall, I. W. *Soils for the Archaeologist.* London: Phoenix House, 1958.

Corte, A. E. "Particle Sorting by Repeated Freezing and Thawing." *Science* 142 (1963): 499–501.

Corte, A. E. "Vertical Migration of Particles in Front of a Freezing Plane." *Journal of Geophysical Research* 67 (1962): 1085–90.

Crawford, O. G. S. *Air-Photography for Archaeologists.* London: Ordnance Survey Professional Papers, n.s., 1929.

Crawford, O. G. S. "Air Survey and Archaeology." *Geographical Journal* 58 (1923): 324–66.

Culling, W. E. H. "Soil Creep and the Development of Hillside Slopes." *Journal of Geology* 71 (1963): 127–62.

Custer, J. F, T. Eveleigh, V. Klemas, and I. Wells. "Application of Landsat Data and Synoptic Remote Sensing to Predictive Models for Prehistoric Archaeological Sites: An Example from the Delaware Coastal Plain." *American Antiquity* 51(3) (1986): 572–88.

Dalan, R. A. "Landscape Modification at the Cahokia Mounds Site: Geophysical Evidence of Culture Change." Ph.D. diss., University of Minnesota, Minneapolis, 1993.

Daniel, G. *A Hundred and Fifty Years of Archaeology.* 2d ed. Cambridge: Harvard University Press, 1976.

Daniel, G., and C. Renfrew. *The Idea of Prehistory.* 2d ed. Edinburgh: Edinburgh University Press, 1988.

Davidson, D. A. "Erosion in Greece During the First and Second Millennia B.C." In *Timescales in Geomorphology*, ed. J. Lewin, D. A. Davidson, and R. Cullingford, 148–58. New York: John Wiley and Sons, 1980.

Davidson, D. A., and M. L. Shackley, eds. *Geoarchaeology.* Boulder, Colo.: Westview Press, 1976.

Davis, L. B. "Late Pleistocene to Mid-Holocene Adaptations at Indian Creek, West-Central Montana Rockies." *Current Research in the Pleistocene* 1 (1984): 9–10.

Davis, L. B., and S. T. Greiser. "Indian Creek Paleo-indians: Early Occupation of the Elkhorn Mountains' Southeast Flank, West-Central Montana." In *Ice Age Hunters of the Rockies*, ed. D. J. Stanford and J. S. Day, 225–83. Denver: Denver Museum of Natural History and the University Press of Colorado, 1992.

Dawson, C. "The Piltdown Skull." *Hastings and East Sussex Naturalist* 2 (1913): 73–82.

Dean, W. E., Jr. "Determination of Carbonate and Organic Matter in Calcareous Sediments and Sedimentary Rocks by Loss-on-Ignition: Comparison with Other Methods." *Journal of Sedimentary Petrology* 44 (1974): 242–48.

De Geer, G. "Early Man and Geochronology." In *Early Man*, ed. G. G. MacCurdy, 323–26. Philadelphia: Lippincott, 1937.

De Geer, G. *Geochronology Suecica Principles*. Stockholm: Almqvist and Wiksells, 1940.

De Morgan, J. *Prehistoric Man: A General Outline of Prehistory*. New York: Knopf, 1924.

Desautels, P. E. *The Jade Kingdom*. New York: Van Nostrand Reinhold, 1986.

Dimbleby, G. W. *The Palynology of Archaeological Sites*. London: Academic Press, 1985.

Dincauze, D. F. *The Neville Site: 8,000 Years at Amoskeag*. Peabody Museum Monographs 4. Cambridge: Harvard University Press, 1976.

Dincauze, D. F. "Strategies for Paleoenvironmental Reconstruction in Archaeology." In *Advances in Archaeological Method and Theory*, ed. M. B. Schiffer, 11:255–336. New York: Academic Press, 1987.

Dittert, A. E., Jr. "Minerals and Rocks at Archaeological Sites: Some Interpretations from Central Western New Mexico." *Arizona Archaeologist* 3 (1968): 1–16.

Doig, R. "2,300-Year History of Seismicity from Silting Events in Lake Tadoussac, Charlevoix, Quebec." *Geology* 18 (1990): 820–23.

Doolittle, W. E. *Canal Irrigation in Prehistoric Mexico: The Sequence of Technological Change*. Austin: University of Texas Press, 1990.

Douglass, A. E. *Climate Cycles and Tree Growth*. Washington, D.C.: Carnegie Institution of Washington, 1919.

Douglass, A. E. *Dating Pueblo Bonito and Other Ruins in the Southwest*. Contributed Technical Papers, Pueblo B Series 1. Washington, D.C.: National Geographic Society, 1935.

Dundes, A. *The Flood Myth*. Berkeley: University of California Press, 1988.

Dunnell, R. C. *Systematics in Prehistory*. New York: Free Press, 1971.

Dye, T. S., and W. R. Dickinson. "Sources of Sand Tempers in Prehistoric Tongan Pottery." *Geoarchaeology* 11(2) (1996): 141–64.

Eidt, R. C. *Advances in Abandoned Settlement Analysis: Application to Prehistoric Anthrosols in Columbia, South America*. Milwaukee: Center for Latin America, University of Wisconsin, 1984.

Eidt, R. C. "Theoretical and Practical Considerations in the Analysis of Anthrosols." In *Archaeological Geology*, ed. G. Rapp, Jr., and J. Gifford, 155–90. New Haven: Yale University Press, 1985.

Eighmy, J. L., and J. B. Howard. "Direct Dating of Prehistoric Canal Sediments Using Archaeomagnetism." *American Antiquity* 56(1) (1991): 88–102.

Eighmy, J. L., and R. S. Sternberg. *Archaeomagnetic Dating*. Tucson: University of Arizona Press, 1991.

Elias, S. A. *Insects and Their Environments*, Washington, D.C.: Smithsonian Institution Press, 1994.

Elias, S. A. "The Timing and Intensity of Environmental Changes During the Paleoindian Period in Western North America: Evidence from the Insect Fossil Record." In *Megafauna and Man*, ed. L. D. Agenbroad, J. I. Mead, and L. W. Nelson, 11–14. Scientific Papers, Volume 1. Hot Springs: Mammoth Site of Hot Springs, South Dakota, 1990.

Evans, A. *The Palace of Minos at Knossos*. Volume 4, Part 2. New York: Biblio and Tannen, 1964.

Evans, J. G. *Land Snails in Archaeology*. London: Seminar Press, 1972.

Faegri, K., P. E. Kaland, and K. Krzywinski. *Textbook of Pollen Analysis*. 4th ed. Chichester, U.K.: John Wiley and Sons, 1989.

Farquhar, R. M., and I. Fletcher. "The Provenience of Galena from Archaic/ Woodland Sites in Northeastern North America: Lead Isotope Evidence." *American Antiquity* 49 (1984): 774–85.

Farquhar, R. M., J. A. Walthall, and R. G. V. Hancock, "Eighteenth Century Lead Smelting in Central North America: Evidence from Lead Isotope and INAA Measurements." *Journal of Archaeological Science* 22 (1995): 639–48.

Farrand, W. R. "Former Shorelines in Western and Northern Lake Superior Basin." Ph.D Diss., University of Michigan. Ann Arbor: University Microfilm, 1960.

Farrand, W. R., and C. W. Dexler. "Late Wisconsin Man and Holocene History of the Lake Superior Basin." In *Quaternary Evolution of the Great Lakes*, ed. P. F. Karrow and P. E. Calkin, 17–32. Geological Association of Canada Special Paper 30. St. John's, Newfoundland: GAC Publications, 1985.

Fedele, F. G. "Sediments as Paleo-Land Segments: The Excavation Side of Study." In *Geoarchaeology*, ed. D. A.

Davidson and M. L. Shackley, 23–48. Boulder, Colo.: Westview Press, 1976.

Feng, Z. D., W. C. Johnson, D. R. Sprowl, and Y. Lu. "Loess Accumulation and Soil Formation in Central Kansas, United States, During the Past 400,000 Years." *Earth Surface Processes and Landforms* 19 (1994): 55–67.

Ferring, R. "Alluvial Pedology and Geoarchaeological Research." In *Soils in Archaeology*, ed. V. Holliday, 1–39. Washington, D.C.: Smithsonian Institution Press, 1992.

Ferring, R. Review of *Principles of Geoarchaeology: A North American Perspective*, by Michael R. Waters. *American Anthropologist* 96(1) (1994): 218–19.

Finlayson, W. D., A. R. Byrne, and J. H. McAndrews. "Iroquoian Settlement and Subsistence Patterns near Crawford Lake, Ontario." *Canadian Archaeological Association Bulletin* 5 (1973): 134–36.

Fladmark, K. R. "Microdebitage Analysis: Initial Considerations." *Journal of Archaeological Science* 9 (1982): 205–20.

Foit, F. F., Jr., P. J. Mehringer, Jr., and J. C. Sheppard. "Age, Distribution, and Stratigraphy of Glacier Peak Tephra in Eastern Washington and Western Montana, United States." *Canada Journal of Earth Sciences* 30 (1993): 535–52.

Foster, J. W., and J. W. Whitney. *Report on the Geology and Topography of a Portion of the Lake Superior Land District in the State of Michigan*. Number 69, Part 1: *Copper Lands*. Washington D.C.: House Executive Documents, 1850.

Fox, C. L., A. Perez-Perez, and J. Juan. "Dietary Information Through the Examination of Plant Phytoliths on the Enamel Surface of Human Dentition." *Journal of Archaeological Science* 21 (1994): 29–34.

Frere, J. "Account of Flint Weapons Discovered at Hoxne in Suffolk." *Archaeologia* 13 (1800): 204–05.

Fritts, H. C. *Tree-Rings and Climate*. London: Academic Press, 1976.

Fritts, H. C., G. R. Lofgren, and G. A. Gordon. "Variations in Climate Since 1602 as Reconstructed from Tree-Rings." *Quaternary Research* 12 (1979): 18–46.

Gatto, L. W., and W. W. Doe III. *Historical Bank Recession at Selected Sites Along Corps of Engineers Reservoirs*. Special Report 83-30. Hanover, N.H.: U.S. Army Cold Regions Research and Engineering Laboratory, 1983.

Geikie, J. *The Great Ice Age and Its Relation to the Antiquity of Man*. 2d ed. London: Daldy, Isbista, 1877.

Gibbard, P. L. *Pleistocene History of the Lower Thames Valley*. Cambridge: Cambridge University Press, 1994.

Gifford, D. P. "Taphonomy and Paleoecology: A Critical Review of Archaeology's Sister Disciplines." In *Advances in Archaeological Method and Theory*, ed. M. B. Schiffer, 4:365–438. New York: Academic Press, 1981.

Gifford, J. A., and G. Rapp, Jr. "The Early Development of Archaeological Geology in North America." In *Geologists and Their Ideas: A History of North American Geology*, ed. E. T. Drake and W. M. Jordon, 409–21. Boulder, Colo.: Geological Society of America, 1985.

Gifford, J. A., and G. Rapp, Jr. "History, Philosophy, and Perspectives." In *Archaeological Geology*, ed. G. Rapp, Jr., and J. A. Gifford, 1–23. New Haven: Yale University Press, 1985.

Gilbert, G. K. "The Topographic Features of Lake Shores." *Report of the Director of the U.S. Geological Survey* 5 (1884): 75–123.

Gladfelter, B. G. "Developments and Directions in Geoarchaeology." In *Advances in Archaeological Method and Theory*, ed. M. B. Schiffer, 4:343–64. New York: Academic Press, 1981.

Gladfelter, B. G. "Geoarchaeology: The Geomorphologist and Archaeology." *American Antiquity* 42(4) (1977): 519–38.

Gladfelter, B. G. "On the Interpretation of Archaeologic Sites in Alluvial Settings." In *Archaeological Sediments in Context*, ed. J. K. Stein and W. R. Farrand, 41–52. Orono: University of Maine, Center for the Study of Early Man, 1985.

Gladwin, W., and H. S. Gladwin. *A Method for the Designation of Cultures and Their Variations*. Medallion Papers 15. Globe, Ariz.: Gila Pueblo Medallion Papers, 1934.

Gleadow, A. J. W. "Fission Track Age of the KBS Tuff and Associated Hominids in Northern Kenya," *Nature* 284 (1980): 225–30.

Gleeson, P., and G. Grosso. "The Ozette Site." In *Excavation of Water-Saturated Archaeological Sites (Wet Sites) on the Northwest Coast of North America*, ed. D. R. Croes, 13–44. National Museum of Man Mercury Series, Archaeological Survey of Canada Paper 50. Ottawa: National Museums of Canada, 1976.

Graubau, A. *Principles of Stratigraphy*. 1924. Rpt. New York: Dover, 1960.

Grayson, D. K. "Eoliths, Archaeological Ambiguity and the Generation of 'Middle-Range' Research." In *American Archaeology, Past and Future*, ed. D. J. Meltzer, D. D. Fowler, and J. A. Sabloff. Washington, D.C.: Smithsonian Institution Press, 1986.

Grayson, D. K. *The Establishment of Human Antiquity*. New York: Academic Press, 1986.

Grayson, D. K. "The Provision of Time Depth for Paleoanthropology." In *Establishment of a Geologic*

Framework for Paleoanthropology, ed. L. F. Laporte, 1–13. Special Paper 242. Boulder, Colo.: Geological Society of America, 1990.

Gruber, J. W. "Brixham Cave and the Antiquity of Man." In *Context and Meaning in Cultural Anthropology*, ed. M. E. Spiro, 373–402. New York: Free Press, 1965.

Hajic, E. R. *Koster Site Archaeology I: Stratigraphy and Landscape Evolution.* Research Series Volume 8. Kampsville, Ill.: Center for American Archaeology, 1990.

Hall, C. M., and D. York. "The Applicability of ^{40}Ar/^{39}Ar Dating to Younger Volcanics." In *Quaternary Dating Methods*, ed. W. C. Mahaney, 67–74. Amsterdam: Elsevier, 1984.

Hamelin, E. B., R. G. Fairbanks, and A. Zindler. "Calibration of the ^{14}C Timescale over the Past 30,000 Years Using Mass Spectrometric U/Th Ages from Barbados Corals." *Nature* 345 (1990): 405–10.

Hammond, E. H. "Analysis of Properties in Landform Geography." *Annals of the Association of American Geographers* 54 (1964): 11–19.

Hammond, N. "Obsidian Hydration Dating of Tecep Phase Occupation at Nohmul, Belize." *American Antiquity* 54(3) (1989): 513–21.

Harbottle, G. "Neutron Activation Analysis in Archaeological Chemistry." In *Chemical Applications of Nuclear Probes*, ed. K. Yoshihara, 58–91. Berlin: Springer-Verlag, 1990.

Harley, J. B., and D. Woodward, eds. *The History of Cartography.* Volume 1: *Cartography in Prehistoric, Ancient, and Medieval Europe and the Mediterranean.* Chicago: University of Chicago Press, 1987.

Harlow, G. E. "The Maya Rediscovered Hard Rock." *Natural History* 100(8) (1991): 4–10.

Harris, E. *Principles of Archaeological Stratigraphy.* 2d ed. London: Academic Press, 1989.

Hassan, F. "Geoarchaeology: The Geologist and Archaeology." *American Antiquity* 44 (1979): 267–70.

Hassan, F. Review of *Formation Processes in Archaeologic Context*, ed. P. Goldberg, D. T. Nash, and M. D. Petraglia. *American Antiquity* 60(3) (1995) 558–59.

Hassan, F. "Sediments in Archaeology: Methods and Implications for Paleoenvironmental and Cultural Analysis." *Journal of Field Archaeology* 5(2) (1978): 197–213.

Hawass, Z., and M. Lehner. "The Sphinx: Who Built It, And Why?" *Archaeology* 47(5) (1994): 30–42.

Haynes, C. V. "The Antevs-Bryan Years and the Legacy for Paleoindian Geochronology." In *Establishment of a Geologic Framework for Paleoanthropology*, ed. L. F.

Laporte, 55–66. Special Paper 242. Boulder, Colo.: Geological Society of America, 1990.

Haynes, C. V. "The Calico Site: Artifacts or Geofacts?" *Science* 181 (1973): 305–10.

Haynes, C. V. "The Geologist's Role in Pleistocene Paleoecology and Archaeology." In *The Reconstruction of Past Environments*, assembled by J. J. Hester and J. Schoenwetter, 61–66. Taos, N.M.: Fort Burgwin Research Center, 1964.

Haynes, H. W. *Man and the Glacial Period.* New York: Appleton, 1893.

Hebda, R. J., and R. W. Mathewes. "Holocene History of Cedar and Native Indians of the North American Pacific Coast." *Science* 225 (1984): 711–13.

Heizer, R. F., et al. "The Colossi of Memnon Revisited." *Science* 182 (1973): 1219–25.

Heizer, R. F., and A. E. Treganza. "Mines and Quarries of the Indians of California." *California Journal of Mines and Geology* 40 (1944): 291–93.

Hennig, G. J., R. Grun, and K. Brunnacker. "Speleothems, Travertines and Paleoclimates." *Quaternary Research* 20 (1983): 1–29.

Herz, N. "Isotopic Analysis of Marble." In *Archaeological Geology*, ed. G. Rapp, Jr., and J. A. Gifford, 331–51. New Haven: Yale University Press, 1985.

Hester, J. J. "The Significance of Accelerator Dating in Archaeological Method and Theory." *Journal of Field Archaeology* 14 (1987): 445–51.

Hoard, R. J., et al. "Neutron Activation Analysis of Stone from the Chadron Formation and a Clovis Site on the Great Plains." *Journal of Archaeological Science* 19 (1992): 655–65.

Hoard, R. J., S. R. Holen, M. D. Glascock, and H. Neff. "Additional Comments on Neutron Activation Analysis of Stone from the Great Plains: Reply to Church." *Journal of Archaeological Science* 22 (1995): 7–10.

Hoch, D. M. "Flake Dispersal Experiments: Noncultural Transformation of the Archaeologic Record." *American Antiquity* 48 (1983): 553–72.

Hohn, M. H., and J. Hellerman. "The Diatoms." In *Paleoecology of the Llano Estacado*, assembled by F. Wendorf. Number 1, 98–104. Taos, N.M.: Fort Burgwin Research Center, Museum of New Mexico Press, 1961.

Holliday, V. T. *Guidebook to the Archaeological Geology of Classic Paleoindian Sites of the Southern High Plains, Texas and New Mexico.* College Station: Texas A & M University, Department of Geography, 1986.

Holliday, V. T., ed. *Soils in Archaeology.* Washington, D.C.: Smithsonian Institution Press, 1992.

Holmes, W. H. "Modern Quarry Refuse and the Paleolithic Theory." *Science* 20 (1892): 295–97.

Hough, W. "Earthquakes and Tribal Movements in the Southwest." *American Anthropologist* 8 (1906): 436.

Howard, E. B. "Evidence of Early Man in North America." *University of Pennsylvania Museum Journal* 24(2–3) (1935): 61–71.

Isaac, G. "Towards the Interpretation of Occupation Debris: Some Experiments and Observations." *Kroeber Anthropological Society Papers* 5(37) (1967): 31–57.

Inglis, D. R. "Particle Sorting and Stone Migration by Freezing and Thawing." *Science* 148 (1965): 1616–17.

Jackson, K. A., and D. R. Uhlmann. "Particle Sorting and Stone Migration Due to Frost Heave." *Science* 152 (1966): 545–46.

Jing, Z., G. R. Rapp, Jr., and T. Gao. "Holocene Landscape Evolution and Its Impact on the Neolithic and Bronze Age Sites in the Shangqiu Area, Northern China." *Geoarchaeology* 10(6) (1995): 481–513.

Johnson, A. W. "Frost Action in Roads and Airfields." Special Report No. 1. Washington, D.C.: National Research Council, Highway Research Board, 1952.

Johnson, D. L., and K. L. Hansen. "The Effects of Frost-Heaving on Objects in Soils." *Plains Anthropologist* 19(64) (1972): 81–98.

Johnson, D. L., D. R. Muhs, and M. L. Barnhardt. "The Effects of Frost-Heaving on Objects in Soils, II: Laboratory Experiments." *Plains Anthropologist* 22(76), Part 1 (1977): 133–47.

Johnson, W. C., and B. Logan. "Geoarchaeology of the Kansas River Basin, Central Great Plains." In *Archaeological Geology of North America*, ed. N. P. Lasca and J. Donohue, 267–300. Centennial Special Volume 4. Boulder, Colo.: Geological Society of America, 1990.

Jones, J. R., and J. J. Fisher. "Environmental Factors Affecting Prehistoric Shellfish Utilization, Grape Island, Boston Harbor, Massachusetts." In *Archaeological Geology of North America*, ed. N. P. Lasca and J. Donohue, 137–47. Centennial Special Volume 4. Boulder, Colo.: Geological Society of America, 1990.

Joyce, A. J., and R. G. Mueller. "The Social Impact of Anthropogenic Landscape Modification in the Rio Verde Drainage Basin, Oaxaca, Mexico." *Geoarchaeology* 7(6) (1992): 503–26.

Judd, N. M. *Arizona's Prehistoric Canals from the Air.* Washington, D.C.: Smithsonian Institution Press, 1930.

Judson, S. "Geology." In *The Identification of Non-Artifactual Archaeological Materials*, ed. W. W. Tay-

lor. National Academy of Sciences Publication 565. Washington, D.C.: National Academy of Sciences—National Research Council, 1957.

Julig, P. J., J. H. McAndrews, and W. C. Mahaney. "Geoarchaeology of the Cummins Site on the Beach of Proglacial Lake Minong, Lake Superior Basin, Canada." In *Archaeological Geology of North America*, ed. N. P. Lasca and J. Donohue, 21–51. Centennial Special Volume 4. Boulder, Colo.: Geological Society of America, 1990.

Julig, P. J., L. A. Pavlish, and R. G. V. Hancock. "INAA Provenance Studies of Lithic Materials from the Western Great Lakes Region of North America." In *Archaeometry '90*, ed. E. Pernicka and G. Wagner. Basel: Birkhäuser Verlag, 1991.

Kamilli, D. C., and A. Steinberg. "New Approaches to Mineral Analysis of Ancient Ceramics." In *Archaeological Geology*, ed. G. Rapp, Jr., and J. A. Gifford, 313–30. New Haven: Yale University Press, 1985.

Kapp, R. O. "Background." In *How to Know Pollen and Spores*, 1–20. Dubuque, Iowa: William C. Brown, 1969.

Karcz, I., and U. Kafri. "Evaluation of Supposed Archaeoseismic Damage in Israel." *Journal of Archaeological Science* 5 (1978): 237–53.

Kayani, P. I., and G. McDonnell. "The Potential of Scanning Electron Microscope Techniques for Non-Destructive Obsidian Characterization and Hydration-Rim Research." In *Archaeological Sciences 1995: Proceedings of a Conference on the Application of Scientific Techniques to Archaeology*, Liverpool, June 1995.

Kempe, D. *Living Underground: A History of Cave and Cliff Dwelling.* London: Herbert, 1988.

Kidder, A. V. "Pottery of the Pajarito Plateau and Some Adjacent Regions in New Mexico." *Memoirs of the American Anthropological Association* 2(6) (1915): 407–62.

Knapp, A. B., and J. F. Cherry. *Provenience Studies and Bronze Age Cyprus: Production, Exchange and Politico-Economic Change.* Monographs in World Archaeology 21. Madison, Wis.: Prehistory Press, 1994.

Kolb, C. R., and J. R. Van Lopik. "Depositional Environments of the Mississippi River Deltaic Plain, Southeastern Louisiana." In *Deltas in Their Geologic Framework*, ed. M. L. Shirley, 17–61. Houston: Houston Geological Society, 1966.

Kolb, M. F., N. P. Lasca, and L. G. Goldstein. "A Soil-Geomorphic Analysis of the Midden Deposits at Aztalan Site, Wisconsin." In *Archaeological Geology of North America*, ed. N. P. Lasca and J. Donohue, 199–

218. Centennial Special Volume 4. Boulder, Colo.: Geological Society of America, 1990.

Konigsson, L. K. "Pollen Analysis in Archaeogeology and Geoarchaeology." In *Geology and Paleoecology for Archaeologists*, ed. T. Hackens and U. Miller. Revello, Italy: European University Centre for Cultural Heritage, 1989.

Kraft, J. C., et al. "The Pass at Thermopylae, Greece." *Journal of Field Archaeology* 14 (1987): 181–98.

Kraus, M. J., and T. Brown. *Pedofacies Analysis: A New Approach to Reconstructing Ancient Fluvial Sequences.* Special Paper 216. Boulder, Colorado: Geological Society of America, 1986.

Kukla, J. G. "Loess Stratigraphy in Central China." *Quaternary Science Reviews* 6 (1987): 191–219.

Kukla, J. G., and Z. S. An. "Loess Stratigraphy in Central China." *Paleogeography, Paleoclimatology, Paleoecology* 72 (1989): 203–25.

LaMarche, V. C. "Paleoclimatic Inferences from Long Tree-Ring Records." *Science* 183 (1974): 1043–48.

Lamothe, M., A. Driemanis, M. Morency, and A. Raukas. "Thermoluminescence Dating of Quaternary Sediments." In *Quaternary Dating Methods*, ed. W. C. Mahaney, 153–71. Amsterdam: Elsevier, 1984.

Lang, A., and G. A. Wagner. "Infrared Stimulated Luminescence Dating of Archaeosediments." *Archaeometry* 38 (1996): 129–41.

Langbein, W., and S. Schumm. "Yield of Sediment in Relation to Mean Annual Precipitation." *Transactions of the American Geophysical Union* 39 (1958): 1076–84.

Larsen, C. E. "Geoarchaeological Interpretation of Great Lakes Coastal Environments." In *Archaeological Sediments in Context*, ed. J. K. Stein and W. R. Farrand. Orono: University of Maine, Center for the Study of Early Man, 1985.

Leach, E. "On the Definition of Geoarchaeology." *Geoarchaeology* 7(5) (1992): 405–17.

Leroi-Gourhan, A. *The Art of Prehistoric Man in Western Europe.* London: Thames and Hudson, 1968.

Libby, W. F. *Radiocarbon Dating.* Chicago: University of Chicago Press, 1955.

Liu, Z. "Paleoclimatic Changes as Indicated by the Quaternary Karstic Cave Deposits in China." *Geoarchaeology* 3(2) (1988): 103–15.

Lock, G., and Z. Stancic. *Archaeology and Geographical Information Systems: A European Perspective.* London: Taylor and Francis, 1995.

Lubbock, J. *Pre-Historic Times.* London: Williams and Norgate, 1865.

Lucas, A. *Ancient Egyptian Materials and Industries*, rev. J. R. Harris. London: E. Arnold, 1962.

Luedtke, B. E. *An Archaeologist's Guide to Chert and Flint.* Volume 7. Los Angeles: Archaeological Research Tools, 1992.

Lyell, C. *Geological Evidences of the Antiquity of Man.* London: J. Murray, 1863.

Lyman, R. L. *Vertebrate Taphonomy.* Cambridge: Cambridge University Press, 1994.

McCauley, J., et al. "Subsurface Valleys and Geoarchaeology of the Eastern Sahara Revealed by Shuttle Radar." *Science* 218 (1982): 1004–20.

MacCurdy, G. G., ed. *Early Man.* London: Lippincott, 1937.

McDonald, W. A., and G. R. Rapp, Jr. *The Minnesota Messenia Expedition: Reconstructing a Regional Bronze Age Environment.* Minneapolis: University of Minnesota Press, 1972.

Mack, G. H., and W. C. James. *Paleosols for Sedimentologists.* Boulder, Colo.: Geological Society of America, 1992.

Mack, G. H., W. C. James, and H. C. Monger. "Classification of Paleosols." *Geological Society of America Bulletin* 105 (1993): 129–36.

McKern, W. C. "The Midwestern Taxonomic Method as an Aid to Archaeological Culture Study." *American Antiquity* 4 (1939): 301–13.

Mallowan, M. *Early Mesopotamia and Iran.* London: Thames and Hudson, 1964.

Mandel, R. D. "Soils and Holocene Landscape Evolution on Central and Southwestern Kansas: Implications for Archaeological Research." In *Soils in Archaeology: Landscape Evolution and Human Occupation*, ed. V. T. Holliday, 41–100. Washington, D.C.: Smithsonian Institution Press, 1992.

Martinez Solarez, J. M., A. Lopez Arroyo, and J. Mezcua. "Isoseismal Map of the 1755 Lisbon Earthquake Obtained from Spanish Data." *Tectonophysics* 53 (1979): 301–13.

Martinson, D. G., et al. "Age Dating and the Orbital Theory of the Ice Ages: Development of a High Resolution 0 to 300,000-Year Chronostratigraphy." *Quaternary Research* 27 (1987): 1–29.

Matson, F. R. *Ceramics and Man.* Viking Fund Publications in Anthropology 41. London: Methuen, 1966.

Mehringer, P. J., Jr., and F. F. Foit, Jr. "Volcanic Ash Dating of the Clovis Cache at East Wenatchee, Washington." *National Geographic Research* 6(4) (1990): 495–503.

Meltzer, D. J. "The Antiquity of Man and the Development of American Archaeology." In *Advances in Archaeological Method and Theory*, ed. M. B. Schiffer, 6:1–51. New York: Academic Press, 1983.

Meltzer, D. J. "North American Archaeology and Archaeologists, 1879–1934." *American Antiquity* 50(2) (1985): 249–60.

Meltzer, D. J., J. M. Adovasio, and T. D. Dillehay. "On a Pleistocene Human Occupation at Pedra Furada, Brazil." *Antiquity* 262(68) (1994): 695–714.

Mercier, N., et al. "TL Dates of Burnt Flints from Jelinek's Excavations at Tabun and Their Implications." *Journal of Archaeological Science* 22 (1995): 495–509.

Mergard, R. O. "Late Quaternary Cladocera of Lake Zeribar, Western Iran." *Ecology* 48 (1967): 179–89.

Michels, J. W. "Obsidian Dating and East African Archaeology." *Science* 219 (1983): 361–66.

Michels, J. W. "Testing Stratigraphy and Artifact Reuse Through Obsidian Hydration Dating." *American Antiquity* 34(1) (1969): 15–22.

Miller, G. F. "Chronology of Hominid Occupation at Bir Tarfawi and Bir Sahara East, Based on the Epimerization of Isoleucine in Ostrich Eggshells." In *Egypt During the Last Interglacial*, by F. Wendorf et al., 241–51. New York: Plenum Press, 1993.

Miller, V. C., and M. E. Westerback. *Interpretation of Topographic Maps.* Columbus, Ohio: Merrill, 1989.

Moeyerson, J. "The Behavior of Stones and Stone Implements Buried in Consolidating and Creeping Kalahari Sands." *Earth Surface Processes* 3 (1978): 115–28.

Moore, P. D., J. A. Webb, and M. E. Collinson. *Pollen Analysis.* 2d ed. Oxford: Basil Blackwell, 1991.

Moss, J. H. "The Geology of Mummy Cave." In *The Mummy Cave Project in Northwestern Wyoming*, ed. H. McCracken et al., 35–40. Cody, Wy.: Buffalo Bill Historical Center, 1978.

Movius, H. L. "The Old World Paleolithic." In *Identification of Non-Artifactual Archaeological Materials*, ed. W. W. Taylor, 26–27. National Academy of Sciences Publication 565. Washington, D.C.: National Academy of Sciences—National Research Council, 1957.

Movius, H. L. "Old-World Paleolithic Archaeology." *Bulletin of the Geological Society of America* 60 (1949): 1443–56.

Naeser, C. W. "Fission-Track Dating." In *Quaternary Dating Methods*, ed. C. W. Mahaney, 87–100. Amsterdam: Elsevier, 1984.

Niemi, T. M., and Z. Ben-Avraham. "Evidence for Jericho Earthquakes from Slumped Sediments of the Jordan River Delta in the Dead Sea." *Geology* 22 (1994): 395–98.

Ningawa, K., et al. "Thermoluminescence Measurements of a Calcite Shell for Dating." *Quaternary Science Reviews* 7 (1988): 367–71.

North, F. J. "Geology for Archaeologists." *Archaeological Journal* 94 (1938): 73–115.

Oldfield, F., et al. "The Role of Mineral Magnetic Measurements in Archaeology." In *Proceedings of the Association for Environmental Archaeology Conference*, Sheffield, England, 1983.

Ortloff, C. R., and A. L. Kolata. "Climate and Collapse: Agro-Ecological Perspectives on the Decline of the Tiwanaku State." *Journal of Archaeological Science* 20 (1993): 195–221.

Palacios-Fest, M. R. "Nonmarine Ostracod Shell Chemistry from Ancient Hohokam Irrigation Canals in Central Arizona: A Paleohydrologic Tool for the Interpretation of Prehistoric Human Occupation in the North American Southwest." *Geoarchaeology* 9(1) (1994): 1–29.

Peacock, E. "Distinguishing Between Artifacts and Geofacts: A Test Case from Eastern England." *Journal of Field Archaeology* 18 (1991): 345–61.

Pearsall, D., B. M. Gilbert, and L. D. Martin. "Late Pleistocene Fossils of Natural Trap Cave, Wyoming, and the Climate Model of Extinction." In *Quaternary Extinction*, ed. P. S. Martin and R. G. Klein, 138–47. Tucson: University of Arizona Press, 1994.

Penhallurick, R. D. *Tin in Antiquity.* London: Institute of Metals, 1986.

Phillipson, D. W. *African Archaeology.* Cambridge: Cambridge University Press, 1994.

Piggott, S. *Ancient Europe from the Beginnings of Agriculture to Classical Antiquity: A Survey.* Chicago: Aldine, 1965.

Pilcher, J. R., and M. Hughes. "The Potential of Dendrochronology for the Study of Climate Change." In *Climatic Change in Later Prehistory*, ed. A. Harding, 75–84. Edinburgh: Edinburgh University Press, 1982.

Piperno, D. R., and D. M. Pearsall. *Current Research in Phytolith Analysis: Applications in Archaeology and Paleoecology.* Philadelphia: MASCA, The University Museum of Archaeology and Anthropology, University of Pennsylvania, 1993.

Potts, R. *Early Hominid Activities at Olduvai.* New York: A. de Gruyter, 1988.

Powell, J. W. "Prehistoric Man in America." *Forum* 8 (1890): 489–503.

Pregill, G. "Body Size of Insular Lizards: A Pattern of Holocene Dwarfism." *Evolution* 40 (1986): 997–1008.

Prestwich, J. "On the Occurrence of Flint Implements, Associated with the Remains of Extinct Mammalia, in Undisturbed Beds of a Late Geological Period." *Proceedings of the Royal Society of London* 10 (1860): 50–59.

Pumpelly, R. *Explorations in Turkestan*. Carnegie Institution Publication 73. Washington, D.C.: Carnegie Institution of Washington, 1908.

Pumpelly, R., et al. *Explorations in Turkestan: Expedition of 1904: Prehistoric Civilizations of Anau: Origins, Growth and Influence of Environment*. Washington, D.C.: Carnegie Institution of Washington, 1908.

Pyddoke, E. *Stratification for the Archaeologist*. London: Phoenix House, 1961.

Raab, L. M., and A. C. Goodyear. "Middle Range Theory in Archaeology: A Critical Review of Origins and Applications." *American Antiquity* 49 (1984): 255–68.

Rapp, G., Jr. "The Archaeological Field Staff: The Geologist." *Journal of Field Archaeology* 2 (1975): 232–33.

Rapp, G., Jr. "Archaeological Geology." In *Encyclopedia of Physical Science and Technology*, 1:688–698. New York: Academic Press, 1987.

Rapp, G., Jr. "Determining the Origins of Sulfide Smelting." *Der Anschnitt* (1989): 107–10.

Rapp, G., Jr. "Geoarchaeology." *Annual Review of Earth and Planetary Sciences* 15 (1987): 97–113.

Rapp, G., Jr. "On the Origins of Copper and Bronze Alloying." In *The Beginning of the Use of Metals and Alloys*, ed. R. Maddin, 21–27. Cambridge: MIT Press, 1988.

Rapp, G., Jr., J. D. Allert, and G. Peters. "The Origins of Copper in Three Northern Minnesota Sites: Pauly, River Point, and Big Rice." In *The Woodland Tradition in the Western Great Lakes*, ed. G. Gibbon, 233–38. Publications in Anthropology 4. Minneapolis: University of Minnesota Press, 1990.

Rapp, G., Jr., and J. Gifford. "Archaeological Geology." *American Scientist* 70 (1982): 45–53.

Rapp, G., Jr., E. Henrickson, and J. Allert. "Native Copper Sources of Artifact Copper in Pre-Columbian North America." In *Archaeological Geology of North America*, ed. N. Lasca and J. Donohue, 479–98. Boulder, Colo: Geological Society of America, 1990.

Rapp, G., Jr., and S. C. Mulholland. *Phytolith Systematics: Emerging Issues*. New York: Plenum Press, 1992.

Rapp, G., Jr., and S. Aschenbrenner, eds. *Excavations at Nichoria in Southwest Greece*. Volume 1: *Site, Environs, and Techniques*. Minneapolis: University of Minnesota Press, 1978.

Reid, K. C. "Fire and Ice: New Evidence for the Production and Preservation of Late Archaic Fiber-Tempered Pottery in the Middle-Latitude Lowlands." *American Antiquity* 49 (1984): 55–76.

Reimnitz, E., and N. F. Marshall. "Effects of the Alaska Earthquake and Tsunami on Recent Deltaic Sediments." *Journal of Geophysical Research* 70 (1965): 2363–76.

Reineck, H. E., and I. B. Singh. *Depositional Sedimentary Environments*. Ithaca, N.Y.: Springer, 1975.

Reinhard, K. J., and W. M. Bryant, Jr. "Coprolite Analysis: A Biologic Perspective on Archaeology." In *Archaeological Method and Theory*, ed. M. B. Schiffer, 4:245–88. Tucson: University of Arizona Press, 1992.

Reinhardt, G. A. "Hydrologic Artifact Dispersals at Pingasagruk, North Coast, Alaska." *Geoarchaeology* 8(6) (1993): 493–513.

Rendell, H. M., and R. W. Dennell. "Thermoluminescence Dating of an Upper Pleistocene Site, Northern Pakistan." *Geoarchaeology* 2(1) (1987): 63–67.

Renfrew, C. "Archaeology and the Earth Sciences." In *Geoarchaeology*, ed. D. A. Davidson and M. L. Shackley, 1–5. Boulder, Colo.: Westview Press, 1976.

Richter, G. "On the Soil Erosion Problem in the Temperate Humid Area of Central Europe." *Geojournal* 4 (1980): 279–87.

Rick, R. J. "Downslope Movement and Archaeologic Intrasite Spatial Analysis." *American Antiquity* 41 (1976): 133–44.

Roberts, N., and H. E. Wright, Jr. "Vegetational, Lake-Level, and Climatic History of the Near East and Southwest Asia." In *Global Climates Since the Last Glacial Maximum*, ed. H. E. Wright, Jr., J. E. Kutzbach, T. Webb III, W. F. Ruddiman, F. A. Street-Perrot, and P. J. Bartlein, 194–220. Minneapolis: University of Minnesota Press, 1993.

Roe, D. A. "Landmark Sites of the British Paleolithic." *Review of Archaeology* 14(2) (1993): 1–9.

Roe, D. A. *The Lower and Middle Paleolithic Periods in Britain*. London: Routledge and Kegan Paul, 1981.

Roosevelt, A. C. *Mound Builders of the Amazon*. New York: Academic Press, 1991.

Rousseau, D.-D., and J.-H. Puisseguir. "A 350,000 Year Climatic Record from the Loess Sequence of Achenheim, Alsace, France." *Boreas* 19 (1990): 203–16.

Rovner, I. "Floral History by the Back Door: A Test of Phytolith Analysis in Residential Yards at Harpers Ferry." *Historical Archaeology* 28(4) (1994): 37–48.

Rowley-Conwy, P. "Was There a Neanderthal Religion?" In *The First Humans: Human Origins and History to 10,000 B.C.*, ed. G. Burenhult. New York: Harper Collins, 1993.

Salisbury, R. "Man and the Glacial Period." *American Geologist* 11 (1893): 13–20.

Saucier, R. T. "Effects of the New Madrid Earthquake Series in the Mississippi Alluvial Valley." U.S. Army Engineer Waterways Experiment Station Miscellaneous Paper S-77-5. Vicksburg, Miss.: U.S. Army Engineer Waterways Experiment Station, 1977.

Saucier, R. T. "Evidence for Episodic Sand-Blow Activity During the 1811–1812 New Madrid (Missouri) Earthquake Series." *Geology* 17 (1989): 103–06.

Saucier, R. T. "Geoarchaeological Evidence of Strong Prehistoric Earthquakes in the New Madrid (Missouri) Seismic Zone." *Geology* 19 (1991): 296–98.

Schick, K. D. "Geoarchaeological Analysis of an Acheulian Site at Kalambo Falls, Zambia." *Geoarchaeology* 7(1) (1992): 1–26.

Schick, K. D. *Stone Age Sites in the Making: Experiments in the Formation of Archaeological Occurrences.* British Archaeological Reports International Series 319. Oxford: British Archaeological Reports, 1986.

Schiffer, M. B. "Archaeological Context and Systemic Context." *American Antiquity* 37 (1972): 156–65.

Schiffer, M. B. *Behavioral Archaeology.* New York: Academic Press, 1976.

Schiffer, M. B. *Formation Processes of the Archaeological Record.* Albuquerque: University of New Mexico Press, 1987.

Schiffer, M. B. "Towards the Identification of Formation Processes." *American Antiquity* 48 (1983): 675–706.

Schoenwetter, J. "Prologue to a Contextual Archaeology." *Journal of Archaeological Science* 8 (1981): 367–79.

Schuldenrein, J. "Coring and the Identity of Cultural-Resource Environments: A Comment on Stein." *American Antiquity* 56 (1991): 131–37.

Schulze, D., et al. "Significance of Organic Matter in Determining Soil Colors." In *Soil Color*, ed. J. Bigham and E. Ciolkosz. SSSA Special Publication Number 31. Madison, Wis.: Soil Science Society of America, 1993.

Schwarcz, H. P. "Absolute Age Determination of Archaeological Sites by Uranium Series Dating of Travertines." *Archaeometry* 22 (1980): 3–24.

Schwarcz, H. P. "The Site of Vertesszollos, Hungary." *Journal of Archaeological Science* 11 (1984): 327–36.

Schwarcz, H. P., and M. Gascoyne. "Uranium-Series Dating of Quaternary Sediments." In *Quaternary Dating Methods*, ed. W. C. Mahaney, 33–41. Amsterdam: Elsevier, 1984.

Schwarcz, H. P., and L. Morawska. "Uranium Series Dating of Carbonates from Bir Tarfawi and Bir Sahara East." In *Egypt During the Last Interglacial*, by F. Wendorf, R. Schild, A .E. Close, and Associates, 205–17. New York: Plenum Press, 1993.

Schweger, C. "Geoarchaeology of Northern Regions: Lessons from Cryoturbation at Onion Portage, Alaska." In *Archaeological Sediments in Context*, ed. J. K. Stein and W. R. Farrand, 127–41. Orono: University of Maine, Center for the Study of Early Man, 1985.

Schwengruber, F. H. *Tree Rings: Basics and Applications of Dendrochronology.* Dordrecht, Holland: Reidel, 1988.

Scollar, I., A. Tabbaugh, A. Hesse, and I. Herzog, eds. *Archaeological Prospecting and Remote Sensing.* Cambridge: Cambridge University Press, 1990.

Shackleton, N. J. "Stratigraphy and Chronology of the KRM Deposits: Oxygen Isotope Evidence." In *The Middle Stone Age at Klasies River Mouth in South Africa*, ed. R. Singer and J. Wymer, 194–99. Chicago: University of Chicago Press, 1982.

Shackley, M. L. "Stream Abrasion of Flint Implements." *Nature* 248 (1974): 501–02.

Shackley, M. S. "Sources of Archaeological Obsidian in the Greater American Southwest: An Update and Quantitative Analysis." *American Antiquity* 60(3) (1995): 531–51.

Shay, C. T. *The Itasca Bison Kill Site: An Ecological Analysis.* St. Paul: Minnesota Historical Society, 1971.

Sheets, P., and Brian R. McKee, eds. *Archaeology, Volcanism, and Remote Sensing in the Arenal Region, Costa Rica.* Austin: University of Texas Press, 1994.

Shepard, A. O. *Ceramics for the Archaeologist.* Carnegie Institution of Washington Publication 609. Washington, D.C.: Carnegie Institution of Washington, 1965.

Shepherd, R. *Ancient Mining.* London: Elsevier, 1993.

Shippee, R. "The Great Wall of Peru." *Geographical Review* 22(1) (1932): 1–29.

Shlemon, R. J., and F. E. Budinger, Jr. "The Archaeological Geology of the Calico Site, Mojave Desert, California." In *Archaeological Geology of North America*, ed. N. P. Lasca and J. Donahue, 301–13. Centennial Special Volume 4. Boulder, Colo.: Geological Society of America, 1990.

Simkin, T., and Fiske, R. *Krakatau 1883: The Volcanic Eruption and Its Effects.* Washington, D.C.: Smithsonian Press, 1983.

Sims, J. D. "Earthquake-Induced Structures in Sediments of Van Normsan Lake, San Fernando, California." *Science* 182 (1973): 161–63.

Sims, J. D. "Records of Prehistoric Earthquakes in Sedimentary Deposits in Lakes." U.S. Geological Survey. *Earthquake Information Bulletin* 11 (1979): 228–33.

Soil Survey Staff. *Soil Taxonomy: A Basic System of Soil Classification for Making and Interpreting Soil Surveys.* Agricultural Handbook 436. Washington, D.C.: U.S. Department of Agriculture, Soil Conservation Service, 1975.

Solecki, R. S. "Prehistory in the Shanidar Valley, Northern Iraq." *Science* 139 (1963): 179–93.

Solecki, R. S. "Shanidar IV: A Neanderthal Flower Burial in Northern Iraq." *Science* 190 (1975): 880–81.

Spencer, F. *Piltdown: A Scientific Forgery.* New York: Oxford University Press, 1990.

Squier, E. G., and E. H. Davis. *Ancient Monuments of the Mississippi Valley.* Smithsonian Contributions to Knowledge 1. Washington D.C.: Smithsonian Institution Press, 1848.

Stanley, D. J. "A Global Sea-Level Curve for the Late Quaternary: The Impossible Dream?" *Marine Geology* 125 (1995): 1–6.

Stanley, D. J., and A. G. Warne. "Nile Delta: Recent Geologic Evolution and Human Impact." *Science* 260 (1993): 628–34.

Steadman, D. W., and N. G. Miller. "California Condor Associated with Spruce-Pine Woodland in the Late Pleistocene in New York." *Quaternary Research* 28(3) (1987): 415–26.

Stearns, C. E. "Uranium-Series Dating and the History of Sea Level." In *Quaternary Dating Methods,* ed. W. C. Mahaney, 53–65. Amsterdam: Elsevier, 1984.

Stein, J. K. "Coring Archaeological Sites." *American Antiquity* 51 (1986): 505–27.

Stein, J. K. "Coring in CRM and Archaeology: A Reminder." *American Antiquity* 56 (1991): 138–42.

Stein, J. K. "Deposits for Archaeologists." In *Advances in Archaeological Method and Theory,* ed. M. B. Schiffer, 11:337–95. New York: Academic Press, 1987.

Stein, J. K. "Earthworm Activity: A Source of Potential Disturbance of Archaeological Sediments." *American Antiquity* 48(2) (1983): 277–89.

Stein, J. K., and W. Farrand. "Context and Geoarchaeology: An Introduction." In *Archaeological Sediments in Context,* ed. J. K. Stein and W. R. Farrand, 1–4. Orono: University of Maine, Center for the Study of Early Man, 1985.

Stein, J. K., ed. *Deciphering a Shell Midden.* San Diego: Academic Press, 1992.

Stein, J. K., and A. R. Linse, eds. *Effects of Scale on Archaeological and Geoscientific Perspectives.* Special Paper 28. Boulder, Colo: Geological Society of America, 1993.

Stockton, E. D. "Shaws's Creek Shelter: Human Displacement of Artifacts and Its Significance." *Mankind* 9 (1973): 112–17.

Stoltman, J. M. "Ceramic Petrography as a Technique for Documenting Cultural Interaction: An Example from the Upper Mississippi Valley." *American Antiquity* 56 (1991): 103–20.

Stoltman, J. M., and D. A. Baerreis. "Evolution of Human Ecosystems in the Eastern United States." In *Late-Quaternary Environments of the United States.* Volume 2: *The Holocene,* ed. H. E. Wright, Jr., 252–68. London: Longman, 1983.

Street, R., and O. Nuttli. "The Central Mississippi Earthquakes of 1811–1812." In *Proceedings, Symposium on the New Madrid Earthquakes,* ed. P. L. Gori and W. W. Hays, 33–63. United States Geological Service Open-File Report 84-770, 1984.

Sutcliffe, A. J., et al. "Cave Paleontology and Archaeology." In *The Science of Speleology,* ed T. D. Ford and C. H. D. Cullingford, 495–549. London: Academic Press, 1976.

Taber, S. "The Mechanics of Frost Heaving." *Journal of Geology* 38 (1930): 303–17.

Taylor, W. W., ed. *The Identification of Non-Artifactual Archaeological Materials.* National Academy of Sciences Publication 565. Washington, D.C.: National Academy of Sciences—National Research Council, 1957.

Terasmae, J. "Radiocarbon Dating: Some Problems and Potential Developments." In *Quaternary Dating Methods,* ed. W. C. Mahaney, 1–14. Amsterdam: Elsevier, 1984.

Thomas, H. "The Source of the Stones of Stonehenge." *Antiquaries Journal* 3 (1923): 239–60.

Thompson, K. S. "Piltdown Man: The Great English Mystery Story." *American Scientist* 79 (1991): 194–201.

Thompson, T. F. "Holocene Tectonic Activity in West Africa Dated by Archaeological Methods." *Geological Society of America Bulletin* 81 (1970): 3759–64.

Thorpe, R., O. Williams-Thorpe, D. Jenkins, and J. Watson. "The Geological Sources and Transport of the Bluestones of Stonehenge, Wiltshire, UK." *Proceedings of the Prehistoric Society* 57 (1991): 103–57.

Thorson, R. M. "Archaeological Geology." *Geotimes* (February 1990): 32–33.

Thorson, R. M. "Geologic Contexts of Archaeologic Sites in Beringia." In *Archaeologic Geology of North America,* ed. N. P. Lasca and J. Donahue, 399–420. Centennial Special Volume 4. Boulder, Colo.: Geological Society of America, 1990.

Thorson, R. M., and T. D. Hamilton. "Geology of the Dry Creek Site, A Stratified Early Man Site in Interior Alaska." *Quaternary Research* 7 (1977): 149–76.

Tite, M. S., and C. Mullins, "Enhancement of the Magnetic Susceptibility of Soils on Archaeological Sites." *Archaeometry* 13 (1971): 209–19.

Tobey, M. H. *Trace Element Investigations of Maya Chert from Belize.* Volume 1. Papers of the Colha Project. San Antonio: Center for Archaeological Research, University of Texas at San Antonio, 1986.

Todd, L. C., and G. C. Frison. "Taphonomic Study of the Colby Site Mammoth Bones." In G. C. Frison and L. C. Todd, *The Colby Mammoth Site: Ta-*

phonomy and Archaeology of a Clovis Kill in Northern Wyoming, 27-99. Albuquerque: University of New Mexico Press, 1986.

Trigger, B. G. *A History of Archaeological Thought.* Cambridge: Cambridge University Press, 1990.

Tushingham, A. M., and W. R. Peltier. "Implications of the Radiocarbon Timescale for Ice-Sheet Chronology and Sea-Level Change." *Quaternary Research* 39 (1993): 125-29.

Upton, W. B., Jr. *Landforms and Topographic Maps.* New York: John Wiley and Sons, 1970.

U.S. Department of Agriculture. *Keys to Soil Taxonomy.* Technical Monograph 6. Ithaca, N.Y.: Department of Agronomy, Cornell University; Agency for International Development, U.S. Department of Agriculture, Soil Management Support Sources, 1987.

Van Andel, T. H., and N. Lianos. "High-Resolution Seismic Reflection Profiles for the Reconstruction of Postglacial Transgressive Shorelines: An Example from Greece." *Quaternary Research* 22 (1984): 31-45.

Van Andel, T. H., and S. B. Sutton. *Landscape and People of the Franchthi Region.* Bloomington: Indiana University Press, 1987.

Van Neer, W. "Fish Remains from the Last Interglacial at Bir Tarfawi (Eastern Sahara, Egypt)." In *Egypt During the Last Interglacial*, by F. Wendorf, R. Schild, A. E. Close, and Associates. New York: Plenum Press, 1993.

Vaughn, C. J. "Ground-Penetrating Radar Surveys Used in Archaeological Investigations." *Geophysics* 51(3) (1986): 595-604.

Vaughn, S. J. "Petrographic Analysis of the Early Cycladic Wares from Akrotiri, Thera." In *Thera and the Aegean World III.* Volume 1: *Archaeology*, ed. D. A. Hardy, 470-87. London: Thera Foundation, 1990.

Wagstaff, J. M., ed. *Landscape and Culture: Geographical and Archaeological Perspectives.* Oxford: Basil Blackwell, 1987.

Walker, R. "Phosphate Survey: Method and Meaning." In *Geoprospection in the Archaeological Landscape*, ed. P. Spoerry. Oxbow Monographs 18. Oxford: Oxbow, 1992.

Wall Paintings of the Tomb of Nefertari: Scientific Studies for Their Conservation. Malibu, Calif.: Getty Conservation Institute, 1987.

Walter, R. C., et al. "Laser-Fusion ^{40}Ar/^{39}Ar Dating of Bed I, Olduvai Gorge, Tanzania." *Nature* 354 (1991): 145-49.

Walthall, J. *Galena and Aboriginal Trade in Eastern North America.* Illinois State Museum Scientific Papers, Volume 17. Springfield: Illinois State Museum, 1981.

Wasburn, A. L. *Geocryology: A Survey of Periglacial Processes and Environments.* 2d ed. New York: John Wiley and Sons, 1980.

Waters, M. R. "The Geoarchaeology of Gullies and Arroyos in Southern Arizona." *Journal of Field Archaeology* 18 (1991): 141-59.

Waters, M. R. *Principles of Geoarchaeology: A North American Perspective.* Tucson: University of Arizona Press, 1992.

Wells, P. V., and C. D. Jorgensen. "Pleistocene Wood Rat Middens and Climate Change in Mojave Desert: A Record of Juniper Woodlands." *Science* 143 (1964): 1171-74.

Wen, G., and Z. Jing. "Chinese Neolithic Jade: A Preliminary Geoarchaeological Study." *Geoarchaeology* 7 (1992): 251-75.

Wendorf, F., et al. "New Radiocarbon Dates on the Cereals from Wadi Kubbaniya." *Science* 225 (1984): 645-46.

Wendorf, F., A. D. Krieger, C. C. Albritton, and T. D. Stewart. *The Midland Discovery.* Austin: University of Texas Press, 1955.

Wendorf, F., R. Schild, and A. E. Close. *The Prehistory of Wadi Kubbaniya.* Dallas: Southern Methodist University Press, 1989.

Wendorf, F., ed. *The Prehistory of Nubia.* Dallas: Southern Methodist University Press and the Fort Burgwin Research Center, 1969.

Wendorf, F., and R. Schild, assemblers. *The Prehistory of Wadi Kubbaniya.* Volume 2: *Stratigraphy, Paleoeconomy, and Environment*, ed. A. E. Close. Dallas: Southern Methodist University Press, 1989.

West, F. H. "Archaeological Geology, Wave of the Future or Salute to the Past?" *Quarterly Review of Archaeology* 3(1) (1982): 9-11.

Weymouth, J. W., and R. Huggins. "Geophysical Surveying of Archaeological Sites." In *Archaeological Geology*, ed. G. Rapp, Jr., and J. A. Gifford, 191-235. New Haven: Yale University Press, 1985.

Wheeler, M. *Archaeology from the Earth.* Oxford: Clarendon, 1954.

Whitley, D. S., and R. I. Dorn. "New Perspectives on the Clovis vs. Pre-Clovis Controversy." *American Antiquity* 58(4) (1993): 626-47.

Whittlesey, C. *The Ancient Miners of Lake Superior.* Cleveland: Academy of Natural Sciences Annals of Science, 1852.

Willey, G., and J. A. Sabloff. *A History of American Archaeology.* New York: W. H. Freeman, 1993.

Willey, G. R., and P. Phillips. *Method and Theory in American Archaeology.* Chicago: University of Chicago Press, 1955.

Williams-Thorpe, O. "Obsidian in the Mediterranean

and the Near East: A Provenancing Success Story." *Archaeometry* 37(2) (1995): 217–48.

Wintle, A. G. "Archaeologically Relevant Dating Techniques for the Next Century." *Journal of Archaeological Sciences* 23 (1996): 123–38.

Wintle, A. G., and M. J. Aitken. "Thermoluminescence Dating of Burnt Flint: Application to the Lower Paleolithic Site, Terra Amata." *Archaeometry* 19(2) (1977): 111–30.

Wintle, A. G., N. J. Shackleton, and J. P. Lautridou. "Thermoluminescence Dating of Periods of Loess Deposition and Soil Formation in Normandy." *Nature* 310 (1984): 491–93.

Wood, W. R., and D. L. Johnson. "A Survey of Disturbance Processes in Archaeological Site Formation." In *Advances in Archaeological Method and Theory*, ed. M. Schiffer, 1:315–81. New York: Academic Press, 1978.

Woolley, L. "Excavations at Ur, 1928–29." *Antiquaries Journal* 9 (1929): 305–39.

Wright, G. F. *Man and the Glacial Period.* New York: Appleton, 1892.

Wright, H. E., Jr. "Environmental Determinism in Near Eastern Prehistory." *Current Anthropology* 34(4) (1993): 458–69.

Wright, H. E., Jr. "Environmental Setting for Plant Domestication in the Near East." *Science* 194 (1976): 385–89.

Wright, H. E., Jr. "Geology." In *The Identification of Non-Artifactual Archaeological Materials*, ed. W. W. Taylor, 48–49. National Academy of Sciences Publication 565. Washington, D.C.: National Academy of Sciences—National Research Council, 1957.

Wymer, J. J. *Paleolithic Sites of East Anglia.* Norwich: Geo, 1985.

Wynn, J. C. "Archaeological Prospection: An Introduction to the Special Issue," *Geophysics: Geophysics in Archaeology* 51(3) (1986): 533.

Young, A. "Soil Movement by Denudational Processes on Slopes." *Nature* 188 (1960): 120–22.

Zangger, E. "Prehistoric Coastal Environments in Greece: The Vanished Landscapes of Dimini Bay and Lake Lerna." *Journal of Field Archaeology* 18 (1991): 1–17.

Zeuner, F. E. *Dating the Past: An Introduction to Geochronology.* 1st ed. London: Methuen, 1946.

Zeuner, F. E. *The Pleistocene Period: Its Climate, Chronology, and Faunal Successions.* 1945. 2d ed. London: Hutchinson, 1959.

Index

People

Abbott, Charles C., 8
Acher, Robert, 14
Adams, Robert McCormick, 14
Adovasio, James, 70
Albritton, Claude, 12, 14
Alexander, J., 37
Ambraseys, N. N., 213
Antevs, Ernst, 9, 11, 12, 154
Aubrey, John, 16

Ball, S. H., 131
Barmore, F., 171
Bate, Dorothy M. A., 10
Ben-Avraham, Z., 212
Bettis, Arthur, 157, 158
Binford, Lewis, 14, 15
Birkeland, Peter, 34
Bolt, B., 212
Boucher de Crèvecoeur de Perthes, Jacques, 5, 7
Boué, Ami, 9
Braidwood, Robert J., 13, 14
Brookes, C. E. P., 106
Bryan, Kirk, 11, 12, 14
Butzer, Karl, 3, 14, 68

Caldwell, Joseph, 15
Cann, J. R., 13
Casteel, R. W., 103
Catlin, George, 124
Chamberlin, Rollin T., 10
Childe, V. Gordon, 106
Clark, A. McFayden, 162
Clark, D. W., 162
Clark, J. D., 164
Clarke, David L., 15, 16
Clinton, DeWitt, 9
Conze, Alexander, 6

Cornwall, Ian W., 13, 14
Curtius, Ernst, 6
Cuvier, Georges, 6

Dall, William H., 7
Dalton, John, 119
Daniel, Glyn, 5, 6, 10
Davis, Edwin H., 7
Davis, Leslie, 64
de Geer, Gerard J., 9, 154
de Heinzelin, Jean, 14
De Morgan, J., 10
de Mortillet, Gabriel, 6
Dincauze, Dena, 28
Doe, W. W., 217
Doig, R., 212
Donahue, Jack, 70
Doolittle, W. E., 200
Dorn, R. I., 161
Dörpfeld, Wilhelm, 6, 9
Douglass, Andrew E., 9, 160
Dundes, A., 214

Eidt, Robert, 28, 195
Ellsworth, Huntington, 106
Evans, Arthur, 210
Evans, John, 5

Falconer, Hugh, 9
Farrand, William, 10, 12
Fedele, F. G., 15
Ferring, Reid, 1, 34
Fiorelli, Giuseppe, 6, 12
Frere, John, 5
Frison, G. C., 52
Fritts, H. C., 89

Gamino, Manuel, 10
Garrod, Dorothy A. E., 10
Gatto, L. W., 217

Gautier, Achilles, 14
Geikie, James, 6, 10
Gifford, John, 5
Gilbert, G. K., 216
Gladfelter, Bruce, 3, 21
Glueck, Nelson, 144
Goodyear, Albert C., 15
Grabau, Amadeus W., 2
Greenwood, P. H., 14

Hajic, Edward, 157, 158
Hammond, N. I., 178
Harbottle, G., 136
Harley, J. B., 181
Harris, Edward, 5
Hassan, Fekri, 3, 15
Haynes, C. Vance, Jr., 8, 12, 14, 66, fig. 1.4
Hebda, R. J., 92
Heizer, Robert E., 13, 131
Herz, Norman, 140
Herodotus, 75, 117
Holliday, Vance, 11, 29
Holman, H. W., 102
Holmes, William Henry, 7, 8
Hough, W., 213
Howard, Edgar B., 11
Hrdlička, Aleš, 10–11

Isaac, Glyn, 14

Jing, Zichun, 193
Johnson, W. C., 156
Jorgensen, Clive D., 103
Joyce, A. J., 66
Judson, Sheldon, 12, 13

Kafri, U., 213
Karcz, I., 213
Kidder, Alfred V., 10

255

Konigsson, Lars-Konig, 1
Krieger, Alex, 12

Lartet, Edward, 6
Leighton, Morris M., 12
Libby, Frank Willard, 12, 165
Lindbergh, Charles, 10
Livy, 75
Logan, B., 156
Lubbock, John, 6, 10
Luedtke, B. E., 113
Lyell, Charles, 5, 6, 7, 10, *fig.* 1.1

MacCurdy, George G., 10
McDonald, William A., 14
McKee, Brian R., 215
MacNeish, Richard, 14
Mallowan, Max, 214
Mandel, Rolfe, 157, 158
Martin, Francine, 14
Martinez Solarez, J. M., 213
Mathewes, R. W., 92
Matson, Frederick R., 13, 150
Megard, R. O., 98
Meltzer, David, 8
Melville, C. P., 213
Michels, Joe, 163
Miller, John, 12
Miller, N. G., 102
Mohs, Friedrich, 113
Moore, Clarence B., 7
Movius, Hallam L., 12, 13
Mueller, R. G., 66

Nelson, Nels C., 10
Niemi, T. M., 212
North, F. J., 16–17

Otto, H., 13

Palacios-Fest, M. R., 97
Pausanius, 75
Peacock, E., 24
Pengelly, William, 5, 9
Petrie, William Matthew Flinders,
   6, 9
Phillips, Philip, 106
Pitt-Rivers, Augustus Henry, 6, 9
Plato, 75, 159
Pliny, 112, 117, 118, 120, 123, 125, 140
Polo, Marco, 115
Powell, John Wesley, 7–8

Pregill, G., 102
Prestwich, Joseph, 5
Pumpelly, Raphael, 9
Putnam, Frederick W., 7
Pyddoke, Edward, 13, 14

Rabb, L. Mark, 15
Rapp G. R., Jr., 5, 14, 79, 129, 138,
   143, 146, 184, 185
Renfrew, Colin, 10, 13
Rigollot, Marcel Jérôme, 5, 7, 9
Rovner, Irwin, 95
Russ, John, 95

Salisbury, Rollin D., 8
Sangmeister, Edward, 13
Saucier, R. T., 212
Sauramo, Matti, 9
Schiffer, Michael B., 15
Schliemann, Heinrich, 6
Schmidt, Hubert, 9
Sears, Paul, 12
Sellards, Elias H., 11, 12, *fig.* 1.3
Shackleton, N. J., 104
Shackley, M. S., 42
Sheets, Payson, 215
Shepard, Anna O., 150
Sims, J. D., 212
Snefru, 198
Squier, Ephraim G., 7
Stanley, D. J., 78
Steadman, D. W., 102
Stein, Julie, 10, 12, 13, 20
Steward, Julian H., 15
Strabo, 75, 200

Taylor, Walter W., 13, 15
Theophrastus, 112, 140
Thomas, Cyrus, 7
Thomas, H. H., 10, 12, 134
Thompson, T. F., 213
Todd, L. C., 52
Treganza, A. E., 131
Trigger, Bruce, 7

von Post, Lennart, 9

Walker, Steven, 7
Walther, Johannes, 75
Waters, Michael, 3
Wells, Philip, 103
Wendorf, Fred, 12, 14

West, Frederick H., 2
Wheeler, Mortimer, 3, 10, 14
White, Leslie A., 15
Whitley, D. S., 161
Willey, Gordon, 106
Williams, David, 13
Williams-Thorpe, O., 138
Winchell, Newton Horace, 8, *fig.* 1.2
Woodward, D., 181
Woolley, Leonard, 214
Wright, George Frederick, 8, 10
Wright, Herbert E., Jr., 12, 13, 14
Wyman, Jeffries, 7

Zeuner, F. E., 10, 14

Places

Abu Simbel (Egypt), 206
Abusir (Egypt), 127
Açigol (Turkey), 138, *fig.* 6.2
Aegean islands (Greece), 127, 137, 138,
   140, 141, 145, 150, 151, 159, 214
Aegean Sea, 215
Agassiz, Glacial Lake, 81
Ain River (France), 68
Akrotiri (Thera, Greece), 150, 159,
   202
Albemarle County (Virginia) quarry,
   142
Altamira (Spain), 66
Anatolia (Turkey), 92, 114, 118, 124,
   126, 137–38, 140, 141, 142, 144, 145,
   180, 201
Anau, site of (southern Turk-
   menia), 9
Andes Mountains, 104, 106, 118
Angel Mounds (Indiana), 183
Arago site (France), 172
Aswan (Egypt), 114, 121, 127, 137, 139,
   202, 206
Avebury (England), 134

Babylon (ancient), 121
Baldachin (Afghanistan), 115
Baltic, 116, 141, 142, 154
Basin of Mexico, 200
Belize, 69, 117, 120, 148, 163
Bent Pyramid (Dashur, Egypt), 198
Bickerton (England), 182
Big Fork River (Minnesota), 176, *figs.*
   8.1, 8.2

Bir Sahara (Egypt), 27, 56
Bohai Sea (China), 214
British Camp shell midden (Washington), 139
British Columbia (Canada), 92
Brixham Cave (England), 5, 9
Bruchsal Aue (Germany), 174
Bunyoro (East Africa), 117
Burnet Cave (New Mexico), 11

Cahokia Mounds site (Illinois), 182
Calico Hills site (Yerma, California), 19
Cap d'Or (Nova Scotia), 119
Carlsbad (New Mexico), 11
Carpathia (Hungary), 138
Carrara (Italy), 140, 205
Carthage (Tunisia), 146
Çatal Höyük (Turkey), 126, 180
Çayonu (Turkey), 142
Cebolleta Mesa (New Mexico), 130
Cerro La China (Argentina), 106
Chaco Canyon (New Mexico), 12
Cheswoanja (Kenya), 109
China, 32, 66, 70, 106, 115, 116, 120, 135, 155–56, 200, 214
China Sea, 214
Chuandong area (Guizhou Province, China), 70
Çiftlik (Turkey), 138, fig. 6.2
Colby site (Wyoming), 52
Colha site (Belize), 148
Colombia (South America), 195
Colossi of Memnon, 136
Copper River (Alaska), 119, 212
Coppermine River (Canada), 119
Cornwall, 120, 144, 146
Cotui (Dominican Republic), 116
Crater Lake (Oregon), 159, 214
Crawford Lake (Ontario, Canada), 92
Crete, 215
Cyprus, 112, 141

Dakhla (Egypt), 216
Danger Cave (Utah), 66
Dashur (Egypt), 198
Dead Sea (Near East), 57, 87, 88, 212
Denbigh site (Alaska), 82
Devil's Lair (Australia), 66
Devil's Tower (Wyoming), 179
Djoser, Step Pyramid of, 127, 202
Drachenloch (Switzerland), 69

Dravidian caves (India), 66
Dry Creek Site (Alaska), 82

eastern desert (Egypt), 113, 144, 145, 192
Eckles site (Kansas), 148
Edfu (Egypt), 206
Egypt, 64, 103, 112, 113, 114, 115, 116, 118, 119, 121, 122, 123, 124, 126, 127, 128, 130, 139, 144, 145, 146, 181, 198, 199, 205, 206
El Castillo Cave (Spain), 68, 69, 165, fig. 3.9
El Chayal (Guatemala), 163, 165
El Kown (Syria), 172
Elk Lake (Minnesota), 155
Elveden (England), 73
Engigstack site (Alaska), 82
Ergani Maden (Turkey), 142
Erzgebirge Mountains (Czech Republic), 144, 146
Esna (Egypt), 216

Fayum (Egypt), 122
Fiji, 141
Finland, 141
Florence (Italy), 220
Folsom (New Mexico), 11, 12, 159–60
Franchthi Cave (Greece), 189
Fraser Cave (Tasmania), 70

Galacia, 145
Ganges River (India), 128
Gebel el Ahmar (Egypt), 137
Giza (Egypt), 127, 145, 198, 202, 207
Glacier Peak volcano (Washington), 159
Gorham's Cave (Gibraltar), 71
Government Mountain (Arizona), 138
Graham Cave (Missouri), 66
Gray's Inn site (England), 65
Great Basin (North America), 103, 109
Great Lakes (North America), 142
Great Plains (North America), 139
Great Salt Lake (Utah), 57
Green River (Kentucky), 20
Grimaldi Caves (Monaco), 9
Grotte de l'Obsérvatoire (Monaco), 9
Guebert site (Illinois), 146
Gulf of Aqabah, 144

Gulf of Malia-Spherchios River floodplain, 79–81, fig. 3.15
Gulf of Mexico, continental shelf, 189
Gypsum Caves (Nevada), 66

Hannaford site (Minnesota), 176, figs. 8.1, 8.2
Harpers Ferry (West Virginia), 95
Haua Fteah (northern Africa), 66, 68, 105
Hearth Cave (Australia), 70
High Lodge (England), 74
Hiscock site (New York), 102
Hissarlik (Troy), 6
Holywell Coombe (England), 98

Iberian Peninsula (Spain), 120, 145
India, 115, 128
Indian Creek site (Montana), 64, 159
Indian Ocean, 214
Indus River (India), 128
Indus Valley (Pakistan), 145
Isle Royale-Minong Mine (Michigan), 143
Isthmus of Panama, 108
Itasca bison kill site (Minnesota), 92

James River (Virginia) drainage, 142
Japan, 117–18
Jericho, 112, 212
Jordan River Delta, 212

Kalambo Falls site (Zambia), 39
Kansas River basin, 156
Kendricks Cave (Wales), 69
Kenniff Cave (Australia), 66
Kent's Cavern (England), 9, 66, 69
Keweenaw Peninsula (Michigan), 7, 136
Khok Phanom Di (Thailand), 110
Klassies River Mouth (Africa), 66, 104
Knife River Indian Villages National Historic Site (North Dakota), 184
Knossos (Crete), 210
Komdraai (Africa), 68
Koobi Fora (East Africa), 169
Korephronisi (Crete), 125
Koster site (Illinois), 158
Krakatoa (Indonesia), 214
Krakow (Poland), 117
Ksar Akil (Lebanon), 12

La Colombière (France), 12, 68
La Grande Pile (France), 160
La Lagunita (Guatemala), 69
La Lomita site (North America), 170
La Olmeda (Spain), 95
Lake Albert (East Africa), 117
Lake Bonneville (Great Basin, North America), 87
Lake Chad (Africa), 57
Lake Lahanton (Great Basin, North America), 87
Lake Magadi (Africa), 57
Lake of the Clouds (Minnesota), 168
Lake Superior Basin, 81
Lake Superior region, 7, 119, 143
Lake Zeribar (Iran), 98
Lamb Spring site (Colorado), 100
Las Acequias (Arizona), 97–98
Lascaux caves (France), 66
Lavrion (Greece), 119
Leaning Tower (Pisa, Italy), 210, *fig.* 9.5
Lehigh Valley (Pennsylvania), 127
Leonard Shelter (Nevada), 66
Les Echets (France), 160
Libyan Desert, 117, 118
Lindsay mammoth site (Montana), 157
Lisbon (Portugal), 213
Llano Estacado, 11
Long Beach (California), 209
Longgu Cave (China), 70
Lubbock Lake site (Texas), 95

Maiden Castle (England), 182
Maikop (Russia), 180–81
Malaysia, 145
Mammoth Cave (Kentucky), 172
Mammoth Junction site (California), 163
Marduk Dam (ancient Mesopotamia), 199
Matapan Formation (Honduras), 120
Meadowcroft Site (Pennsylvania), 66–67, 70
Mecca (Saudi Arabia), 171
Mediterranean, 75, 92, 104, 109, 119, 120, 123, 124, 125, 138, 139, 140, 142, 144, 145, 146, 159, 205, 210, 215, 218
Mekong River (Vietnam), 128
Melanesia, 214
Melbourne (Florida), *fig.* 1.3

Mesopotamia, 91, 128, 198, 200, 214
Messenia (Greece), 14
Michipicoten Island (Ontario, Canada), 143
Midland (Texas), 161
Milling Stone Horizon (California), 83
Mississippi Delta, 63
Mississippi River, 63, 117, 146, 180, 212, 213, *fig.* 8.3
Mississippi Valley mounds, 7
Missouri River, 217, 218
Modoc Cave (Illinois), 66
Mokattam hills (Egypt), 202
Mono Lake (California), 87
Monte Alban (Mexico), 116
Montezuma Well (Arizona), 95–96
Mordor caves (Australia), 70
Mount Carmel (Asia), 66
Mount Mazama (Oregon), 19, 65, 159, 214
Mount Saint Helens (Washington), 159
Mount Vesuvius (Italy), 127
Mueilha (Egypt), 145
Mummy Cave (Wyoming), 71
Mutsu Province (Japan), 114

Natural Trap Cave (Wyoming), 93–94
Nelson County (Virginia) quarry, 142
Nenezi Dag (Turkey), 138
Neville site (New England), 28
New Madrid (Missouri), 212
Nichoria (Greece), 25, 121, 185, *figs.* 8.5, 8.7, 8.8
Nile Delta (Egypt), 63–64
Nile River, 128, 199
Nineveh (ancient), 214
Nippur (ancient), 181
Nohmul (Belize), 163
North China Plain, 200, 214
Nubia (ancient), 14, 117, 118

Oaxaca (Mexico), 200
Obsidian Cliff (Yellowstone National Park), 124
Ogallala aquifer (Great Plains, North America), 110
Olduvai Gorge (Tanzania), 164, 169
Olorgasailie (Kenya), 14

Olympia (Greece), 6
Ontonogan (Michigan), 142
Ozette site (Washington), 19

Palace of Fine Arts (Mexico City), 210
Palestine, 214
Pecos (New Mexico), 10, 150
Pedra Furada site (South America), 24
Peking Man Cave (Zhoukoudian, China), 66, 70
Périgord rock shelters (France), 68
Peten (Guatemala), 69
Pickering, Glacial Lake (England), 107
Picketpost Mountain (Arizona), 138
Pingasagruk (Alaska), 79
Pink Hill (London, England), 98
Pommeroy Park (England), 208
Pompeii (Italy), 6, 16, 139, 202
Pontine marshes (Italy), 200
Portales (New Mexico), 11
Pozzuoli (Italy), 127
Preseli Mountains (Wales), 134
Proconessus (Island of Marmora, Turkey), 140
Prospect Farm site (Kenya), 163
Pueblo Bonito (New Mexico), 218

Rainy River (North America), 176
Real Alto (Peru), 79
Rio Tinto (Spain), 119
Rio Verde Valley (Oaxaca, Mexico), 66
Rudna Glava (Serbia), 130
Russell Cave (Alabama), 66

Sahara desert (Africa), 106, 172
St. Acheul (France), 9
St. Anthony Falls (Minnesota), *fig.* 1.2
St. Paul's Cathedral (London, England), 209
Salisbury Plain (England), 134
Salzburg (Austria), 117
Samothrace (Greece), 6
San Francisco, 212
San Jon site (New Mexico), 12
Sandia Cave (New Mexico), 66
Santa Clara Valley (San Francisco), 209

Saqqara (Egypt), 127
Sardinia, 144
Sea of Marmara (Turkey), 114
Shanidar Cave (Iraq), 66 , 92, 123
Shiraz (Iran), 213
Sidi Abderrahman quarry (Morocco), 71
Silver Springs (Florida), 208
Sinai (Egypt), 130
Skara Brae, 10
Slovakia, 114
South Dakota, 148, 195
Starr Carr (England), 29, 107
Sterkfontein (Africa), 66, 68
Stonehenge (England), 12, 134, *fig.* 6.1
Swartkrans (Africa), 68

Tabun Cave (Israel), 172
Taung (Africa), 68
Tel Michal (Israel), 75–77, *fig.* 3.12
Tell es-Sultan (Jericho), 112
Teotihuacan (Mexico), 71
Terra Amata (France), 92
Tesuque Valley (New Mexico), 12
Thailand, 145
Thames River (England), 193–94, 209
Thames River Valley (England), 65
Thebes (Egypt), 136, 216
Thera (Greece), 127, 159, 202, 214
Thermopylae (Greece), 79–81, 180, *fig.* 3.15
Thorne Moor (England), 100
Tigris River, 199
Timna (Israel), 144
Tiryns (Greece), 199
Todos los Santos Formation (Guatemala), 120
Tollund, Denmark, 29
Tonga islands, 141
Tower of London (England), 209
Towosahgy State Archaeological Site, 212–13
Two Creeks boreal forest (Wisconsin), 72, 92, 93, *fig.* 3.11

Ugarit (ancient), 125
Upper Delaware Valley (Pennsylvania), 107
Upper Mississippi Valley (North America), 151

Ur (ancient), 214
Ust-Kanskaiya Cave (Siberia), 66
Utalan site (Quiche Maya), 69

Valley of the Kings (Egypt), 216, *fig.* 216
Valley of the Queens (Egypt), 205
Venice (Italy), 205, 210
Ventana Cave (Arizona), 66
Vero (Florida), 10–11, 12, *fig.* 1.3

Wadi Kubbaniya (Egypt), E-84-1 site, 65, 93
Wadi Natrun (Egypt), 118
Wenatechee site (Washington), 159
West Africa, 213
western desert (Egypt), 120
Weyerhauser Number 3 Mine (Wisconsin), 143
Whitby (England), 116
Windover site (Florida), 29
Wyoming, 195

Yangtze River (China), 200
Yellow River (China), 200, 214
Yellow River Plain (China), 128, 193, 214, *fig.* 8.11
Yucatan Peninsula (Mexico), 69, 117

Zagros Mountains (Asia Minor), 92

Subjects

A. islandica, 96
A soil horizon, 31, 32, 34, 35, 44, 110, 158
Ap soil horizon, 37
A1 soil horizon, 35
abiotic indicators, 90
abrasion, 19, 39, 54, 90, 203–04, 220; artifact, 42, 59, 65; mechanical, 24, 25, 82
abrasives, 127
accelerator mass spectrometry (AMS), 86, 149, 155, 165
accretion, 81; lateral, 59, 66; vertical, 66, 193. *See also* eluviation
Acheulian, 14, 39, 56, 57, 61, 71, 92, 106, 165; artifacts, 172, 192; hand axes, 73–74
acid rain, 124, 133, 206, 207, 220

acidic soil, 204
acidity, 159, 204, 221
acids, amino, 161–62; carbonic, 124, 131, 208, 220, 221; deoxyribonucleic (DNA), 103, 134; humic, 171; nitrogen, 206; sulfuric, 143, 205, 220, 221; succinic, 142
additive dose technique. *See* thermoluminescence
adobe, 131, 140; bricks, 128; structures, 210, 213
agate, 112, 114
Aggie Brown Member, 157
aggradation, 31, 60, 61, 109, 110; bar, 59; lateral, 64; vertical, 64
aggradational events, 61, 63
agricultural features, 190, 194
agriculture, 29, 32, 66, 79, 87, 88, 91, 93, 98, 110, 174, 178, 184, 188, 190, 195, 199, 200, 213–14; crops, 111; in Guatemala, 109; Iron Age, 99; Mayan, 192; origins, 106, 109; use of water, 131
alabaster, 112, 116, 117
alcohol, 184
Alfisols, 29, 32, 33, 36, 158
algae (habitat tolerance), 95
alkaline, 33, 90, 126, 129, 205; earth, 44, 204
alkalinity, 82
alloys, 112, 199; copper, 221; tin-lead, 221
alluvial, 108, 140, 145, 147; chronology, 12; depositional systems, 59–66; deposits, 128, 157, 158, 172; fans, 19, 55, 59, 65, 176; ferric sediments, 158; fill, 63, *figs.* 3.5, 3.6; plains, 55; sediments, 54; sequences, 60–63, 158; sites, 34; soil formation, 34; terraces, 33, 34, 60–63, 193, *figs.* 3.5, 3.6; valleys, 34, 130
alluviation, 66
alluvium, 59, 64, 128, 155–58, 183, 188, 192, 193, 210
alpha particles, 169
aluminum, 31, 33, 195; phosphate, 28
Amazon River mound builders, 182
amazonstone, 115–16
amber, 135; Baltic, 116, 142; sources in the Americas, 116
American Geologist, 8

amethyst, 112, 114

amino acid epimerization and racemization: controls in amino acid dating, 161–62; D/L ratio conversion, 161–62

amphibians, 88, 102

amphibole, 115, 151

Anasazi Warm Period (climatic event), 98

Andean prehistory, 79

andesine, 142

andesite, 122, 142

anglesite, 119 (*see* lead sulfate)

anhydrite, 28, 36, 57

anhydrous conditions, 204

animals: body size related to climate, 102; browsers versus grazers, 101; burrows, 44; extinction in North America, 111; waste, 195. *See also specific animals*

anomalies, 185; dipolar, 184; geologic versus archaeological, 187; in geophysical prospecting, 182; magnetic, 183

Anomoeoneis sphaerophora, 96

anoxic, 29, 91

anthropogenic: biogeochemistry, 194; context of buried sites or features, 182; disturbances, 184; impacts, 195; soil-forming processes, 184

anthropological archaeology, 3

anthrosol, 195, 197

antimony, 143, 144

antlers (deer and elk), 107

Apache (Native Americans), 115

apatite, 28, 113, 142, 169

aragonite, 57, 98

ARC/INFO, 196

archaeogeology, 1

archaeological: geology, 2, 3, 4–8; materials dating chart, *fig.* 7.1; record, 1, 2, 3, 4, 7, 12, 14, 15, 16, 18, 50–52, *fig.* 3.1; sediments, 20–21; strata, 210; survey, 130, 177, 199, 222

Archaeological Society of Greece, 159

archaeology: bridging theory approach, 52; classical, 6; classified as a subdivision of the natural sciences, 2; closely connected with historic geology and paleontology, 15; collaboration with geology and the natural sciences, 8–12; contextual approach to, 14, 15; distinct from anthropology, 4; earth-sciences and, 4, 8; excavations, 208; goal of, 2; historic, 4, 103, 165, 195; middle-range theory in, 15; multidisciplinary, 177, 222; New Archaeology, 1; processual, 14–15; relation of geology to, 13, 16; salvage, 199; and soils, 29–30; taphonomic approach to, 53; thematic periods in, 4; theoretical basis for studies, 13; wetland, 103

archaeosedimentary column, 68

archaeosediments, 4, 20–21

Archaic (North America), 20, 28, 88, 92, 106–07, 109, 120, 158

Archimedes screw, 192

argillaceous clasts, 151

argillic soil horizon, 33, 38, 44, 158

Argillisols, 35

argilliturbation, 83

Aridosols, 33–34

Army Corps of Engineers, U.S., 178, 216

arroyos, 55

arsenic, 34, 118, 143, 144, 195

articlast, 21, 24, 59

artifact(s), 18, 25, 47, 48, 70, 219; abrasion, 42, 59, 65; and American Paleolithic, 7; assemblages, 56; carbonate incrusted, 168; chemical alteration of, 161; contemporaneity, 159; in desert settings, 54; deterioration of stone, 203–04; and formation processes, 53; geologic interpretation of deposits, 25; as "index fossils," 159; mixing, 59, 163; orientation, 50; patterning, 50, 52, 53; primary and secondary accumulations, 18, 57, 65, 83; redeposition, 65, 78; secondary context, 18, 65; secondary zone, 27; size distribution, 39–40; size sorting, 83; Stone Age, 5; taphonomy, 32, 50, 65

ash tree, 100

ash, volcanic, 19, 33, 64, 65, 69, 89, 107, 127, 141, 154, 158–59, 164, 214–15; column, 203; fall, 202–03; flow, 202–03; layers, 159, 214; lenses, 70; plume, 203

ash, wood, 126

ashlar masonry, 127

Atlantis, legend of, 159

atomic absorption spectrometry (AA), 137, 147–48, 149

attapulgite, 129 (*see* palygorskite)

augering, 192

Aulacoseira granulata, 96

Aurignacian, 68

Australopithecus, 101

australopithecine, 38, 68, 86

authigenic, 81; carbonate deposition, 81; components, 44; mineralization, 35; sulfate, 35

Aztecs, 115, 116, 121, 124, 127, 215

azurite, 112, 119, 131; pigment, 120, 129; smelting, 144

B soil horizon, 31, 158

Bt soil horizon, 44, 158

Btn soil horizon, 44

Babylonians, 181

back-scattered electron petrography, 138

backswamps, 63

bajada, 55

balloons, and aerial photography, 186, 190

bank(s): canal, 199; erosion, 64, 199, 216, 217; overflow, 213–14; stability, 199

bar(s), 59, 74

barium, 137

basalt, 33, 112, 131, 139, 200; basaltic obsidian flows, 137; basaltic rock, 127; lava, 143; trap rock, 122

bases (chemical), 33

basin(s), 19, 24, 27, 28, 44, 47, 53, 56–59, 63, 87, 91; deep, 77, *fig.* 3.13; drainage, 88, 95; Great Basin (North America), 87, 103, 106; Lake Superior Basin, 81; lake, 44, 47; Mediterranean, 109

bays, 75, 79, 189

beach, 75, 81; cobble, 24, 79; deposition, 71, 77, 79, *fig.* 3.13; recession, 216; sands, 27, 41, 79, 141; sediments, 41, 71; terraces, 81

beaches, 40, 41, 57, 58, 74, 75, 79, 189; lake, 106

beavers, 87

bedrock, 31, 32, 33, 67, 68, 69, 70, 71, 73, 115, 151, 166, 178, 180, 184, 210; canals, 200; geology of, 137, 202, 212; maps of, 175, 178, 180; quarries, 121; toxicity, 195

beetles, 100

bentonite, 128, 142

berms, 219, 220

beta rays, 165

bioclasts, 91

biofacts, 219

biologic activity, 29, 30, 99, 216

biologic processes, 19–20, 24, 25, 195–96; and artifacts, 52; mixing, 20; and phosphates, 28; trampling, 19

biosphere: modified by human activity, 109

biostratigraphic: deposits, 18; markers, 48; units, 30, *fig. 2.5*

biostratigraphy, 159

biotic, 81, 89, 100, 102, 109, 111; activity, 30, 33, 35, 44, 70; attributes, 31; contexts associated with humans, 106; damage, 219; extinction of communities, 110; habitats, 101, 108; indicators, 88, 90; inputs, 70; intervention, 87; remains, 50; signals, 88

bioturbation, 18, 32, 44, 58, 81, 82, 83–85, 154, 155, 168, 184, 215, *fig. 3.16*

bird fossil remains, 101–02

bison, 101 (extinct), 159–60

bitumen, 201

bivalve crustacea, 96, 98

"black amber." *See* jet

bleaching, 118, 171

"blue mud of the meadows," 201

"blue stones" (Stonehenge), 134

bog people, 103

bogs and boglands, 29, 57, 91, 95, 96, 99, 100, 131; peat, 103–04, 176; preserved prehistoric human remains, 29

bone, 65, 131, 168, 171, 174, 195, 204, 208, 219; antlers, 107; buried, 131, 160; Late Holocene: oracle, 120; rabbit, 161; remains, 83

boron, 195

boulder clay, 73

boulders, 21, 107, 115, 122, 130; copper, 142; obsidian, 163

Brady soil, 157

breccia, 70, 71, 165

brick, 127–28, 183, 198, 205; adobe, 128; burnt, 128; concentrations, 188; making, 128; mud, 26, 28, 126, 128, 210; sun-dried, 198

brickearth, 65

brine, 117, 118; boiling of, 117; springs, 117

bronze, 120, 130, 135, 144–46, 221; and cassiterite, 145; Chinese, 146; composition, 145; Egyptian, 144; Old World deposits, 145

Bronze Age, 13, 25, 69, 100, 108, 118, 119, 120, 121, 130, 158, 197, 218

Brule Formation, 148

Buckner Creek paleosol, 158

building: materials, 116, 117, 126–28, 130; stone, 127–28, 178, 205

Bureau of American Ethnology, 7

burial(s), 195, 216; mound construction, 110; Neanderthal, 92; processes, 204; protective, 199, 200; rate and depth, 216; Viking ship, 103

buried: bone, 160; features, 184, 188, 219; materials, 208; river valleys, 192; sites, 78, 202–03, 208, 216, 219; soils (*see* paleosols); structures, 187, 188, 190–91, *fig. 8.9*; walls, 184, 187, 188

burned features, 183, 190

burnt flint, 172–73

burnt lime, 127

C soil horizon, 31

cadmium, 195

calcareous, 37; concretions, 129; mud deposits, 107; nodules, 34; ostracod shells, 96; precipitates, 27–28; sand, 73; sandstone, 27; soils, 205

calcic soil horizon, 31, 35

Calcisols, 35

calcite, 27, 28, 38, 44, 57, 67, 81, 113, 115, 116, 118, 126, 129, 131, 162, 204, 205, 220; cement, 38, 220; pigments, 129; veins, 104

calcitic formations, 172

calcium, 97, 133, 137, 161, 195, 204

calcium carbonate, 20, 26, 27, 28, 31, 33, 81, 97, 117, 118, 126, 127, 133, 155, 165, 200, 204, 220, 221; crusts on sherds, 165, 204; in paleosols, 34, 35

calcium oxalate, 93

calcium oxide, 127, 151

calcium phosphate, 28

calcium sulfate, 28, 118, 205, 220

calcium-magnesium carbonate, 68, 129

calcrete, 35, 44, 47, 168

caldera, 138, 214–15

caliche. *See* calcrete

canal(s), 199–201

cap rock, 179, 180

capillary: action, 208; fringe, 81; rise, 44, 81, 131

carbon, 221; "dead," 47, 166; isotope fractionation, 167, *figs. 7.4, 7.6*; old, 155, 166, 168; photosynthetic pathways, 93; reservoir, 155, 166; stable isotopic values, 105

carbon-12 (^{12}C), 165–66, 167, *fig. 7.6*

carbon-13 (^{13}C), 165–66, 167, *fig. 7.6*

carbon-14 (^{14}C), 155, 157, 165–66, 167, *fig. 7.6*; chronology, 163; cycle, *fig. 7.5*; half-life, 165; sample contamination problems, 165. *See also* radiocarbon dating

carbon dioxide (CO_2), 127, 131, 194, 208

carbonaceous, 29; deposits, 47; layers, 65; particles, 220

carbonate(s), 57, 68, 206, 218; analysis, 195; deposition, authigenic, 81; dissolution, 220; enrichment, pedogenic, 81; forms of, 27–28, 35; incrustation on artifacts, 18; lake, 172; microfossils, 151; organic, 165; precipitates in lakes, 57; proportions to clastics, and deposition, 44–48, *figs. 2.12, 2.13, 2.14*; Quaternary, 171; rocks, 208, 209; secondary accumulation, 81; shell, 166

carbonation, 204

carbonic acid, 124, 208, 220, 221

carnallite, 118

carnelian, 114

casing blocks, 202

cassiterite, 130, 144–46

cast iron, 221

catacombs, 202
cation, 161, 204
catlinite, 124
cave(s), 53, 66–71, 199, 208; art in, 69–70, 121; deposits, 165; igneous rock, 70–71; limestone, 67–70, *fig. 3.7*; mechanical disintegration of rocks within, 19; pseudo karst, 69; sediments, 91
cement: calcite, 38, 220; portland, 127; pozzolanic, 127; silica, 124; underwater, 201
cementation and induration, 38
Cenozoic, 108
ceramic, 169, 205; clays, 124, 125–26, 127, 128, 131; glaze, 118, 126, 146; temper, 126; thin sections, 149–51
cerium, 141
cerrusite, 119, 120, 146, 220
cesium, 141
Chaconnes placentula var. *Lineata*, 96
Chadron Formation, 148
chalcedony, 112–14, 131, 148
Chalcolithic, 9, 119
chalcopyrite, 119, 121
chalk, 28, 113, 180, 206
channel(s), 63; aggradation, 59; braided, 64; branches, 64; drainage, 192; fill, 59; margins, 213; migration, 65, 66, 108; pattern, 66; river, 64–65, 188, 189, 211, 212
charcoal, 65, 92, 93, 158, 168, 173
chemical: alteration of artifacts, 81–82, 161; analysis, 160, 220; compatibility of fill, 219; composition of buried bone, 160; composition of ostracod shell, 97; dating techniques, 160–61; decomposition, 204; deposition, 21, 27; dissolution of stone, 203–04; nutrients, 194; precipitates and precipitation, 28, 155; prospecting to locate sites, 195; ratios, 104–05; stone treatments, 220; weathering, 174, 220
chernozems, 33
chert, 112–14, 122, 130, 131, 139–40, 149, 202; Hudson Bay Lowland, 140; nodules, 128, *fig. 5.3*; red, 113 (*see also* jasper); sourcing, 139
chisels, 115

chloride, 118, 129
chlorine, 195
chlorine-36 (^{36}Cl), 174
chlorite, 38
chroma, 36
chronology, 153; absolute, 153, 158, 161; relative, 153, 159, 160, 161
chronometric techniques, 153
chronostratigraphy, 156
chronozones, 160
Chumash (Native Americans), 109
cinnabar, 120, 129
Cladocera, 98
clams, 98, 212
clastic(s), 21; basin deposits, 57; and deposition, 44–48, 57, 66–67, 97, *figs. 2.12, 2.13, 2.14*; deposits, 21–27; materials, 67; particle(s), 21, 23–27, 44, 57, 122, 220, *fig. 2.10*; in sediments, 80, 110; units, 73
clasts, 21, 42, 65; argillaceous, 151; eroded, 174; non-artifact, 59
clay, 13, 21–24, 26–27, 31, 34, 35, 63, 65, 69, 70, 96, 107, 109, 124, 125–26, 129, 131, 135, 140–41, 183, 187, 188, 198, 202, 214, 218, 220, *figs. 2.2, 2.3, 2.4*; adobe bricks, 128; beds, 32, 140; boulder, 73; burnt brick, 128; defined, 125; deposits, 125, 171, 178; expansion and contraction, 83, 126; as geologic term, 127; glacial, 141; halloysite, 126; illite, 126, 204; kaolinite, 125–26, 128; load bearing, 209–10; matrix, 205; micaceous, 151; mineral formation, 204; minerals, 125, 149, 212; montmorillonite, 126, 128, 212, 216; mortar, 128; paste, 150; petrographic study of pottery, 149; pottery, 124, 125–26, 127, 128, 131, 140; sand-silt-clay ratios, 127, 128; saturated, sandy clay, 210; size, 21–23, 26–27, 125, *figs. 2.3, 2.4*; smectite, 126; sourcing, 140, 151; structural strength, 127
climate, 86–92, 106, 107–11, 131, 133, 168, 180, 182, 184, 196, 207; and animal body size, 102; Bronze Age, 109; change, 9, 75, 86–92, 99, 100, 102, 104, 105, 108, 160, 164, 222; cold, 65; and insects, 100; in

oxygen isotope ratios, 104; and pack-rat middens, 103; and pollen assemblages, 91; in the prehistoric Near East, 91; temperate, 208; tree remains as indicators of, 93; tropical, 198; and use of diatom taxa, 95–96; variation, 56
Clovis, 11, 24, 52, 148, 159, 161
cluster analysis, 152
coal, 129, 131, 168; burning, 195, 196; clinker, 123; mining, 201
coastal: and marine depositional settings, 74–78; areas, 74–75, 92, 189; change studies, 2; environments, 168, 189, 192, 216; erosion, 202, 216, 219; harbors, 180; landscape context, 79–80; Mediterranean studies, 75; plains, 180; processes and site formation, 71, 78–79; ridges, 76, *fig. 3.12*; settings, 63, 75; sites, 180; systems, 63; uplift, 79
coasts, 75, 98, 103, 189
coating (water repellent), 218
cobalt, 141, 143, 195
Coleoptera (beetles), 100
collagen degradation, 161
colloidal, 28; ferric oxides, 28; silica, 126
colluvium, 64, 158, 174
color, 36–38, 53, 158
Columbia, space shuttle, 192
Columbus, Christopher, 116
compaction, 35, 82, 112, 192, 198, 212, 215, 216, 219
computer: and imaging technology, 162; digital processing, 181; software, 196
concretions, 121, 125, 126, *fig. 5.2*; chert nodules, 128, *fig 5.3*; ferrous, 221; septarian, 129
conductivity: electrical, 10, 187; electromagnetic (EM), 188; subsurface, 187
conglomerate, 24, 29, 122, 127
conservation, 207, 220–21
construction (large scale), 198, 199–201
contamination: detrital, 165; of potable water, 199
context: primary, 18, 19, 20, 24, 25, 42, 48, 57, 59, 83–84; secondary,

18, 25, 40, 48, 65; systemic, 15, 16, 52, 54, 59, 65, 85
continental crust, 107
continental shelf (Gulf of Mexico), 183
contour intervals, 175, 176, 197
contraction cracks, 74
convergent light, 150
copper, 25, 113, 118, 120, 127, 130, 135, 140, 142–44, 195, 219, *fig.* 6.4; alloy metallurgy, 119, 221; complex copper minerals, 143; deposits, 116, 136, 140, 143, 144; hydroxycarbonate (*see* azurite); iron sulfide, 119, 121 (*see also* chalcopyrite); native, 8, 119, 135, 142–44; ore, 121, 130, 135, 146; slag dumps, 130; smelting, 112, 119, 130, 135, 144, 146, 196; sourcing, 119, 143–44, 149; sulfide deposits, 119, 120, 143, 144; sulfide ores, 119, 135
coprolites, 90
coquina, 28
coral, 165
core drilling, 75, 80–81, 107, 155, 176, 177, 179, 182, 184, 185, 187, 189, 192–94, 196, 219, *fig.* 8.10
corn, 122
corrosion, 131, 221
corundum, 113, 127
cosmic-ray intensity, 166
cracking, 201, 206
creep: downslope, 180, *fig.* 9.1; seasonal, 202; soil, 82, 215; surface, 40
crinoid, 125
crop(s), 190, 195
cross bedding, 40, 59, 79
cryostatic pressures, 82
cryoturbation, 74, 82–83, 168, 216
crystal(s), 149, 204–05
cultivation, 180, 203
cultural resource management, 184, 193
cummulic soil horizon, 158
currents: longshore, 63; wind driven, 87
cut and fill, 55, 59, 61, 63

D-amino acid (right handed), 161–62
D/L ratio conversion, 161–62

dacite, 139
dams, 64, 65, 110, 199–200, 204, 217
data analysis, 151–52, 181
databases: digital, 196; geoarchaeological, 196; of marble isotope analyses, 140; modeling, 196; of obsidian trace elements, 138; of trace elements in native copper, 143
datable materials and geoarchaeological applications, 168–69; loess deposits, 156; organics in soils, 268; wood, 158, 168
dating methods: absolute, 9, 74, 153, 154, 158, 160, 161, 162; accelerator mass spectrometry (AMS), 86, 142, 155, 165; archaeomagnetic, 169–71; argon-argon, 163–64; cation-ratio, 161; dendrochronology, 9, 160, *fig.* 7.7; of exposed surfaces, 174; fission track, 169; hydration (obsidian), 162–63; infrared stimulated luminescence (IRSL), 174; loess deposits, 156, 174; optical stimulated luminescence, 174; paleomagnetic and archaeomagnetic, 169; paleosols in loess and alluvium, 155–58; pollen stratigraphy, 12, 154, 166; potassium-argon(K/Ar), 12, 86, 157, 158, 163, 164–65; radiation, 169–74; radiocarbon, 12, 34, 103, 155, 157, 165–68, 176, 197, *figs.* 7.2, 7.4, 7.5, 7.6; radiometric, 163–69; rate of weathering, 174; relative, 153, 159, 160, 161; rind, 174; shell-midden deposits, 104; and travertine, 28; uranium series (U-series), 86, 164–65; using animal and plant remains, 159–60; varves, 160; volcanic ash, 158–59
dating site formations, 163
debitage (flaking debris), 39, 41, 56, 139, 173
debris flow, 19, 24, 55, 64, 74
deer, 100, 101, 107, 109
deflation, 48, 54, 55, 56, 219
degradation, 60, *figs.* 3.5, 3.6
dehydration, 44, 115, 162; of paleosols, 35; seasonal, 110
delta, 166

delta(s), 2, 58, 59, 63–64, 74, 75, 81, 110
deltaic deposits, 72, 209
Delvin Quadrangle topographic map, 176
dendrites, 129, 130, *fig.* 5.4
deoxyribonucleic acid (DNA), 103, 134
Department of Agriculture, U.S., 34
deposition, 18, 20, 25, 31, 34, 35, 38, 40, 42, 43, 48, 90, 214; ash, 19, 32; calcite, 57; carbonate, 57, 70; chemical, 21, 27–28, 67; of chemical precipitates, 57; clastic, 91, 97; in coastal and marine settings, 74–81; contexts, 25, 59–66; eolian, 54, 67, 70, 202; episodic, 81; flood, 56, 65, 107; fluvial, 65, 67, 70, 108; human, 110–11; lake-related, 57–58; loess, 106; overbank, 66, 193; patterns, 110; pollen, 90–91; processes, 98, 110 (*see also* depositional systems); post-depositional conditions, *fig.* 2.12; sediment, 44; stream, 59, 61; surfaces (dating), 174; of tufa and other carbonates, 59; and Walther's Law of Correlation of Facies, 75; wind, 67
depositional systems, 53–71
deposits: alkaline, 90; alluvial, 128, 157, 158, 159, 172; cassiterite, 145; chert, 139; clay, 70, 125, 140, 171, 178; copper ore, 116; copper sulfide, 119, 120, 143, 144; deltaic, 209; eroded or reworked, 168; evaporite, 117; fluvial, 59, 65, 70, 99; galena, 146; glacial, 174; gold, 147; Holocene, 64, 87, 158, 213; lag, 48, 55, 119; lake, 27, 65, 87, 100, 125, 165, 172; lode, 130, 142, 147; loess, 19, 40, 98, 106, 155–56, 174; mass wasting, 202; midden, 78, 104, 163; obsidian, 124, 137–38, 140; placer, 118, 120, 130, 144, 145; point bar, 212; pyroclastic, 137; prodelta, 63; Quaternary, 19, 29, 86, 98, 100; salt, 117; sedimentary, 93, 143, *fig.* 2.1; tephra, 141, 164; travertine, 80, 172; volcanic ash, 64, 154, 158, 202
desert varnish (cation-ratio), 161

desert(s), 32, 40, 53, 54–57, 58, 113, 114, 117, 118, 121, 144, 145, 180, 202, *fig.* 3.2

destruction, 203–07

detrital: contamination, 165; quartz sourcing, 142; remanent magnetism, 170; silt, 27; zone, 72

diagenesis, 18, 20, 38, 135, 208, 215, 216, 219

diagenetic, 16, 27, 52, 82, 150, 219

diamond, 113, 114, 127

diatomites, 65, 96

diatoms, 57, 60, 90, 95–96, 141

diorite, 112, 123, 126, 127, 139

discoloration, 205

discontinuities, 48

discriminant analysis, 136, 148, 151–52

distal segment, 59

ditches, 10, 98, 110, 117, 186, 187, 190, 200

dolerite, 127, 134

dolomite, 57, 68, 113, 126

dosimetry, 172

downslope creep, 180, 210, *fig.* 9.1

drainage, 38, 52, 64, 66, 74, 91, 103, 110, 131, 142, 180, 200, 208, 215, 218; basin, 88, 95; channels, 192; networks (ancient), 192, 196

dripstone, 67, 165

drought, 97, 108, 217

drumlins, *fig.* 3.10

dumps and refuse areas, 130, 194, 195

dune(s), 54, 55, 71, 75, 79; eolian deposits, 41, 72; formations, 19; interdunal ponds, 56; sand, 27, 41, 42, 56, 65, 74, 175, 176, 202; sediments, 65; stabilization, 65

dung, 168

dwellings, 19, 29, 79, 96, 103, 126, 210, 195

dye, 125, 129

E soil horizon, 31, 35

"early man" controversy, 7

earthenware, 204–05

earthquake(s), 44, 88, 99, 107, 108, 180, 189, 209, 210–13, 215, 218; Copper River Delta (Alaska), 212; eastern Mediterranean earthquake zone, 210; fissures, 212, 213; Jeri-

cho (Israel), 212; Knossos (Crete), 210; Lisbon (Portugal), 213; Modified Mercalli Scale, 210, 212; *table* 9.1; New Madrid (Missouri), 212; Richter magnitude scale, 210; San Francisco earthquake of *1906*, 212; Shiraz (Iran), 213

earthworms, 83

East African Rift system, 88

ecofacts, 107

ectotherms, 102

edaphic conditions, 177

edge effects, 188

efflorescence, 204

electrical conductivity, 10, 187

electrical resistivity, 184, 186–88

electromagnetic (EM) conductivity, 188

electromagnetic spectrum, 182, *fig.* 8.4

electron spin resonance (ESR), 171–74, *fig.* 7.9

electron traps in minerals, 171, 172

electronic scanner images, 191

electrum, 119, 221

element concentrations (rare earth), 142

elements, 119

elephants, 101, 160

elk, 101, 107

eluvial horizon, 35

eluviation, 81

emery, 127

engineering geology, 218

Entisols, 32, 33, 36

environmental change and archaeological interpretation, 9, 12, 22, 48, 92, 100, 105–11, 160, *fig.* 4.3; evidence for, 88; human habitats and geoecology, 105–07; inferring environmental change, 88–89

environmental determinism, 106

environments, geologic, 75, 86, 119, 143, 217

Eocene Type Formation (Oregon), 142

eolian, 19, 40, 41, 42, 54–56, 65, 67, 70, 72, 106, 172, 202, *fig.* 2.9

epidote, 38

epigraphy, 140

epipedon, 33

erosion, 19, 27, 32, 33, 34, 35, 38, 54, 57, 59, 61, 66, 70, 81, 86, 88, 106, 108, 110, 128, 130, 180, 199, 212, 215, *fig.* 3.12; bank, 64, 216, 217; coastal, 202, 219; and cultivated fields, 203; events, 48, 60, 63; features, 41, 55, 75, 176, 217; intervals, 109; lateral, 200, 209; processes, 64, 216; and redeposition, 64, 74, 78, 84; and reservoirs, 216–17; and slopes, 218; surfaces, 48, 78 (dating), 174; and transport, 79, 84–85

escarpments, 175, 218

Eskimos, 116

estuary, 75, 168, 180

europium, 143

eustatic: change, 75, *fig.* 3.14; rise curves, 78

evaporation, 28, 44, 57, 68, 81, 87, 104, 117, 118, 204, 205

excavation (ancient), 201–02

exfoliation, 204

exogenic sediments, 40

extinction, 110–11

facies, 4, 41, 64, 75, *fig.* 2.4; freshwater lake, 57; marsh, 57; microfacies, 61; plant, 57; sedimentary, 41, 75; Walther's Law of Correlation of Facies, 49, 75, 77

faulting, 88, 107, 108, 213, 218

faults, 43, 88, 204, 209, 212–13, 215, 218

fauna. *See* animals

faunal: change in communities, 79, 92; remains as indicators of environment, 100–03

features: archaeological, 10, 16, 18, 20, 24, 48, 53, 68, 84, 90, 98, 100, 153, 160, 168, 169, 176, 182, 183, 184, 186, 187, 189, 190, 195, 197; buried, 10, 182, 184, 188, 190, 218; burned, 183; depositional, 55, 72, 176; discrete, 182; erosional, 41, 55, 72, 75, 176, 217; karst solution, 70; lake-margin, 58; pedological, 180; ridge and swale, 60; shoreline, 59, 64, 78; solution, 69; stranded, 74

feldspar(s), 122, 128, 131, 151, 172, 174, 204; alteration, 126; amazonstone, 115–16; in archaeological contexts, 115; moonstone, 115; potassium, 163–64; sunstone, 115; weathering, 126, 204

felsite, 122–23, 131

fen carr, 107

ferric: oxides (colloidal), 28; sediments (alluvial), 158; sulfate, 143

ferrous, 28; concretions, 221; iron compounds, 37; iron sulfide, 221; salts, 28

ferruginous quartzite, 136

fill, 19–21, 61, 63, 71, 158, 174, 187, 210, 218, 219

fingerprint: chemical, 137, 143; isotope, 140; non-overlapping, 136; trace-element, 139, 143, 147, 152

fire, 109–10

firestone, 121

fish, 103, 193

flagstone, 201

flint, 25, 107; burnt, 172; defined, 113; knapping, 113; Knife River Flint, 139–40; mines, 130, 186

flood legends, 213–14

flooding, 58, 59, 64–66, 70, 98, 108, 180, 199, 200, 213–14

floodplain(s), 18, 34, 38, 63, 64–66, 75, 108, 110, 128, 176, 180, 193, 209, 213–14, 216; canals built in floodplain sediments, 200; deposits, 27, 70; Gulf of Malia-Spherchios River (Greece), 80; Yellow River (China), 128, 193, 214

floods, 25, 32, 66, 97, 108, 200, 213–14, 216, 217, 220

floors, 48, 186, 188

flora (fossil), 98, 90, 141. *See also* plants

floralturbation, 83

flow: ash, 202; debris, 10, 24, 55, 64, 74; lava, 70, 174; obsidian, 137, 138

flowstone, 28, 67–68, 165

fluorine, 161

fluorite, 113

fluvial, 59–64, 67, *fig. 3.5*

flux, 135, 148

Folsom artifacts, 159–60

food: and phytolith analysis, 95; resources, 176; waste, 195

footslope areas, 110

forest, 28, 32, 33, 36, 72, 108, 109, 110, 203; boreal habitat, 72, 101; boundaries, 92; clearing, 100, 174; species, 98; spruce, 92

forges, 183

Formative Period in Mesoamerican prehistory, 65–66

fortifications, 188, 218

fossils, 5, 47, 50, 56, 66, 67, 89, 90, 99, 101, 102, 129, 131, 159; australopithicene, 38; hominid, 12, 164; shell, 124–25, 126

foundations: historic buildings, 183, 186, 188, 209, 210; stability, 198

fractionated, 104

fracture, 113, 114, 116, 122, 123, 124, 126, 204

fragmentation, 204

freeze-thaw, 24, 70; cycles, 74, 82, 205, 219; phenomena, 216

frost: action, 19, 82–83, 133, 206, 207, 215; damage, 205; effects on building stone, 205; heave, 36, 74, 82

fumarole (gas emissions), 168

fungi, 90

galena, 119, 120, 131, 146, 147

gamma, 183, 185

gamma rays, 148

gangue, 118, 130

garnet, 142

gas chromatography, 142

gas emissions (fumarole), 168

gas extraction, 215

gastropods, 57, 98, 125

geoarchaeology, 1–18, 26, 32, 34, 50–52, 86, 90, 122, 144, 149, 153, 158, 174, 175, 188, 190, 192, 197, 212, 218

geochemical contamination, 161, 168

geochemical environments (ancient), 195

geochemical prospecting and analysis, 182, 194–96

geochemical surveys, 177

geochemistry, 2, 139, 220

geochronology, 2, 9, 12, 16, 161

geoecology, 2, 4, 86, 87–88, 105–07

geofacts, 1, 24, 25, 82

geographic information systems (GIS), 196

geologic: anomalies, 187; aspects of land transportation networks, 201; deposits, 120, 135–37, 142–43, 146, 147, 152, 168, 169, 174, 213, 215–16; environments, 143; maps and mapping, 175–81, 196, 212; time horizons, 218; units, *fig. 2.5*

Geological Society of America, 8, 197

Geological Survey, U.S., 7, 175, 178, 192, 216

Geological Survey of England, 175

geomagnetic field master curve, 170

geomorphic: change and geologic processes, 75; features, 175; stability, 180

geomorphology, 2, 75, 176, 180, 218, 222

geophysical prospecting, 192; electrical resistivity (ER), 186–88; electromagnetic conductivity, 188; ground-penetrating radar (GPR), 188–89; magnetic susceptibility (MS), 184; magnetometry, 182–86

geotechnology, ancient, 199–202

Giddings corers, 192

glacial: advance, 72, 74, 89, 163; clay, 141; deposits, 174; ice, 91; loess, 174; maximum, 73; melting, 71, 74, 168; moraines, 72, 163; outwash, 72; periglacial conditions, 71, 74, 82; and postglacial landscapes, *fig. 3.10*; proglacial lakes, 72, 81; system, 71–74; till, 72, 119, 121

glaciers, 19, 24, 40, 41, 53, 71–74, 78, 89, 209

glaciofluvial deposits, 74

glass, 118, 169

glaze, 118, 126, 146

gley soils, 38

gleyed horizons, 81

gleying, 35

Gleysol, 35

global warming and cooling events, *fig. 7.3*

gneiss, 127

goethite, 37, 121, 129

gold, 118, 130, 135, 142, 147, 221

gophers, 83

gossan, 121
grain size, 113, 140, 151, 190, 202, 212, *fig.* 2.8
graminae, 95
granite, 112, 122, 123, 126, 127, 142, 220
granular disintegration, 70
graphite, 129
grass, 93
gravel, 21, 23-24, 59, 64, 65, 81, 130, 194, 202, 217
graves, 184, 189, 194
gravity, 19, 200, 202, 208
Greek Archaeological Service, 159
greywacke, 122
grog, 126, 128
ground penetrating radar (GPR), 188-89
groundmass, 142
ground-surface irregularities, 175
groundwater. *See under* water
gypsic soil horizon, 36
Gypsisols, 35
gypsum, 28, 31, 57, 112, 113, 117, 127, 128, 172, 205

Hackberry Creek paleosol, 158
hafnium, 141
halite, 28, 117-18, 131, 206
Hallein mine, 117
Hallmundarhraun lava flow (Iceland), 70
halloysite, 126
Hallstatt mine, 117
harbors, ancient, 180, 189
hardpans, 35
hearths, 184, 185
hematite, 28, 37, 113, 120-21, 125, 129, 131, 184
histograms, 40, *fig.* 2.7
Histosols, 34
hog-back ridges, 175
Hohokam (North America), 97-98, 170, *fig.* 4.2
Holocene, 19, 65, 66, 70, 74, 79, 88, 92, 98, 100, 102, 106, 109, 160, 161, 192, 193, 212; climate change, 108; coastlines, 75, 189; deposits, 64, 87, 158, 213; environmental change, 91, 110; loess, 157
hominids, 12, 14, 16, 27, 70, 71, 73, 86, 101, 160, 161, 164

Homo erectus, 70, 86, 101
Hopewell (culture), 117, 119
horizons. *See under* soil
horses, 160, 161
Hudson Bay Lowland chert (HBL), 140
human-environmental interactions, 109-10, 174, 195, *fig.* 3.1
humates, 157, 158
humic: acid radicals, 171; material, 37, 131, 184
humification, 81
humus, 33, 155, 168, 198
huntite, 129
hydration, 162-63, 204, 205, 220
hydraulic cement, 127
hydrocarbons, 195
hydrocerrusite, 221
hydrogen bond, *fig.* 9.4
hydrogeologic conditions, 178
hydrology, 3, 175, 177, 201, 218
hydrolysis, 204
hydrosphere, 108, 176, 195

ice, 74, 78, 82, 91, 215
Ice Age, 4, 5, 8, 10, 24, 69, 93
ice core, 104, *fig.* 4.4
illite, 126, 128, 204
illuvial, 31, 36
illuviation, 81
Inceptisols, 32-33, 36
indigo, 129
indium, 147
Inductively Coupled Plasma spectrometry (ICP), 147-48
infrared light, 174
infrared spectroscopy, 142
infrared stimulated luminescence (IRSL), 174
Ingram-Wentworth size scale, 21
insects, 99-100
Instrumental Neutron Activation Analysis (INAA), 137, 138, 140, 143, 148-49, 172
interfacies, 48
interglacial and glacial episodes, 104, 108, 160, 174
International Society of Soil Science, 36
interstadials, 160, 174
Inuit, 121, 124
Inupiat, 79

invertebrates, 96-100
iridium, 143
iron, 28, 35, 37, 38, 81, 113, 118, 126, 127, 133, 143, 144, 168, 170, 183, 184, 195; ancient, 221; cast, 221; in sedimentary rocks, 31; meteoric, 121; Mohs hardness, 115; ore mines, 121; red, 120; wrought, 221
iron oxide, 20, 27, 28, 35, 37, 38, 43, 113, 121, 129, 133, 144, 151, 184, 190, 191, 205, 221
iron phosphate, 195
irrigation, 64, 110, 200, *fig.* 4.2
isoleucine (amino acid), 162
isotope analysis, 149, 195, 196
isotopes: carbon, 140; fingerprints, 140; fractionated, 104, 195; lead, 147; oxygen, 104, 140; provenance, 140; strontium, 149
isotopic: fractionation, 164, 166, 167, *fig.* 7.4; ratio variation in tree rings, 93; signals in marine sediments, 104; stable value of nitrogen, 105
ivory, 79

jade, 113, 115, 135
jasper, 113, 131
jet, 116
jointing patterns, 139
joints, 19, 68, 70, 130, 204, 212, 218
Jurassic, 128

K soil horizon, 31
kaolinite, 125-26, 128
karst: settings, 68, 69, *fig.* 3.9; soils, 199; solution features in caves, 70, 189; topography, 71, 180, 199
KBS tuff (Kenya), 169
kilns, 183
Klamath Indians, 214
K-means cluster analysis, 151-52
kurkar, 76, *fig.* 3.12
kurtosis, 41

L-amino acids (left handed), 161
lag: deposits, 48, 119; gravels, 54
lagoons, 189, 205, 212
lake(s), 26, 28, 38, 53, 90, 99, 103, 107, 110, 118, 154, 189, 201, 207, 216, 217, 219; artificial, 212; basins,

57–59, *fig.* 3.3; beaches, 106; bottoms, 180; clastic deposition in, 57; closed, 87; cycles, *fig.* 2.14; deposits, 27, 65, 87–88, 100, 125, 165, 172; desert, 56; freshwater, 57, 59; glacial meltwater, 74; ice margin, 74; level changes, 87–88; with outlets, 87; oxbow, 60, 66; proglacial, 72, 81; reservoir, 58; saline, 57; sediments, 65, 86, 165, 172, 212, *fig.* 2.13; shoreline features, 59; types, 57; wave energy in, 57

lamellae, 43

laminae, 43, 154

laminations, 154–55

land transportation networks, 201. *See also* roads and roadbeds

land use, 184, 192, 202

landscape(s): as cultural artifact, 178; change, 65, 66, 89–90, 191, 222; features, 176, 192; glacial and postglacial, *fig.* 3.10; initial, and original occupation, 52–53; paleolandforms, 79; preservation, 180; stability, 193, 203

landslides, 82, 88, 210, 212, 213, 215

lanthanum, 137, 143

lapis lazuli, 112, 115

Laurentide Ice Sheet (North America), 88

lava, 70, 137, 143, 151, 184

lava tubes, 70

Law of Superposition, 34

leaching, 35, 81, 161, 199, 216

lead, 113, 118, 126, 144, 164; carbonate, 119, 120, 146 (*see* cerrusite); deposits, 146; glaze, 126, 146; isotopes, 135, 146–47, 149, 165, *fig.* 6.4; litharge, 119–20; mining, 119; pigment, 119–20; as a preservative in Roman times, 119; provenancing, 146–47; salts, 221; smelting, 119, 146; sulfate (anglesite), 119; sulfide (galena), 119, 120; use, 195

lemmings, 101

lenses, 70

Leonard Paleosol, 157

lepedocrocite, 37, 221

levee, 63, 213

lime, 127–28

limestone, 28, 29, 67–71, 112, 113, 116, 126, 127, 128, 130, 131, 155, 165, 166,

168, 180, 184, 201, 202, 203, 205, 206, 207, 216, 220, *fig.* 3.7

limonite, 28, 121, 131

liquefaction, 44, 199, 212–13

litharge, 119–20

lithic, 65, 81; cores, 41, 56; debitage (flaking debris), 41, 56, 139; defined, 112; flakes, 56; material, 142, 149, 161; raw materials, 123, 130, 131; resources, 126; tools, 122

lithification, 20, 38, 43, 112

lithofacies sequences, 64

lithology, 112, 170, 193, 198

lithosphere, 108, 112

Little Ice Age, 88–89, 104

loam, 23, 37

lode(s), 119, 130, 142, 144, 147

lodestone, 121

loess, 19, 27, 34, 98, 151, 172; Bignell, 157; dating, 156; deposits, 19, 41, 98, 106, 155–56, 174, *fig.* 7.4; Holocene, 157; loess-soil chronostratigraphy, 156; paleosols in, 154, 155–58; Peoria, 156; plateau, 214; sequences, 106, 155–56, 173, 174

"Lucy" hominid remains, 164

macrofossil(s), 29, 87, 92–93, 103

macronutrients (plant), 195

mafic, 28; igneous rocks, 28, 124, 143; intrusives, 143; lava, 143; volcanic rocks, 119

Magdalenian, 98

maghemite, 37, 184

magma, 122, 123

magnesite, 129

magnesium, 126, 127, 129, 133, 137, 195, 204

magnetic: analysis of soil, 182; anomalies, 183–84; compass, 171; declination, 171, *fig.* 7.8; field of the earth, 166, 169–70, 183; poles, 169–70; properties, 184; reversal chronology, 156; shield intensity, 166; susceptibility, 139, 182, 184; variation (time transgressive), 171

magnetite, 121, 127, 184, 221

magnetometry, *figs.* 8.6, 8.7, 8.8; and anomalies, 183–84; as complement to electrical resistivity, 186; magnetic analysis of soils, 182; magnetic properties of minerals,

184; magnetic susceptibility, 182, 184; at Nichoria (Greece), 185

maize (Zea mays), 92, 94–95, 105

malachite, 112, 116, 119, 120, 131

malacology, 98

mammal fossil remains, 100–101

mammoth, 100–101, 157

manganese, 81, 129, 137, 141, 171, 195

manganese oxide, 27, 28, 113, 129, *fig.* 5.4

maps and mapping: ancient, 180–81; base, 175, 190; classification in, 175; geologic, 175, 181, 196, 212; intensity, 218; isopach, 178; landslide susceptibility, 178; photomaps, 191; Quaternary maps, 175; scale, 175, 177, 179, 190, 197; soil, 174, 177–78, 185; structure contour, 178; surficial geology maps, 175; terrain, 177; thematic, 175, 196; topographic, 175, 176, 177, 170, 180, 190, 196, 197

marble, 113, 124, 126, 131, 135, 149, 204, 220; of Aegean area, 140; of Carrara (Italy), 140, 205; and corrosion of monuments, 131; database of isotope analyses, 140; sourcing, 140

marine: depositional settings, 74–81; geophysical techniques, 189; microfauna, 168; oxygen isotope curve, 156; regression, 78–79; sediments, 87, 95, 104, 172; sites, 221; transgressions, 64, 209

marker horizons, 19, 159

marl(s), 26–29, 33, 65, 73, 96, 106, 128

marlstones, 26, 28

marshes, 57, 75, 176

mass wasting, 55, 81, 82, 202, 215

mastic, 131

mastodon, 100–101

matrix, 24

matte, 135, 136

Maya, 69–70, 115, 116, 117, 120, 121, 129, 163, 192, 198

Maya blue, 129

meander: belts, 64; channels, 66; scar pattern, 176

mechanical disintegration, 19, 203–04, 205

meerschaum, 129 (*see* sepiolite)

megaliths, 134

mercury, 28, 118, 120, 195
mesas, 176, 180
Mesolithic, 29, 98, 107, 110, 163, 189
metal, 10, 21, 25, 112, 118–22, 141,
148; artifacts, 9, 131, 146; Bronze
Age, 13; concentrations, 188;
corrosion, 221; conservation
techniques, 221; deposits, 178; detector, 184; ores, 198; probes, 186;
scrap, 135; trace amounts, 195. *See
also specific metals*
metalliferous zones, 144
metallurgy, 118–19
metamorphic rocks, 122, 124, 126,
131, 136, 140, 204, 220; *table* 5.3
meteorites, 121, 174
mica, 112, 116–17, 126, 131, 151, 163,
169
micrite, 58, *fig.* 3.3
micro-artifacts, 25, 40, *fig.* 2.2
microclimates and microclimatology,
111, 162, 201
microcline, 115
microcrystalline quartz, 113, 139
microdebitage, 25
microdepositional conditions, 59
microfauna, 25, *fig.* 4.3; in loess deposits, 157, *fig.* 7.4; marine, 168;
remains, 75
microfloral remains, 75
microfossil(s), 87, 134, 141, 151
micronutrients (plant), 195
micro-organisms, 208, 219
microscope, 149–150, 160
midden deposits, 163, 184; pack rat,
103; shell, 78, 104
Middle Ages, 117
Middle Minoan, 125
migration, 148
millet, 95
mineralogic analysis, 220
minerals, 112–18, 125, 169; carbonate and sulfate, 204; defined, 112;
evaporate, 28; hardness, 13, 114; in
igneous rocks, 164; isometric, 144
mines and mining, 113, 135, 136, 209,
215; ancient, 135; coal, 201; flint,
130, 186; King Solomon's, 144;
lead, 119; open pit, 142, 201; ore,
121; placer, 130; prehistoric North
American, 7, 131; prospecting (ancient), 130; salt, 117; Slovakian,

114; spoil heaps, 110; tin, 146; tunnels, 188; underground, 124; waste
dumps, 126
Minnesota Messenia Expedition, 7
Minoan, 117, 159
Mississippian (North America), 120
mixing, 20, 48, *fig.* 3.6
Modified Mercalli Scale, 210, 212;
table 9.1
Mohs scale of hardness, 113
moisture, 161, 204, 206; content of
soil, 35, 81, 110, 187–88, 190; effects
of, 55
Mollisols, 33, 36, 158
mollusks, 98–99, 161, 165
molybdenum, 195
montmorillonite, 126, 128, 212, 216
monuments: deterioration, 203–04;
preservation, 216
moonstone, 115
moraines, 72
mortar: clay, 128; gypsum, 128; lime,
128, 199, 205; mud, 210; paint, 131
mortuary sites, 120
mosques (Turkish), 171
mosses, 90
mottling, 38, 81
mound builders (Amazon River), 182
Mound Builders (Hopewell), 117, 119
Mousterian (Middle Paleolithic), 68,
74, 121, 165, 172
MSA I/II soil horizon, 104
muck, 201
mud, 18, 21, 23, 26–27, 57, 59, 75, 107,
127, 128; cracks, 43; deep water,
75; indicators of climate change,
27; particle size, 23, 66; playa, 64;
used by humans, 27
mudbrick, 26, 126, 128, 210
mudflows, 82
mudslides, 19
mudstone, 26, 126, *fig.* 2.2
multi-element analyses, 147–49
mummification (Egyptian), 118
Munsell color order system, 36, 190
murex shells, 125, *fig.* 5.1
muscovite, 116–17
musk ox, 101

native copper, 7, 135, 136, 140, 142–
44; boulder (Michigan), 142;
chemical characterization of,

143; geologic environments of,
142; North American deposits
of, 142; sourcing, 136–37, 143;
trace-element "fingerprinting,"
143
natric soil horizon, 31, 44
natron, 118
Neanderthal burial, 92, 172
Neogene, 16
Neolithic, 9, 29, 91, 98, 109, 110, 115,
116, 118, 121, 122, 123, 129, 163, 174,
180, 189, 193
nephrite, 115 (*see* jade)
New Kingdom (Egyptian), 116, 216
nickel, 121, 143
nitrates, 204
nitrogen, 105, 194, 195, 206, 219
noncalcareous: precipitates, 28; sand,
141; soils, 37
novaculite, 113
Nubian sandstone, 206
nucleated settlement patterns, 180
nuts, 92

O soil horizon, 31
oak pollen frequency curve, 92
obelisks, 202, 206
obsidian, 13, 25, 112, 122, 131, 135,
141, 149, 169; cobbles and boulders, 163; deposits, 124, 137–38,
140; flows, 138; hydration dating,
123, 162–63, 174; mirrors, 124;
provenancing, 136; trace-element
database, 138
ocher, 120–21, 129
oil: extraction, 209, 215; shale, 131
old carbon, 155, 166, 168. *See also*
carbon-14 (^{14}C)
Old Kingdom (Egypt), 122, 130
Olmec canal irrigation, 200
oncolite, 57
onyx, 114, 115
opal, 93, 114–15
optical microscopy, 138, 149, 162
optical stimulated luminescence
(OSL), 174
optical-emission spectroscopy, 147
orbital imaging radar, 192
ore(s), 116, 118–22, 130, 135–36,
143–44, 146, 198
orthoclase, 113, 115
orthopyroxene, 142

osmotic pressure, 208
ostracod(s), 57, 96–98, *fig.* 4.2
otoliths, 103
outcrop(s), 129, 130, 136, 179
outwash (glacial), 72, 74, 163
overbank: deposition, 193; mud, 64
oxbow lakes, 60, 66
oxidation, 29, 35, 37, 38, 91, 143, 199, 204; mottling, 81; processes in groundwater, 208
oxide ores, 121
oxidized colors, 158
Oxisols, 35, 36
oxygen, 37, 81, 96, 104, 140, 149, 156, 165, 172, 194, 207, 208, 221
oxyhydroxides, 221

paleoclimates, 67, 86
paleoecologic indicators, 57, 86
paleoecology, 14, 222
paleoenvironmental reconstruction, 86–111, 178
paleogeography, 4, 75, 80
paleogeomorphic reconstruction, 74–75, 202
paleoherpetology, 102
Paleo-Indian (North American), 4, 11–12, 65, 81, 92, 95, 100, 111, 157, 158
Paleolithic, 5, 24, 27, 44, 56, 70, 71, 72, 100, 103, 106, 110, 121, 123, 160, 165, 172, 189; American, 7–8; artifacts, 65, 68–69; archaeology, 164; deposits, 12; divisions of, 6; flint mine (Hungary), 186; Nubian, 14; studies, 10, 11
paleontology, 2, 3, 4, 9, 16, 49, 89–90, 134, 153, 159–60
paleopathology (human), 195
paleoseismic, 218
paleosols, 34–36, 93, 109, 172, 182; in archaeological contexts, 31; Buckner Creek, 158; Hackberry Creek, 158; as indicators of environmental conditions, 36; in loess, 155–58, *fig.* 7.4; as time indicators, 154, 155–58
palygorskite, 129
palynology, 90, 92
paramagnetic defects, 171
particle morphology, 42–43, 142, *fig.* 2.10

paste, 151
patina, 161, 221
patination. *See* desert varnish
patterned ground, 82
peat, 36, 47, 103–04, 168; bogs, 103, 160, 176; deposits, 29, 57; histosols, 34; reed, 107
pebbles, 21, 122
pediments, 59
pedogenesis, 32, 44, 168
pedogenic, 57, 89; alteration, 158; carbonate enrichment, 81; horizons, 27, 35; zones, 81
peds, 44
pelecypods, 57
perched, 81
periglacial, 71, 74, 82
permeability, 82, 133, 178, 202, 204
petrocalcic zones, 31
petroglyphs, 161
petrography, 2, 3, 9, 13, 138–39, 141, 149–51, 220
petroleum products, 131
petrology, 149
pewter, 119, 144, 221
pH, 96, 37, 178, 195, 204, 205, 208, 216, 219
phenocrysts, 122
Phoenicians, 145
phosphates, 27, 28, 177, 195
phosphorus, 195
photography, aerial, 10, 176, 190–91, 197, 216, 217
photomaps, 191
photosynthesis, 57
photosynthetic pathways of carbon, 93
phylogenetic change, 96
phytoliths, 34, 60, 93–95, *fig.* 4.1
phytoplankton, 131
pigments, 114, 116, 119, 120, 121, 129, 131
pigs, 160
Piltdown Man, 12, 161
pine (white), 155
pipestone, 124 (*see* catlinite)
pisé, 128
pitchstone, 131
pits, 20, 174, 183, 187, 194, 213
placer deposits, 118, 120, 130, 141, 144, 145
plagioclase, 115

Plains Woodland, 158
plant(s), 57, 117, 131, 168, 204; communities, 79, 90, 92–93; material, 128; nutrients, 125; particle size, 125, 195; remains, 83, 92, 93
plaster, 127, 128, 205
plaster of Paris, 117
plastered surfaces, 108
plasticity, 126
plate tectonic theory, 107
platinum, 147
playa, 56, 64, 106
Pleistocene, 9, 10–11, 19, 44, 100, 106, 157, 159, 161, 164, 168, 192, 193, *fig.* 7.4; American, 12, 13; coastal areas, 189; extinction of North American large mammals, 111; extinction of plant communities, 111; geography, 14; glaciers, 71; gravel beds, 64; transition to Holocene, 92, 102, 111
Pliocene, 101, 164, 185
Plio-Pleistocene, 86, 160
plowing, 110
pluvial, 106
Poaceae (graminae), 95
pocket gophers, 83
Podzols, 33
point bar, 60, 63, 64, 176, 212
polar bear, 101
polarity reversals, 164
polarizing microscope, 149–50, *fig.* 6.5
polje, 180
pollen, 29, 90–92, 93, 103, 109; analysis, 107; dating, 12; diagrams, 110; fen carr, 107; fossil, 60, 90; oak, 92; preservation, 90–91; spores, 90; stratigraphy, 47, 90, 92, 102, 154, 160; tree, 160
pollution, 75, 87, 124, 131, 195, 205, 206, 208
ponds, 27, 56–58, 66, 96, 99, 103, 201
porcelain, 120
porosity, 82, 133, 187, 204, 205, 212, 220
porphyry (red), 139
postdepositional processes, 81–85
postglacial landscapes, *fig.* 3.10
potassium, 125, 126, 161, 163, 172, 195, 204. *See also* dating methods
pottery, 21, 26, 27, 42, 79, 119, 184;

pottery (*continued*)
Black Sand (Early Woodland), 158; Bronze Age, 197; clay, 124, 125–26, 127, 128, 131, 140; dating by TL, 172; grog, 128; Middle Minoan, 125; Neolithic painted, 121; sub-Neolithic, 141; temper, 13, 126, 141, 151, 205; thin sections, 149–51
precipitates: calcareous, 27–28; chemical, 57, 67, 154; noncalcareous, 28
precipitation, 54, 55, 56, 58, 87–88, 89, 91, 95, 105, 108, 110, 111, 131, 202, 203, 204, 206, 208, 210, 213
Predynastic Period (Egypt), 64, 112, 114, 115
proglacial, 71, 72, 81
prograding sequence, 27
Protoclassic Period (Maya), 69
protons, 143
Protosols, 35
provenance, 3, 123, 134–52; analytic techniques, 147–51; defined, 134
provenience, 38, 134
Pueblo III (New Mexico), 218
pumice, 36, 124, 127, 159, 214, 215
pyramids, 26, 69, 127, 198, 199, 202, 206–07
pyrite, 121, 126, 143
pyroclastic deposit, 137
pyroxene, 115
pyrrhotite, 221

quarries, 130, 137, 182; ancient, 115, 136, 202; bedrock, 121; building stone, 126; catlinite, 124; discard piles of, 115; marble, 140; sandstone, 127, 206; sites, 163; soapstone, 142
quarrying, 136, 201–02, 220
quartz, 38, 112–14, 122, 123, 124, 125, 131, 151, 172, 220; detrital (sourcing), 142; inclusions, 150; microcrystalline, 113, 139; Mohs hardness, 113; stream sedimented grains, 172. *See also specific types*
quartzite, 24, 113, 122, 124, 127, 131, 135, 136–37, 151, 204, 213
quartzose, 130, 131
Quaternary, 89, 99, 101, 106, 108, 193, 209; climates, 86; deposits, 19, 29, 86, 98, 100; fossil record, 102; ge-

ology, 2, 4; maps, 175; sediments, 8; stratigraphic studies, 12
Queleccaya ice cap (South America), 104–05
querns, 122

R soil horizon, 31
racemization. *See* amino acid epimerization and racemization
radar, 182
radiation dose (past), 172
radioactivity (background), 172
radio-isotope timescale, 160
rainfall. *See* precipitation
rainforests, 192
rammed earth, 128. *See* pisé
rare earth, 142
rasters, 196
ravines, 201
reducing, 35; atmosphere, 119; conditions, 35, 38, 81
reduction (chemical), 81, 204, 208
reed peat, 107
reef limestone, 207
refractory, 125
regression (marine), 78–79, 180
reindeer, 101
relative humidity, 163, 205, 206
remote sensing: electrical resistivity, 186–88; geophysical prospecting, 182–89; ground-penetrating radar (GPR), 188–89; magnetometry, 182–86; pattern recognition, 181; satellite and airborne, 182, 191–92; seismic profiling, 189–90; terrain conductivity, 188
reservoir effects, 168
Reservoir Salvage Act, U.S., 199
reservoir(s), 216–218
resin (fossilized tree), 116
retrograding sequence, 27
revetment (riprap), 220
rhinoceros, 101
rhyolite, 122, 123
rhyolitic volcanic glass, 162
rhythmites, 154–55. *See also* varve(s)
Richter magnitude scale, 210
ridge (hogback), 179
ridge and swale topography, 60, 176
Rift system (East Africa), 117
rifting, 107, 108
rims (hydration), 162

"rind" (obsidian), 162
riprap, 200, 204, 216, 219, 220
river(s), 18, 40, 66, 68, 71, 74, 125, 128, 130, 131, 176, 192; anastomosing, 60, 63; bank terraces, 217; beds, 59, 137; braided, 63; changes due to earthquakes, 213; channels, 64, 65, 188, 189, 211, 212; deposits, 119; drainage patterns, 180; environments, 192; erosion, 216; lateral migration, 219; meandering, 179, 200, 201, 203, 209, 213, 215; runoff, 108; sands, 41–42; types, 59–60
roads and roadbeds, 110, 175, 201, 202
rock: beds, 133; berms, 219; cap, 170; classification, 122–24; damage to, 205; dams, 199; dating, 170; defined, 112; deserts, 202; diversion dams, 200; fired, 184; friable, 218; layers (igneous), 218; outcrop surfaces, 174; "plant rocks," 93; porous, 205, 218; properties, 204; weathering, 187, 202
rock crystal, 114
rock salt, 117
rock shelters, 19, 53, 67–71, 161, *fig. 3.8*
rockfall, 70, 213, 218
rocks: high silica, 118; igneous, 12, 115, 118, 121, 122–123, 124, 126, 134, 139, 164, 170, 172, 179, 202, 218; *table* 5.1; pyroclastic, 124; quartzite, 124; quartzose, 130; siliceous, 113; volcanic, 164
root action, 83
rotary drill rigs, 192
routes: communication, 180; water transportation, 176. *See also* roads and roadbeds
rubidium, 137
runoff, 66, 201
rust (iron oxide), 221

sagebrush, 155
salinity, 75, 87, 95, 96, 97, 98, 133
salt: crystal formation, 205, 219; deposits, 117; table (*see* halite)
saltpans, 118
sand: alluvial, 63; beach, 42, 141; color, 38; dikes, 212; dunes, 27, 41, 42, 56, 65, 71, 74, 175, 176, 202; fill,

219; in fluvial settings, 25; laminated, 65; layers, 210; mineralogic composition, 25; non-calcareous, 141; particle size, 24–26; permeable, 180; pipes, 212; Pliocene, 185; quartz, 127; sand-filled valleys, 192; seas, 55; sheets, 55; shore margin, 75; tar, 131; volcanic temper, 141; wedge, 82

sandblows, 212

sand-silt-clay ratios, 127, 128

sandstone, 26, 27, 122, 129, 131, 218; caves and rock shelters, 70–71; and deterioration of buildings, 205–06, 220; dikes, 44; granular disintegration, 70; isotopic provenancing, 142; Nubian, 124, 206; quarries, 127; quartz, 124

sanukite, 142

Sapropels, 47

sard, 114

sardonyx, 114

sarsens, 134

Satellite Positioning and Tracking (SPOT), 192

scandium, 137, 141, 143

scarps, 59, 189

scatter plots, 196

schist, 112

scoria, 123

sea, 74; margins, 78; regression, 180; water, 117

sea level: rise, 64, 75, 189, 215; variations in, 78, fig. 3.14

seasonal: creep, 202; dehydration, 110; migration, 102

seasonality, 103

seaweed, 118

sediment(s), 8, 18–21, 27, 30, 32, 36–49, 75, 174, 188, 192, 195, 198, 199; aggradation, 31; alluvial, 54; alluvial fan, 158; analysis, 13, 15, 36, 182, 184; archaeological, 3, 9, 20–21, 187; beach, 42; burial, 54; carbonaceous, 29; cave, 71, 91; chemical deposition of, 21, 28; classification of deposits, 21–23, fig. 2.2; clastic exogenic, 21; composition, 44–48; cones, 55; contortion, 82, 83; deformation, 82; dielectric properties, 188; distribution in lakes, 57; dune, 56–

57; eroded, 110; fill, 180; illitic, 128; indurated, 21; infilling of harbors, 180; input, 202; lake, 57, 86; liquefaction, 199; load, 155, 213; marine, 104, 172; mixing, 192; and Munsell color order notation, 36–38; organic, 58; proglacial lake, 81; postdepositional alterations of, 82; resuspension, 211; saturated, 211; siliceous, 151; size distribution, 38–43; slumped, 212; spring, lake, and marsh, 41; structure, 43–44; texture, 38–43, fig. 2.3; transport, 19–20, 162; unconsolidated, 210; undeflated, 56; volcanic pyroclastic, 141; waterlogged, 188; weathering, 19

sedimentary: deposits, 48, 93, 143, fig. 2.1; facies, 26, fig. 2.4; features, 202; rocks, 204, 220; table 5.2; sequences, 26, 77, 157, figs. 2.4, 2.5

sedimentation, 70, 87, 170, 200

sedimentology, 48, 195

seeds, 25, 92

seepage (groundwater), 56

seiches, 212

seismic: damage, 218; disturbance, 210–13; induced sedimentary structures, 211; load, 218; profiling, 189–90; waves, 212. See also earthquake(s)

seismicity, 175, 213, 218

selenite, 117

selenium, 195

semiprecious stones, 114–18. See also individual stones

sepiolite (meerschaum), 129

septarian, 129

serpentine, 38, 112, 124, 129

serpentinite, 115, 124, 135, 142

sesquioxides, 35

settlement patterns, 177, 180–81

shale, 122, 124, 126, 131, 129, 210, 216

sheet flood, 55

sheetwash, 56, 70, 158

shell(s), 64, 79, 83, 124–25, 168, 171; clam, 79, 211; fossil, 125, 126; gastropod, 125; implements, 125; middens, 78, 81–82, 104; mollusk, 98, 156, 157, 168, 172, fig. 7.4; murex, 125; ostracod, 96; ostrich egg, 161; temper, 141

shellfish procurement (Holocene), 99

Shoshone (Native Americans), 109

shotcrete, 218

Side-Looking Airborne Radar (SLAR), 129

signatures (mineralogic or geochemical), 159

silica, 20, 27, 28, 93, 126

silicate components, 220

silicates, 126, 148, 218

siliceous: rock, 113; sediments, 151; shale, 124; varves of diatoms, 141

silicic volcanic rocks, 137

silicone compounds, 218

silt, 21, 23, 27, 28, 63, 69, 114, 118, 122, 124, 125, 126, 157, 185, 187, 212, 214, 217

Silt Complex, 65

silting, 200

siltstone, 131

silver, 113, 119, 120, 144, 146, 149, 221

Sinagua, 96

sinkholes, 208, 209

site(s): abandonment, 216; in arid settings, 56–57; associated with deltas, 64; boundaries, 195; burial, 78, 202–03, 208, 216, 219; catchment, 179, 222; formation, 50–53, 58–59, 64–65, 71, 162, 199, figs. 3.2, 3.3; frozen or snow covered, 188; geomorphic context, 176; habitation, 218; historic, 184, 189; location by geochemical prospecting, 195; near lakes and basins, 57–59; potential, 189; preservation, 65, 215–19, 222; primary, 53, 59; protection, 218; and settlement patterns, 177; stabilization, 218–19; stratigraphy, 189, 195; surface, 219

size categories of artifacts and particles, fig. 2.2

size distribution: of sediments and artifacts, 39; of temper, 141

size fraction data, fig. 2.12

skewness, 39, 41

slag, 119, 135

slate, 124

slickensides, 36

sliding, 202

slip, 126

slope(s), 203, 218
slopewash, 70
slumping, 19
smectite, 126
smelting, 25, 116, 119, 121, 135, 144, 146, 147, 195, 196
snails, 98, 168
soapstone, 124, 142
sodium, 97, 117, 126, 204
sodium chloride, 133
sodium sulfate, 205
Soho phase (Hohokam Classic), 171
soil: acidic, 204; biochemical development, 131; calcareous, 21; color, 36–38, 190; cover, 202; creep, 82, 215; definitions of, 30; description and analysis, 36–49; development, 222; disturbance, 190; failure, 213; formation, 18, 34, 38, 48, 108, 155, 158, 174, 193; gley, 38; horizon(s), 27, 30, 31–36, 37, 38, 44, 65, 81, 104, 110, 111, 151, 158, 188, 190, 195, 198, *fig.* 2.6; humates, 157, 158; liquefaction, 199; loosening, 110; maps, 174, 177, 178, 185; mechanics, 218, 219, *fig.* 9.5; moisture variations, 188; morphology, 158; profile, 20, 31–34, *fig.* 2.6; scientists, 197; sediment-soil analysis, 192; selenium deficiency, 195; sorting, 202, 221; terminology, 31–32; textural variation, 190; types, 32–36; waterlogged, 188. *See also specific soil horizons*
soil clay, 126
Soil Conservation Service, 178
soil data forms, 178
Soil Survey, U.S., 36
soil-organic fractions, 168
solifluction, 70, 82
soluble salts, 219
sorting, 40–41, 56, 59, 82–83, 202
sourcing, 134, 136, 142. *See also* provenance
spall, 127
spalling, 162, 163, 204
spectral reflectance curves, 190
speleothems, 165
spits, 74
Spodosols, 33, 35, 36
spoil heaps, 110
spring(s), 41, 58, 95, 98, 133, 175,

fig. 5.5; brine, 117; changes due to earthquakes, 213; conduits, 59; deposits, 28, 44, 165; disruption of groundwater system, 213; permanent, 200; tar, 131
spruce, 155
stability, 193, 198, 203
stabilization, 218
stable isotope analysis, 195–96
stable isotope series technique, 156
stadial events, 174
stalactites and stalagmites, 67, 165
stalactitic lenses, 70
stalagmitic flowstone, 68
Statistical Analysis Systems (SAS), 151
Statistical Package for the Social Sciences (SPSS), 151–52
steatite, 114, 124, 142
steel, 221
steppe, 91, 101
stone: artifact deterioration, 203–04; artifacts, 161; "blue stones," 134; building, 127–28, 220, 221; cut, 210; frost action on, 205; geologic definition, 112; lining canals, 200; monuments, 221; pavements, 83; quarried, 126; semiprecious, 113–16; structures, 220; treatments (chemical), 220
storage: areas, 195; dam (Olmec), 200; pits, 183
strandlines, 80
stratigraphic: chronology, 5; column, 75; levels, 182; markers, 158; principles, 7, 10; profiles, 195; sequences, 67–68, 182, 215; studies, 12; units, *fig.* 2.5
stratigraphy, 64, 68, 153–54, 189, 192, 195
streak (geological term), 120
stream(s), 103, 180; braided, 65–66; channeled, 219; ephemeral, 64; gravels, 130; meandering, 66, 200, *fig.* 3.4; patterns, 66; related deposits, 158; tributary, 212; valleys, 63, 176
strontium: isotope analyses, 140, 149; ratios, 97, 137
subsidence, 82, 202, 209–10, 211, 212
succinic acid, 142
Sui Dynasty (China), 200

sulfur, 159, 195, 196
sulfuric acid, 143, 220, 221
sunspot activity, 166
sunstone, 115
superposition, principle of, 163
surface: cracks, 213; creep, 40; materials, 178; runoff, 108; sites, 219; surveys, 175, 182, 190; wash, 19; water, 175, 180, 200; water features, 175
surficial geology, 175, 178, 201, 202
surveys: surface archaeological, 175, 190; surface geophysical, 182
swamps, 57, 103, 107, 131, 175
syenite, 122
systemic context, 52, 65

taiga, settings, 36
talc, 124
talus, 68
tannic acid, 29
taphonomic: mixing, 101; processes of deposition, 98; trajectories, 93
taphonomy: artifact, 32, 50–53; defined, 2, 50; fossil, 48
tar, 131
Tecep phase (Maya), 163
tectonic: event, 44; forces, 208–09; processes, 107; vertical movement, 75
tectonics, 107–08
tectonism, 75
teeth, 95, 100, 101, 171, 195
tell, 6, 76, 110, *fig.* 3.12
temper, 13, 126, 141, 151, 205
temperature: ambient, 161; change, 57, 104, 205, 206; flux, 191; moisture change, 102; Little Ice Age, 104; variations, 188
temporal scale, 197
tephra, 141, 159, 164
tephrochronology, 154, 158–59
terraces, 110, 176; alluvial, 33, 34, 193, *fig.* 3.6; fluvial, 60; systems, 60; surface, 61; types and fill, *fig.* 3.5
terrain: classification of geologic phenomena, 178; conductivity, 188; elevation, 175; mapping, 177, 178; patterns, 177
terrigenous, 28, 201
test excavations, 185, 186
textiles, 103

textural terms for sediments and soils, 21–27, *fig. 2.3*

texture, 21, 38–39, 53; exogenic, 40; mean particle size, 40; size distributions, 38, 41

thermal: annealing, 169; infrared images, 191; maximum (North America), 109

thermoluminescence, 140, 156, 159, 172–74, *fig. 7.4*; additive dose technique, 172, *fig. 7.10*; flint TL chronology, 173; infrared stimulated luminescence (IRSL), 174; optical stimulated luminescence (OSL), 174

Third Dynasty (Egypt), 126

thorium, 172, 165

till, 71, 72, 73, 74, 107, 119, 121

timescale resolution, 196

tin, 144–46, *fig.* 6.3

titanium, 161

Tiwanaku civilization (Peru), 104–05

"Tollund man," 103

topography, 201, 202

toxic elements and toxicities, 119, 195

trace element: analyses, 34, 147–49; composition, 90; concentrations, 152; fingerprints, 139, 142; signatures for native copper, 143

trace metal contaminants, 195

trading patterns, 148

trampling, 19, 27, 52, 83

transgressions, 64; coastline, 189; marine, 209

transgressive: conditions, 27; lake events, 59; marine, 64, 78–79; shorelines (postglacial), 189

translocation, 82

transport, 40, 57, 202, *figs.* 2.8, 2.9

transportation: artifact, 56; and biologic processes, 19, *figs.* 2.8, 2.9; and energy levels, 19, 27; of objects by water, 19; saltation, 40; of sediments, 18, 19, 56, 108, *fig.* 2.9; suspension, 40; in viscous medium, 24; and volcanic eruptions, 19

trap rock, 122

trash pits, 213

travertine, 28, 67, 68, 200; lenses, 70; deposits, 80, 172; spring deposited, 165, 171, 172

tree ring: calibration curves, 168; chronology, 160, 168; dating (*see under* dating methods: dendrochronology); series, 160

tree throw, 83, 84, *fig.* 3.16

trenches and trenching, 186, 192

troughs, 200

truncation, 48

tsunamis, 214, 215

tufa, 28, 59, 68, 91, 165, 166

tuff, 127, 137; beds, 164; breccia, 71; KBS, 169

tumbaga, 221

turbation, 32, 81

turquoise, 115

ultramafic intrusives, 143

unconformity, 48, 64, 212

uniaxial crystals, 149

uniformitarianism, 75

unit: depositional, 163; geologic, *fig.* 2.5; lithostratigraphic, 178

uranium, 165, 169, 172. *See also under* dating methods

Utisols, 33, 36

Valdivia, 79

valley(s), 64, 70, 72, 111, 157, 188, 202; alluvial, 34, 130; alluvium filled, 192; bottoms, 200; buried, 192; forms, 180; river, 60–61, 68; sand-filled, 192; stream, 61, 63, 71, 176

vanadium, 34

varve(s), 154, 160, *fig.* 7.2; analysis, 9; chronology and dating. *See also under* dating methods

Vegas occupation (Ecuador), 79

vegetation, 175, 203, 222; boundaries, 108; changes, 155; cover, 202; landscapes and past climates, 91; removal by humans, 196

ventifacts, 202

vertebrate(s), 100–103, 164

vertic soil horizon, 36

Vertisols, 32, 35, 83

vesicular andesite, 122

vibracorers, 192

Vinca culture (Serbia), 130

visible light spectrum, 190

vitric soil horizon, 36

volcanic: activity, 107, 108; arcs and chains, 137; ash, 33, 64, 65, 69, 89, 107, 126, 127, 141, 154, 159, 164, 202–03, 214–15; bedrock, 71, 184; deposits, 154, 158, 159, 202; destruction, 214; eruptions, 19, 89, 107, 108, 159, 214–15, *fig.* 9.6; gas emissions (fumarole), 168; glass, 123, 162; hazards, 215; lava, 70, 137, 143, 151, 184; layers, 214, 215; mafic rocks, 119; neck, 179; pyroclastic sediments, 151; rocks, 137, 164; temper sands, 141; zones, 215

volcanism, 107, 164, 214

wadis, 55, 118, 192

wall paintings, 205

walls: ancient, 218; berm, 220; buried, 187, 188; canyon, 218; distortion of, 213; mud brick, 126

Walther's Law of Correlation of Facies, 49, 75–77, *fig.* 3.13

waste, 130, 195

water, 19, 27, 28, 29, 32, 33, 34, 35, 37, 38, 40, 41, 42, 44, 47, 48, 53, 54, 56, 58, 67, 68, 69, 71, 72, 74, 75, 78, 79, 81, 82, 87, 88, 91, 93, 95, 96, 97, 98, 103, 104, 107, 110, 111, 115, 116, 118, 125, 126, 127, 135, 143, 162, 164, 184, 195; acid rain, 124; agricultural use of, 131; atomic configuration of, 207; bacteria in, 131; circulating, 121; contamination, 100; content, 171–72, 212; erosion and, 218; expansion, 207; flow, 59–66, 208; frost action, 207; ground, 131–33, 208, *fig.* 5.5; heat energy and, 207; level change, 217; ocean, 117, 168; potable, 176, 180; removal, 209; repellent coatings, 218; runoff, 198; springs, 131; standing, 57; surface, 168, 175, 180, 200; supply, 213; table, 192, 208; transport, *fig.* 2.8; turbidity, 131; upwelling, 168; velocity, 130; as weathering agent, 207

waterlogged environments, 110; fen, 107; peat bogs, 103, 160, 176

waterlogging, 183

waterproofing, 215

watershed size, 202

wave regimes, 75

waves (seismic), 189

Index

wave-cut notches, 78
weather, 111
weathering, 12, 18, 19, 20, 27, 28, 29, 33, 34, 35, 36, 48, 50, 83, 115, 127, 128, 131, 161, 164, 179, 180, 182, 204–07, 216, 219; chemical, 70, 125, 133, 174, 220; debris, 130; destruction by, 54; feldspar, 126, 204; frost, 68; mechanical, 68; physical, 70; processes, 81, 174; rate of, 174; rock, 30, 202; scientific analyses of, 220; volcanic ash, 126, 130; zones, 38, 158
wells, 184, 213

wetland, 64
wheat, 122
White River Group silicates, 148
wind, 19, 27, 56, 57, 90, 91, 95, 111, 168, 202, 203, 215, 220; deposits, 65; effects of, 54–55; eolian processes, 56; erosion, 48, 218; velocities, 218. *See also* eolian
wood, 158; burning, 195; cells, 160; charred, 182; pilings, 209; structures, 210; waterlogged, 104
Woodland (North America), 106–07, 120, 176

X-ray analyses, 220
X-ray fluorescence spectrometry (XRF), 134, 138, 140, 147, 149

Yabrudian artifacts, 172
Younger Dryas event, 89

zinc, 34, 118, 143, 195
zircon, 169
zirconium, 137
zooarchaeology, 3